Existential Theology

Existential Theology

—— An Introduction ——

Hue Woodson

WIPF & STOCK · Eugene, Oregon

EXISTENTIAL THEOLOGY
An Introduction

Copyright © 2020 Hue Woodson. All rights reserved. Except for brief quotations in critical publications or reviews, no part of this book may be reproduced in any manner without prior written permission from the publisher. Write: Permissions, Wipf and Stock Publishers, 199 W. 8th Ave., Suite 3, Eugene, OR 97401.

Wipf & Stock
An Imprint of Wipf and Stock Publishers
199 W. 8th Ave., Suite 3
Eugene, OR 97401

www.wipfandstock.com

PAPERBACK ISBN: 978-1-5326-6840-1
HARDCOVER ISBN: 978-1-5326-6841-8
EBOOK ISBN: 978-1-5326-6842-5

Manufactured in the U.S.A.   09/25/20

Contents

Preface: The Question of the Meaning of Existential Theology | vii
Acknowledgments | xi

Introduction: Situating Existential Theology | 1

Chapter 1: Themes of Existential Theology | 15
    Augustine's *Enchiridion: On Faith, Hope, and Love* 15
    A Brief History of the Forgiveness of Sins in the Early Church 20
    Ideals of Medieval Theology and the Pre-Constantinian Church 25
    Ontological Arguments: Anselm of Canterbury, Duns Scotus, and William of Ockham 28
    Aquinas's Cosmological Arguments in *Summa Theologica* 31
    Martin Luther, Theodicy, and the Problem of Evil 32
    Sin and *The Heidelberg Catechism* 34
    The Justification by Grace through Faith: Three Reformed Perspectives 38
    The Point of View of Truth and Selfhood in Kierkegaard's *The Point of View* 43

Chapter 2: Modern European Traditions of Existential Theology | 50
    The French School 50
    The German School 67
    The Russian School 92

Chapter 3: Countertraditions of Existential Theology | 109
    Liberation Approach 109
    Feminist Approach 136
    Womanist Approach 173

Chapter 4: Postmodern Traditions of Existential Theology | 204
    Anthropological Approach 204
    Political Approach 231
    Ethical Approach 255

Conclusion: Theologizing Beyond the Question of the Meaning of Existential Theology: Toward Posthumanism | 282
- "What It Means to Be Human" and Bruno Latour's Posthumanism 283
- "What It Means to Be Human" and Rosi Braidotti's Posthumanism 285
- "What It Means to Be Human" and Sylvia Wynter's Posthumanism 287
- "What It Means to Be Human" and Catherine Malabou's Posthumanism 289
- "What It Means to Be Human" and Cary Wolfe's Posthumanism 292

Appendix A: An Introduction to Robert Boyle's *The Excellency of Theology, Compared with Natural Philosophy* (1665) | 299

Appendix B: Pluralism and Ecumenism: The Development of Pluralistic Theology and Ecumenical Ecclesiology in the Nineteenth-Century European Religious Culture | 305

Appendix C: "The March of God in the World": American Ideological Monumentality, Hegel's State, and the Second Great Awakening | 307

Appendix D: The Hermeneutical Significance of the Doctrine of Creation to Theological Thought: From Karl Barth and Emil Brunner to Paul Tillich and Karl Rahner | 308

Appendix E: Paul as Tragic Hero and the Use of the Soliloquy: An Exegesis of Acts 20:17–38 | 310

Appendix F: Vision, Seeing, and Sight: An Exegesis of Acts 9:1–22 | 313

Appendix G: Christophanic Moments, Ontological Proof, and Existential Truth in the Conversion of Saul: An Exegesis of Acts 9:1–18 | 317

Bibliography | 323
Names Index | 333
Subject Index | 337

PREFACE

The Question of the Meaning of Existential Theology

The question of the meaning of existential theology seems simple, straightforward, and fairly transparent, particularly when attending to the two words that unavoidably make up its orientation, task, and method: "existential" and "theology proper." It should be clear that, on the surface, the business of "existential theology" traverses the respective businesses of existential philosophy and theology proper, such that, in the relationship between the two, "existential theology" becomes concerned with a connection between issues that are fundamental to the two fields of studies. In that way, we may be able to conclude that "existential theology" is a synthesis of the tasks and methods of existential philosophy and those of theology proper—that synthesis, as such, seems to suggest that existential philosophy informs and speaks to something in theology and theology, likewise, informs and speaks to something in existential philosophy.

What do the two fields inform the other about? How do they speak to one another? Perhaps, what these questions ask is: do "existential philosophy" and "theology proper" have anything meaningful to say to one another within a plane of understanding emanating between the two? And, if there is, indeed, something in the former's secularism and the latter's sacredness, *the question of the meaning of existential theology* may, in fact, be much more opaque than it initially seems.

If we remain steadfast to the extent that there is more than just a synthesis at work between "existential philosophy" and "theology proper," we still must not overlook that a mere synthesis, as I make explicit in *Heideggerian Theologies* (2018), is "an important place to begin, [even if] it is certainly only a superficial understanding of what existential theology is and does."[1] In recognizing this first, it becomes all the more possible to conceptualize "existential theology" as not only being unique to what traditional theologizing intends to do, but also unique to what existential philosophizing espouses. We can say, then, that, if "existential theology is concerned

---

1. Woodson, *Heideggerian Theologies*, 1.

with expressing theology by way of existential errands,"[2] those errands must be enumerated and outlined as taking hold to a kind of philosophizing and theologizing that goes un-philosophized by "existential philosophy" and goes un-theologized by "theology proper." If these errands are intent on "meaning-making,"[3] we might ask: what is the meaning that is being made? How does "meaning-making" bring us closer to *the question of the meaning of existential theology*? In one sense, given that "meaning" is respectively presented in "existential philosophy" and "theology proper," and some sort of "making" takes place in both within the framework for the secular and the sacred, it behooves us to ask: what is existential theology fashioning through its philosophizing and theologizing that is not fully fashioned by "existential philosophy" or "theology proper"?

We need not ask that question to suggest that either "existential philosophy" or "theology proper" purposefully overlook certain phenomena and entities within their different frameworks of inquiry, investigation, and explication—on the contrary, clearly "existential philosophy" and "theology proper" both have something significant to say about our world of both the infinite and the finite, and the temporal and the atemporal, if I may use Kierkegaard's categorization in *Sickness unto Death* (1849). In fact, when working within a purely existential-philosophical framework, we can easily arrive at important insights about the world and our standing in it, just as much as the meaning of human being and our worldhood can be aptly translated through a properly-theological framework. However, what is missed—what falls outside of the purview of "the existential-philosophical" and "the properly-theological" is what "the existential-theological" has to say, when comporting ourselves to what is required of us as *a task* and what we require as *a method* from an "existential-theological dialogue."[4]

In *Heideggerian Theologies*, I align "the existential-theological" to Martin Heidegger, and distribute the issues of scripture, tradition, reason, and experience to four theologians with four kinds of theologizing that are largely-openly influenced by and make use of Heidegger's philosophizing—the fact that John Macquarrie, Rudolf Bultmann, Paul Tillich, and Karl Rahner are "existential theologians" has as much to do with how they handle and are handled by their "Heideggerian" influences as it has to do how each calibrates the dialogue between "the existential" and "the theological." These influences serve different roles in the theologizing of each. What any one of them does theologically with Heidegger is not necessarily out of the scope of the other three—each individual Heideggerian influence does not place each of their respective theologizing within an exclusivity. Rather, because the Macquarrie, Bultmann, Tillich, and Rahner "speak" to one another from where they are each grounded theologically, through how they make use of Heidegger, and about what the "existential-theological" is. The extent to which the *question of*

2. Woodson, *Heideggerian Theologies*, 1.
3. Woodson, *Heideggerian Theologies*, 1.
4. Woodson, *Heideggerian Theologies*, 3.

the meaning of existential theology is expressed differently from Macquarrie to Bultmann to Tillich to Rahner is grounded on how each purposefully aligns themselves with Heidegger—for each, Heidegger becomes a means to an end, but not the very end of *the question of the meaning of existential theology*.

In whatever way—in terms of qualifications, aims, or intentions—we can call a "Heideggerian theology" a kind of existential theology, I do not think too fine a point can be made on the fact that making use of Heidegger is not the only way to handle *the question of the meaning of existential theology*. As largely as Heidegger looms philosophically within however he may be problematically aligned with the concerns of existentialism (i.e., to Sartre's, more generally and problematically than anyone else), and as crucial as Heidegger becomes theologically—which is the central, guiding claim made in my *A Theologian's Guide to Heidegger* (2019)—"existential theology" is much larger than any single philosopher or any individual theologian. *The question of the meaning of existential theology* unfolds itself, as itself, through a community of voices, all of which negotiate the secular and the sacred, ground a voice firmly between "the existential' and "the theological," and embark on a quest that inextricably philosophizes and theologizes.

The question of the meaning of existential theology is posed in the attunement of "the existential" and "the theological," and the meaningful manner with which the former attunes itself to the latter, and the latter meaningfully attunes itself to the former. What is offered in *Heideggerian Theologies* is just one representation of "existential theology"—it is one that attunes and is attuned by what I have called a "Heideggerian pathmark," and, to be sure, "express[es] only a specific kind of existential theology."[5] Here, as a way to further explicate the question of the meaning of existential theology beyond a "Heideggerian pathmark," this book, *Existential Theology: An Introduction*, wishes to explore what it means to do existential theology more comprehensively as far as the pathmarks of "the existential' and "the theological" go.

---

5. Woodson, *Heideggerian Theologies*, 4.

Acknowledgments

A SPECIAL THANKS TO James O. Duke and David J. Gouwens, both of whom inspired this book and to whom this book is dedicated.

I am always indebted to the past and present mentorship of Stacy Alaimo, David R. Brochman, Warren Carter, Valerie Forstman, Namsoon Kang, Peter L. Jones, Joretta Marshall, Kevin J. Porter, Masood Raja, Stephen G. Ray Jr., Timothy Richardson, Kenneth Roemer, Allan Saxe, Jacqueline Vanhoutte, Jim Warren, Kathryn Warren, Jeffrey Williams, Newell Williams, and Kenneth W. Williford.

Many thanks to my Tarrant County College family of colleague-friends: Rahma Aboutaj, Cindy Allen, Rebecca Balcarcel, Lisa Benedetti, Jim Baxter, Angela Chilton, Adrian Cook, George Edwards, Ryan Ferguson, Angela Jackson-Fowler, Curtis Fukuchi, Natalie Garcia, Nicole Hall, Scott Heaton, Kim Tapp Jackson, Leslie Genz Johnson, Liz Lounsbury, Joél Madore, Erin Mahoney-Ross, LeeAnn Olivier, Melissa Perry, Wendi Pierce, Krista Rascoe, Carroll Clayton Savant, Joan Shriver, Steve Smiley, Stacy Thorne Stuewe, Cecilia Sublette, Kristi Ramos Toler, Audrey Haferkamp Towns, Zainah Usman, and Michelle York.

Thanks to my family at Northway Christian Church of Dallas, Texas: Jennifer G. Austin, Judd Austin, Sarah Talbott Brown, Ted Brown, Rev. John G. Burton, Chrissy B. Cashion, Gail G. Coburn, Roderick Fisher, Tim Gilger, Paula Hammond, Kim Hetzel, Rev. Derry Henry, Rev. Ruby H. Henry, Emily Hohnstein, Karen S. Hohnstein, Roger Hohnstein, Rev. Virzola Law, Shane Mullin, Andrew Reinhart, Kelsey Reinhart, William Schick, Rev. Cheryl Scramuzza, and Rev. Megan Turner.

Lastly, I am extremely thankful for Samantha Woodson (my wife), Shirley J. Woodson (my mother), and Jeanne McKinnis (my mother-in-law).

INTRODUCTION

Situating Existential Theology

The question of the meaning of existential theology, as it exists in the history of ideas, must be defined separately from the history of existentialism, since *the question of the meaning of existential theology* is not the question of the meaning of existentialism. For existentialism, the question of "meaning" is regulated by and relegated to a kind of philosophizing about existence, which, in itself, grounds itself to itself—the question for existentialism can be non-theological, or even a-theological, to the extent that "meaning," when mere philosophizing existence is not entirely dependent on human existence's relationship to God's existence. Not only is *the question of the meaning of existential theology* not concerned with simply philosophizing about existence, but it is also concerned with the role that existence plays in the theologizing about God. In this way, *the question of the meaning of existential theology* seeks to ground human existence to God as the point of grounding—the "question," then, is: what kind of relationship does human existence have in relation to God's existence, how is the former grounded to the grounding of the latter, and what does it mean to theologize about God from the standpoint of human existence?

Though "existentialism" informs *the question of the meaning of existential theology*, what existentialism provides is merely cursory, even if it is relatively fundamental—yet, the contributions of existentialism need not be underestimated or overlooked in its influence on *the meaning of existential theology*, as such, *per se*. This is certainly so, when contextualizing both existentialism and existential theology to the mid-twentieth century, to the philosophizing of Soren Kierkegaard and Friedrich Nietzsche—indeed, both Kierkegaard and Nietzsche play critical roles in both existentialism and existential theology, even if there is some disagreement on whether only Kierkegaard, only Nietzsche, or both equally loom largely at the origins of existential thought.

In what is considered as the earliest critical study of existentialism, Marjorie Grene's *Dreadful Freedom: A Critique of Existentialism* (1948) cites Kierkegaard over Nietzsche, and includes Sartre, Marcel, Jaspers and Heidegger within "existentialism." More precisely, Grene's study is concerned with presenting five philosophies of existence—while Marcel and Jaspers author texts explicitly referring to a "philosophy of existence" and Sartre provides *Existentialism Is a Humanism* (1946), Heidegger distances himself from "existentialism" altogether in "Letter on Humanism" (1946) in a way that Grene does not fully acknowledge. Nonetheless, Grene's grouping of the five thinkers methodologically set a standard for subsequent studies of existentialism throughout the 1950s: Blackham's *Six Existentialist Thinkers* (1952), James Collins's *The Existentialists* (1952), E. L. Allen's *Existentialism from Within* (1953), Heinemann's *Existentialism and the Modern Predicament* (1953), and William Barrett's *Irrational Man* (1958).

The birth of existentialism, as such, whether its origins are in Kierkegaard or Nietzsche, is tied to the birth of *the question of the meaning of existential theology*, particularly when we considering "existential theology" in the postmodern sense—what ties the former to the latter is the degree to which the latter acts as a theological counterweight to the philosophical preoccupations of the former. The former's use of either Kierkegaard or Nietzsche as a foundation for the further philosophizing of existence seems to suggest that "existentialism" is grounded on a divided mind, which proceeds into "the philosophical" and the secular. By its very mature, we read existentialism as being unconcerned with theologizing about God and, instead, chiefly and predominantly preoccupied with the matters of human existence. This is derived, at the least, in part, by Sartre's fingerprints on "existentialism" and, to a certain extent, Grene's earliest grouping of thinkers into a formal study. For "existentialism" to begin with either Kierkegaard or Nietzsche, existentialist thought seemingly recognizes that the matters of human existence cannot ground human existence alone, without the theologizing of Kierkegaard and Nietzsche. To be sure, though Kierkegaard and Nietzsche respectively approach theologizing differently—a difference that could easily view Nietzsche as atheistic—theology is undoubtedly a silent partner in "existentialism," with which Sartre and Heidegger have conflict. It has been noted, however, that Sartre is an atheist and Heidegger purposefully avoided a theological voice—to whatever degree either speak to the concerns of existentialism, just as Heidegger denied an alignment with existentialism, Sartre, too, struggled with such a label. We may ask, then: what is the question of the meaning of existentialism?

Answering such a question is impossible. There is no definitive way to answer the question of the meaning of existentialism—all that can be done is merely an approximation based on specific thinkers and the unfolding of specific thoughts on existence.

From Grene's earliest study to all the subsequent studies following in the 1950s, there is no one way to do existentialism, even if there is some consensus on a set of themes that broadly concern what existentialism means to do. What makes "existentialism" so difficult to pinpoint is that it grounds itself to itself when it attends to the matters of human existence. In that way, the question of the meaning of existentialism is a perpetual question that is as paradoxical as the meaning of human existence, when situating that meaning, as Kierkegaard describes in *Sickness unto Death*, between "the infinite and the finite, the temporal and the eternal, of freedom and necessity."[1] These extremes are negotiated by existentialism from the standpoint of providing limitations to human existence—for existentialism, the focus is primarily on the finite, the temporal, and necessity over the "existential" dialectical counterparts of each.

The question of the meaning of existential theology, in its own directedness, theologically ventures into "the infinite," "the eternal," and "of freedom," in order to attend to states of affair that are not explicitly handled by the philosophical question of the meaning of existentialism. In doing so, even though the path taken by existential theology is largely parallel to that of existentialism, existential theology's path diverges on the issue of what it means to theologize about God. The joint-influence of Sartre and Heidegger—to their respective consternation about such an association—on the very meaning of existentialism prevents existentialism from fully theologizing about God, even if it is clear that existentialism does so implicitly. The use of Kierkegaard and Nietzsche in existentialism point toward the need for theologizing, but tend to limit that work to merely philosophical reflection.

To even wrestle with *the question of the meaning of existential theology* means we have already wrestled with the philosophical questions raised by existentialism, and to what extent can we even understand the nature of human existence's "modern predicament." Existential theology's "question" and its "meaning" is more than philosophical reflection—the question of the meaning of existential theology requires theological reflection in order to theologize about God adequately, meaningfully, and existentially. That task is more than just a philosophical reflection of human existence and its modern predicament, but more so about a conceptualization of God's existence, what it takes to theologize about God from the human standpoint, and how the theologizing about God lifts up, frees, and expands the meaning of human existence as such.

Though the path of existentialism begins, at least scholarly speaking, with Grene's *Dreadful Freedom* in 1948 as an expansion, perhaps, of Sartre's offering in "Existentialism Is a Humanism" in 1946, the path of existential theology, in my view, does not begin until 1954 with John Macquarrie's dissertation, "An Existentialist Theology: A Comparison of Heidegger and Bultmann" (1955), at the University of Glasgow—under the doctoral supervision of Ian Henderson, Macquarrie's study is a notable beginning point since it is, here, that the terms "existentialism" and "theology" are first joined into a single manner of theologizing.

I wish to make the first of two points of privilege about Macquarrie. First, when situating Macquarrie's 1954 dissertation at the very beginning of the development of what has become, as I have defined it, "existential theology," we must not draw too much of a difference between what is termed as "existential theology" and Macquarrie's term, "existentialist theology"—I take the two terms synonymously, since both grammatical uses are as adjectives (just as "existentialistic" holds a comparable meaning). Whether using "existential theology" or "existentialist theology," the same

---

1. Kierkegaard, *Sickness unto Death*, 1.

is being said: we are speaking about a kind of theologizing that is "existentialistic" in nature, attending to a certain referential: "existentialism."

Setting aside the genesis of the term itself, another point of privilege that must be advanced about Macquarrie's 1954 dissertation is whether it appears *ex nihilo*. I would be remiss to not contextualize Macquarrie's study of the "existential" comparisons between Heidegger and Bultmann outside of Henderson's influences on Macquarrie—even if, when taking into account Macquarrie's own recounting of his writing of *Existentialist Theology*, Macquarrie's separate introductions to Heidegger and Bultmann revealed, without any other influence, a comparative, existential thread between the two thinkers. I have written about this in *Heideggerian Theologies* (2018).[2] Still, I wish to question this context just a bit. To go further than what has assumed to be true, it may be possible to argue that Macquarrie was also influenced by James Brown's 1953 Croall Lecture delivered at the University of Edinburgh, entitled *Subject and Object in Modern Theology*, which Brown would later publish as *Kierkegaard, Heidegger, Buber, and Barth: A Study of Subjectivity and Objectivity in Existentialist Thought* (1955). Let us consider this carefully. Given that Macquarrie was at Glasgow and Brown's Croall Lecture was at Edinburgh, it is certainly not out of the realm of possibility that Macquarrie either attended Brown's lecture or, at a minimum, was marginally aware of its content. Geographically, the two universities are roughly fifty miles apart, so Macquarrie's attendance at the Croall Lecture in 1953 seems plausible. Yet, to the best of my knowledge, no proof exists verifying such a suspicion—Macquarrie simply does not directly or explicitly mention Brown's Croall Lecture. Nevertheless, given Macquarrie's proclivity to the zones of conflict tion in the relationship between Heidegger and Bultmann, through Henderson, it stands to reason that Macquarrie would have been interested in Brown's grouping of Heidegger and Barth within the foursome with Kierkegaard and Buber under the broader scope of the relationship between existentialism and theology. It seems to me that the relationship Brown draws between Heidegger and Barth—"the existential," as it was erroneously ascribed in the 1950s, and "the theological"—would have informed Macquarrie's "comparison" between Heidegger and Bultmann.

Whether or not Macquarie knew about Brown's Croall Lecture in real time—rather than coming in contact with it through its 1967 publication just as Macquarrie reconceptualizes "existentialist theology" into the notion of the "existential theologian" in Macquarrie's 1968 collection *Contemporary Religious Thinkers from Idealist Metaphysicians to Existential Theologians*—the question of the meaning of existential theology undoubtedly begins, in a forthright way and in earnest, with Macquarrie's *Existentialist Theology*. When placing these origins here, we find that Heidegger and Bultmann are at the center of what it means to do existential theology. To be more precise, it is Heidegger's philosophical influence on Bultmann's theologizing that becomes the foundation for *the question of the meaning of existential theology*. However foundational this

---

2. See the "Heidegger and Macquarrie" section in *Heideggerian Theologies* (2018).

INTRODUCTION: SITUATING EXISTENTIAL THEOLOGY

is, Macquarrie's subscription of Heidegger and Bultmann to an "existentialist theology" is only the beginning point, since Heidegger's philosophical influence reaches into the thought of Karl Jaspers, Jean-Paul Sartre, and Paul Tillich. When returning to Kierkegaard by citing Kierkegaard's own influence on Heidegger and situating Barth in the fold (which reminds us of Brown's *Subject and Object in Modern Theology*), with the inclusion of Etienne Gilson, we see an expansion of *the question of the meaning of existential theology* in Arthur Cochrane's *The Existentialists and God: Being and the Being of God in the Thought of Soren Kierkegaard, Karl Jaspers, Martin Heidegger, Jean-Paul Sartre, Paul Tillich, Etienne Gilson, Karl Barth* (1956), which is derived from Cochrane's lectures delivered in during the Fall 1954 semester at Presbyterian College in Montreal, when Cochrane was a guest professor, while he was Professor of Systematic Theology at the University of Dubuque Theological Seminary. In Cochrane, not only is there a labeling of the seven thinkers, three of which are theologians, as "existentialists," but there is a suggestion that Cochrane is providing an examination of existential theology, if his intent, as the subtle of the work offers, to explicate how the seven thinkers work through "being and the being of God."

From Cochrane, while the "being" of "being and the being of God" undoubtedly points to the thought of Jaspers, Heidegger, and Sartre, "the being of God" element largely points to Tillich, though only one of Tillich's *Systematic Theology* volumes would have been published at the time—the other two would not appear until 1957 and 1963. Even though "the being of God" attends to the thought of Gilson (as a scholar of medieval philosophy, specializing in the tradition of Aquinas) and Barth (with majority of the volumes of *Church Dogmatics* completed), it seems to me that Cochrane's language of "the being of God" is devoted to Tillich's theologizing. It is Tillich that stands between the concerns of Kierkegaard, Jaspers, Heidegger, and Sartre, and those of Gilson and Barth—the centrality of Tillich speaks more directly to *the question of the meaning of existential theology*. Not only does this seem to be derived from the first volume of Tillich's *Systematic Theology* (1951), in which Tillich writes of "the actuality of God," in terms of "God as being and knowledge," but there is also a similar articulation found in Tillich's *Courage to Be* (1952), in which Tillich asserts that "the God of the theological theism is a being besides others and as such a part of the whole reality."[3] In this way, Cochrane's use of Tillich brings together "being" and "the being of God," so that Tillich, more so than the other figures highlighted by Cochrane, is best situated to confront the question of *the meaning of existential theology*.

Like Bultmann, as examined by Macquarrie, Cochrane's handling of Tillich presents Tillich as engaged in an "existentialist theology," particularly when remembering that both are philosophically influenced by Heidegger. Given Tillich's own relationship with Heidegger, which I outline in *Heideggerian Theologies*,[4] the kind of theologizing found in the theological thinking of Bultmann and Tillich chart important paths

3. Tillich, *Courage to Be*, 184.
4. See the "Heidegger and Tillich" section in *Heideggerian Theologies* (2018).

through the 1950s and 1960s. While Bultmann is engaged in growing debates on the relevance of demythology in the wake of Bultmann's essay "The New Testament and Mythology" (1941), *The Gospel of John* (originally published in 1941) and *Theology of the New Testament* (originally published in 1948), Tillich is engaged in growing discussions on the relationship between philosophy and theology due to his three volumes of *Systematic Theology*. Through their respective relationships with Heidegger, Bultmann, and Tillich mitigate "the philosophical" and "the theological," or what was deemed as the relationship between existentialism and theology, since there remained a continued tendency to align Heidegger's philosophizing to existentialism. What Bultmann and Tillich would come to represent toward *the question of the meaning of existential theology* at the close of the 1950s is evidenced in George W. Davis's *Existentialism and Theology: An Investigation of the Contribution of Rudolf Bultmann to Theological Thought* (1957), Will Herberg's selected collection *Four Existentialist Theologians: A Reader from the Works of Jacques Maritain, Nicolas Berdyaev, Martin Buber, and Paul Tillich* (1958), and Quintin R. De Young's doctoral dissertation, "A Study of Contemporary Christian Existential Theology (Kierkegaard and Tillich) and Modern Dynamic Psychology (Freud and Sullivan) Concerning Guilt Feelings" (1959), presented to the Graduate School of University of Southern California (which, to the best of my knowledge, has yet to be published in monograph form).

While Davis's "investigation" is narrowly devoted to understanding the implications of Bultmann's existentialism to "theological thought" and Young's dissertation examines what he considers as "contemporary Christian existential theology," in a narrow sense of Kierkegaard and Tillich, against what he defines as "modern dynamic psychology," Herberg's collection *Four Existentialist Theologians* provides a broader exploration of *the question of the meaning of existential theology* beyond the narrow confines of Davis and Young. We see, of course, that Davis and Young respectively approach this "question"—with Davis grounding the question in Bultmann, and Young grounding it in Kierkegaard and Tillich—by either drawing a relationship between existentialism proper and theology proper, or as "contemporary Christian existential theology." Though Herberg curiously excludes Bultmann, Herberg's inclusion of Tillich broadens to include Buber—also acknowledged earlier in Brown's *Subject and Object in Modern Theology*—as well as Maritain and Berdyaev as "existentialist theologians." To the best of my knowledge, Herberg is the first to use the term "existentialist theologian." It is unclear if this use is influenced by Macquarrie's reference to "existentialist theology." Given the close proximity of the publication of Herberg's collection to that of Macquarrie's dissertation, there appears to be some marginal influence of the latter on the former, which stands to reason why Herberg excludes Bultmann. This seems certainly so, if considering Herberg's collection as a deviation from Macquarrie, with Herberg's meaning of the "existentialist theologian" resisting any relationship between Bultmann and Heidegger and, instead, making use of a set of themes that tie together Tillich, Buber, Berdyaev, and Maritain. In that case, how Herberg attends to *the question of the meaning of existential theology* becomes altogether separate from how Macquarrie works through *the question of the meaning of existential theology*—for Herberg's purposes, there are "common themes that give unity to the thinking of men so diverse in outlook and tradition as Maritain, Berdyaev, Buber, and Tillich."[5]

When taking into account the "common themes" highlighted by Herberg, these five dimensions Herberg assigns to Maritain, Berdyaev, Buber, and Tillich attempt to work through *the question of the meaning of existential theology* as a matrix of ontology, existentialism, personalism, social concern, and apologetic-cultural interest. If these five are collective nonnegotiables for Herberg, we can see how Bultmann would not necessarily fit into such a Herberg's overall scheme, when assuming that, for Herberg, Bultmann does not "develop [his] thought in philosophic form."[6] This holds true, if assuming that Herberg finds Bultmann's demythology as an example of those that "present [their thought] as the elaboration of revealed truth,"[7] Bultmann stands outside of Herberg's conceptualization of "existentialist theology" and, for that matter, Herberg's Bultmann stands outside of Herberg's understanding of *the question of the meaning of existential theology*—Bultmann's exclusion from Herberg's definition of the "existentialist theologian" cannot be on the grounds of Bultmann's lack of "ontology" or even "existentialism," but must be on account of the trickiness of locating "personalism," "social concern," or "apologetic-cultural concern" in Bultmann's demythology.

The problem with Herberg's possible characterization—or what can be seen as a mischaracterization, perhaps—of Bultmann's thought as falling outside Herberg's view of "existentialist theology" is that Herberg does not adequately handle *the question of the meaning of existential theology* as that which lies beyond the five themes that he insists on identifying. It seems to be that, though Herberg's five themes assist us in understanding the meaning of "existentialist theology," we need not assume that these five themes are the only way that "existentialist theology" can be defined. The fact that these are not all-inclusive dimensions in the making of an "existentialist theologian" is evidenced in Bultmann's exclusion. However, when bringing Macquarrie into dialogue with Herberg, we find that Bultmann, Maritain, Berdyaev, Buber, and Tillich are all "existentialist theologians" by a definition that must be broader than Herberg's five specific themes, whether considering the term "existentialist theology" or "existential theology."

Indeed, the very meaning of "existential theology," as I define it, does reckon with Herberg's five themes and does so in a way that falls loosely within prescribed bounds. To do "existential theology" or adhere to an "existentialist theology," means locating the relationship between "the existential" and "the theological," so that the bounds that can be possibly prescribed to *the question of the meaning of existential theology* form a foundation building up the dynamic relationship between "the question" and "the meaning" on the thought of key thinkers—these thinkers, or what

---

5. Herberg, *Four Existentialist Theologians*, 2.
6. Herberg, *Four Existentialist Theologians*, 2.
7. Herberg, *Four Existentialist Theologians*, 2.

we can describe as "existential theologians," include: Bultmann, Tillich, Maritain, Berdyaev, Buber, and Kierkegaard.

What this also means is that, if we align the variants of "existential theology"—that is, Macquarrie's use of "existentialist theology" and Herberg's use of "existentialist theologian"—these meanings, in an effort to approach *the question of the meaning of existential theology*, allow for a broadening landscape of themes in the 1960s. This notably begins with Bernard Martin's *The Existentialist Theology of Paul Tillich* (1963), which, as the title suggests, is devoted to considering Paul Tillich's "existentialist theology," through assessing the relationship between "philosophy and theology in Tillich's system" and how this explicates "the structure of man's being" in light of "man's estranged existence." What follows, in G. M. A. Jansen's *An Existential Approach to Theology* (1966), is not a rearticulation of the "existential approach" of Bultmann, Tillich, Maritain, Berdyaev, Buber, or Kierkegaard, but an inaugural presentation of Karl Rahner as an "existential theologian" that, in Jensen's words, espouses "[a] new theology [that] tries to bring [our] religious experiences into the open, to let full light fall upon them."[8] In Harry M. Kuitert's *The Reality of Faith: A Way Between Protestant Orthodoxy and Existentialist Theology* (1968), we find reconstitution of Bultmann to "existentialist theology," which, to the best of my knowledge, is the earliest reference of Dietrich Bonhoeffer's "existentialist theology"—however, for Kuitert, as much as "there is a clear conjunction between him and the existentialist theologians . . . there is also a tangible difference,"[9] through an assessment of Bonhoeffer's *The Cost of Discipleship* (in English in 1948), *Ethics* (in English in 1955), and *Letters and Papers from Prison* (written in 1943–1945). After this, in Norman J. Young's *History and Existential Theology: The Role of History in the Thought of Rudolf Bultmann* (1969), we not only find a devotion to Bultmann and an analysis of three "characteristic features" of Bultmann's approach to history, but also the use of the term "existential theology," rather than "existentialist theology," which conceptually mirrors Jensen's use of the term in *An Existential Approach to Theology*.

By the 1970s and 1980s, there are three notable texts that expand on *the question of the meaning of existential theology*: the first, Howard A. Slaatte's *The Paradox of Existentialist Theology: The Dialectics of a Faith-Subsumed Reason-in-Existence* (1971), which aligns Kierkegaard, Tillich, and Barth with dialectical theology, and primarily concentrates on Bultmann's "existentialist theology," the second, Eugene T. Long's *Existence, Being and God: An Introduction to the Philosophical Theology of John Macquarrie* (1985), which introduces Macquarrie's "philosophical theology" in terms of Macquarrie's situatedness of "the experience of existence and Being" toward "a new style of natural theology," and the third, David Jenkins's *The Scope and Limits of John Macquarrie's Existential Theology* (1987), which expands upon Long's use of Macquarrie by more firmly labeling Macquarrie's theologizing as an "existential

---

8. Jensen, *Existential Approach to Theology*, 19.
9. Kuitert, *Reality of Faith*, 76.

theology" and ultimately highlighting Macquarrie's "phenomenological ontology" as well as Macquarrie's "philosophy of language"—it is in the two studies devoted to Macquarrie that both make use of Macquarrie's *Principles of Christian Theology* (1966), *God-Talk* (1967), *Thinking about God* (1975), *In Search of Humanity* (1983), and *In Search of Diety* (1984).

Though my *Heideggerian Theologies* (2018) brings together Macquarrie, Bultmann, Tillich, and Rahner in terms of Heidegger's influence on each, to the extent that the kind of theologizing on which each theologians focuses brandishes a "Heideggerian theology," it must be made clear that Heidegger is not the only means by which we can understand the theologizing of Macquarrie, Bultmann, Tillich, and Rahner. For that matter, when we assess the kind of theologizing in each, and configure what is being theologized toward *the question of the meaning of existential theology*, we quickly find that Heidegger's influences only go so far. Heidegger certainly positions Macquarrie, Bultmann, Tillich, and Rahner on the path toward existential theology and, as I argue in *Heideggerian Theologies*, each of them expand upon Heidegger's own unwillingness or inability to employ a theological voice. In this way, Heidegger is a means to an end for Macquarrie, Bultmann, Tillich, and Rahner, if we cite this end as attempting to confront *the question of the meaning of existential theology*.

Still, if Heidegger's philosophizing is, indeed, incompatible with the philosophizing of existentialism—if we are to take heed to Heidegger's own stance on this issue—and if we ask what role does existentialism actually play in the theologizing of Macquarrie, Bultmann, Tillich, and Rahner, we find that it is not enough to simply say that the relationship between existentialism and theology gives birth to the "existential theologian." In effect, though Heidegger does help us explain what motivates the theologies of Macquarrie, Bultmann, Tillich, and Rahner, we must be reminded of the fact that Heidegger does not hold the same motivations for and have the same influences on the theologies of Maritain, Buber, Bonhoeffer, and Berdyaev. As much as Heidegger figures into what it means to do existential theology, what ties existential theologians together is *the question of the meaning of existential theology*.

If what it means to be an "existential theologian" is always-already about fundamentally working through *the question of the meaning of existential theology*, it becomes important to outline the answers that existential theologians seek. These answers not only predate Heidegger but also expand beyond the bounds of Heidegger's thought—if we can conclude that Kierkegaard is an "existential theologian," Heidegger not only does not hold any influence on Kierkegaard's theologizing, but, instead, Kierkegaard serves as an influence on Heidegger's philosophizing. From this, if locating Kierkegaard's own influences, we uncover thinkers such as Hegel, Kant, Aquinas, and Augustine—just to name a few—all of which are as concerned with "the existential" as they are with "the theological." In this case, if recognizing how Hegel, Kant, Aquinas, and Augustine all influence, in varying ways, Heidegger's own ventures into "the theological," which I carefully examine in *A Theologian's Guide to Heidegger* (2019), this leads to us to ask whether or not Heidegger himself is an "existential theologian."

Even though it is certainly impossible—and even irresponsible—to categorize Heidegger as a "theologian" engaged in theology proper, calling Heidegger an "existential theologian" seemingly becomes something of a compromise. The term itself points to two kinds of thinking in one thought—a philosophizing that occurs simultaneously with a theologizing. As I present in *A Theologian's Guide to Heidegger*, Heidegger's theological roots are grounded, in part, on working through the theologies of Aquinas and Augustine in early lectures and seminars Heidegger taught, insomuch as Heidegger's confrontations with Aquinas and Augustine influence Heidegger's later decidedly philosophical confrontations with Hegel and Kant.

To even propose Heidegger's status as an "existential theologian" requires us to determine how Heidegger theologizes about God—to be sure, in light of Heidegger's theological roots, we can read a theologizing into *Being and Time*, even though this theologizing, as such, can just as easily be refuted. This is because Heidegger does not make God explicit in *Being and Time*. There always remains an implicit theologizing embedded in his philosophizing about the question of the meaning of being—it is this implicitness that I trace in *A Theologian's Guide to Heidegger*. It is precisely because of this implicitness that Heidegger cannot be fully explained as an "existential theologian," even if Heidegger's philosophizing in *Being and Time* comes dangerously close to a kind of theologizing. This closeness is not enough. To engage with *the question of the meaning of existential theology*, as an existential theologian, means explicitly theologizing about God, even if that explicitness is framed philosophically.

While Heidegger falls short as an "existential theologian," Buber also falls short. Like Buber, the existential Judaism of Abraham Heschel (1907–1972), Lev Shestov (1866–1938), Franz Rosenzweig (1886–1929), and even Emmanuel Levinas (1906–1995) also fall outside what is meant by "existential theologian." Though Jose Ortega y Gasset (1883–1955) and Miguel de Unamuno (1864–1936) display some variations of a relationship between "the existential" and what can be deemed as "the theological" in a sense, these two are also not necessarily representative of the "existential theologian." This is so, when considering what the theologies of Maritain, Bonhoeffer, Berdyaev, Macquarrie, Bultmann, Tillich, and Rahner have in common, how these theologies theologize about God, and the manner with which these theologies handle *the question of the meaning of existential theology*: there is a relation to and a relatedness with the Christian tradition, which unfolds through a guiding and being guided by Christian thought. By "Christian thought," I am not making a distinction between Catholicism, Protestantism, or Russian Orthodoxy, but, rather, bringing together these historicized traditions into a single kind of theological thought anchored historically in the "primitive Christianity" spawned from the teachings of Jesus, dated to the early first century CE.

INTRODUCTION: SITUATING EXISTENTIAL THEOLOGY

Because *the question of the meaning of existential theology*, at its most fundamental, is a questioning and a meaning developing within the theoretical bounds of Christianity, the relationship between "existential theology" and Christianity is inextricable. This means that, in order to theologize about God, the necessary theologizing is relegated to and regulated by the Christian God—the "existential theologian" and *the question of the meaning of existential theology* is calibrated by the concerns of Christian theology and how these concerns present themselves to the meaning of human existence in relation to God's existence. It is this regard that "existential theology," as a term, becomes connected to three terms: "Christian existentialism," "Christian humanism," and "Christian philosophy"—if we wish to understand what these terms contribute to *the question of the meaning of existential theology*, and how these terms, though antiquated now, conceptualize the "existential theologian" in a way that excludes Heidegger and Buber, and gathers together Augustine, Aquinas, Kant, Hegel, Kierkegaard, Maritain, Bonhoeffer, Berdyaev, Macquarrie, Bultmann, Tillich, and Rahner, it would be prudent to consider the terms "Christian existentialism," "Christian humanism," and "Christian philosophy" in their respective origins.

"Christian existentialism," as a term, to the best of my knowledge, seems to originate in the 1960s with the following texts published in close proximity to one another: the collection of texts entitled *Christianity and Existentialism* (1963), John Macquarrie's *Studies in Christian Existentialism* (1965), Donald A. Lowrie's edited collection entitled *Christian Existentialism: A Berdyaev Anthology* (1965), and John B. Cobb Jr.'s *The Structure of Christian Existence* (1967). First, *Christianity and Existentialism*, based on six lectures delivered at Northwestern University from October 11 to November 15, 1961, in the prefatory note to the collection, suggests that the collected texts are meant "to explore in a series of dialectical discussion the impact of the existential viewpoint in philosophy on religious thought, particularly in its relevance to Christian philosophy." These texts include: William Earle's "Faith as Existential Choice," focusing on the Punic Fathers, James M. Edie's "Christian Rationalism," focusing on Aquinas, Gilson, and Maritain, and John Wild's "The Paradox and Death of God," focusing on Kierkegaard and Nietzsche. What these texts demonstrate, under the overall relationship set up between Christianity and existentialism, is the notion that figures such as the Punics, Aquinas, Gilson, Maritain, Kierkegaard, and Nietzsche are concerned with how "the existential" speaks to Christian thought and Christian thought, in itself, is embodied in "the existential." What is also demonstrated in these texts are themes that not only connect "Christianity" to "existentialism," but also connect the texts to that larger Christianity-existentialism relationship: faith, choice, rationalism, paradox, and the death of God. These same themes carry over into John Macquarrie's *Studies in Christian Existentialism*, in which Macquarrie defines additional themes under the notion of "some philosophical presuppositions": "selfhood and temporality," "the language of being," sin, grace, and authenticity. Published in the same year as *Studies in Christian Existentialism*, Donald A. Lowrie's edited collection entitled *Christian Existentialism:*

A Berdyaev Anthology (1965), or what is also referred to as "A Berdyaev Synthesis," presents an "anthology" of selections of Berdyaev's work thematically oriented toward the concerns of epistemology, metaphysics, philosophy-theology relations, the nature of man, God-man relations, society, and history. John B. Cobb Jr.'s *The Structure of Christian Existence* (1967) devotes its largest section to "Christian Existence," which considers it as "spiritual existence that expresses itself in love"[10]—this spiritual existence, for Cobb, "is explained as a structure of radical self-transcendence, and its power for both good and evil is emphasized."[11]

"Christian humanism," as a term, seems to have its origins in the work of Friedrich Niethammer (1766–1848) as "humanism," which, as such, is believed to have developed from Cicero's "humanitas." Niethammer's use of "humanism," as a nineteenth-century idea, became differentiated from what was known as the "renaissance humanism" of the fourteenth century to the sixteenth century—this "renaissance humanism" is embodied in the work of Thomas More (1478–1535). Considered together, when acknowledging that Niethammer is a Lutheran and More is a Catholic, the notion of "Christian humanism," in my view, becomes a bridge between the concerns of Protestantism and Catholicism. In this way, the concerns of Protestantism are shaped by Catholicism, particularly if we heed Cobb's sentiment about "radical self-transcendence, and its power for both good and evil." When contextualizing Cobb within Christian humanism, we still see an emphasis on "Christian existence" as an explication of spiritual existence—for Christian humanism, the question of the meaning of existential theology becomes predicated in calibrating human existence by a spiritual existence by way of an actualizing Christian existence. William S. Urquhart's *Humanism and Christianity* (1945), based on Croall Lectures delivered in 1938–1939 at the University of Edinburgh, locates a tension between "human existence," "spiritual existence," and "Christian existence" as a "modern tension." Urquhart is guided by the supposition that "humanity cannot be delivered from its wretchedness by being faithless to its freedom."[12] This leads Urquhart to consider that humanity must be "delivered from its wretchedness" either as an "escape through psychology" or in terms of "salvation through humanism."[13] It is the latter, in particular, that thematically guides the collection *Readings in Christian Humanism* (1982), which draws on readings as early as Plato's *Republic* books 6 and 7, and the opening books to Aristotle's *Politics* and *Ethics*—for the editors of the collection, Christian humanism is defined as "the interest in human persons and the positive affirmation of human life and culture which stems from the Christian faith."[14] The editors go on to say that, in Christian humanism, there arises "the motiv[ation] of discovering and supporting whatever enhances human existence, but is distinctive in finding the

10. Cobb, *Structure of Christian Existence*, 124.
11. Cobb, *Structure of Christian Existence*, 124.
12. Urquhart, *Humanism and Christianity*, 10.
13. Urquhart, *Humanism and Christianity*, 37–55.
14. Shaw, *Readings in Christian Humanism*, 23.

source and goal of human powers in God, the Creator, Redeemer, and Spirit."[15] In light of this, the editors conclude that "Christian humanism seeks to an understanding of the whole range of human experience in the light of God's revelation to humanity in the person and work of Jesus Christ."[16] Because "Christian humanism," as an idea, as noted by the editors, "emerged with Christianity itself," *the question of the meaning of existential theology* has always been connected to "Christian humanism" *per se*—this, of course, is made all the more clear with the inclusion of the following thinkers in *Readings in Christian Humanism*: Augustine, Aquinas, Anselm, Luther, Calvin, Pascal, Schleiermacher, Bonhoeffer, and Niebuhr, all of which contribute to the formulation of *the question of the meaning of existential theology*.

"Christian philosophy," as a term, has the same roots and the same trajectory as those of "Christian humanism," insomuch as the extent to which "Christian philosophy" emerges and develops with respect to the emergence and development of Christianity and the unfolding Christian tradition from the Hellenistic era to the medieval era to the Renaissance and Reformation eras to the Modern era beginning in the seventeenth century. The scope and range of "Christian philosophy" is best illustrated in Étienne Gibson's *God and Philosophy* (1941), which includes sections on "God and Greek Philosophy," "God and Christian Philosophy," "God and Modern Philosophy," and "God and Contemporary Philosophy."

Taken together, "Christian existentialism," "Christian humanism," and "Christian philosophy"—two of which Heidegger vehemently rejects in one fell swoop in his "Letter on Humanism" (dated to December 1946, but edited by Heidegger and published in 1947)—are all oriented toward *the question of the meaning of existential theology*. To be an "existential theologian" means theologizing at the epicenter of "Christian existentialism," "Christian humanism," and "Christian philosophy," so that what it means to do existential theology grounds itself to the groundedness of the Christian tradition. To even theologize about God through existential theology requires standing theologizing itself against the very concerns of "Christian existentialism," "Christian humanism," and "Christian philosophy," so that existential theology, as such, provides a unified field of thinking a kind of thought about God, dedicated to handling God's existence in relation to human existence, attuned to a set of dynamic existentializing themes that shape and calibrate what it means to be human, and predicated on tending to *the question of the meaning of existential theology* as an ongoing ontotheological actualization of humanity's "being" and God's "Being."

Chapter 1 carefully outlines the "themes" associated with *the question of the meaning of existential theology* by presenting Augustine as a historical beginning point with *Enchiridion: On Faith, Hope, and Love* and what unfolds through a brief history of the forgiveness of sins in the early church. Further themes are considered within the ideals associated with the medieval theologizing of the pre-Constantinian church, as

15. Shaw, *Readings in Christian Humanism*, 23.
16. Shaw, *Readings in Christian Humanism*, 23.

well as what can be thematically ascertained from Aquinas's *Summa Theologica*. More themes are assessed through Luther's theologizing the problem of evil as well as the role of sin in *The Heidelberg Catechism*. From here, the roles of justification, grace, and faith are examined through reformed perspectives, with Kierkegaard rounding out a discussion of selfhood, identity, and perspective.

Chapter 2 works through what I have defined as "modern European traditions" of existential theology by exploring *the question of the meaning of existential theology* across the French, German, and Russian schools of thought. This is accomplished by determining how a variety of thinkers handle *the question of the meaning of existential theology* through various ways and means of theologizing about God.

Chapter 3 considers what I have referred to as the "countertradition" of existential theology, particularly positioned in the kind of theologizing about God that make use of the approaches of liberation theology, feminist theology, and womanist theology. These approaches attempt to reckon with, challenge, and reconceptualize the existential foundations laid by traditional, Eurocentric conceptualizations of *the question of the meaning of existential theology*.

Chapter 4 presents what I have offered as a "postmodern tradition" of existential theology, as that which is rooted in how theological anthropology, political theology, and ethics respectively translate *the question of the meaning of existential theology* by working through the existential implications set by the previous chapter's conceptualizations of a countertraditions. This "postmodern" tradition, in itself, counters the countertradition, such that the countertradition, in itself, becomes limited to a modern kind of theologizing about God that postmodern theologizing must surpass.

The pursuit of *the question of the meaning of existential theology* forces us to follow a pathmark leading us to not just what it means to do existential theology, but also what it means to theologize about God. It is the pursuit of "the question" and "the meaning" as the task and method of the existential theologian, negotiating human existence by way of God's existence and, in turn, ascertaining God's existence fundamentally and existentially mitigated by our human existence. The interplay between human existence and God's existence is at the heart of *the question of the meaning of existential theology*, insomuch as the manner by which we theologize about God becomes, in itself, a theologizing about ourselves and our "being" as that which is theologically *imago Dei*. And yet, when the existential theologian, defined as such, theologizes about God, the mere nature of human existence and the worldhood of what it means to be human is always-already impugning us with a plenitude of worldly trappings that shape, oppress, marginalize, limit, ground, situate, repress, and tether our humanity to the world in which we are humanized. To work through *the question of the meaning of existential theology*, when posed authentically, means theologizing about God in a way that takes into account all that we must theologize ourselves out of, from, and toward, if we wish to truly grapple—at an existential level—with what stands between human existence and that of God.

CHAPTER 1

Themes of Existential Theology

WHEN CALIBRATING THE QUESTION *of the meaning of existential theology* to broader themes—or key inquiries that seek to answer specific questions about human existence in terms of how the meaning of human existence expresses itself meaningfully through varying, intersecting ideas—I wish to focus on the following key thinkers as general guideposts: Augustine, Aquinas, Martin Luther, and Soren Kierkegaard. From them, and through other thinkers contemporary to them, *the question of the meaning of existential theology* unfolds through guiding movements: the early church, medievalism, the Reformation, and the nineteenth century. Across each of these guiding movements, *the question of the meaning of existential theology* is further delineated through the specific concerns of faith, hope, love, sin, cosmology, theodicy, the justification by grace through faith, and selfhood.

Augustine's *Enchiridion: On Faith, Hope, and Love*

In chapters 3 and 4 of *Enchiridion: On Faith, Hope, and Love* (ca. 420), Augustine discusses God as the creator of all, both representing the goodness of all creation and, by way of God's innate nature, allowing for the existence of evil.

What Augustine seems to propose is a concept of theodicy[1] as a means to articulate the personification of God's goodness in everything God has created. Not only, then, is there an attempt to "characterize the topic of God's govern[ing] of the world in relation to the nature of man," but it allows for "[a] justification of God's goodness and justice in view of the evil in the world."[2] Subsequently, when considering the relationship between good and evil as possibilities in the created world, Augustine is able

---

1. This term was first introduced by Gottfried Wilhelm Leibniz, a German philosopher (1646–1716), who argued that a world containing moral and physical evil is better, because it is metaphysically richer that one containing good only, and that, furthermore, God must have created the best of all possible worlds. What theodicy asks is how we can believe that God is both good and sovereign in the face of the world's evil. Ferguson and Wright, *New Dictionary of Theology*, 381; 679.

2. Reese, *Dictionary of Philosophy and Religion*, 573.

to postulate that "in this [world], even what is called evil, when it is rightly ordered and kept in its place, commends the good more eminently, since good things yield greater pleasure and praise when compared to the bad things.[3] It is precisely through this fashioning of theodicy[4] that Augustine operates from the supposition that God, as creator of all and the origin of all goodness, imparts an innate "goodness [into] all creation"[5] that provides for evil to exist innately. Evil, as Augustine argues, can never exist as such unless goodness can be brought forth from it by God's omnipotent power and goodness,[6] where it can be further presumed that, if "God is the author of everything [and], if evil is something, it follows that God is the author."[7] What this means, then, is that just as goodness comes from God, evil must come from goodness, even if God embodies only goodness and evil exemplifies a distortion of that goodness[8]—the relationship between good and evil as it is woven into this contradiction[9] can be better explained, as a take on Augustine's own argument, as "two poles, two opposite directions, the two arms of a signpost pointing to right and left [that] are understood as belonging to the same place of being, as the same in nature, but the antithesis of one another."[10] In other words, since goodness cannot exist without God,[11] evil, as the antithesis of goodness, could never exist without God, existing not as goodness does but, instead, as a form of nonbeing.[12] In this, subsequently, it is necessary to argue for the existence of evil being possible only out of the existence of goodness when both

---

3. See ch. 3, para. 11 of Augustine, *Enchiridion*.

4. All theodicies, in effect, view evil as making for a good that is ultimately greater than what is attainable without it. Ferguson and Wright, *New Dictionary of Theology*, 679.

5. The title Augustine uses for chapter 3, which, perhaps, suggests that Augustine realizes that, in order to understand the problem of evil (the title of chapter 4), it is first important to embrace the notion that humankind "cannot resolve the problem of evil by denying or limiting either the reality of evil or the goodness and power of God." Ferguson and Wright, *New Dictionary of Theology*, 241.

6. The Omnipotent God, as having the Supreme Power over all, would not allow any evil in his works, unless in his omnipotence and goodness, as the Supreme Good, he is able to bring forth good out of evil. See ch. 3, para. 11 of Augustine, *Enchiridion*.

7. Ferguson and Wright, *New Dictionary of Theology*, 242.

8. To use Augustine's own words: "*Esse qua esse bonum est.*" This means "being as being is good." In order to be "a being" from something that is already "a being" implies that evil is a distortion of something which has being, becoming pseudo-real only as much the undistorted state of goodness has ontological realness. Evil, as a result, is only a distortion of a good creation. Tillich, *History of Christian Thought*, 53–54.

9. Ferguson and Wright, *New Dictionary of Theology*, 241.

10. Martin Buber, *Good and Evil*, 121.

11. The Christian believes that nothing exists save God himself and what comes from him. See ch. 3, para. 9b of Augustine, *Enchiridion*.

12. To this, Berdyaev states the following: "Evil is a return to non-being, a rejection of the world, and at the same time it has a positive significance because it calls forth as a reaction against itself could not exist. The possibility of evil is the condition of the good. A forcible suppression or destruction of evil would be a great evil. And good easily turns into evil. God's toleration of evil is a paradox which is not sufficiently dwelt upon. God tolerates evil, allows evil for the sake of the good of freedom. Toleration of evil is a part of God's provincial plan." Berdyaev, *Destiny of Man*, 41.

are considered as existing along the same timeline,[13] whereby evil is not evil without having first been in a state of goodness. Specifically, when assuming more ontological terms, "evil is not a positive power; it is the negation of the spiritual. It is participation in matter, in non-being, in that which has no power of being by itself. Evil arises when the soul turns to non-being,"[14] where goodness has being and substance. For Augustine, evil "is not a substance [but] the wound or the disease [that] is a defect of the bodily substance which, as a substance, is good. Evil, then, is an accident, [for example], a privation of that good which is called health."[15] In effect, Augustine provides a "double interpretation of evil [which] is non-being, a privation, and nothing positive,"[16] in order to define evil not just as an entity in and of itself but, particularly, in relation to God and the goodness of God's creation.

Augustine's argument, then, does not necessarily insinuate that the existence of evil allowed through "a defect of the bodily substance" or some imperfection embedded in the goodness of God's creation is a result of a weakness in God's omnipotent power to overcome and eradicate evil from the world through God's response to the problem of evil by way of the doctrine of atonement.[17] Instead, when utilizing Augustine's articulation of evil being an accident that deprives goodness through "health," what Augustine asserts with "health"[18] is a Kierkegaardian notion of sickness,[19] which, as a result, is substantiated in the possibility of freedom. This freedom, created by God during the creation of all creation, is a meonic freedom,[20] which provides for goodness and evil to coexist as being and nonbeing, respectively, within each and every one of God's creations. In effect, this represents the double possibility of human existence,[21] to which Augustine concludes not only that goodness and evil can't exist

13. Friedrich Nietzsche refers to this in the following terms: "What time experiences as evil is usually an untimely echo of what was formerly experienced as good." Kaufmann, *Basic Writings of Nietzsche*, 280.

14. Tillich, *History of Christian Thought*, 53–54.

15. See ch. 3, para. 11 of Augustine, *Enchiridion*.

16. Reese, *Dictionary of Philosophy and Religion*, 161.

17. Urban, *Short History of Christian Thought*, 100–101.

18. In the Christian understanding, health is the complete well-being of a person who is in a right relationship to God, to himself, to his fellows and to his environment. Ferguson and Wright, *New Dictionary of Theology*, 287.

19. Kierkegaard believed that "sickness," as a relation to Augustine's "health," is the source of humankind's despair as much as it is the means toward which humankind suffers a "sickness unto death," dying not in the physical sense, but in the spiritual. This, undoubtedly, illustrates the Augustinian notion that evil is the result of Kierkegaard's notion of the "sickness of the soul" as evidenced in Kierkegaard's *The Sickness unto Death* (1847). Bretall, *Kierkegaard Anthology*, 341–44.

20. In the first act of creation God appears as the maker of the world. But that act cannot avert the possibility of evil contained in meonic freedom, which utilizes the Greek term "meon" referring to the creation of two, one as being and another as nonbeing. See Berdyaev, *Destiny of Man*, 25, and Reese, *Dictionary of Philosophy and Religion*, 350.

21. In the concept of existence, there are possibilities of decision. These concepts "gain all their meaning from the question of human existence, and express the double possibility in man's existing."

independently of one another but that, "since every being, in so far as it is a being, is good, if we then say that a defective thing is bad, it would seem to mean that we are saying that what is evil is good, that only what is good is ever evil and that there is no evil apart from something good."[22] Despite the double possibility of human existence toward goodness and evil, goodness, as Augustine points to, is the focal point of every being[23] made evident in human nature. By this, Augustine proposes that "from a human nature, which is good itself, there can spring forth either a good or an evil will."[24] In this Augustinian ideology of will, there is free choice:[25] humankind's ability to perform either goodness or evil.

If goodness and evil coexist in human nature—in order words, that they don't exist independently of one another, as Augustine proposes—and having had developed from what can only be described as a dual inception,[26] the freedom that is apparent in free choice—that is to say, the possibility to choose good over evil or vice versa—is relatively tragic. To that end, that tragedy is even fatal.[27] This is because the "paradoxical, tragic and complex character of moral life lies in the fact that not only evil and the wicked are bad, but that good and evil may be bad also."[28] To put this more plainly, the tragedy of freedom in moral character occurs through the relationship between good and evil subsisting without a clear ideological dividing line but, rather, occurring dualistically to the point that "[what can be assessed as] 'good' may be evil because [anything exhibiting goodness] may believe in an evil 'good' [until] evil is, so to speak, the retribution for spurious good."[29] Furthermore, in light of this, Augustine finds this tragedy of freedom in the fact that "[all of God's creation] is not supremely and immutably good as is the Creator of it [since] the good in created things can be diminished

---

That double possibility is to live from God, or to live from human resources—for man to be himself as the child of God, or to lose himself in the world. Macquarrie, *Existentialist Theology*, 47.

22. Augustine goes on to suppose that this is because every actual entity is good and that nothing evil exists in itself, but only as an evil aspect of some actual entity. As a result, there can be nothing evil without something good. See ch. 4, para. 13 of Augustine, *Enchiridion*.

23. Goodness must be defined as the essential nature of a thing and the fulfillment of the potentialities implied in it. However, this applies to everything that is and describes the inner aim of creation itself. See Tillich, *Systematic Theology*, 3:67.

24. Augustine furthers this with saying, "There was no other place from whence evil could have arisen in the first place except from the nature—good in itself—of an angel or a man." See ch. 4, para. 15 of Augustine, *Enchiridion*.

25. See Ferguson and Wright, *New Dictionary of Theology*, 242.

26. Berdyaev finds the following: "The distinction between good and evil had an origin in time and had been preceded by a state of being 'beyond' or 'prior to' good and evil. 'Good' and 'evil' are correlative and in a sense it may be said that good comes into being at the same time as evil and, therefore, disappears together with it." Berdyaev, *Destiny of Man*, 35.

27. The tragedy of freedom shows that there is a struggle between the conflicting principles which lie deeper than the distinction between good and evil. Fate is the child of freedom—this means that freedom itself is fatal. Berdyaev, *Destiny of Man*, 31.

28. Berdyaev, *Destiny of Man*, 32.

29. Berdyaev, *Destiny of Man*, 32.

and augmented."[30] The way through which good is diminished and augmented, since it coexists with evil, comes by way of stages of living reality, so that "[in] the first stage of living reality, the purpose of man is to overcome the chaotic state of his soul, the state of undirected surging passion."[31] In this stage, humankind is innately good but struggles to remain so by resisting against physio-psychological drives within the heart[32] until, when in the second stage of living reality, humankind is presented with the choice to remain good or wicked[33]—the difference between these two stages of living reality does not just lie in "being" with the choice to continue as such or become "nonbeing," but with the notion of evil coexisting with good before it becomes radicalized,[34] albeit, to use Augustine's terms, diminished and augmented.

Not only does Augustine, then, invoke Matt 12:35 by paraphrasing "an evil man brings forth evil out of the evil treasure of his heart,"[35] but he proceeds to objectify the heart, or, for the sake of argument, a heart conceived in goodness. Consequently, the "good heart" as it was conceived, when confronted with meonic freedom[36] and the process of the turning away of the soul,[37] is the place where goodness is diminished and augmented wickedness, where the good becomes evil. Since "evils have their source in the good, and unless they are parasitic on something good, they are not anything at

---

30. See ch. 4, para. 12 of Augustine, *Enchiridion*.

31. This occurs in "appearance only, instead of really overcoming it and breaking violently out of it wherever a breach can be forced, instead of achieving direction by unifying his energies—the only manner in which [living reality] can be achieved." Buber, *Good and Evil*, 139.

32. According to Nietzsche, "a proper physio-psychology has to contend with unconscious resistance in the heart of the investigator, it has 'the heart' against it: even a doctrine of the reciprocal dependence of the 'good' and the 'wicked' drives, causes (as refined immorality) distress and aversion in a still hale and hearty conscience—still more so, a doctrine of the deprivation of all good impulses from wicked ones." Kaufmann, *Basic Writings of Nietzsche*, 221.

33. Augustine's term for evil—this is drawn on the relationship between good and evil, and goodness and wickedness.

34. Buber proposes the following: "In the first stage man does not choose, he merely acts; in the second, he chooses himself, in the sense of his being-constituted-thus or having-become-thus. The first stage does not yet contain a 'radical evil'; whatever misdeeds are committed, their commission is not a doing of the deed but a sliding into it. In the second stage evil grows radical, because what man finds in himself is willed." Buber, *Good and Evil*, 140.

35. Though Augustine makes a reference to Matt 12:35, when considering the entity of Matt 12:33–35, the complete context of Jesus' words are the following: "Either make the tree good, and its fruit good; or make the tree bad, and its fruit bad; for the tree is known by its fruit. You brood of vipers! How can you speak good things, when you are evil? For out of the abundance of the heart the mouth speaks. The good person brings good things out of a good treasure, and the evil person brings evil things out of an evil treasure."

36. Augustine does not use the term "freedom" but, instead, implicates the term "will" when assuming the language of Matt 12:33–35 about good trees versus bad trees with, "Just as a bad tree does not grow good fruit, so also an evil will does not produce good deeds." See ch. 4, para. 15 of Augustine, *Enchiridion*.

37 The turning away of the soul from the nous toward matter, toward the bodily realm, is the source of evil. Tillich, *History of Christian Thought*, 53.

all [and] there is no other source whence an evil thing can come to be,"[38] the existence of evil occurs along with the existence of good, so that the possibility of something becoming evil is triggered only by the freedom of choice.

The fact that goodness is inherently evident in all of creation, due to the premise that, according to Augustine, "the creator of all nature is supremely good,"[39] the knowledge of evil comes from a kind of knowledge of God. For Augustine, this knowledge is "not sought in the exploration of the nature of things . . . after the manner of those whom the Greeks called 'physicists,'"[40] which, undoubtedly, refers to natural philosophy.[41] Since Augustine believes this manner to be too empirical, he surmises that the natural philosopher is more concerned with "exploring [the nature of things] by human conjecture and others through historical inquiry [to the point that they] have not yet learned everything there is to know."[42] In effect, what Augustine seems to argue for is a natural theology to develop knowledge of God, because natural theology, unlike natural philosophy, approaches the "study [of] God according to what existing things can tell [humankind] about [God]."[43] Rather than utilizing theology in the more strict sense of the term and discipline in a sacred or revealed form,[44] Augustine's application of "natural theology," then, has the distinct purpose of investigating what reason can inform humankind about God, how this knowledge of God can explain the relationship between good and evil as coexisting in forms of being and nonbeing, and the means through which such an extrapolation can further examine the problem of evil and the notion of freedom in a created world generated by an all-powerful, supremely-good God.[45]

A Brief History of the Forgiveness of Sins in the Early Church

Sin as an act committed against humankind or a transgression against God, and the act of the forgiveness of sins are inextricably linked to the concept of salvation, which is "the Christian term for that state in which [humankind] is redeemed and reconciled to God [where] the mediator in this event is Jesus Christ, who atones for

---

38. See ch. 4, para. 14 of Augustine, *Enchiridion*.

39. See ch. 4, para. 12.

40. See ch. 3, para. 9.

41. Up to the thirteenth century, philosophy as a whole, and natural philosophy in particular, were viewed as the handmaidens of theology. As we saw, natural philosophy was regarded as a tool or instrument for explicating theology and the articles of faith. In terms of the study of the natural sciences such as biology, chemistry, and physics, theologians and natural philosophers all recognized that natural philosophy was a powerful instrument for the study and analysis of both physical world and the faith. Grant, *History of Natural Philosophy*, 242; 248.

42. See ch. 3, para. 9 of Augustine, *Enchiridion*.

43. Holloway, *Introduction to Natural Theology*, 17.

44. Holloway, *Introduction to Natural Theology*, 18.

45. Joyce, *Principles of Natural Theology*, 1–2.

[humankind's] sins."[46] This, then, can be construed in terms of a Christian doctrine on the relationship between sin, forgiveness, and salvation, of which, at the center, lies the redemptive nature of Jesus Christ. Though the early church canonized a text based on the resurrected Jesus Christ imparting to his disciple, "thus it is written, that the Messiah is to suffer and to rise from the dead on the third day, and that the repentance and forgiveness of sins is to be proclaimed in his name to all nations,"[47] the relationship between sin, forgiveness, and salvation is seen differently in Augustine of Hippo (354–430), Origen of Alexandria (184–253), Gregory of Nyssa (335–395), Irenaeus of Lyons (130–202), and Athanasius of Alexandria (ca. 296–373).

Augustine of Hippo

Operating first from Platonism, then moving toward a kind of Neoplatonism that he believed "to be a preliminary and necessary step in the acceptance of Christianity,"[48] Augustine of Hippo viewed sin through a relationship between freedom and will. For Augustine, then, "the power of sin is such that it takes hold of our will, and as long as we are under its sway we cannot move our will to be rid of it."[49] What this incites is a struggle with the "will," which is based on Plato's tripartite doctrine of the soul,[50] until that struggle is the most that can be accomplished. Augustine believed that the human soul struggles between willing and not willing to such an extent that not only is there a relative powerlessness in humankind's will against itself but, more importantly, because of this struggle, "the sinner can will nothing but sin."[51] For the sinner, there remains freedom to choose other options other than a sinful act but, nevertheless, "all these [options] are sin, and the one alternative that is not open is to cease sinning."[52] Augustine refers to this as the freedom to sin which is the only freedom a sinner has. Essentially, this perpetual freedom to sin can't be reconciled as a true freedom until "[the sinner is] redeemed [by] the grace of God [working] in [them], leading [their] will from the miserable state in which it found itself to a new state in which freedom is restored, so that we are now free both to sin and not to sin."[53] It is here, then, where

---

46. Reese, *Dictionary of Philosophy and Religion*, 506.

47. Refer to Luke 24:46–47; similar language is used in Matt 28:19, where the resurrected Jesus tells his disciples, "Go therefore and make disciples of all nations, baptizing them in the name of the Father and of the Son and of the Holy Spirit," with the intent to bring about widespread salvation through the forgiveness of sins, in order to Christianize the Christian faith.

48. Reese, *Dictionary of Philosophy and Religion*, 443.

49. Gonzalez, *Story of Christianity*, 1:214.

50. In the tripartite doctrine of the soul advanced by Plato, the will stands between reason and the appetites. It is the function of the reason to control the will, and humankind is obliged to build good habits allowing such control. Reese, *Dictionary of Philosophy and Religion*, 626.

51. Gonzalez, *Story of Christianity*, 1:214.

52. Gonzalez, *Story of Christianity*, 1:214.

53. Gonzalez, *Story of Christianity*, 1:214.

freedom actually exists as it should in mortality, where humankind has two options to either sin or not to sin. For Augustine, this is possible "only by the power of grace itself [are we able to make the decision to accept grace], for before that moment we are not free not to sin, and therefore we are not free to decide to accept grace."[54] In other words, Augustine viewed sin as something innate and fundamentally intrinsic within humankind's character which was brought about by the fall[55] and, because of this, humankind can do nothing else but inevitably, albeit hopelessly, sin, even under the guises of freedom and will. It is only through the power of grace—specifically, the act of God's forgiveness and subsequent salvation—that humankind can choose to not sin by way of an "initiative in conversion [that] is not human, but divine."[56]

Origen of Alexandria

Having studied under Clement of Alexandria,[57] Origen is considered more Platonist than Christian, which stands to reason why he "reject[ed] the doctrines of Marcion[58] and of the Gnostics that the world is the creation of an inferior being [and, by this, arriving at the] conclusion that the existence of the physical world is the result of sin."[59] Sin was, in effect, the result of the fall.[60] Because of the fall and the act of sin, humankind was punished by being condemned to a physical existence subordinate to their previous spiritual existence. For Origen, then, before sinning and before the fall, all human souls preexisted as pure spirits "before being born into the world, and that the reason why we are here is that we have sinned in that prior, purely spiritual existence."[61] Moreover, Origen believed that because the devil and his demons hold us captive in this present world, in this physical existence, evidence of God's forgiveness of the sins committed in that prior, purely spiritual existence is in Jesus Christ "[coming] to break the power of Satan and to show us the path to follow in our return to

---

54. Gonzalez, *Story of Christianity*, 1:215.

55. Between the fall, or the original sin of Adam and Eve, and redemption, or the God's act of forgiveness and the promise of salvation, the only freedom left to humankind is the freedom to sin. Refer to Gonzalez, *Story of Christianity*, 1:214.

56. Gonzalez, *Story of Christianity*, 1:215.

57. One of the beliefs that Origen surely carried forward from Clement of Alexandria, would have been the idea that God the Father is the Absolute, the Monrad, devoid of all characteristics because of God's superiority to sensible distinctions. Refer to Reese, *Dictionary of Philosophy and Religion*, 95.

58. Marcion of Sinope held the belief that humankind was created by the Demiurge (or maker of the world in Platonism), a just and wrathful God who placed humankind under a rule of law. Since humankind couldn't keep the law, the whole human race fell under a divine curse. Refer to Reese, *Dictionary of Philosophy and Religion*, 331.

59. Gonzalez, *Story of Christianity*, 1:81.

60. It is evident that, for Origen, the prehistorical fall explains not only the limitations of human finitude such as death and bodily material existence, but also the reality of human sinfulness. Urban, *Short History of Christian Thought*, 139.

61. Gonzalez, *Story of Christianity*, 1:79.

our spiritual home."[62] Once that occurs, not only will Satan be saved due to the devil being a spirit fashioned similarly to that of the human soul, but "the entire creation will return to its original state, where everything was pure spirit."[63] Even though all of creation's return to its original state of being pure spirits will mark a sort of salvation by way of the redemptive powers of Jesus Christ, Origen viewed this as not a singular, one-time event but, instead, a cycle of fall and salvation that could possibly go on forever since spirits are irrevocably free.

Gregory of Nyssa

Being one of the three great Cappadocians,[64] Gregory of Nyssa was a follower of Origen in the belief of universal redemption, or, more aptly, the universalism of salvation as being afforded to all of creation including the devil. But, Gregory had a significant theological point of divergence with Origen by "[denying] the Platonic doctrine of [the] pre-existence of souls, [and instead], believing them to be created by God."[65] From this, not only does Gregory believe that humankind's creation is made in a "likeness which consists in being in the image of God [and] a summation of all the characteristically divine attributes [but] namely that in [humankind's] origins our nature was good and [we were] surrounded by goodness."[66] What he postulated was that the presence of evil in human life does not suggest that humankind, at some point in time, had never been in a state of goodness but, rather, that "evil comes in some way or another from within [because] it is the product of free choice, whenever the soul withdraws in any way from the good." For Gregory, God wasn't the cause of humankind's evil state but was, simply, a provider of humankind's free and independent nature. Therefore, in terms of freedom and will, "evil has no existence of its own outside the will."[67] It is by way of the same will and freedom in which humankind makes choices to engage in evil that, according to Gregory, the sickness of the soul and the body "aim to bring us to our senses and induce us to flee from evil by fear of a painful retribution [in order to bring forth] a healing remedy provided by God for the restoration of [his] special creation to its original state."[68]

---

62. Gonzalez, *Story of Christianity*, 1:80.

63. Gonzalez, *Story of Christianity*, 1:80.

64. From the region of Cappadocia in southern Asia Minor, in lands now belonging to Turkey, Gregory of Nyssa was one of three church leaders known under the collective title of "the Great Cappadocians" along with Basil of Caesarea and Gregory of Nazianzus. Refer to Gonzalez, *Story of Christianity*, 1:181.

65. Reese, *Dictionary of Philosophy and Religion*, 203.

66. Wiles and Santer, *Documents in Early Christian Thought*, 103.

67. Wiles and Santer, *Documents in Early Christian Thought*, 108.

68. Wiles and Santer, *Documents in Early Christian Thought*, 110.

Irenaeus of Lyons

Opposing Gnosticism and relying heavily on the writings of Paul to the extent of increasing the influence of the Johannine gospel, Irenaeus of Lyons viewed the presence of sin, the act of God's forgiveness, and the process of salvation in terms of "divinization," where "God's purpose is to make us ever more like the divine."[69] The concept of divinization, for Irenaeus, is embodied in the idea of human communion with a divine God and, more importantly, that the supposition of God's creation of humankind was based on this need for divine communion. What can be gleaned further from this is that forgiveness and salvation are the ultimate goals of God for humankind with the intent of restoring this communion. With the introduction of sin and the resulting fall, this is approached through the incarnation of God in Christ not as the result of sin but, instead, "what has happened because of sin is that the incarnation has taken on the added purpose of offering a remedy for sin, and a means for defeating Satan."[70] Specifically, then, the incarnation of God in Christ is meant to create a new humanity in salvation, whereby all of the actions of Jesus, both physically and spiritually, are meant to "correct what was twisted because of sin [and] defeat Satan [so that humankind can] live in a new freedom."[71]

Athanasius of Alexandria

As an opponent of Arianism,[72] Athanasius of Alexandria's declaration that "it was acceptable to refer to the Father, Son, and Holy Spirit as 'one substance' as long as this was not understood as obliterating the distinction among the three"[73] becomes a significant means to understand, particularly, his view of salvation. This belief rests in the notion of the redemptive powers of God the Son as being homoousian.[74] For Athanasius, sin, then, "is overcome by forgiveness, and death, which is the curse of sin, is overcome by the new life. Both are given by Christ."[75] What this means, too, is

---

69. Gonzalez, *Story of Christianity*, 1:70.

70. Gonzalez, *Story of Christianity*, 1:70.

71. Gonzalez, *Story of Christianity*, 1:70.

72. This was the name given to a dispute in the early church from 318 to 381 CE that required eighteen councils, beginning with the Council of Nicaea in 325 CE and ending with the Council of Constantinople in 381 CE. The subject of the dispute was the meaning of incarnation in relation to the Christian belief of monotheism. In this dispute, while Arius believed in a sharp distinction between God the Father and God the Son, subordinating the latter to the former, Athanasius believed that the Father and the Son were of the same essence. Reese, *Dictionary of Philosophy and Religion*, 27; 36.

73. Gonzalez, *Story of Christianity*, 1:179.

74. This is based on the doctrine established at the Council of Nicaea and the councils thereafter about God the Son being of the same essence or substance as God the Father. Reese, *Dictionary of Philosophy and Religion*, 231.

75. Tillich, *History of Christian Thought*, 73.

Ideals of Medieval Theology and the Pre-Constantinian Church

that the forgiveness of sins through salvation can occur "only by Christ who, as true man, suffers the curse of sin and, as true God, overcomes death."[76]

In order to ascertain the notion that the dominance of the ideals of medieval Christianity during the Middle Ages[77] originated in the earlier ideals of the pre-Constantinian[78] church, this means that the principles that shaped the early Christian church are not only the foundational ideologies of the medieval church but are, undoubtedly, interwoven into medieval theology.[79] The ideological framework of medieval theology, then, is based and crafted on prominent individuals and movements of the pre-Constantinian era. Four of these influential early Christian theologians and philosophers that had a long-lasting impact on medieval Christianity are Augustine of Hippo, Tertullian of Carthage (155–240), and Origen of Alexandria.

Augustine, the Return to the Monasticism, and New Doctrine of Salvation

The main element of medieval theology is monastic theology, which "refers not just to the local setting of the theologians but to the approach that they adopted."[80] This adopted approach involved a discipline of life characterized by a relative withdrawal from the material world, in order to focus on meditation, self-abnegation, and asceticism.[81] What these aspects of monasticism, as an institution, did, as a result, was not only provide "a way to live out the total commitment that had been required in earlier times,"[82] but create a new Christian church of the Middle Ages that attempted

---

76. Tillich, *History of Christian Thought*, 73.

77. This period that can, roughly, include the era between 500 and 1500 CE. More specifically, this can be considered from 590 CE with the inauguration of Gregory as bishop of Rome and 1517 CE with Martin Luther's Protestant Reformation. Ennis, *Moody Handbook of Theology*, 433.

78. This is in reference to Constantine, who became emperor of the Roman Empire in 312 CE. To suggest a "pre-Constantinian era" in relation to a, perhaps, "post-Constantinian era," denotes the influence Constantine had as the champion of Christianity following his own conversion to the faith and ascension to the supreme seat of power in the Roman Empire. Constantine allowed for Christianity to flourish in the empire as it never had before his rule by his readiness to support Christianity in every way he could, such as, among many other examples, generously endowing Christian shrines, particularly in the Holy Land, and, in 321 CE, making Sunday an official holiday. MacGregor, *Dictionary of Religion and Philosophy*, 139.

79. Ennis, *Moody Handbook of Theology*, 433.

80. Ferguson and Wright, *New Dictionary of Theology*, 441.

81. Reese, *Dictionary of Philosophy and Religion*, 365.

82. Gonzalez, *Story of Christianity*, 1:238.

to redefine many of the important early church teachings of Augustine, who was responsible for molding Christian thought.[83]

Augustine of Hippo, subsequently, became the central ideological figure in the medieval church's doctrines of purgatory and salvation in relation to their return to monasticism. For Augustine, when considering the possibility of salvation from sin, there was "a place of purification for those who died in sin, where they would spend some time before going to heaven."[84] The medieval church, then, not only affirmed the existence of such a place that Augustine described, but developed a doctrine of purgatory. Where the medieval church differed, however, was with Augustine's doctrine of salvation that involved predestination[85] and irresistible grace,[86] both of which are concepts built into Augustine's doctrine of purgatory. Despite Augustine's doctrines on purgatory and salvation with respect to predestination and God's irresistible grace, the medieval church "was more concerned with the question of how we are to offer satisfaction to God for sins committed."[87] Consequently, the medieval church developed an ideology of penance, which consists of contrition and confession, as well as priestly absolution, which confirms the forgiveness granted by God.[88] For the medieval church, since "those who die in the faith and communion of the church without having offered satisfaction for all of their sins will [ultimately] go to purgatory before they attain their final salvation,"[89] the participation of the living in a mass or a communion[90] helped the dead out of purgatory.

Tertullian, the Trinitarian Formula, and the Use of Sacraments

Though he is connected to Montanism,[91] which was, eventually, transformed into Tertullianism by 400 CE, before the influence of Montanist-Tertullianist movement

---

83. MacGregor, *Dictionary of Religion and Philosophy*, 47.

84. Gonzalez, *Story of Christianity*, 1:247.

85. Originating with Augustine, this term refers the belief that the individual, left to himself, is so lost in sin and rebellion against God that he will not seek God. His fallen will is so corrupted that he cannot seek salvation. In that sense, humanity has no free will. So, if there is to be salvation for man, it must come at God's initiative. Ferguson and Wright, *New Dictionary of Theology*, 528.

86. This is based on the notion that God not only provides grace but the will to receive it, with the intent of an individual's inability to refuse it. If it cannot be refused, then grace is irresistible. Reese, *Dictionary of Philosophy and Religion*, 200.

87. Gonzalez, *Story of Christianity*, 1:247.

88. Gonzalez, *Story of Christianity*, 1:247.

89. Gonzalez, *Story of Christianity*, 1:247.

90. This permitted Christ to be sacrificed anew. Gonzalez, *Story of Christianity*, 1:247.

91. This was the name of the second-century CE movement which, along with Gnosticism, provided the early Christian church with its greatest challenge. The movement, initially led by Montanus, was otherworldly, stressed the importance of martyrdom, and awaited the coming of the Lord. Montanism, as a religious movement, forced the early church to become Catholic. Reese, *Dictionary of Philosophy and Religion*, 367.

subsided altogether,[92] Tertullian offered two very significant contributions that survived to become part of the theological and doctrinal stance of the medieval church: the Trinitarian Formula and the use of sacraments as church practice.

The Trinitarian Formula, which was first used by Tertullian[93] during the development of the early church, "viewed [God] as three persons in one substance."[94] This view of God was influenced by what is known as economic Trinitarianism, through "the belief that God the Father brought forth two hands, [which were] the Son and the Holy Spirit, to serve as mediators in creating the world."[95] By viewing God as three persons in one substance and explaining the meanings of "person" and "substance" in terms drawn from their legal use,[96] this became incorporated into not only Trinitarianism but Christology,[97] where it is evident that Tertullian "coined the formulas that would eventually become the hallmark of orthodoxy."[98]

What would also become just as significant a hallmark of orthodoxy is the use of sacraments,[99] which was a term that Tertullian was the first to use and "did so to denote not only particular signs, like the water of baptism, but also the whole rite of which the sign was a part."[100] Since the term "sacrament," then, "came to mean more than simply 'sign' or even 'ritual' and [to that end] carries with it the idea that sacred action changes the lives of the participants,"[101] it came to represent the objectivity of the grace of Christ and the continuation of the basic sacramental reality of God's manifestation in Christ.[102] To that end, when considering religious life in the Middle Ages, sacraments were, perhaps, the most important thing in medieval church history,[103] which are exemplified

---

92. Reese, *Dictionary of Philosophy and Religion*, 367.

93. What must be taken into consideration, first, is that Tertullian was part of a religious fringe movement that acted in opposition to the early church. But, the Trinitarian speculation begins in the second century, with Athenagoras (ca. 177 CE), who defended the doctrine as being an essential part of the church's faith. This stance was expounded at length by Tertullian. Ferguson and Wright, *New Dictionary of Theology*, 692.

94. Reese, *Dictionary of Philosophy and Religion*, 572.

95. Ferguson and Wright, *New Dictionary of Theology*, 692.

96. Perhaps this is due to the fact that Tertullian was either a lawyer or had been trained in rhetoric, and that his entire output bears the stamp of a legal mind. Gonzalez, *Story of Christianity*, 1:74.

97. The doctrine of Christ, in terms of his person and nature. Ferguson and Wright, *New Dictionary of Theology*, 137.

98. Gonzalez, *Story of Christianity*, 1:77.

99. In its original meaning as "sacred sign," it was used in the Roman army as the name for the oath to the emperor. The word "sacrament" does not appear in Christian writing until the early third century. Urban, *Short History of Christian Thought*, 255.

100. Urban, *Short History of Christian Thought*, 256.

101. Urban, *Short History of Christian Thought*, 256.

102. Tillich, *History of Christian Thought*, 155.

103. Tillich, *History of Christian Thought*, 154.

in the use of water, bread, wine, oil, a word, the laying on of hands as all becoming "sacramental if a transcendent substance is poured into them."[104]

Origen, Scholasticism, and the Practice of Hermeneutics

Monastic life, by the thirteenth century, marked the height of papal power and the birth of the mendicant orders. By this time, scholasticism arose, which, as a term, is "the name given to a theology that developed in the [cathedral] schools [that] became the center of theological activity."[105] In these cathedral schools, scholasticism sought to make "an immense intellectual effort to investigate and bring into a single system the articles of faith and reason."[106] The ways and means by which faith and reason were investigated were through the use of hermeneutics, which involve "all methods of interpreting philosophical or literary texts, including biblical ones [with the intent of] being more involved in the problem of how to achieve an authentic understanding of a culture and an age other than one's own."[107] This was, of course, an essential aspect of monastic life as a theological activity. Hermeneutics, then, was "Origen's most enduring influence on the [early] church [which endured into the medieval church, surmising that] every text has a spiritual meaning [and] the interpreter [must] discern this meaning, and divine power must be added to the words to make them effective."[108] As a result, Origen's use of hermeneutics had a major impact on scholasticism in the medieval church, which, eventually, "was the determinative cognitive attitude of the whole Middle Ages [and] is the methodological explanation of Christian doctrine."[109]

Ontological Arguments: Anselm of Canterbury, Duns Scotus, and William of Ockham

As Scholasticism grounded itself further on the use of hermeneutics in the high to late medieval period, the two joined in an effort to conceptualize and articulate one important preoccupation of the medieval church: the ontological argument. This concern is centered, if you will, on how to theologize about God and, in doing so, on how this kind of theologizing situates itself in a unique period influenced by the early church fathers of Augustine, Gregory of Nyssa, Irenaeus, Athanasius, Tertullian, and Origen. Together, with the growth of scholasticism, the development of hermeneutics, and the methodological merging of "the philosophical" with "the theological" to handle the

---

104. Tillich, *History of Christian Thought*, 155.
105. Gonzalez, *Story of Christianity*, 1:311.
106. Reese, *Dictionary of Philosophy and Religion*, 514.
107. MacGregor, *Dictionary of Religion and Philosophy*, 306.
108. Ferguson and Wright, *New Dictionary of Theology*, 482.
109. Tillich, *History of Christian Thought*, 135.

doctrine of God, three key thinkers emerge: Anselm of Canterbury (1033–1109), Duns Scotus (1266–1308), and William of Ockham (1285–1347).

Generally speaking, "the ontological argument" is predicated on an explicitly philosophical approach to defining and explaining the existence of God through the framework of ontology. As such, what makes "the ontological argument" oriented toward "the ontological" is the degree to which it presents a foundational argument that attends to the nature of existence. That is to say, "the ontological" for this kind of argument articulates the nature of existing and the extent of being, which extends itself from the guiding *a priori* conceptualization—in beginning here, what it means to construct an "ontological argument" is based on presupposing, through an *a priori* construct, an organizational structure to the universal, which is built upon the notion that the construction of reality itself is centralized by an unmoved mover, as Aristotle defines it, and the organization of this reality requires an argument that intends to express a series of propositions validating and existentializing God's existence by necessity.

In *Proslogion* (1077–1078), considered as the very first articulation of what is now known as "the ontological argument," Anselm begins, in the first chapter, entitled "That There Is Something That Is Best and Greatest and Supreme among All Existing Things," with the following:

> If anyone does not know, either because he has not heard or because he does not believe, that there is on nature, supreme among all existing things, who alone is self-sufficient in his eternal happiness, who through his omnipotent goodness grants and brings it about that all other things exist or have any sort of well-being, and a great many other things that we must believe about God, or his creation, I think he could at least convince himself of most things by reason alone, if he is even moderately intelligent.[110]

Though Anselm concedes that "there are many ways in which he could [convince himself of most things by reason alone],"[111] what follows, for Anselm, is an outline that Anselm "think[s] would be easiest for him" to understand "by reason alone." To do this, Anselm defines the meaning and importance of "something supreme" in relation to everything else—in this regard, "something supreme," according to Anselm, is defined as that which "surpasses others in such a way that nothing is equal to or more excellent than it."[112] This "something supreme" can only be thought of and expressed through a kind of theologizing, insomuch as that theologizing allows Anselm to conceive of "something supreme" as "that which is supremely good [and] is also supremely great."[113] The theologizing of "something supreme" by Anselm is, at its most fundamental, based on outlining a set of parameters about the existence of "something

---

110. Anselm, *Monologion*, 10.
111. Anselm, *Monologion*, 10.
112. Anselm, *Monologion*, 11–12.
113. Anselm, *Monologion*, 12.

supreme" and how these parameters, when defined, formulate the parameters of the existence of everything else that "something supreme" necessarily "surpasses," by the very fact that "something supreme," by defining it as such, "is supremely good [and] is also supremely great." It is on this point that Anselm logically arrives at the subsequent conclusion: "There is, therefore, some one thing that is supremely good and supremely great—in other words, supreme among all existing things."[114]

Anselm's explication of "some one thing that is supremely good and supremely great," as that which is fundamentally, existentially, and predominantly "supreme among all existing things" is advanced further by Duns Scotus in *A Treatise on God as First Principle*. As a text that is considered as "a short but important compendium of Scotus' natural theology,"[115] it is undoubtedly a representation of Scotus's handling of "the theological" and "the philosophical" at the intersection of the meaning of the existence of God. As such, it is generally believed that *A Treatise on God as First Principle* "draws heavily on [Scotus's] *Ordinatio*"—the latter, being dated to 1300–1304, serves as a commentary on *Sentences* (around 1150) written by Peter Lombard (1096–1160). Yet, it remains difficult to accurately date the writing of *A Treatise on God as First Principle*, and it is only in the extent to which it stands in relation to *Ordinatio* that is possible to conclude that it is "one of [Scotus's] latest works."[116]

At the outset of *A Treatise on God as First Principle*, Scotus directly addresses Anselm's conceptualization of "some one thing that is supremely good and supremely great" with the following proclamation: "May the First principle of things grant me to believe, to understand and to reveal what may please his majesty and may raise our minds to contemplate him."[117] For Scotus, God's existence, as a "first principle," is that "some one thing," from which everything that exists is able to exist at all. This conceptualization of the meaning of the existence of God is carried forward by William of Ockham in what is the first maxim representing "the guiding principles of all of Ockham's work"—that first maxim, then, is that "all things are possible for God, save such as involve a contradiction."[118] As with Scotus, Ockham unfolds a "treatise on God" grounded on a fundamental first question: "whether in essentially ordered causes the second cause depends on the first?"[119] To this first question, Ockham answers in the affirmative, arguing that "for in causes of this kind the second cause cannot cause an effect of the same kind as itself without the first cause, though the reverse is possible."[120]

---

114. Anselm, *Monologion*, 12.
115. Scotus, *Philosophical Writings*, xxvii.
116. Scotus, *Philosophical Writings*, xxvii.
117. Scotus, *Treatise on God as First Principle*, 2.
118. Ockham, *Philosophical Writings*, xix.
119. Ockham, *Philosophical Writings*, 115.
120. Ockham, *Philosophical Writings*, 115.

What is expressed by Anselm, Scotus, and Ockham, through what has been referred to as "the ontological arguments," is a kind of theologizing about God focused on the meaning of God's existence toward the meaning of human existence. These two meanings actualize one another, such that what it means to be human is actualized by and actualizes the meaning that can be made through the actualizing and actualization of God as "the first cause."

Aquinas's Cosmological Arguments in *Summa Theologica*

Largely influenced by Aristotle—and to a lesser extent, precisely within the traditions of the medieval church, also influenced by Augustine—Aquinas (1225–1274) serves an essential role in the development of medieval theology and how that theologizing speaks to questions of God's existence. The manner with which Aquinas speaks about God's existence is, in itself, generally drawn from Aristotle's articulation of the "unmoved mover," or what is also called "the primary cause," or "the first uncaused cause"—Aristotle expresses this concept in both book 8 of *Physics* and book 12 of *Metaphysics*.

While Aristotle's notion of an "unmoved mover" is not particularly new, given that Aristotle was influenced by the cosmological speculations of Greek pre-Socratics such as Parmenides and Heraclitus, Aristotle's situating the "unmoved mover" as the centerpiece of a first philosophy that becomes the framework for a theologizing about the meaning of "primary cause" and "first uncaused cause," as an independent, eternal, unchanging, divine, immaterial substance. By essentially theologizing "the unmoved mover," if attending to the decidedly theistic implications to Aristotle's "first philosophy," Aquinas's more purposeful theologizing of Aristotle's "unmoved mover" becomes delineated into five logical arguments about the existence of God in article 3, question 2 of part 1 of Aquinas's *Summa Theologica* (1265–1274): metaphysical motion, efficient causation, contingency, degrees of being, and the teleological.

In the "Treatise on the One God" of *Summa Theologica*, Aquinas presents question 2 as "The Existence of God," which is considered in the following way:

> Because the chief aim of sacred doctrine is to teach the knowledge of God, not only as He is in Himself, but also as He is the beginning of things, and their last end, and especially of rational creatures, . . . therefore, in our endeavor to expound this science, we shall treat: 1. Of God; 2. Of rational creature's advance towards God; 3. Of Christ, Who as man, is our way to God.[121]

From this, Aquinas finds that "in [the] treat[ment] of God there will be a three-fold division," which are delineating along "whatever concerns the Divine Essence," "whatever concerns the distinction of Persons," and "whatever concerns the procession of creatures from Him."[122] From Aquinas's notion of "the Divine Essence," he further

---

121. Aquinas, *Summa Theologiae*, 1:18.
122. Aquinas, *Summa Theologiae*, 1:18.

considers three aspects or themes in terms of "whether God exists," "the manner of His existence, or, rather, what is not the manner of His existence," and "whatever concerns His operations—namely, His knowledge, will, power."[123]

In light of these, "concerning the first," Aquinas suggests that "there are three points of inquiry," with article 3, in particular, focusing on "whether God exists?"[124] It is with respect to this third article that Aquinas writes, in response to two objections to the question of "whether God exists," the following: "The existence of God can be proved in five ways."[125] What follows is two "replies" to the two objections Aquinas provides to the question of "whether God exists": Aquinas's first reply makes reference to and adjudicates the problem of theodicy seen in Augustine's *Enchiridion*, while, in his second reply, Aquinas makes use of Aristotle's "first cause" through the notion "nature works for a determinate end under the direction of a higher agent [such that] whatever is done by nature must needs be traced back to God."[126]

Martin Luther, Theodicy, and the Problem of Evil

In reading Daniel Migliore's chapter entitled "The Providence of God and the Mystery of Evil," from *Faith Seeking Understanding* (1991) along with the excerpt from *The Bondage of the Will* (1525) by Martin Luther (1483–1546), one of the most predominant challenges to human existence, human being's faith in God, and the means by which humans interact and form relationships with God through the appropriation of theological language is the coexistence of goodness and evil. What arises in this challenge is the fact that evil should exist at all in our world, when our world is created by a God of transcendent Good that embodies the highest of all good. In other words, the existence of evil threatens human existence's fundamental knowledge of what goodness is, shapes their faith in God as the ultimate source of that goodness, and defines the language they use to address God, particularly at times of human suffering. These three things are, on one hand, wielded by the presence of evil and necessity of validating the superiority of goodness, but, on the other hand, they become components of a theological existence that is constantly tested and influenced either negatively or positively.

The issue of evil and goodness coexisting is at the heart of the problem of theodicy that can, at least on the surface, be articulated by Migliore's idea of God's goodness being providential and evil being a mystery. Evil and goodness both exist in juxtaposition, not only in theory but in practice. They are, perhaps, as a relationship, dialectical within the human nature of reality, where, as Hegel would argue, their mere coexistence represents a contradiction that restructures a thesis by an antithesis in order to

---

123. Aquinas, *Summa Theologiae*, 1:18.
124. Aquinas, *Summa Theologiae*, 1:19.
125. Aquinas, *Summa Theologiae*, 1:23.
126. Aquinas, *Summa Theologiae*, 1:26.

arrive at a synthesis.[127] In Hegelian logic, then, the thesis would be that God's goodness is providential, the antithesis would be that evil does not adhere to God's providential goodness, and the synthesis would be that the coexistence of good and evil contradict, at best, to provide a conflict in the notion of theosophy. Not only is Hegel's concept of dialectics essential to, perhaps, understanding the relationship between goodness and evil, but also as a way of articulating that the juxtaposed natures of goodness and evil create an existential dilemma in human existence.

While Voltaire (1694–1778), in his *Candide* (1759), suggests, through the text's fictional character Pangloss, that, in this existential dilemma in the goodness-evil dialectic, everything in our world exists in the best of all possible worlds—the notion that the balance between goodness and evil is theosophical, because God creates a world that contains the least amount of ethical or moral suffering possible so that goodness and evil can coexist. This train of logic about our world being the best of all possible worlds originates with Leibniz who argued, in short, that, though God is the creator of all things good, God is also the creator of evil.[128] For Leibniz, the creation of evil in tandem with the creation of good denotes a balance between them that is determined by God through God's creation of free will and human freedom—the gift of choice to human existence, which is especially evident in the fall of Adam and the original sin. What Leibniz and Voltaire are both articulating, perhaps from two different perspectives, is not only does the existence of evil undermine the existence of goodness, at least in theory, when understanding the providence of God, but that God's goodness creates human beings' free will which, in turn, creates the possibility of evil. Essentially, de facto, then, at least in Leibniz's view, God is the creator of evil.

What arises from this, consequently, is that free will, or human freedom frees human existence to act by the power of their will and to make decisions through their autonomy. But, unfortunately, free will, as Martin Luther correctly posits in his Bondage of the Will, becomes something that frees us, true, but it also binds us.

Migliore echoes Luther through the essential supposition that the coexistence of goodness and evil presents a problem: a theodicy. To take Migliore a bit further on this note, what he describes as the providence of God as the creator of goodness addresses theosophy, while, unfortunately, that same theosophy seems less theosophical due to the inherent mystery surrounding the creation of evil. The initial question, then, is how can evil and goodness coexist? The next question, if appropriating Migliore's argument, must be, particularly in reference to the first: does the coexistence of evil and goodness affirm the providence of God, refute it, or simply redefine it? Moreover, if faith in God is meant to validate the providence of God, does that same faith function as a means of theorizing that the coexistence of evil and goodness is theosophical, transcending the human understanding?

---

127. Hegel discusses his concept of dialectics as a "negative movement," which I would argue redefines any thesis. Hegel, *Phenomenology of Spirit*, 124.

128. Wiener, *Leibniz Selections*, 509.

To that extent, for Aquinas, God has a transcendental good, where all things are good by God's goodness, particularly working under the perspective that "everything is therefore called good from God's goodness . . . everything is called good by reason of the likeness of God's goodness inheriting it."[129] This, in turn, is extending Aristotle's argument about the nature of the whole having the good and the highest good.[130] This, in some regard, presents a final question within the theoretical framework of theodicy and theosophy: Is the existence of evil actually a form of goodness, since it is created by God through God's providential nature and God's ordination of free will onto human existence?

Sin and *The Heidelberg Catechism*

As an instructional document of Christian doctrine that has become "acknowledged as a symbolical book of the Reformed churches,"[131] *The Heidelberg Catechism* (1563) espouses a uniform rule of Christian faith, from which the reformed movement in the Christian church could be systematically voiced. What is voiced, undoubtedly, by the authors of *The Heidelberg Catechism*,[132] is a concerted truth about Christianity, a means of structuring what it means to be a Christian in the reformed era, and an underlying supposition that, as an extrapolation of the reformed movement, it "clearly set[s] forth the true Christian doctrine."[133] If *The Heidelberg Catechism* represents an organized articulation of a "true Christian doctrine," then it, more specifically, assumes the functionality of catechization, which is a "brief and elementary instruction [that] is given by word of mouth in relation to the rudiments of the [Christian doctrine, in order to] signif[y] a system of instruction relating to the first principles of the Christian religion [as] designed for the ignorant and unlearned."[134] With the "ignorant and unlearned" in mind as the audience of this text, the authors utilize an interactive, question-and-answer format, where *The Heidelberg Catechism* embodies a specific method and language that is "well-chosen [for anyone who generally might] desire the knowledge of the truth, [so that] they may live by it."[135] In this respect, then,

---

129. Anderson, *Introduction to the Metaphysics of St. Thomas Aquinas*, 87.

130. Apostle, *Aristotle's Metaphysics*, 210.

131. Bethune, *Expository Lectures*, 10.

132. The two authors were: Zacharias Ursinus, a learned professor at Heidelberg, and Casparus Olevianus, a court preacher, a favorite of Frederic III of Germany. Both Ursinus and Olevianus took part in the composition of the book, where Olevianus arranged his part as a simple illustration of the covenant of grace and Ursinus prepared two forms of a catechism: one of children in the schools and another suited for the more advanced. Though the labors of both Ursinus and Olevianus, ultimately, play equally important roles in the overall production of the Heidelberg Catechism, the system of the book must be attributed mainly to Ursinus. Bethune, *Expository Lectures*, 7.

133. Bethune, *Expository Lectures*, 6.

134. Williard, *Commentary of Dr. Zacharias Ursinus*, 11.

135. Bethune, *Expository Lectures*, 3.

for a Christian to live a distinctly Christian life of faith in reference to a theological desire to know the truth of a true Christian doctrine—albeit, to acknowledge a true Christian doctrine as the existential reference point for any Christian[136]—there, first, should be a theologically most adequate understanding of sin.

In addition to certain inextricably linked[137] understandings that can be derived from the gospel, or salvation, and how God's grace and human faith are related, the concept of sin is the impetus behind the concept of humanity as much as it is the theological starting point for developing a definition of what it means to be human. What this means is that, if the concept of sin is, as aforementioned, an existential reference point for a Christian, then, if being a Christian invokes a state of being, sinfulness must also be a state of being, an alternate one.[138] Though, in the Christian tradition, the source of sin "is held to be hubris or pride, and concupiscence or lust [as being] attitudes [that] are interpreted as stemming from the failure to recognize the divine authority,"[139] as an alternate state of being, there remains "the central idea that sin is a state of our being that separates us from the holy God."[140] Not only does sin, as a separation from God through separating the holy and the secular,[141] incorporate a state of being in which God is not at the center but at the periphery,[142] but it presents the possibility for alienation. Sin as a form of alienation can be extrapolated from the Heideggerian notion of "being-in-the-world."[143] By way of this approach, sin can, in turn, be defined as "being tempted and being tranquilized"[144] to the point that being human becomes being alienated, where "this [overriding] alienation drives [the

---

136. In using the term "existential," what is being addressed is the concept of "being Christian" as equating to an understanding, an interpretation, and a perception of what is means to exist, in the most fundamental way, as a Christian. This, more importantly, presumes that "being Christian" personifies a certain state of being.

137. The concepts of sin, salvation, and God's grace are linked not just theologically by way of their interrelationships and interdependence, but, more poignantly, with the christological assertion of Jesus Christ being the conduit for salvation from sin through the utilization of God's grace-giving, divine power.

138. To say that sin is an "alternate" state of being is to be in conflict with the Augustine-based view of sin as nonbeing due to assertion that sin has no reality and that it is a lack of perfect realization; this logic pertains the belief that sin has no positive ontological standing, where the term "nonbeing," as applied to sin, refers to resistance against being and perversion of being. Tillich, *Systematic Theology*, 1:188.

139. Reese, *Dictionary of Philosophy and Religion*, 530.

140. Ferguson and Wright, *New Dictionary of Theology*, 641.

141. The act of separation from God can also be viewed as the resistance to reunion with God. Since the act of forgiving for sins focuses on the particular sin as the symbol of forgiveness, the human mind concentrates on that particular sin and the moral quality of that sin rather than on the underlying estrangement from God and its religious quality. Tillich, *Systematic Theology*, 3:225.

142. Tillich, *Systematic Theology*, 1:218.

143. This refers to Heidegger's idea of human existence, as it relates to being, is always in reference to the meaningful relations that occur between beings that encounter each other. Gordon, *Dictionary of Existentialism*, 37.

144. Heidegger, *Being and Time*, 222–23.

sinner] into a kind of Being which borders on the most exaggerated 'self-dissection,'" which becomes, in turn, "[an] alienation [that] closes off from Dasein its authenticity and possibility, even if only the possibility of foundering."[145] Dasein, or what it means to exist as a human being when a human, as a subject, can come to address an object as such,[146] can be adopted to explain the relationship between humanity and sin. If the human is the subject and sin is the object, how human existence encounters sin comes to bear not just in the psychological, mental, spiritual, and physical awareness of sin but becomes protracted in the extenuating effects sinfulness has on the underlying dimensions of human authenticity and possibility. To that end, consequently, if sin is a form of alienation that predisposes a sinner to another state of being, then sin encompasses a "course of life [that] betrays the divine intent for created being . . . it alienates from God, divides the sinner from God's community, disorders the life of the sinner, and in that measure disorders creation itself."[147] Here, at the hub of this argument, is the impression that any alienation from God, through the act of sinning against God,[148] denotes both a discomfort in life and in death.

This stands to reason, then, why *The Heidelberg Catechism*, from its outset, is concerned with addressing the notion of having comfort in life and in death. In response to the first question that is specifically posited as, "What is your only comfort in life and in death," the answer that follows states, in part, "That I, with body and soul, both in life and in death, am not my own, but belong to my faithful Savior Jesus Christ, who with His precious blood has fully satisfied for all my sins."[149] The ten questions and answers that ensue further develop a theologically most adequate understanding of sin by appealing to the five following personifications of sin: sin as the core of the three things that are necessary for a Christian to know in order to live and die happily,[150] sin as a misery that arises from the law of God,[151] sin as something which makes humankind "prone by nature to hate God and [their] neighbor,"[152] sin as a "wicked and perverse" state of human existence that is the result of "the fall and disobedience of our first parents, Adam and Eve, in Paradise, whereby our nature became so corrupt that we are all conceived and born in sin,"[153] and sin as the "depraved nature of man"

---

145. Heidegger, *Being and Time*, 222–23.

146. "Dasein" was a term coined by Martin Heidegger to explain human existence as being an interactive experience between objects and subjects, where a human subject encounters an object, can name an object as being an object, and develops a greater awareness of an object's relative objectification to human subjectivity. Gordon, *Dictionary of Existentialism*, 100.

147. Musser and Price, *Handbook of Christian Theology*, 442–44.

148. Ferguson and Wright, *New Dictionary of Theology*, 641.

149. See question and answer #1 of *The Heidelberg Catechism*.

150. See question and answer #2.

151. See question and answer #3–4.

152. See question and answer #5.

153. See question and answer #6–7.

that employs God's justice, mercy, and punishment.[154] Each of these personifications of sin contributes to the doctrine of sin in *The Heidelberg Catechism*—subsequently, what is constituted within this doctrine of sin, then, is a systematic means of explaining what sin is, why sin exists, where sin originates in humankind, and how sin came to be manifested in human existence.

So, for *The Heidelberg Catechism*, the doctrine of sin is, essentially, an expository on the doctrine of original sin. To say original sin is to refer to the first sin of Adam and Eve. With Adam and Eve's sinful act, not only does death become the wage of their sin,[155] but it is their first transgression that directly caused a "loss of the divine image [which] was followed by a universal corruption of the powers of the soul . . . which kindled within them unlawful passions [and] it was in this way that they began to die, since they revolted from God the author of life; and thus the divine sentence began to be put in force."[156] Not only were the consequences of Adam and Eve's first sin that they "lost their holiness and righteousness [along with] the principal features of [their] divine likeness [being] destroyed,"[157] but the ramifications of their first transgression were extended to their posterity. The wickedness and perversion projected onto all of humanity counted among the posterity of Adam and Eve, as *The Heidelberg Catechism* theologizes, makes sin and sinfulness interwoven into our human nature since "we are all conceived and born in sin."[158] Moreover, the first sin, or first transgression, and all of humanity's connection to that act through an existential lineage with Adam and Eve's humanity suggests that "it has somehow become second nature for [humankind] to oppose the will of God, and thereby to fall into contradiction with [their] fellow [humankind], with [itself], and with the world."[159] This contradiction is between the depravity in human nature, as mentioned in *The Heidelberg Catechism*, and the full seriousness of sin as an affront to "the full potentialities of human existence as created in the image of God."[160] What becomes further crystallized in this contradiction is the inevitability of sin, which *The Heidelberg Catechism* describes as something that humankind is prone to exhibit by nature.[161] In this, it can be ascertained that "[humankind] sins inevitably [doing so] without escaping responsibility for [its] sin [to the extent that] the temptation to sin lies [therefore] in the human situation itself."[162] Within this human situation, "[humanity's] spirit transcends the temporal and natural

---

154. See question and answer #8–11.
155. Barth, *Evangelical Theology*, 137.
156. Pictet, *Christian Theology*, 199.
157. Pictet, *Christian Theology*, 199.
158. See question and answer #6–7 of *The Heidelberg Catechism*.
159. Horton, *Christian Theology*, 147.
160. Macquarrie, *Principles of Christian Theology*, 259.
161. See question and answer #5 of *The Heidelberg Catechism*.
162. Niebuhr, *Nature and Destiny of Man*, 251.

processes in which [it] is involved and also transcends [itself, and] thus [its] freedom is the basis of [its] creativity but it is also his temptation."[163]

Since sin is conceptually equated as having an inevitability that predisposes humanity to temptation, there still exists the implicit notion that sin is linked to freedom, choice, and free will. To that end, with sin always being an act, "it seems that all acts of will presuppose a reason for willing and that this reason is naturally prior to the act of will."[164] In speaking of "acts of will" as objectifications of the acts of sin, there is an underlying action of the body that connects to the act of will by the bond of causality,[165] where action, in itself, can only be action if it is exuded with freedom and choice. Through this assertion, the possibility of being free does not justify sin nor simply make an excuse for it, but, rather, it puts forth an argument that "man becomes free and is free by choosing, deciding, and determining himself in accordance with the freedom of God [and, therefore, a] sinful man is not free."[166] What this suggests, then, is, if "a sinful man is not free," just "by coming into existence, [the human] becomes a sinner [because the human] is not born as a sinner in the sense that [they are] presupposed as being a sinner before [they are] born, but [they are] born in sin and as a sinner."[167]

It is for this reason that *The Heidelberg Catechism* expresses the theologically most adequate understanding of sin: the notion that the totality of humankind is born as sinners because they are conceived in sin, have an inevitable nature that predestines the act of sinning through being enslaved by sin,[168] and have a situational existence that functions in relation to temptation and opposing God.

The Justification by Grace through Faith: Three Reformed Perspectives

Faith, for the Protestants of the Reformation movement, proved to be more than just "an attitude which goes beyond [any] available evidence"[169] but, more importantly, seemingly "[had] a moral rather than an intellectual meaning [to it, conceptually]."[170] What this means, in other words, is that faith, as a standalone moral concept, represented a measuring stick by which Protestants came to understand the meaning of living a Christian life. In this connotation, then, "the [Protestants] stressed the

---

163. Niebuhr, *Nature and Destiny of Man*, 251.
164. Ariew and Garber, *G. W. Leibniz*, 36.
165. Schopenhauer, *World as Will and Representation*, 100.
166. Barth, *Humanity of God*, 77.
167. Bretall, *Kierkegaard Anthology*, 218.
168. The term "enslaved by sin" is an adaptation of John Calvin's notion of humanity being the slaves of sin. See Calvin, *Institutes of the Christian Religion*, 10.
169. Reese, *Dictionary of Philosophy and Religion*, 166.
170. MacGregor, *Dictionary of Religion and Philosophy*, 241.

importance of living by faith, which alone makes a person righteous."[171] Right
ness, in this regard, points to faith as the prime, overarching ingredient of a Chri
character—it "refers to dogma, [as something] which is believed [as well as] trust in a
person which is essentially relational to character."[172] So, while a Christian is expected
to live their life by faith with the intent of personifying righteousness, faith, for the
Christian character, is an essential point of justification, since "it is not so much in
strict terms that we are saved by [faith]: rather we are not saved without it."[173] To be
saved, specifically, refers to God's grace. It is from this linking God's grace to faith, faith
to the Christian life, the Christian life to righteousness, and the possibility of righteousness to an underlying justification comes to bear in each of the aforementioned
interrelationships that Protestants arrived at the idea of justification by grace through
faith—this idea attempts to address "the problem of how one is absolved, or acquitted,
of [their] past actions, or how [they] acquire [their] new being as a Christian."[174] Subsequently, in the justification of grace through faith, there exists justification through
Christ as it is defined in the Pauline doctrine of justification of faith.[175]

Though Protestants preached in favor of a justification of grace through faith,
they, concurrently, railed against works of righteousness.[176] Nevertheless, there was,
indeed, a general consensus among the Protestant faithful about the necessity of
Christians leading a classically defined Christian life built upon the notions of obeying
the law and doing good works. As connected as the concept of justification of grace
through faith is to the notion of achieving good works in accordance with the law,
there are three noteworthy Protestant leaders that crafted their respective reformed
movements by advocating differing views about that connectedness: Martin Luther
and the Lutheran movement, Ulrich Zwingli (1484–1531) and the Swedish reform
movement, and John Calvin (1509–1564) and the Calvinist movement.

---

171. MacGregor, *Dictionary of Religion and Philosophy*, 241.

172. Ferguson and Wright, *New Dictionary of Theology*, 246.

173. Ferguson and Wright, *New Dictionary of Theology*, 246.

174. Reese, *Dictionary of Philosophy and Religion*, 275.

175. This is referring to Paul's doctrine of justification of faith which is contrasted with the justi-
fication simply by way of law. Of this, Paul not only writes, in Gal 2:21, "I do not nullify the grace of
God; for if justification comes through the law, then Christ died for nothing," but further explains, in
Gal 5:4–6, "You who want to be justified by the law have cut yourselves off from Christ; you have fallen
away from grace. For through the Spirit, by faith, we eagerly wait for the hope of righteousness. For in
Christ Jesus . . . the only thing that counts is faith working through love."

176. Clearly, works of righteousness denotes something tangible that can be tested or expressed
evidentially, which points to Paul, who implores in 2 Cor 13:5a-b, "Examine yourselves to see whether
you are living in the faith. Test yourselves."

Martin Luther and the Lutheran Movement

For Martin Luther, the doctrine of justification by grace through faith afforded the possibility of seeing "the Word of God as law."[177] Perhaps, Luther's view of the doctrine developed from his being "guided by the work of the divine Spirit upon his own understanding and heart, through the word."[178] At any rate, by seeing the Word of God as law, Luther came to define salvation and all its blessings as being "purchased for men by Christ [to the extent that they are] freely imparted to them individually by God's grace through the instrumentality of faith"[179] as a fundamental principle of Christian truth, which, in turn, is extrapolated by the dimensions of human merit[180] in accordance with the law. To this end, Luther viewed the doctrine of the justification of grace through faith as "the gospel of justification alone, an inexhaustible gospel."[181] As far as Luther was concerned, "to preach Christ is to feed the soul, to justify it, to set it free, and to save it, if it believes the preaching. For faith alone, and the efficacious use of the word of God, bring salvation."[182] What arose from this, for Luther, was that "the message of God's forgiveness"[183]—as it is exemplified in the justification of grace through faith—suggests that forgiveness is the gospel.[184] Even in this case, there is still the contention that "this gospel does not contradict or obliterate the law."[185] Instead, in terms of Lutheran logic, there is a dialectic connection between the law and the gospel, where what it means to be a Christian is to be "at one and the same time both sinful and justified."[186] From this, not only is it important to concede that "the sinner does not cease to be such upon being justified" but that justification "is not the absence of sin but the fact that God [by way of God's grace] declares us to be just, even while we are still sinners."[187] What God declares to be just for a sinner who does not cease to be as such, then, is always in accordance with the law and the notion of good works. To this end,

---

177. Gonzalez, *Story of Christianity*, 2:51.

178. Cunningham, *Reformers*, 103.

179. Cunningham, *Reformers*, 103.

180. This is in respect to the notion that Luther never totally avoided the risk of making faith a substitute for works, and, therefore, itself a meritorious performance on humankind's part. Ferguson and Wright, *New Dictionary of Theology*, 360.

181. Luther further perceived the gospel of justification alone as being "full of reformatory vigor, capable not only of destroying the old, but in [the reforming movement] breaking by its inner fullness the traditionary chains . . . [which] is the complete, perfect, divine gospel, which tolerates neither addition nor decreases [so that those whom abide by it and supplement it into their Christian lives] receive its precious contents, and find spiritual quickening thereby." Sohm, *History of Christianity*, 220–21.

182. Luther, *Christian Liberty*, 9.

183. Gonzalez, *Story of Christianity*, 2:51.

184. Gonzalez, *Story of Christianity*, 2:51.

185. Gonzalez, *Story of Christianity*, 2:51.

186. Gonzalez, *Story of Christianity*, 2:52.

187. Gonzalez, *Story of Christianity*, 2:52.

then, being in accordance with the law and expressing oneself with one's good works is what it takes to be considered not just a righteous person, but having lived an ideal Christian life. This is not just Lutheran theology here, because such a premise is directly linked to Pauline theology about what it means to live in a manner that is appropriate and obedient in order to live a righteous life that becomes a life in Christ.[188] From this, Luther and the Lutheran movement shaped their view of the justification by grace through faith by way of adopting the Pauline doctrine of justification of faith, which they believed to be "the cardinal doctrine of Christianity."[189]

Ulrich Zwingli and the Swedish Reform Movement

Ulrich Zwingli, like Martin Luther, found the connection between the gospel and the law irrefutable. At this theological point of convergence, Zwingli not only perceived "the law of the gospel [as] law [and, by extension did] accept Luther's doctrine of the forgiveness of sins, as did all Reformers"[190] but developed a new concept of law that he referred to as a "new evangelical law [that] should be the basis of the law of the state."[191] Here, at this particular point of contention with Luther, Zwingli is operating more from a philosophical point of view, having been influenced by nominalists and humanists.[192] As a result, rather than finding solace in the biblical message of justification by faith as Luther was moved to do, "Zwingli's [approach to understanding justification by grace through faith] was that of the humanist, who studied Scripture because it was the source of Christian faith, and humanism encouraged such return to the sources."[193] Evidently, Zwingli "had a more positive view of the power of reason"[194] as it is evidenced in history and nature, which is directly at odds with Luther who "wanted everything as non-rational, non-legal, as possible"[195] so that the process of salvation, history and nature could be interpreted by a kind of new law that "exists by nature, by created nature, and is [something] which we are essentially."[196] What becomes distinctly evident about Zwingli's "new law" is that it incorporates, through the importance placed on human reason, a specter of natural theology,[197] since it is formulated on the premise that God, in the form of law, is exhibited in nature. Unlike the Lutheran view of the gospel being about grace and nothing more than a grace that

---

188. Rom 6.
189. Reese, *Dictionary of Philosophy and Religion*, 275.
190. Tillich, *History of Christian Thought*, 259.
191. Tillich, *History of Christian Thought*, 259.
192. Tillich, *History of Christian Thought*, 259.
193. Gonzalez, *Story of Christianity*, 2:62–63.
194. Gonzalez, *Story of Christianity*, 2:63.
195. Tillich, *History of Christian Thought*, 259.
196. Tillich, *History of Christian Thought*, 259.
197. Joyce, *Principles of Natural Theology*, 1.

can never be a "new law,"[198] Zwingli's humanist view was influenced by a Neoplatonic interpretation of Christianity.[199] Zwingli's Swedish movement, then, interpreted this new law as "valid not only for the moral situation but also for the state, the political sphere [to the extent that] politically, the law of the gospel determines the laws of the city."[200] Essentially, for Zwingli and the movement he led, the relationship between the law and the justification through faith by grace is one that theologically builds upon the Lutheran theology but further advocates a merging of societal laws with gospel laws so that "the law of the gospel [becomes] the basis of the law of the state."[201]

John Calvin and the Calvinist Movement

John Calvin not only found an important theological line of agreement with Zwingli about viewing nature in terms of law, but, more importantly, Calvin agreed with the Zwinglian notion of the law of the gospel being incorporated into the law of the state. Here, Calvin advocated the role the state must play in "punish[ing] the impious [who] were criminals because they are against the law of the state which is based on God's law."[202] As a result, for Calvin and his movement, "it [became] their duty to make the civil government conform to the law of God."[203] This, of course, undoubtedly, aligns Calvin's perception of the oneness between the law of the state and God's law with that of Zwingli's but, simultaneously, places him in opposition to Luther who "detested the idea that God has established a law between himself and his world, between himself and finite actions and things and decisions."[204] These "finite actions and things and decisions," as Calvin would have defined them by way of how they manifest themselves from "the impious" that violate the law of the state as well as God's law, would have been just as easily construed in light of the issue of justification. This is because justification by grace through faith is inarguably based on "finite actions and things and decisions," the embodiment of righteousness and what is considered as "good works." By extension, therefore, this leads Calvin to define the doctrine of justification by grace through faith as: "Christ given to us by the kindness of God [which] is apprehended and possessed by faith by means of which we . . . reconciled by the righteousness of Christ . . . sanctified by his Spirit [so that] we aspire to integrity and purity of life."[205] The fact that Calvin invokes the need to "aspire to integrity and purity of life" means that he interprets the importance of Christians obeying the law and

198. Tillich, *History of Christian Thought*, 259–60.
199. Gonzalez, *Story of Christianity*, 2:64.
200. Tillich, *History of Christian Thought*, 259–60.
201. Tillich, *History of Christian Thought*, 260.
202. Tillich, *History of Christian Thought*, 259.
203. Gonzalez, *Story of Christianity*, 2:86.
204. Tillich, *History of Christian Thought*, 259.
205. Calvin, *Institutes of the Christian Religion*, 445.

doing good works. Though this seemingly abides by Luther's views on the matter, Calvin does not focus exclusively on the doctrine of justification as the be-all and end-all of the Christian faith but, instead, "was able to pay more attention to several aspects of Christian faith which Luther had virtually ignored—in particular, the doctrine of sanctification."[206] For Calvin, justification and sanctification, "which we perceive to be united together in him, are inseparable."[207] In this respect, the Calvinist movement sees both justification and sanctification as a divine act of God receiving someone into God's favor in order to present that person with the Spirit of adoption, "whose agency forms them anew in his image."[208] It is, perhaps, in view of the justification-sanctification doctrinal relationship that Calvin asserts that "there is so wide a difference between justification by faith and by works, that the establishment of the one necessarily overthrows the other."[209]

The Point of View of Truth and Selfhood in Kierkegaard's *The Point of View*

When reading *The Point of View for My Work as an Author* (1848), it is impossible to not interpret from the explicit title that Soren Kierkegaard (1813–1855) set out, as David Law describes, "to explain the meaning and purpose of his authorship up to the time of the composition of [the work]."[210] This, of course, is Kierkegaard's chief concern with the work, even if it may have been intended to, according to Law, bring his authorship to a conclusion.[211] Be that as it may, it becomes rather simple, then, to assume that Kierkegaard's *The Point of View*, in its entirety, was meant to sum up the totality of his work. It is, in fact, functioning as much more than just a kind of "concluding postscript"[212] to his body of work. What it is doing, instead, is providing the reader with a blueprint by which that reader can understand, in Kierkegaard's own words and through what Kierkegaard describes as direct communication,[213] the meaning of his authorship with respect to his use of pseudonyms. As a blueprint, Kierkegaard is not concerned with simply giving an apologia, or defense, for his use of pseudonyms, but, rather, is interested simply in explaining their usage.

---

206. Gonzalez, *Story of Christianity*, 2:78.
207. Calvin, *Institutes of the Christian Religion*, 449.
208. Calvin, *Institutes of the Christian Religion*, 449.
209. Calvin, *Institutes of the Christian Religion*, 456.
210. Law, "Cacophony of Voices," 16.
211. Law, "Cacophony of Voices," 16.
212. I am thinking here of Kierkegaard's pseudonym Johannes Climacus authoring *Concluding Postscript to Philosophical Crumbs* as a "postscript" to *Philosophical Crumbs*, which was authored by the same Kierkegaardian pseudonym.
213. That is, rather than indirect communication.

For Kierkegaard, there is a clear distinction between defense, or apologia, and an explanation, as Law rightly notes. In this regard, operating under the notion that it is "an explanation" becomes a very important way to read *The Point of View*. Not only would I agree with Law, but I find such a premise fairly straight forward when considering Kierkegaard's own words in the introduction to *The Point of View*, where he states, in no uncertain terms, that, "I know with God, before whose eyes the undertaking found and finds favor as it rejoices in his assistance, that in connection with my authorship I am not one who must defend myself before my contemporaries."[214] By "defending [him]self," Kierkegaard believes this "undertaking" would become "an untruth," because, as he puts it, it would be rather meaningless and would, in that respect, be the impetus for his downfall.[215] In saying this, what Kierkegaard is, undoubtedly, worried about is what it would look like—not for his reputation with his contemporaries but his posthumous reputation in posterity—if he defended the purposes of his work in *The Point of View*. In fact, it would seem to Kierkegaard that defending himself, in any measurable way, implies that he has committed an offense, or is guilty of an act, or counsel for the defense; if he sees himself as anything it would be as counsel for the prosecution.[216] Taking this into account, therefore, for Kierkegaard, the mere act of defending himself becomes viewed as an impropriety and self-contradiction to the point that it presents not only an impossibility for him but an impossibility in itself.[217]

If I incorporate Kierkegaard's logic as is, but extrapolate it just a bit further, I would argue that the "impossibility," as Kierkegaard accurately sees it, lies in defending a totality of work that was created with the assistance of God, having been "prompt[ed] of an irresistible need,"[218] which was meant to exact a virtuous good in its aim. What I mean, then, is that Kierkegaard's approach to writing *The Point of View* as an explanation of his authorship, rather than a defense, is by way of his fundamental understanding of moral philosophy and ethics, in general. It is, I contend, an enactment of Aristotle's own notion, in book 1, chapter 1 of *Nicomachean Ethics*, that "every art and every inquiry, and similarly every action and pursuit, is thought to aim at some good; and for this reason the good has rightly been declared to be that at which all things aim."[219] Kierkegaard's aim in *The Point of View* contains a good will, which Immanuel Kant suggests is good "not because of what it effects or accomplishes, nor because of its fitness to attain some proposed end; it is good only through its willing."[220] In other words, any aim is good because it is created through

---

214. Kierkegaard, *Point of View*, 24.
215. Kierkegaard, *Point of View*, 24.
216. Kierkegaard, *Point of View*, 24–25.
217. Kierkegaard, *Point of View*, 24.
218. Kierkegaard, *Point of View*, 24.
219. McKeon, *Basic Works of Aristotle*, 935.
220. Kant, *Grounding for the Metaphysics of Morals*, 7.

good will—this is, as Kant theorizes, because good will does not need qualification in the same manner that anything regarded as good does.[221] To suggest that something was created through good will is to qualify it as good.

This is specifically important, I would argue, when considering that Kierkegaard felt that his body of work and how he approached *The Point of View* to discuss that body of work "found and finds favor as it rejoices in [God's] assistance." What he is describing, in effect, is that all his work was created through good will from God's goodness and had "good" as its chief aim—it is, as a result, good by virtue. To defend something that is inherently good in itself is to put forth an unfortunate untruth about it. Doing so, it would completely contradict Kierkegaard's mission in *The Point of View*, which is, as Law argues, "to provide a direct explanation which will make clear the Christian character of the aesthetic authorship."[222] So, at first blush, what becomes apparent about Kierkegaard's *The Point of View* is that it is concerned with putting forth the truth about his authorship. If this is, indeed, what Kierkegaard is groping for in *The Point of View*, he is, by extension, appropriating the truth about his authorship as a collective statement that is, as William James proposes, "reference then to something determinate, and some sort of adaptation to it worthy of the name of agreement [as] constituent elements in the definition of any statement . . . as true."[223] Nevertheless, James's definition of the truth is not the kind of truth that Kierkegaard is concerned with. That is to say this: expressing the truth about his authorship through true statements in *The Point of View*. It is because there is no definitive truth in the sentences and propositions[224] that populate *The Point of View*—it is absent of any statement that can be construed as true, even if the underlying premise is to reconsider his work as an author,[225] even if construed through a direct explanation. Though Kierkegaard's direct communication functions on presenting not "the truth" but "a truth,"[226] I propose that he is approaching truth as, according to Nikolai Berdyaev, something that is "not given to [humankind] in a ready-made form, as though it were an article, or one of the realities in a world of things."[227] When considering that Kierkegaard wants his direct explanation to contain what he calls a "historical truth [that] gets it due by

221. What I am articulating here is Kant's supposition that "there is no possibility of thinking of anything at all in the world, or even out of it, which can be regarded as good without qualification, except a good will." Kant, *Grounding for the Metaphysics of Morals*, 7.

222. Law, "Cacophony of Voices," 16.

223. James, *Meaning of Truth*, 218.

224. I am applying what Robert McKim says of the truth, suggesting that is it, first, based on sentences and propositions that act as bearers of the truth so that they become either perceived as true or false. McKim, *On Religious Diversity*, 7.

225. Kierkegaard, *Point of View*, ix.

226. This is working under the notion that, if using Nikolai Berdyaev, "the nature of truth is not intellectual and purely cognitive . . . it must be grasped integrally by the whole personality." In saying this, I would extend the following: the truth cannot be objectified with "the," but, instead, is existential as an "a." Berdyaev, *Truth and Revelation*, 25.

227. Berdyaev, *Truth and Revelation*, 25.

way of a direct communication,"[228] it becomes possible to agree with Law's assertion that Kierkegaard cannot give a "complete explanation."[229] In this, I would argue that Kierkegaard is not attempting to be purposefully deceptive or illusive in his efforts but, instead, seeks to protect, as he explains, "my private character, which of course for me contains much of the explanation of my author-character."[230]

I find that there is more at work in Kierkegaard not giving a complete explanation in *The Point of View* than just protecting his "private character." I see this as especially the case when he has gone through great pains to explicitly label the work itself as a direct communication in lieu of the indirect style that his pseudonymous works employ.[231] To get at this problem, Law surmises that Kierkegaard "wishes to explain enough to enable the reader to grasp the overall meaning of the authorship,"[232] in order to prevent himself from giving away elements of personal existence which motivated the production of his authorship. Obviously, the use of indirect communication and his pseudonyms are meant to protect his personal existence and, to that end, provide Kierkegaard with considerable anonymity. But, to give up that anonymity in *The Point of View* by discarding the veil of pseudonymity, I would argue that Kierkegaard is not just concerned with his own personal existence but, also, the personal existence of the reader. If taken just a bit further, I find that Kierkegaard, through being concerned about his personal existence and the personal existence of the readers, is, likewise, concerned with the readers' ability to ascertain their own existence as readers existing within Kierkegaard's readership and, consequently, project that existence back toward Kierkegaard's own personal existence as the author that makes the readers' existence possible, in the first place. This is, with extreme brevity and condensing, a rudimentary articulation of Martin Heidegger's "Dasein,"[233] which is defined by Haim Gordon as "[an] encounter between subject and object [yielding an] opening within which a subject can come to address an object."[234] The way in which Gordon explains "Dasein"

---

228. Kierkegaard, *Point of View*, 271.

229. Law, "Cacophony of Voices," 17.

230. Kierkegaard, *Point of View*, 26.

231. This is a very important distinction to make when understanding that the pseudonyms that Kierkegaard uses throughout his body of work, prior to the composition of *The Point of View*, put forth a "literary style of philosophical interest." The philosophical interest, of course, is that Kierkegaard, through his indirect communicative style "does not express his philosophical insights in straightforward academic prose." This makes *The Point of View* all the more interesting in its use of a decidedly direct approach. Aumann, "Kierkegaard on Indirect Communication," 295.

232. Law, "Cacophony of Voices," 17.

233. Heidegger uses this term when explaining how a being uses existence to establish selfhood. For Heidegger, this occurs only when the basic structures of human existence, or what he calls "Dasein," has been adequately worked out with explicit orientation toward the problem of "being" itself. What must be noted in this regards, therefore, is, within the concept of "Dasein," there is the expression of individual beings harboring "being-in-itself." "Being-in-itself" is an existential justification that is gained from the interpretation of human existence. Heidegger, *Being and Time*, 37.

234. Gordon, *Dictionary of Existentialism*, 100.

is essential to what I propose Kierkegaard is doing with the relationship between his personal existence as an author and what he perceives[235] as the personal existence of the reader—there is an "encounter" in *The Point of View*, through which Kierkegaard, by way of his personal existence, is addressing the reader's personal existence. I would go so far as to assert, then, that this encounter develops from what Gilles Deleuze offers as an "immanent event," which, Deleuze writes, "is actualized in a state of things and of the lived that make it happen." On either side of this immanent event, Kierkegaard is just as much aware of the personal existence of his readership as his readership would be of his personal existence. What occurs across this plane of immanence has a significant influence on how Kierkegaard categorizes his personal existence and comes to address his readership.

In fact, while Kierkegaard's personal existence behind *The Point of View* is constructed by the two authorial voices of "Kierkegaard as the Author" and "God as the Author,"[236] the personal existence Kierkegaard perceives in his readership is stratified by their multiplicity.[237] The significance in this, I would argue, is that regardless of which authorial voice Kierkegaard employs and which strata of readership he is addressing, Kierkegaard's main concern with *The Point of View* is to speak of himself in the third-person. I am not suggesting that his use of "I" or addressing the reader with "you"—respectively, first-person and second-person approaches, of course—is not concerned with direct communication, or the plane of immanence. What I am suggesting, however, is that the uses of "I" and "you," or the communal "us" and "we" for that matter, are meant to distance himself and his own personal existence as the person writing *The Point of View* from *The Point of View* itself, as well as everything else he has authored pseudonymously. In other words, Kierkegaard treats his body of work and even his explanation of it in *The Point of View* as if the author is someone other than himself.

This tactic is important, I believe, in understanding the purposes of *The Point of View* as a representation of Kierkegaard's moral philosophy. Through this tactic, Kierkegaard is implementing Jacques Derrida's deconstructionist theory about "there

---

235. I use the term "perceives" because, for Kierkegaard, the reader must be perceived through an impression as in an exchange of impressions that occurs between two beings engaged in interpersonal contact. What this further points to, then, is the idea of existence and external existence as it is postulated by David Hume in *Treatise on Human Nature*. Hume suggests, in this work, that a being never remembers any idea or impression without attributing existence to it because the idea of existence must either be derived from a distinct impression, conjoined with every perception or object of our thought, or must be the very same with the idea of the perception or object. Hume, *Treatise on Human Nature*, 41.

236. Law labels these two authorial voices as the following: "Kierkegaard the Author," where Kierkegaard speaks of his authorship and states in his intention to explain that authorship, and "God as the Author," where Kierkegaard claims that God has guided his writing. Law, "Cacophony of Voices," 31.

237. Law lists the multiplicity of Kierkegaard's readership as the ideal reader, the single individual, God, Kierkegaard's contemporaries, Kierkegaard's "Lover," Kierkegaard himself, and Kierkegaard's "Poet." Law, "Cacophony of Voices," 34–42.

is nothing outside of the text."[238] But, what is also at play with this kind of deconstructing, is that, in turn, once anything he has written has been written, "Kierkegaard the Author" has died in the process, because, as Roland Barthes surmises, "to give a text an Author is to impose a limit on that text, to furnish it with a final signified, to close the writing."[239] This is so, as Barthes theorizes, due to the birth of the reader, since, in order to give writing a future, "the birth of the reader must be at the cost of the death of the author."[240] If Kierkegaard hopes to actually "report to history,"[241] either in terms of the past readership that has read or the future readership that will read his body of work, or, specifically, *The Point of View*, Kierkegaard understands that the text and the author must be separated. To that end, Kierkegaard is separating the relationship that Michel Foucault ascertains "as the singular relationship that holds between an author and a text, the manner in which a text apparently points to this figure who is outside and precedes it."[242] What I am suggesting, then, is that by Kierkegaard removing himself from the authorship of his body of work, it presents the possibility for Kierkegaard to not only report to history but allow for the historical truth of his authorship to manifest itself more fully in *The Point of View*.

In other words, by removing the authorial point of reference, or the "figure who is outside the text and precedes it," Kierkegaard, I believe, is allowing for the reader to fully engage with moral philosophy inherent in the work as it is set forth in *The Point of View*. I would argue that this is accomplished through two distinct methods: the pragmatic method and the polarity method. While the former makes it possible for the reader to arrive at a meaning in his body of work as it is outlined in *The Point of View* through what William James describe as "try[ing] to interpret each notion by tracing its respective practical consequences,"[243] the latter, as Edward Mooney explains, "keeps alive a sense that the path we follow is of ultimate concern, that our particular commitments are at risk."[244] These two methods are essential to the point of view that Kierkegaard assumes in his *The Point of View*.

Kierkegaard is, in effect, interested in not just providing a meaning that the reader can assess as meaningful about his authorship but, more importantly, projecting that that meaning is seated in moral value that is worthy of being assessed for the sake of finding the virtue in it—when this moral value is being considered, as Immanuel Kant suggests, "the concern is not with the actions, which are seen, but rather with their inner principles, which are not seen." In other words, the actions

---

238. Derrida, *Of Grammatology*, 158.
239. Barthes, "Death of the Author," 1325.
240. Barthes, "Death of the Author," 1326.
241. This is "in the sense of an accounting," as Walter Lowrie states in his preface to his translation of *Point of View*. Kierkegaard, *Point of View*, xiv.
242. Foucault, "What Is an Author?," 1476.
243. James, *Pragmatism*, 23.
244. Mooney, "Perils of Polarity," 235.

Kierkegaard takes with his pseudonyms and the direct communicative approach in *The Point of View*, which are seen, is not as important to finding the moral value he wished to extend to his readership as it would seem. Such clarity of understanding, or meaningful meaning, comes, in fact, from the inner principles that are seen only by creating "a truth" from them.

CHAPTER 2

Modern European Traditions of Existential Theology

As THE QUESTION OF *the meaning of existential theology* unfolds further through the making of modernity, what it means to do existential theology is articulated through European traditions arising from the French School, the German School, and the Russian School, all of which include key thinkers that negotiate the philosophical with the theological when understanding the relationship between human existence and God's existence. In each of the schools of thought, between the thought of key thinkers and certain associated thinkers, *the question of the meaning of existential theology* is grounded on the historical, sociological, psychological, and cultural contexts, which are oriented toward an intersection that defines the nature, limits, and concerns of human existence.

The French School

The French school of existential theology is chiefly defined by four key thinkers: Gabriel Marcel (1889–1973), Jacques Maritain (1882–1973), Pierre Teilhard de Chardin (1881–1955), and Jean-Luc Marion (1946–). While all of these four thinkers theologically aligned themselves with Catholicism—with Teilhard, in particular, being a Jesuit priest—all four have a diversity of influences that philosophically influence how they respectively comport themselves to theology.

However, before even considering the existential theologies of Marcel, Maritain, Teilhard, and Marion, as they are firmly rooted in the convergence between twentieth-century French philosophy and twentieth-century Catholic thought, the seventeenth-century thought of Blaise Pascal (1623–1662) must be considered as a seminal figure that influences what eventually becomes, as it has been defined, the French school of existential theology. It is particularly with Pascal's *Pensées*—left largely incomplete at the time of Pascal's death, but published in 1670—consisting of a collection of fragments on theology and philosophy, which offers an origin point not just for this

French school's comportment to existential theology, but also a foundational text for existentialism more generally. The most noted concept derived from *Pensées* is what has been called "Pascal's wager"—it is Pascal's idea that it is better for a rational person to live by way of the fundamental belief that God exists, in order to mitigate the difference between finite sacrifices in the world and infinite rewards in heaven. Conversely, to disbelieve in the existence of God, in light of God's existence, means relegating oneself to the infinite losses of hell. This concept is quintessentially an existential theology, since it presents a relationship between theology and philosophy, between God and humanity, and between issues of doubt and certainty—clearly, Pascal's approach to theology and philosophy has some kind of tangible influence on Marcel, Maritain, Teilhard, and Marion, even if, at best, that influence is rather secondary as a bridge between the Renaissance and the Enlightenment.

To a larger extent, excluding Maritain, Marcel and Teilhard are contingently influenced by nineteenth-century German thought, such as Schelling (for Marcel) and Marx, Nietzsche, Hegel, and Schleiermacher (for Teilhard), while Marion's influences reach into late seventeenth-century German thought with Kant. With the exception of Maritain and Teilhard, the other two are also influenced by twentieth-century German thought by way of Edmund Husserl's phenomenology, with Marion more influenced by Martin Heidegger than Marcel—both Marcel and Marion were influenced by Husserl's *Cartesian Meditations* lectures, though only Marcel was more directly influenced by the original lectures as they were delivered at the Sorbonne in the Amphithéatre Descartes on February 23 and 25, 1929. Maritain and Teilhard, on the other hand, have their influences traced to Aristotle and Aquinas (for Maritain) or the early church fathers, such as Origen, Gregory of Nyssa, and (for Teilhard) Ignatius of Loyola (1491–1556)—Marion, too, is informed by the Patristic thought of Augustine and the early medieval thought of Pseudo-Dionysius. While Marion and Teilhard have very long relationships with Catholicism, insomuch as Marion is considered as a Roman Catholic theologian and Teilhard's earliest educational roots were in the Jesuit college of Mongré, the childhoods of Maritain and Marcel were largely agnostic, with both converting to Catholicism respectively in 1906 and 1929.

What unifies the four thinkers is how each approach metaphysics and ontology, though the work and thought of Marion veers predominantly toward phenomenology and the same of Teilhard ventures exclusively toward philosophical biology. Nevertheless, all four thinkers, to a certain extent, are concerned with conceptualizing, defining, and explicating the meaning of being from the standpoint of what existence is, the nature of existing, and what it means to exist—how each thinker handles their respective approach to the question of the meaning of being is based on how their own philosophical influences come to bear on their theological stances, both of which are ultimately and unapologetically predicated on the demands of Catholicism.

Gabriel Marcel

Though, historically speaking, Marcel is often classified as one of the earliest existentialists and, through this classification, he is often grouped alongside Sartre, philosophically aligning Marcel with Sartre is certainly unfair to Marcel's thought. It is true, as it has been noted by a handful of studies into the historical roots of existentialism, that Marcel is responsible for coining the term "existentialism" sometime in the mid-1940s.[1] By 1945, as Ann Fulton points out in *Apostles of Sartre: Existentialism in America 1945–1963* (1999), Marcel applied the term "existentialism" to Sartre's philosophy at a colloquium, which Sartre rejected.[2] However, Sartre soon embraced the Marcel-coined term, by October 29, 1945, in a public lecture to the Club Maintenant in Paris—this would eventually become the text, *L'existentialisme est un humanisme* (1946), subsequently translated as *Existentialism Is a Humanism* (1948), which, in itself, would popularize and systemize the aim and scope of existentialist thought. Be that as it may, Marcel, in his own right, would distance himself from the term "existentialism" altogether and any association with Sartre's "existentialism."[3] As a means of opposing "existentialism," Marcel chose to deem his philosophical thought as "Neo-Socratic" which arose from a purposeful alignment with Kierkegaard's essay "On the Concept of Irony" (1841).

What arises from Marcel's revolt against being absorbed conceptually into Sartre's existentialism and situating himself as a self-ascribed "Neo-Socratic" is the necessity for Marcel to forge his own way philosophically. In *Gabriel Marcel* (1963), having appeared in Marcel's lifetime, Seymour Cain's study of Marcel begins by describing Marcel in the following way:

> [He] has doggedly and courageously followed his own way throughout a philosophical career that covers half a century. An existential philosopher decades before the term "existential" became fashionable, a phenomenological thinker long before phenomenology became a central concern of European philosophy, a religious thinker at a time when religion had not yet regained respectability in philosophical circles—Gabriel Marcel has been a herald of our times.[4]

While Cain is certainly correct to say that Marcel can be viewed as "a phenomenological thinker" and "a religious thinker" before either were fully in vogue, calling Marcel

---

1. Three notable studies make this case: D. E. Cooper's *Existentialism: A Reconstruction* (1990), Thomas Flynn's *Existentialism: A Very Short Introduction* (2006), and Christine Daigle's *Existentialist Thinkers and Ethics* (2005).

2. Fulton, *Apostles of Sartre*, 18–19.

3. To be sure, Sartre's existentialism is, in actually, a French existentialism, though Sartre's existentialism is a humanism became a general introduction to the themes that pervade all forms of existentialism beyond the specific concerns of French existentialism.

4. Cain, *Gabriel Marcel*, 11.

"an existential philosopher" is a bit outdated and problematic. Given what Marcel explicitly thought about his own philosophical work, Cain unfortunately conflates Marcel's philosophical proclivities into those of existentialism. This is only further complicated by Cain's suggestion that "[Marcel] is a leading existential philosopher—associated in histories of contemporary thought with Martin Heidegger and Jean-Paul Sartre."[5] In this way, Cain's assessment of Marcel carries forward problems with associating Marcel to existentialism from the 1950s, especially in Blackham's *Six Existentialist Thinkers* (1952) and F. H. Heinemann's *Existentialism and the Modern Predicament* (1953), without taking greater heed to Majorie Grene's *Dreadful Freedom* (1948), which quarantines Marcel from Sartre and Heidegger, in what is considered as the earliest study of existentialism. With all of this in mind, Cain's grouping of Marcel, Heidegger, and Sartre together within "existentialism" is not just a simplistic view of the meaning of existentialism, which is likely due to the dating of Cain's study, but it also fundamentally ignores both Marcel's and Heidegger's own refusal to be associated with Sartre's existentialist thought.

If, as Cain notes, Marcel "proclaims a human community centered on God,"[6] this does not present itself in Heidegger—who generally refuses to adopt a theological voice—or in Sartre—who generally employs an atheistic perspective. This religiosity to Marcel is centered on a "nonconformist" view of Catholicism, as Cain rightly points out, such that Marcel's handling of Catholicism is both "non-Thomistic and anti-Thomistic."[7] Cain revisits Marcel's religiosity by later defining it as a theory of religious experience in the aptly titled work *Gabriel Marcel's Theory of Religious Experience* (1995), which concludes that Marcel's basic thought on human existence is rooted in Marcel's locating in human existence a human condition that carries an ultimate religious meaning. In light of this, in a more recent study of Marcel, Brendan Sweetman's *The Vision of Gabriel Marcel* (2008) defines Marcel's philosophy as predicated on "clarifying his perspectives and insights about the nature of human knowledge, the human person, and Transcendence."[8] All these themes articulated by Sweetman previously come to bear in Clyde Pax's *An Existential Approach to God: A Study of Gabriel Marcel* (1972), in which, as Pax writes, "the focus of the work is only incidentally on the writings of Marcel; the direct focus, as for Marcel, is on man's seeking to know and to draw near to God."[9] By way of Pax's unifying theme of self-identity "in all of its fullness and obscurity," Pax's conceptualization of Marcel's "existential approach to God" is chiefly surmised from Marcel's major works.

Generally, if following Pax's views on Marcel, these major works include: *Metaphysical Journal* (1927, translated in 1950), *Being and Having: An Existentialist Diary*

---

5. Cain, *Gabriel Marcel*, 12.
6. Cain, *Gabriel Marcel*, 12.
7. Cain, *Gabriel Marcel*, 11–12.
8. Sweetman *Vision of Gabriel Marcel*, xv.
9. Pax, *Existential Approach to God*, vii.

(1933, translated in 1949), *The Philosophy of Existence* (1948, translated in 1956, and often entitled *The Philosophy of Existentialism*), and the two-volume *The Mystery of Being* (1951), which is based on Gifford Lectures delivered in Aberdeen, Scotland, in 1949 and 1950. While Marcel's *Metaphysical Journal* traces, as Cain describes, "his major metaphysical and 'metapsychical' concerns, without feeling bound to conform to any finished philosophical system or prescribed habits of thought"[10] on the way to Marcel's conversion to Catholicism, *The Philosophy of Existence*, too, is not "bound to conform" to existentialism, even if Marcel characterizes *The Philosophy of Existence* as "an exposition of the character of existentialist philosophy, including an analysis of the theories of Jean-Paul Sartre."[11]

As much as *Being and Having* and *The Mystery of Being* are also not "bound to conform," the two texts as major works, unlike *Metaphysical Journal* and *The Philosophy of Existence*, more firmly present Marcel's philosophical approach to theology. Not only do the two texts resist functioning philosophically solely within the boundaries of existentialism and subsequently avoid the parameters of Catholicism, they offer Marcel's existential theology focus on the question of the meaning of being.

In *Being and Having*—a text that was especially influential for the phenomenology and Thomism of Karol Wojtyla (1920–2005, as Pope John Paul II)—Marcel finds that,

> as we raise ourselves towards Reality, and approach it more nearly, we find that it cannot be compared with an object placed before us on which we can take bearings: and we find, too, that we are ourselves actually changed in the process.[12]

What is apparent, here, is that Marcel wishes to make an important distinction between "being" and "having" in terms of the extent to which "being" itself is epistemological and in what way "having" is itself epistemological. This distinction is based on how "we raise ourselves towards Reality"—in this case, "Reality" not only shapes how we encounter "being" and "having" in the level of our most immediate context of the world, but it also influences, more broadly, how we encounter "Reality" through "being" and "having" in the world. For Marcel, while the relationship between "being" and "having" is an essential epistemological endeavor that allows us to engage with the world around us, our ultimate engagement with "Reality" is all the more important, since it dictates how we phenomenologically situate ourselves to the concerns of both "being" and "having." Because Marcel is not just concerned with the vertical relation between us and the relationship between "being" and "having" but he is also

---

10. Cain, *Gabriel Marcel*, 11.

11. This is Marcel's subtitle to *The Philosophy of Existence*. Through the use of this subtitle, the three papers that Marcel collects in *The Philosophy of Existence* outline his philosophical position since 1933, present a critical survey of Sartre's philosophy, and define Marcel's understanding of the "existentialist' doctrine" in terms of "certain reservations in regard to a vocabulary which has become fashionable but which is, in many ways, open to criticism." Marcel, *Philosophy of Existentialism*, 5.

12. Marcel, *Being and Having*, 169.

concerned with the horizontal relation with "Reality," Marcel's conceptualization of "being," "having," and "Reality" is predicated on an existential theology—it is about meaning that is made between "being" and "having," as well as meaning that can be made out of the transcendence of "Reality," such that we not only self-identify with what is adjudicated between "being" and "having," but also the extent to which "Reality" reflects itself upon our self-consciousness.

Later, in the second volume of *The Mystery of Being*, Marcel seemingly describes self-consciousness, "Reality," and what he assessed in the relation between "being" and "having" in the following way:

> I have to think not only for myself, but for us; in other words for everyone who may have contact with the thought which is mine. There is a sense in which we are all historical beings; that is to say, that we come after other beings from whom we have received a great deal, and this precisely in a way which gives us something by which we are differentiated from them: but at the same time we come before other beings, and these will find that they have the same relation to us as we have to those who came before us.[13]

From this, there arises a tension between Marcel's understandings of how "we are all historical beings" and the extent to which "we come before other beings." This tension is, in fact, existential at a philosophical level, but is also theological in the sense that Marcel draws from the idea that, as beings, we "have the same relation"—the existential-theological tension, as articulated by Marcel, between the historical demands of being and what can be seen as the spatial demands of being is the very meaning of being. Negotiating between the historical and the spatial, for Marcel, becomes a negotiation between "being" and "having" as much as it becomes a negotiation between the mystery of being and how being reveals itself. Nevertheless, even though Marcel's existential theology is grounded on existence and, to some extent, formulating a set of parameters by which the meaning of being can be compartmentalized and thusly managed and understood, he is careful to suggest that:

> In any case existence cannot be reduced to a mean or to a collection of means; in reality it comes to us as something which contains and also goes beyond everything to which we might seek to reduce it.[14]

Essentially, the question of the meaning of being is a question that, in itself, does not propose, by soliciting an answer, that "existence" is readily accessible to us. Because the meaning of being, by the fact of its very nature, tends to hide itself in what Marcel calls a "mystery," he is correct to assert that "existence cannot be reduced to a mean or to a collection of means." And yet, the task of Marcel's existential theology navigates between what can be reduced and what cannot, and what can become

13. Marcel, *Mystery of Being*, 5.
14. Marcel, *Mystery of Being*, 33.

a collection of means and what cannot. Marcel's existential theology threads the needle between the definable and the undefinable, between revealed being and the mystery of being, and, if reconceptualizing Marcel's words, between being as that which "comes to us as something which contains" and being as that which "goes beyond everything to which we might seek to reduce it."

Because the question of God is always the context by which Marcel's existential theology threads its needle, this becomes, in turn, the challenge at the root of the task and method of Marcel's existential theology. *Being and Having* and *The Mystery of Being* represent the height of Marcel's existential theology and the challenge with which he confronts the question of the meaning of being. This challenge is explored in other Marcel works that have been translated into English include: *Man Against Mass Society* (1962), *Royce's Metaphysics* (1956)—which is a study devoted to Josiah Royce—*Homo Viator: Introduction to the Metaphysic of Hope* (1962), *The Existential Background of Human Dignity* (1963)—which is based on Marcel's William James Lectures at Harvard in 1961–1962—*Creative Fidelity* (1964), *Presence and Immortality* (1967), *Problematic Man* (1967), and *Tragic Wisdom and Beyond* (1973).

Jacques Maritain

Even though Maritain's thought is not absorbed into the philosophy of existentialism in the same manner that Marcel has often been throughout the 1940s, 1950s, and into the 1960s, the relationship between Maritain and Marcel within the context of Catholic thought remains unavoidable. They are, in fact, philosophical and theological contemporaries that share important commonalities—both harbor proclivities toward the analysis of the meaning of being from a theological stance. Yet, with Marcel often grouped—and rather unfairly—with Sartre and Heidegger under the umbrella of "existentialism," Maritain is largely marginalized and even quarantined from this sort of characterization, even though Maritain, like Marcel, is concerned with what "the existential" means to "the theological" and vice versa. Rather, Maritain can be discussed alongside the thought of Berdyaev, Buber, and Tillich, particularly and notably in the Will Herberg–edited volume *Four Existentialist Theologians* (1958).

In the collection's "general introduction," Herberg identifies a series of "common themes that give unity to the thinking of men so diverse in outlook and tradition as Maritain, Berdyaev, Buber, and Tillich."[15] For Herberg, the four thinkers "may be reduced to five heads,"[16] and though Herberg outlines these "five heads" across the thought of the four thinkers to which *Four Existentialist Theologians* is dedicated, I will focus more exclusively on how Herberg's assessment of "common themes" to what he has referred to as "existentialist theology" come to bear on the thought of Maritain—I must, of course, set aside Herberg's use of the term "existentialist

15. Herberg, *Four Existentialist Theologians*, 2.
16. Herberg, *Four Existentialist Theologians*, 2.

theology." Herberg's "common themes" are ontology, existentialism, personalism, social concern, and apologetic-cultural interest.[17]

First, Herberg's understanding of Maritain's ontology finds that Maritain grounds "[his system] on an analysis of true being," such that Maritain's "philosophical approach is therefore basically ontological."[18] Because of this, in Herberg's view, Maritain "[has] much to say about being and non-being, and [he says] it in quite explicit terms."[19] What Maritain is chiefly interested in, as Herberg points out, is how the ontological ushers forth "the conclusions of philosophical reflection and analysis."[20] Maritain's articulation of the ontological, for Herberg, "indubitably possesses theological relevance, and indeed we may suspect the operation of unexpressed theological presuppositions."[21] These theological presuppositions are not just Catholic in nature for Maritain, but they are also especially Thomistic in specificity. It is at this point of specificity—through Maritain's preoccupation with Thomism—that, as Herberg notes, "it is not in an authoritative Scripture and tradition that [his] teachings seek their explicit sanction," but rather, "[his] teachings make their claim to validity primarily on [his] appeal to human reason and experience, however differently these terms are understood."[22] In light of this, Herberg suggests that Maritain is an ontologist "in [his] point of departure," instead of a theologian.[23] This is certainly true, if Maritian's existential theology—which must be made more explicit from denoting it as an "existentialist theology"—is a thought that negotiates ontology and theology. In this way, because of Maritain's focus on the ontological, Maritain is not strictly a theologian, but, as rightly pointed out by Herberg, a "philosopher-theologian."[24]

The extent to which Maritain is a "philosopher-theologian" and how he philosophically comports his theologizing to ontology is conceptualized against the context of Herberg's second theme: existentialism. Herberg's recognition that there is an "existentialist bent to [Maritain's] thinking" is certainly "obvious,"[25] even if Herberg assesses the "existentialism" in Maritain's thought as undefinable, since "it is probably impossible to achieve a single unequivocal definition of this much used, much disputed term."[26] What makes this especially insightful, given that Herberg's volume appears in 1958 and the tendency, at this time, was to define existentialism more broadly in terms of Sartre's thought—Herberg distances his understanding of an "existentialist

---

17. Herberg, *Four Existentialist Theologians*, 2–6.
18. Herberg, *Four Existentialist Theologians*, 3.
19. Herberg, *Four Existentialist Theologians*, 3.
20. Herberg, *Four Existentialist Theologians*, 2.
21. Herberg, *Four Existentialist Theologians*, 3.
22. Herberg, *Four Existentialist Theologians*, 3.
23. Herberg, *Four Existentialist Theologians*, 3.
24. Herberg, *Four Existentialist Theologians*, 3.
25. Herberg, *Four Existentialist Theologians*, 3.
26. Herberg, *Four Existentialist Theologians*, 3.

bent of [Maritain's] thinking" from the mainstream understanding of existentialism through Sartre. Nevertheless, without directly referencing Sartre at all, Herberg concedes that "generally we can describe thinking as existentialist if it makes existence rather than essence the starting point of its ontological reflections."[27] If connecting this to Herberg's first theme of ontology, and how that first theme "possesses theological relevance," Sartre's existentialism is out of bounds—the lack of theological relevance to Sartre, then, leads Herberg to define existentialism in terms of a theological relevance found in Kierkegaard, "in the sense this term has acquired since Kierkegaard." This is especially so, if, for Maritain, "it is human existence, the 'human situation,' that is the starting point."[28] As such, as Herberg continues, "existential thinking then becomes (to employ some of Kierkegaard's own expressions) the thinking of the existing subject about his existence as he 'exists' his existence."[29] When thinking of existentialism this way, it becomes all the more possible to understand why, just as Herberg highlights, Maritain "made a point of defining his way of thinking as existentialist."[30] This thinking is tied to Maritain's Thomism, which, as recognized by Herberg, is based on the idea that Thomism, "properly understood," is the most authentic form of existentialism, if it, too, is "properly understood."[31] This means that Maritain cleaves his "existentialist thinking" to Aquinas rather than Kierkegaard, insomuch as, in being "true to his Thomist traditions," Herberg writes, "[Maritain] has meant something rather different by [existentialism]: his ontological emphasis is not on the 'human situation' or the 'human predicament,' nor for that matter on anything specifically human at all, but on the act of existence as an enactment of being."[32] In order to examine "the act of existence as an enactment of being," Maritain's ontology comes to bear on Maritain's existentialist tendencies as they are predicated on Maritain's theological preoccupations through what becomes Maritain's existential theology.

A way to further assess "the act of existence as an enactment of being" becomes interpreted through personalism—this third theme, for Herberg, through Maritain's Catholicism, "insist[s] on the primacy of the person, on his uniqueness and integrity, in the varying relations of life; and each makes this affirmation a cornerstone of his social philosophy."[33] Through this "personalism," Maritain, as Herberg sees it, "see[s] true personal being fulfilled, not in isolation, but in community."[34] Herberg goes on to say that Maritain's personalism "understand[s] community in the same personalistic way, as involving mutual relation of man with man, rather than a system of external

27. Herberg, *Four Existentialist Theologians*, 3.
28. Herberg, *Four Existentialist Theologians*, 3.
29. Herberg, *Four Existentialist Theologians*, 3.
30. Herberg, *Four Existentialist Theologians*, 4.
31. Herberg, *Four Existentialist Theologians*, 4.
32. Herberg, *Four Existentialist Theologians*, 4.
33. Herberg, *Four Existentialist Theologians*, 4.
34. Herberg, *Four Existentialist Theologians*, 4.

institutions in which the self is diminished and distorted."[35] And yet, "this personalism," Herberg asserts, "is not something superadded to [Maritain's] ontological and existentialist orientation, but flows directly from it."[36] According to Herberg, "the three—ontology, existentialism, and personalism—fall together into a coherent whole, as three facets of the same fundamental outlook"[37]—this "fundamental outlook" for Maritain's existential theology is rooted in, as Herberg's fourth and fifth themes, a "social concern" construed through "Maritain's 'Christian democracy'"[38] and an "apologetic-cultural interest" represented in Maritain's "writings on philosophy, poetry, art, psychology, and politics,"[39] so that, "when [Maritain] theologize[s], [he] theologize[s] in the midst of life, and with relevance to all the issues of life."[40]

In light of Herberg's focus on the themes of ontology, existentialism, personalism, social concern, and apologetic-cultural interest, what remains at the intersection of Maritain's rather large body of work is the interconnectedness of metaphysics, epistemology, ethics, and logic through Maritain's explication of Thomism, which are best exemplified in the following texts, as they have appeared in English translation: *Introduction to Philosophy* (1930), *An Introduction to Logic* (1937), *The Degrees of Knowledge* (1938), *True Humanism* (1938), *A Preface to Metaphysics* (1939), *Science and Wisdom* (1940), *Scholasticism and Politics* (1940), *Religion and the Modern World* (1941), *Saint Thomas and the Problem of Evil* (1942), *Essays in Thomism* (1942), *Philosophy of Nature* (1951), *The Range of Reason* (1952), *An Essay on Christian Philosophy* (1955), *God and the Permission of Evil* (1963), and *Moral Philosophy* (1964). Among these works, there are four texts in particular that are often cited as Maritain's most important works, as they have appeared in English translation: *The Person and the Common Good* (1947), *Existence and the Existent* (1948), *Man and the State* (1951), and *Approaches to God* (1954)—all of these prove to be especially pertinent to understanding Maritain's existential theology and his contributions to the field more broadly.

Considered together, *The Person and the Common Good* and *Man and the State* are both concerned with the intersection of metaphysics, epistemology, ethics, and logic in terms of how the meaning of being is constituted by way of being's worldhood. In effect, Maritain's analyses in both hinge on the relationship between human existence and the world—it is, in one sense, the assessment of what the meaning of being offers to the meaning of worldhood and, in another sense, what the meaning of worldhood offers to the meaning of being. Through Maritain's use of Thomism, *The Person and the Common Good* expresses a social philosophy, which, as described by Maritain, is "centered in the dignity of the human person from every social philosophy

---

35. Herberg, *Four Existentialist Theologians*, 4.
36. Herberg, *Four Existentialist Theologians*, 4.
37. Herberg, *Four Existentialist Theologians*, 4–5.
38. Herberg, *Four Existentialist Theologians*, 5.
39. Herberg, *Four Existentialist Theologians*, 6.
40. Herberg, *Four Existentialist Theologians*, 6.

centered in the primacy of the individual and the private good."[41] This is "rooted in the doctrine of St. Thomas,"[42] such that, Maritain goes to say, "Thomistic personalism stresses the metaphysical distinction between individuality and personality."[43] From this social philosophy, Maritain develops a political philosophy in *Man and the State*, which wishes to confront "the confusion between, of the systematic identification of, *Nation* and *Political Society*—or *Political Society* and *State*—or *Nation* and *State* [which] has been a woe to modern history."[44] As a means of settling this "confusion," Maritain draws a distinction between the meaning of community and society,[45] another distinction that asserts that "the Nation is a community, not a society,"[46] and "in contradistinction to the *Nation*, both the *Body Politic* and the *State* [as they] pertain to the order of society, even society in its highest or 'perfect' form,"[47] and the degree to which "the body politic differs from the State."[48]

In *Existence and the Existent*, subtitled *An Essay on Christian Existentialism*, Herberg's themes of ontology, existentialism, personalism, social concern, and apologetic-cultural interest, at the interconnectedness of metaphysics, epistemology, ethics, and logic comes to bear on Maritain's development of an authentic existentialism that directly confronts Sartre's existentialism as what Maritain deems as an inauthentic existentialism. While Maritain argues for an authentic existentialism rooted in Thomism, he finds that Sartre's existentialism originates from Cartesianism. Maritain is careful to say that he is not interested in "rejuvenating" Thomism for the purposes of establishing what he means by "authentic existentialism"—in this regard, too, how he wishes to define "authentic existentialism" is not from the position of a neo-Thomist, since "[he] would rather be a paleo-Thomist than a neo-Thomist."[49] That is to say, he considers himself to be a Thomist, "who speaks of St. Thomas's existentialism [that] is merely reclaiming his own, recapturing from present-day fashion an article whose worth that fashion itself us unaware of."[50] In doing so, Maritain, as a Thomist, he "is asserting a prior right."[51] This "prior right" is what establishes a Thomistic existentialism as "authentic" and views Sartre's Cartesian existentialism as "inauthentic"—this, in turn, distinguishes Maritain's understanding of a Thomism-influenced existentialism that is decidedly theistic from "the atheistic existentialism of to-day; wherefore the author of

---

41. Maritain, *The Person and the Common Good*, 12.
42. Maritain, *The Person and the Common Good*, 12.
43. Maritain, *The Person and the Common Good*, 12.
44. Maritain, *Man and the State*, 2.
45. Maritain, *Man and the State*, 2.
46. Maritain, *Man and the State*, 4.
47. Maritain, *Man and the State*, 9.
48. Maritain, *Man and the State*, 12.
49. Maritain, *Existence and the Existent*, 11.
50. Maritain, *Existence and the Existent*, 11–12.
51. Maritain, *Existence and the Existent*, 12.

L'Etre et le Néant has more reasons than he reali[z]es to hark back to the philosophy of the *cogito*."[52] To what Sartre harks back, in Maritain's view, is a kind of "lay ethics" that "abolish[es] God and fall[s] back upon bourgeois respectability and the Kantian Decalogue."[53] It is in this that Maritain locates Sartre's imitation of "Descartes' God in arbitrarily setting up standards of justice and injustice and establishing an objective measure of morality."[54] Not only does a Thomistic existentialism make an account for the problems Maritain sees in Sartre's use of "Descartes' God," but it also grounds Aquinas's God, so to speak, to a more meaningful "measure of morality" that more concretely formulates "standards of justice and injustice."

Maritain's concerns in *Existence and the Existent* are further systematized in *Approaches to God*, particularly in its final section, entitled "The Desire to See God." Leading up to this final section, Maritain begins by discussing "[a] primordial way of approach" as a means of grounding a "natural or prephilosophic knowledge of God,"[55] proceeds into explicating his understanding of "philosophical knowledge of God" outlined in five Thomist themes,[56] which ushers forth what he acknowledges as "a sixth way,"[57] and offering "the ways of the practical intellect."[58] All these sections come to bear on "The Desire to See God" section, which furthers Maritain's existential theology through the recognition that, Maritain argues—and what is included in Herberg's selection from Maritain in Herberg's *Four Existentialist Theologians*—"it is as First Cause of things that all the proofs of the existence of God make us know God."[59] Maritain's existential theology, then, becomes a negotiation between "proofs of the existence of God" and what "makes us know God," such that human existence itself is calibrated by the "First Cause." It is in this regard that Maritain concludes:

> Thus the natural desire to see that First Cause whose existence is shown to us through the natural approaches to God is, in human reason, the mark of the possibility—through a gift which transcends the whole order of nature, and in which God communicates what belongs only to Himself—of a knowledge of God superior to reason, which is not due to reason, but to which reason aspires.[60]

For Maritain, the very meaning of "to which reason aspires" as it points to "a knowledge of God superior to reason" comes to bear not just through "proofs of the existence of God" but, more importantly, precisely toward what "makes us know God."

52. Maritain, *Existence and the Existent*, 15.
53. Maritain, *Existence and the Existent*, 15.
54. Maritain, *Existence and the Existent*, 15.
55. Maritain, *Approaches to God*, 15–26.
56. Maritain, *Approaches to God*, 27–66.
57. Maritain, *Approaches to God*, 67–76.
58. Maritain, *Approaches to God*, 77–94.
59. Herberg, *Four Existentialist Theologians*, 37.
60. Herberg, *Four Existentialist Theologians*, 40.

Pierre Teilhard de Chardin

Within the section entitled "Roman Catholic Christianity" and the subsection entitled "Theological Developments" in his second volume of *The Story of Christianity* (2010), Justo Gonzalez provides an interesting and noteworthy discussion of Teilhard's approach to the theory of evolution. Though Gonzalez notes that Teilhard accepted the theory of evolution's general principles, Gonzalez explains that "Teilhard rejected the proposal that the survival of the fittest is the guiding force behind evolution."[61] What Teilhard proposed, however, in its place, was the cosmic law of complexity and consciousness, which served as "a pull in evolution toward the more complex and the more highly conscious."[62] I found this premise to be a particularly poignant way to reinterpret evolution through a theological lens. Hence, as Gonzalez outlines, by reinterpreting evolution theologically, Teilhard suggests that "what we see at any given stage of evolution is a number of organisms that represent different stages or spheres in the evolutionary process."[63] These stages are the "geosphere" (i.e., matter organized into molecules, and molecules into bodies), the "biosphere" (i.e., the way or the means by which life appears), and the "noosphere," in which life attains consciousness of itself. At the "noosphere" stage, what Teilhard's logic contends is that "evolution does not end, but rather takes on a conscious dimension."[64] In this respect, human beings, as we—that is to say humanity—know them as such, are not at the end of the evolutionary process. To suggest this, then, Gonzalez explains that Teilhard believed that "[humanity is] still part of ongoing evolution, leading to human hominization."[65] Of Teilhard's "hominization," Gonzalez explains it by offering this: "What is characteristic of this new stage is that, as conscious being, we are involved in our own evolution." To this end, consequently, it can be ascertained, according to Gonzalez, that Teilhard combined science and theology. In light of this, through Teilhard, there are many connections to existential phenomenology, which further extend examinations about the various ways and means by which existence can be viewed through the parameters of the consciousness, and, in turn, a possible understanding of Teilhard's brand of existential theology at the intersections of the work of Hegel, Merleau-Ponty, Ricoeur, and Husserl.

Jean-Luc Marion

As both a philosopher hailing from the Continental tradition and a Roman Catholic theologian, the influences that notably come to bear on Marion's "existential

---

61. Gonzalez, *Story of Christianity*, 2:450.
62. Gonzalez, *Story of Christianity*, 2:450.
63. Gonzalez, *Story of Christianity*, 2:450–51.
64. Gonzalez, *Story of Christianity*, 2:451.
65. Gonzalez, *Story of Christianity*, 2:451.

theology"—if we call it this, in order to take account for how his philosophical and theological converge in the aim and scope of his thought—are Derrida, Louis Althusser, and Gilles Deleuze with respect to Marion's philosophizing (all of whom taught Marion during his graduate studies in philosophy at École Normale Supérieure in Paris) and a theologizing simultaneously informed by Louis Bouyer (a Lutheran), Henri de Lubac (a Jesuit), and Hans Urs von Balthasar (a Swiss).

These influences especially converge into an existential theology that is grounded on Marion's understanding of phenomenology—through his phenomenological studies marked in the trilogy, *Reduction and Givenness: Investigations of Husserl, Heidegger and Phenomenology* (1989, translated in 1998), *Being Given: Toward a Phenomenology of Givenness* (1997, translated in 2002), and *In Excess: Studies of Saturated Phenomena* (2001, translated in 2002), Marion not only expands upon Husserl's phenomenology predicated on a first reduction of a transcendental nature, but also broadens Heidegger's phenomenology, which is, in itself, a second reduction of an existential nature. While Husserl's transcendental reduction is oriented toward constituted objects and Heidegger's existential reduction is oriented toward the phenomenon of Being, Marion's third reduction is oriented toward the givenness of phenomena.

As an overarching theme to his phenomenology, Marion suggests, in the *In Excess* volume, that, in terms of how he construes "givenness," he wishes to "radically reduce the whole phenomenological project beginning with the primacy in it of givenness."[66] Though Marion's notion of givenness is a phenomenological advancement of both Husserl and Heidegger, it holds a certain theological significance for Marion's philosophical thought, particularly as a project that is an expansion of a theological stance begun earlier in *God Without Being* (1982, translated in 1991). As a theological reading of Heidegger, through *God Without Being*, as Laurence Hemming explains, "Jean-Luc Marion is one of the first theologians to take seriously the force of Heidegger's critique of metaphysics *as a whole*, which means he takes seriously Heidegger's claims about the 'overcoming' (Überwindung) of metaphysics."[67] For Hemming, *God Without Being*— as a work through which we can anticipate Marion's phenomenological studies—is a special reading of Heidegger, by which Marion comports that reading theologically. As it has been pointed out by Hemming, "when in the work of Martin Heidegger the whole of metaphysics is thrown into question,"[68] Marion's reading of Heidegger, then, is one that attempts to take Heidegger's questions in a theological direction. That is to say, through Marion's understanding of how Heidegger "throw[s] into question" how we do metaphysics and the extent to which "any and all of [metaphysics's] determinations become 'questionable,' that is, worthy of being questioned," Marion's take on what Heidegger means to theology takes on a relevance in much the same manner as it does in the theologies of John Macquarrie, Rudolf Bultmann, Paul Tillich, and Karl Rahner,

---

66. Marion, *In Excess*, xxi.
67. Hemming, "Reading Heidegger," 343.
68. Hemming, "Reading Heidegger," 343.

which I have explored in *Heideggerian Theologies* (2018). While, as Hemming writes, "Marion concedes the impact [of what Heidegger has thrown into question] may have for theology,"[69] I would be remiss to not acknowledge the similar efforts made by Macquarrie, Bultmann, Tillich, and Rahner—while each undoubtedly reconceptualizes metaphysics and the meaning of being in their own respective aims and scopes, Marion remains unique in his approach. Yet, what makes the theologies of Macquarrie, Bultmann, Tillich, and Rahner "existential" in nature, is also precisely what makes Marion's work in *God Without Being* undeniably "existential," when considering the work at the head of Marion's larger phenomenological project.

Marion's existential theology—through *God Without Being* in particular, as a means for providing the directedness for Marion's phenomenology—is rooted in Marion's (well-known but rather controversial) examination of God as being free of all categories of Being. Not only does Marion, through Heidegger, confront the fundamentals of metaphysics, but he also, through Aquinas's assertion about God's Being, confronts neo-Thomist theology—in doing so, Marion grounds his conceptualization of "God without Being" on the Christian understanding of love, or the notion of charity. In *Jean-Luc Marion: A Theo-logical Introduction* (2005), Robyn Horner devotes a chapter to *God Without Being*, intending to "assess, at least in a preliminary way, the possibilities of the theological destitution of metaphysics and 'non-metaphysical thought' by love."[70] Horner finds that, in *God Without Being*, "Marion first seeks to identify a non-metaphysical thought of being (and overcoming of metaphysics exemplified in Heidegger's work) and then to subject it, in a second stage, to theological destitution."[71] According to Horner, there is "something of a tension in Marion's treatment of Heidegger," insomuch as that tension arises in the relationship between a non-metaphysical thought of Being and a non-metaphysical thought of God. Horner reads this "tension" occurring within how "[Marion's] stated focus is on a non-metaphysical thought of being (which will be overcome), [such that] his overwhelming interest is in the way God has been thought in metaphysics."[72] In particular, this tension, as such, is grounded on the extent to which "Marion follows Heidegger in relation to the thinking of God in metaphysics, rather than the thinking of being as such."[73] It is through "thinking of God," instead of "thinking of being as such" that Marion is able to take a reading of Heidegger further theologically—the pathmark that Marion takes from Heidegger is one that is altogether different from the respective pathmarks of Macquarrie, Bultmann, Tillich, and Rahner, as they have been laid bare in *Heideggerian Theologies* (2018), especially when considering the controversial nature of Marion's desire to delimit "being" from his conceptualization of God in order to more faithfully

---

69. Hemming, "Reading Heidegger," 343.
70. Horner, *Jean-Luc Marion*, 89.
71. Horner, *Jean-Luc Marion*, 90.
72. Horner, *Jean-Luc Marion*, 90.
73. Horner, *Jean-Luc Marion*, 90.

confront the question of God through overcoming the categories that prevent that question from completely being asked.

With this in mind, Horner recognizes that, "when Marion 'overcomes' Heidegger's non-metaphysical thought of being, he does so on the basis of the inadequacy of such a thinking to deal with the question of God."[74] In this way, rather than viewing Marion's approach as engaging in a brand of Heideggerian theology, Marion can be better explained within a more general understanding of existential theology—this is so, in particular, with the way that Marion believes that, as Horner writes, "when considering the question of being, the question of the existence of God becomes secondary."[75] We see, here, that while it has been noted by Hemming in *Heidegger's Atheism* (2002) about the degree to which Heidegger refuses to present a "theological voice," through what Horner has pointed out, it becomes possible to say that Heidegger's "refusal" to have a theological voice is grounded on a consideration of the "question of being" without necessarily or even contingently working through "the question of the existence of God."[76]

It is precisely because of Heidegger's focus on the "question of being" to the "secondariness" of the question of the existence of God that Marion believes, as Horner cites, that "the thought of being exhibits its own idolatry."[77] Horner correctly notes that "there are two ways in particular in which [idolatry] is confirmed" for Marion.[78] While the first idolatry "does not depend on the aim of a human gaze, Marion locates in the analytic of *Dasein* [the] very tendency to reduce the divine to the scope of the human," the second idolatry "concerns Heidegger's search for a 'more divine God,' to which Marion objects on the grounds that the judgment about the measure of divinity again inevitably proceeds on the basis of a human gaze."[79] These two forms of idolatry are important to what can be described as Marion's existential theology, such that the two idols, as Marion finds them, only distance us from the meaning of the question of the existence of God—that distance forces us to erroneously locate the meaning of God in the question of being, and it is with respect to this that Marion raises objections, particularly when the question of the existence of God, in itself, is placed as a secondary concern and inquiry to that of the question of being. What Horner has suggested about Marion's objections are, in Marion's own words, in the preface to *God Without Being*, in

> following the thematic elaborated by Heidegger, I admit that metaphysics imposes on what it still designates under the disputable title of "God" a function in the onto-theo-logical constitution of metaphysics: as supreme

---

74. Horner, *Jean-Luc Marion*, 90.
75. Horner, *Jean-Luc Marion*, 91.
76. Horner, *Jean-Luc Marion*, 91.
77. Horner, *Jean-Luc Marion*, 91.
78. Horner, *Jean-Luc Marion*, 91.
79. Horner, *Jean-Luc Marion*, 91.

being, "God" assures the ground (itself grounded according to the Being of beings in general) of all other derived beings.... Inevitably, though it did not become apparent for three centuries, [metaphysical] names reflect purely metaphysical functions imposed on "God" and hide that much more the mystery of God as such.[80]

Not only is Marion clearly attempting to avoid the "metaphysical names" as they are "imposed" on God, but he also interested in avoiding "metaphysical functions" assigned to God—both, according to Marion, "hide that much more the mystery of God as such." Such a point is crucial to how Marion theologizes about the philosophical understanding of the meaning of the question of God and, in turn, philosophizes about the theological understanding of the meaning of the question of God.

Having considered Marion's words, when returning to Horner and his conclusion that "for the Marion of *God Without Being*, God gives Godself in a gift of love that can be recognized but not appropriated,"[81] David Tracy's foreword to *God Without Being* furthers Horner's explication of Marion's theological and philosophical concerns in terms of explaining the path that Marion takes toward the meaning of God as "a gift of love" and away from all the "metaphysical names" and all the "metaphysical functions" customarily assigned to the question of God. To this, Tracy acknowledges that "Marion's other path away from modernity leads into a path of postmodernity, a postmetaphysical and post-Heideggerian attempt to think of God outside the horizon of *Sein* altogether, that is, within the horizon of God's own self-revelation as ['a gift of love']."[82] Because of this, Tracy cites the following, which provides an excellent way to gather together Marion's significance to existential theology:

> The deeply French Catholic theological sensibility in Marion's philosophy and theology will take even most Catholic theological readers, whether conservative or liberal, on paths they may not usually choose to read. Conservatives will be led to wonder whether the familiar paths of thought for understanding God in terms of Being from Thomas Aquinas to modern Thomism (Gilson) is a path that genuinely allows the theologian or the philosopher to understand the priority of goodness over being in God's self-revelation as Love. Liberals will be led to question, in more postmodern than antimodern terms, their own commitments to modernity, and thereby to the modern subject, to metaphysics, and to a correlational model for theo-logy.[83]

---

80. Marion, *God Without Being*, xxiii.
81. Horner, *Jean-Luc Marion*, 101.
82. Marion, *God Without Being*, xvi.
83. Marion, *God Without Being*, xvi.

The German School

The German school of existential theology, as I intend to define it, is best comprised of three key philosophers: Friedrich Nietzsche (1844–1900), Karl Jaspers (1883–1969), and Dietrich Bonhoeffer (1906–1945). If considering the contributions of the German school to the theological development of existential theology by way of the philosophical development of existentialism, Nietzsche and Jaspers undoubtedly stand prominently in relation to what we can, perhaps, refer to as "German existentialism."

However, as a variant of the term, "German existentialist," seems to originate, to the best of my knowledge, to Marjorie Grene's article "The German Existentialists" (1959)—in it, Grene provides an examination of Heidegger and Jaspers, insomuch as "they are both acknowledged to practi[c]e a kind of philosophy derived at least in part from Kierkegaard and called *Existenzphilosophie*."[84] In addition to Heidegger and Jaspers, Grene considers the contributions of Tillich as "a theologian . . . with similar interests."[85] Together, Grene concludes that "Heidegger and Jaspers still rank as the two outstanding philosophers of the German-speaking world, and Tillich is certainly in the forefront of contemporary theological philosophers."[86] That said, Grene seemingly attempts to draw the three figures under the umbrella of producing a thinking that can be described as "German existentialism." To the extent that all three can be called "German existentialists," as Grene references, comes with a disclaimer that Grene readily provides by saying: "Only Tillich accepts the term 'existentialism' as meaningful; both Heidegger and Jaspers reject it."[87] From here, Grene is very careful to add that "both Heidegger and Tillich have linked what we should call their 'existentialism' with ontology, a step which so far as I know is not taken by Jaspers."[88]

What Grene is referencing as "what we should call their 'existentialism'" is undoubtedly pointing to the "existentialism" that had been branded and popularized by Sartre by the time of Grene's article. Not only did Grene study with Heidegger and Jaspers up until 1933—at which point she left Germany—but Grene also wrote the earliest study of existentialism, *Dreadful Freedom* (1948), which recognized Sartre's influences on the development of existentialism. With this in mind, as well as Grene's study entitled *Heidegger* (1957) and another work on existentialism, entitled *Introduction to Existentialism* (1959), by the time of "The German Existentialists" article, it is clear that Grene is intent on further defining the German school of existentialism from that of Sartre (and even Marcel), in order to lay bare the philosophical concerns of the German school, especially if we can find that these concerns arise as early as the 1930s. Because Tillich does not officially arrive within the purview of what we

---

84. Grene, "German Existentialists," 49.
85. Grene, "German Existentialists," 49.
86. Grene, "German Existentialists," 49.
87. Grene, "German Existentialists," 49.
88. Grene, "German Existentialists," 49.

can call "existentialism" until the 1950s with his three-volume *Systematic Theology* (1951–1963), *The Courage to Be* (1952), and *The New Being* (1955), Jaspers can be dated to the notion of "existentialism" in the 1930s, more so with the three-volume *Philosophy* (1932) and *Philosophy of Existence* (1938) than the later work *Reason and Existenz* (1955). Jaspers's "existentialism," then, can be viewed a form that is unique from Heidegger's—and yet, when considering the meaning of "German existentialism," this term is more closely associated with Heidegger than Jaspers. While this association is somewhat blurred with Grene's 1959 article—keeping in mind that Grene's purpose is to draw a connection between Heidegger, Jaspers, and Tillich as a particular kind of school of thought—the term "German existentialism," in itself, is not explicitly used until it is applied to a collection of Heidegger's political papers entitled *German Existentialism* (1965). This collection espouses a specific meaning that does not especially have anything to do with Grene's article, or even whatever degree Jaspers can be aligned with the term—here, it is a term that seeks to conceptualize Heidegger's relationship with Nazism and National Socialism.

In the introduction to the *German Existentialism* collection, Dagobert D. Runes—who also translated the texts appearing in the collection from German—clearly acknowledges the controversial milieu of the collected texts, insomuch as they "are bound to throw the light of simple reasoning and simple ethical awareness upon [Heidegger] who, by joining the National Socialist Party of Adolf Hitler, brought discredit not only upon his distinguished teacher, Edmund Husserl, but also upon the philosophical profession."[89] For Runes, there arises a tragic irony from the collection as the espousal of a kind of philosophy in relation to the fact that "Heidegger himself once defined philosophy as the search for the meaning of being."[90] Still, Runes claims that, with respect to what kind of philosophy can be construed from the decidedly political texts collected in *German Existentialism*, "I am not at the moment interested in interpreting the existentialist philosophy or theology of this follower of Soren Kierkegaard who turned into a follower of Adolf Hitler."[91] Be that as it may, it is clear that Runes is making an assessment of Heidegger's "existentialist philosophy," particularly under Runes's banner of "German existentialism" as Heidegger's philosophical comportment to Hitler—having juxtaposed Heidegger's stature as a "follower of Soren Kierkegaard" with that of a "follower of Adolf Hitler," Runes is seemingly understanding that Heidegger's alignment with Hitler is as much about existentialism as his alignment with Kierkegaard is. Indeed, how Runes views Heidegger as "a follower" of Hitler becomes predicated on an existentialism that is different in aim and scope than that of Kierkegaard—it is an existentialism that is uniquely German, and calibrated by way of the National Socialist ideology. Along these lines, Runes is able to be astonished at "how masterfully Martin Heidegger managed to weave into the

89. Heidegger, *German Existentialism*, 9.
90. Heidegger, *German Existentialism*, 9.
91. Heidegger, *German Existentialism*, 9.

sanguinary pattern of National Socialism the pseudo-profundity of his metaphysical terminology."[92] How Heidegger philosophizes the ideology National Socialism through the use of "metaphysical terminology" allows Runes to consider Heidegger as a "neo-existentialist."[93] Such a label acknowledges, on one hand, the philosophical underpinnings that Heidegger ascribes to the aphilosophical National Socialist ideology, while, on the other hand, the label explicitly connects Heidegger's focus on *the question of the meaning of being* to the extent to which the Nazi Party was concerned, too, with the question of the meaning of being.

For Heidegger, when considering three texts found in *German Existentialism*, "German Students," "Avowal to Adolf Hitler and the National State," and "The Call to Labor Service," the term "German existence" best defines the synthesis of Heidegger's philosophical, nonpolitical concerns with *the question of the meaning of being* with National Socialism's aphilosophical, political concerns with the question of the meaning of being—"German existence," as Heidegger uses it, is at the core of what "German existentialism" fundamentally means for Runes. For Heidegger, in particular, "German existence" is more than just about the philosophical meaning of being, or even about the political meaning of being for the National Socialist agenda, but more so about finding a means through which the German people, as a national identity, could be at the very center of the disclosure of the meaning of being for all humanity—to Heidegger, the National Socialist platform presented by the Nazi Party became a means to an end: a way for Heidegger read the question of the meaning of being through the elevated stature of German existence as that which will allow being to authentically and fully reveal itself. Because of this, Heidegger clearly viewed his role on the National Socialist movement as pivotal to Hitler's larger plan, to the extent that Heidegger found himself, through his development of the meaning of German existence as the answer to the question of the meaning of being, as the *Führer* of the *Führer*—or Hitler's guide. In a way, by believing that he was laying the philosophical and theoretical framework for National Socialism, Heidegger seemingly constitutes *the question of the meaning of being* as an existential theology to Nazism.

When summoning forth the idea of "existential theology" in the context of German existentialism, not only does Heidegger loom largely in it—mostly because of Heidegger's involvement with National Socialism—but, as Grene acknowledges, Tillich holds a significant place in it, as well as, though unmentioned by Grene, Rudolf Bultmann. But, what cannot be reiterated enough is how crucial Heidegger's development of an existential theology figures into what becomes the existential theologies of Tillich and Bultmann, as I argue in *Heideggerian Theologies* (2018) and, speaking more generally, how it contributes to what it means to theologize from a philosophical stance, as I attempt to make clear in *A Theologian's Guide to Heidegger* (2019), by definitively recognizing Heidegger's theological roots. These roots—as they functionally predate the

92. Heidegger, *German Existentialism*, 11.
93. Heidegger, *German Existentialism*, 11.

tangible emergence of the existential theologies of Tillich and Bultmann—are inevitably filtered through the culmination of Hitler's rise to power in 1933 and Heidegger officially joining the Nazi Party on May 1, 1933. In that year—almost two decades before Tillich's three-volume *Systematic Theology* and almost a decade before Bultmann's "New Testament and Mythology" essay (1941) and *The Gospel of John* (1941)—Heidegger's existential theology, in light of his understanding of "German existence," functions within a much broader theologizing under the German school of Protestant theology, which, in itself, becomes exploited by National Socialism.

In *Theologians under Hitler* (1985), Robert P. Erickson provides the earliest study of German Protestant theology at the time of Hitler's rise to power in 1933. In it, through focusing on three German Protestant theologians, Paul Althaus (1888–1966), Emanuel Hirsch (1888–1972), and Gerhard Kittel (1888–1948), with each "represent[ing] different approaches to theology."[94] Nonetheless, together, they openly welcomed and unabashedly supported National Socialism and the Nazi Party, such that, as Erickson illustrates, they undoubtedly embody a kind of existential theologizing operating in the vein of Heidegger's. Like Heidegger, Althaus, Hirsch, and Kittel were all official members of the Nazi Party, having all joined in 1933—though Heidegger's philosophizing comports itself theologically, Althaus, Hirsch, and Kittel all seemingly attempt to theologize the meaning of "German existence" from the standpoint of National Socialism. The difference between what can be referred to as the "existential theology" of Heidegger and those that can be projected upon Althaus, Hirsch, and Kittel is that Althaus, Hirsch, and Kittel were all affiliated with the "*Deutsche Christen*" (or the "German Christians"), an evangelical movement that sought to synthesize German Protestantism with the *Führerprinzip* ideological principles of Nazism into what was coined as "positive Christianity." At its core, "positive Christianity" is, in my view, a form of existential theology, which presents a more radicalized version of "German existence" predicated on rejecting the entirety of the Hebrew Bible, advocating for a non-Jewish, Aryan identity of Christ, eliminating Catholicism, and promoting a national unity through uniting Protestantism under a single Unitarianism. With all of this in mind, the overarching understanding of existential theology became based largely on reconceptualizing the meaning of German existence in terms of theologizing the meaning of Aryanhood, in order to establish an Aryan Homeland.

Yet, in order to even speak of "German existence" in the purview of the development of positive Christianity to the posthumous exploitation of Nietzsche, the German school itself must be further contextualized historically, with respect to the kind of theologizing that occurred prior to the rise of National Socialism, Nazism, and Hitler. These critical nineteenth-century philosophical-theological antecedents include: Immanuel Kant (1724–1804), Johann Fichte (1762–1814), Friedrich Schelling (1775–1854), Friedrich Schleiermacher (1768–1834), Georg W. F. Hegel (1770–1831), Arthur Schopenhauer (1788–1860), and Karl Marx (1818–1883)—each

94. Ericksen, *Theologians under Hitler*, 1.

of these thinkers, through specifically philosophizing about God in ways that purposefully venture into theological territory, set the stage for what can be conceptualized as Nietzsche's existential theology, insomuch as Nietzsche becomes, as argued by Heidegger, the consummation of metaphysics.

Because of this, it behooves me to briefly discuss each antecedent, so that we may understand not just how Nietzsche arrives at his own existential theology, but also how Nietzsche's philosophizing and theologizing about God become exploited by National Socialism, when recognizing that each of these antecedents, in different ways, through their connections to secondary influences, contribute to what becomes the German school of existential theology by the mid-1930s.

Immanuel Kant

Kant represents an important starting point for what can be described as modern German philosophy at the height of the Enlightenment era in Germany, insomuch as Kant, generally speaking, sought to synthesize rationalist thought with religious belief—not only is Kant a significant figure of the Age of Enlightenment, he also becomes just as significant a figure at the turn of the nineteenth century, ultimately shaping German thought and the whole of European philosophy which lasts well into the twentieth century and certainly with respect to what becomes National Socialism.

Though Gottfried Leibniz (1646-1716) and Christian Wolff (1679-1754) serve as influences on Kant and Johann Gottfried von Herder (1744-1803) stands contemporaneously to Kant's career, Kant, in particular, can be best contextualized philosophically and theologically with respect to Leibniz's "Essays of Theodicy on the Goodness of God, the Freedom of Man and the Origin of Evil" (1710) and *Monadology* (1714) and Wolff's development of theoretical philosophy as comprised of three special metaphysics: rational psychology, rational cosmology, and rational theology. What Wolff develops both philosophically and theologically is developed, in itself, from Leibiniz's own philosophical-theological articulations—in the sixth volume of his *A History of Philosophy* (1960), Copleston describes, in what is, to my knowledge, the best assessment of Wolff via Leibniz, the philosophical-theological connection between Leibniz and Wolff in the following way:

> Wolff adopted Leibniz's distinction between truths of reason, the opposites of which cannot be asserted without contradiction and which are necessarily true, and truths of fact, which are not necessarily but contingently true. He applied the distinction in, for example, this way. The world is the system of interrelated finite things, and it is like a machine which works or moves necessarily in a certain way because it is what it is. But this necessity is hypothetical. If God had so willed, the world could have been other than what it is. . . . For

when we conceive essences, we abstract from concrete existence and consider the order of possibility, irrespective of God's choice of this particular world.[95]

Here, it becomes all the more apparent that Wolff's use of Leibniz positions Wolff's approach to the "philosophical-theological," and it is this positioning that allows Wolff to serve as an influence on Herder.

As Kant's contemporary, Herder's work within "the philosophical-theological" is best represented in *Essay on Being* (1763), *Letters concerning the Study of Theology* (1780–1781), *Ideas on the Philosophy of the Human of Mankind* (1784–1791), and *God: Some Conversations* (1787), all of which provide a relationship between mainstream Enlightenment thought, deism, and "Radical Enlightenment." More importantly, Herder's alignment with classicism brought about a Romantic nationalism to his understanding of the "philosophical-theological" and what has been referred to as "Weimar Classicism," both of which positioned Herder in opposition with the general ideals of eighteenth-century Enlightenment as what has come to be known as "Counter-Enlightenment" and what has become understood as "German Romanticism" (i.e., of Fichte, Schelling, Schleiermacher, and Hegel).

Though Herder certainly plays an important role in the transition of the "philosophical-theological" from the concerns of Leibniz, Wolff, and the German Enlightenment era, Herder's influence does not reach as widely and as far as Kant does into the nineteenth-century German thought—while Herder unmistakably serves as an influence on the thought of Fichte, Schelling, Schleiermacher, and Hegel, it is without question that this influence is overshadowed by Kant's own influence and the extent to which Kant goes much further into the "philosophical-theological" than Herder. Generally speaking, Kant's approach to philosophical-theological inquiry was innovative and asserted a paradigm shift away from Leibniz, Wolff, and even the contemporaneous work of Herder—Kant's shift, within the "philosophical-theological," is especially noteworthy in "Answering the Question: What Is Enlightenment?" (1784) and *Groundwork of the Metaphysics of Morals* (1785). Yet, when particularly pointing out Kant's philosophizing at the point of theologizing, his three most important works as a trilogy come to mind: *Critique of Pure Reason* (1781), *Critique of Practical Reason* (1788), and *Critique of Judgment* (1790)—these three texts representing Kant's "critical philosophy." Not only does philosophizing about God frequently figure into Kant's "critical philosophy" across the three *Critiques*, but it also becomes more significantly articulated in three other lesser-known works that can be viewed as a second trilogy: *The One Possible Basis for a Demonstration of the Existence of God* (1763), *Lectures on Philosophical Theology* (ca. 1783–1784), and *Religion within the Limits of Reason Alone* (1793). Of this second trilogy—as I have called it—the first and second make a "philosophical-theological" contribution to what might be called Kant's existential theology.

---

95. Copleston, *History of Philosophy*, 6:107.

In *The One Possible Basis for a Demonstration of the Existence of God*, as an essay, Kant interrogates two arguments that explore the existence of God: the ontological argument for God as it originates with Anselm of Canterbury, and the teleological argument for God. In it, in what constitutes part 1, Kant presents four "observations" that become "the basis for a demonstration of the existence of God." These observations are: (1) "existence in general," (2) "on internal possibility insofar as it presupposes an existence," (3) "on positively necessary existence," and (4) "the argument for a demonstration of the existence of God."[96] While the first three observations outline how Kant philosophizes about human existence in general—and we may, in effect, think of this understanding of existence as a proto-existentialism—the fourth observation, in particular, makes use of the meaning of human existence, as Kant has defined it, as a "necessary being [that] is a simple substance in that not only are all other realities given through it as a ground, but also since the maximum possible that may be contained in a being as determinations inheres in it."[97] For Kant, to be a "necessary being" means having "a spirit."[98] What makes the "necessary being," according to Kant, "a spirit" is that "the necessary being has will and understanding."[99] It is from this that Kant finds that "there exists something positively necessary"[100]—that which is "positively necessary" grounds the manner in which "necessary being is a spirit." Kant defines this that is "positively necessary" in the following way:

> This is an entity which is unitary in its essence, simple in its substance, a spirit in its nature, eternal in its duration, immutable in its constitution, and sufficient in respect to everything possible and actual. It is a God.[101]

It is notable, here, that Kant says "it is a God" and not something more definitive such as "it is God," without the qualifying article. Even if, as Kant writes, "I am not giving a definite definition of the concept of God,"[102] it is clear that what he describes as "positively necessary" is based on a theologizing. As much as Kant wishes to philosophize what he means by "something positively necessary," and does not wish to "giv[e] a definite definition of the concept of God," he, nevertheless, concedes that "the definition of the concept of divinity meanwhile may be arranged as one finds apt."[103] Kant further concedes: "But I am certain that that being whose existence we have just demonstrated is precisely the divine being whose defining characteristics

---

96. Kant, *One Possible Basis*, 53–97.
97. Kant, *One Possible Basis*, 87.
98. Kant, *One Possible Basis*, 87.
99. Kant, *One Possible Basis*, 87.
100. Kant, *One Possible Basis*, 87.
101. Kant, *One Possible Basis*, 91.
102. Kant, *One Possible Basis*, 91.
103. Kant, *One Possible Basis*, 91.

will quickly be designated in one way or the other."[104] This eventually leads Kant to think of "divine being," in light of a "definite definition of the concept of God," as "not the only substance which exists, and all others are only dependent upon him."[105] From this point, Kant concludes that

> the ground of proof we give for the existence of God is built simply upon [the fact] that something is possible. Thus it is a proof which may be adduced completely a priori. Neither my existence nor that of other minds nor that of the corporeal world is presupposed. In fact it is deduced from the internal mark of absolute necessity. In this way the existence of this being is known from what really constitutes its absolute necessity and thus entirely genetically.[106]

This notion of "the ground of proof" is continued but broadened by Kant, beyond the Anselm framework, particularly in the lectures Kant delivered at the University of Königsberg presumably around 1783–1784, as they are comprised in the text entitled *Lectures on Philosophical Theology*.

In the lectures delivered some twenty years after *The One Possible Basis for a Demonstration of the Existence of God* essay, Kant's *Lectures on Philosophical Theology* outlines a transcendental theology consisting of "ontotheology" as "ontological proof," "cosmotheology" as "cosmological proof," and "physicotheology" as "physicotheological proof," and a moral theology predicated on "moral theism." These tenets, as they appear in the *Lectures on Philosophical Theology* text, are, as noted by Allen W. Wood and Gertrude M. Clark, the text's translators, "our main source for Kant's views on many of the traditional issues of philosophical theology: the nature and attributes of God, God's relation to the world, God's causality, creation, and divine providence."[107] The translators go on the add, "and they show, perhaps surprisingly, that despite Kant's generally critical stance toward the transcendent metaphysics of the scholastics and rationalists, he remained quite sympathetic to traditional theology on many points."[108] Because of this, the *Lectures on Philosophical Theology* text can be viewed as a more authoritative text on how Kant's theologizing at the intersection of how he philosophizes than what can be mined from the three *Critiques*—even as the most significant representation of Kant's thought in general, it is clear that the *Lectures on Philosophical Theology* text embody a more forthright and sophisticated handling of Kant's understanding of God. Nonetheless, given the dates of the materials that are collected in *Lectures on Philosophical Theology* text, it has a contemporaneous relationship with *Critique of Pure Reason* and predates *Critique of Practical Reason*. With this in mind, though the first critique contains a much more frequent reference to "God" than the

104. Kant, *One Possible Basis*, 91.
105. Kant, *One Possible Basis*, 95.
106. Kant, *One Possible Basis*, 95.
107. Kant, *Lectures on Philosophical Theology*, 10.
108. Kant, *Lectures on Philosophical Theology*, 10.

second critique—and, the first critique and the third critique seems relatively comparable with their respective frequency of "God" references—the *Lectures on Philosophical Theology* text offers Kant's most sustained and concentrated discussion of God, theologizing, and theology in general.

From its outset, in its introduction, the *Lectures on Philosophical Theology* text discusses "the idea of God," by which Kant asserts that "human reason has need of an idea of highest perfection, to serve it as a standard according to which it can make determinations."[109] It is possible, to some extent, to read into this opening a reference to Kant's intentions with *Critique of Pure Reason*. What is different, here, is that, while the first critique is Kant's theologizing from a philosophical standpoint through any reference to God throughout the text, the *Lectures on Philosophical Theology* text is all about theologizing for theology's sake, such that the latter is more concerned with building a functional relationship between Kant's understanding of theology and philosophy. This comes to bear, then, on what he means by "the idea of God," and how the variations of this "idea" makes appearances throughout *Critique of Pure Reason*—for the *Lectures on Philosophical Theology*, Kant finds that "the idea of God" is constituted by "three elements," which Kant delineates as the following "for any idea of this kind":

> (1) Completeness in the determination of the subject with respect to all its predicates (for instance, in the concept of God all realities are met with); (2) completeness in the derivation of the existence of things (for instance, the concept of a highest being which cannot be derived from any other, but which is rather that from which everything else must be derived); (3) completeness of community, or the thorough determination of community and connection of the whole.[110]

These "elements," for Kant, point to how "the idea of God" is determined, and how that determination is further constituted by the extent to which "the world depends on a supreme being [and] the things in the world all mutually depend on one another."[111] Kant considers the idea of "supreme being" synonymously with "the idea of a highest being"—it is through this latter idea, in particular, that Kant conceptualizes God as:

> (1) A being which *excludes every deficiency* . . . (2) A being which contains all realities in itself. Only in this way will the concept be precisely determined. This concept can also be thought as the most perfect nature, or the combination of everything belonging to a most perfect nature. . . . (3) It can be considered as the highest good, to which wisdom and morality belong. The first of these perfections is called transcendental perfection; the second is called physical, and the third, practical perfection.[112]

---

109. Kant, *Lectures on Philosophical Theology*, 21.
110. Kant, *Lectures on Philosophical Theology*, 21–22.
111. Kant, *Lectures on Philosophical Theology*, 22.
112. Kant, *Lectures on Philosophical Theology*, 23.

Here, what Kant denotes as three "perfections" seems to point to a similar rule of three in the *Critiques*, which seems to align "transcendental perfection" with *Critique of Pure Reason*, "physical [perfection]" with *Critique of Judgment*, and "practical perfection" with *Critique of Practical Reason*—what seemingly links all three kinds of "perfection," by way of what Kant points out as an example of the second "perfection," is "will and understanding,"[113] which, in itself, is similarly and previously articulated in *The One Possible Basis for a Demonstration of the Existence of God* essay.

What is also of note in the *Lectures on Philosophical Theology* text is Kant's definition of theology. For Kant, when considering how he understands the meaning of "highest being," and how this "highest being" expresses itself epistemologically, he defines theology in the following manner:

> What is theology? It is the system of our knowledge of the highest being. How is ordinary knowledge distinguished from theology? Ordinary knowledge is an aggregate, in which one thing is placed next to another without regard for combination and unity. In a system, the idea of the whole rules throughout. The system of knowledge of God does not refer to the sum total of all possible knowledge of God, but only to what human reason meets with in God.[114]

In this, not only do we find that Kant wishes to distinguish between "ordinary knowledge" and "the system of knowledge of God," but it becomes all the more apparent that Kant seems to align the former with philosophizing and the latter with theologizing. If the latter is, indeed, about theologizing, Kant sees in that theologizing a means to venture beyond "ordinary knowledge," even that such a venture—when it proceeds toward God—"does not refer to the sum total of all possible knowledge of God." This is because there are limits to what can be theologized about "the system of knowledge of God." Similarly, even when engaging in a philosophizing about "ordinary knowledge," there also arises a limit to it as well. Yet, Kant sees a difference between what is possibly attained through "ordinary knowledge" and what can be attained through "the system of knowledge of God"—in my view, it would seem the "aggregate" nature of the former limits how we can grasp "combination and unity." It is only through "the system of knowledge of God" that we are able to conceive of how "the idea of the whole rules throughout." But, more importantly, it is through "the system of knowledge of God," through theologizing, which becomes a kind of knowing "to what human reason meets with in God."

From here, with respect to the role that human reason plays in the theologizing process, Kant makes a distinction between theologizing about "the system of knowledge of God" between what he calls "*theologia archetypa*" and "*theologia ectypa*"[115]—while the former is denoted as "the knowledge of everything in God,"

---

113. Kant, *Lectures on Philosophical Theology*, 23.
114. Kant, *Lectures on Philosophical Theology*, 23.
115. Kant, *Lectures on Philosophical Theology*, 23.

as "knowledge is only to be found in God himself,"[116] the latter is grounded on "the system of knowledge of that part of God which lies in human nature is called *theologia ectypa*, and it can be very deficient."[117] Even with such a distinction, Kant finds that "to what human reason meets with in God" is fundamentally and pragmatically predicated on the fact that "the sum total of all possible knowledge of God is not possible for a human being, not even through true revelation."[118] This means that, for Kant, theologizing about God has limitations, which are defined by human reason. Nevertheless, the directedness "to what human reason meets with in God," even with its inherent limitations, is what Kant believes to be "one of the worthiest of inquiries to see how far our reason can go in the knowledge of God."[119]

Interestingly, Kant truly believed in "the worthiest of inquiries," and did, indeed, wish "to see how far our reason can go in the knowledge of God," such that "the idea of God" preoccupied Kant in his very last work during the final years of his life up to the time of his death in 1804. Setting aside the problematic composition and publication history of this text entitled *Opus postumum*, it seems that Kant intended for this text to go further than the three *Critiques*, not just to the extent that *Opus postumum* was meant to serve as a "transition" from what Kant had already done with critical philosophy, but also since "this task occupied him virtually until his death."[120] In this text—which, according to Eckart Förster's introduction to the 1993 translation of the work, is believed to be "virtually completed by the middle of 1801"[121]—Kant devotes its final two sections, as they have been ordered posthumously, to "the idea of God." Together, these final two sections are given about fifty-seven pages in the Cambridge edition. In the penultimate section, entitled "Practical Self-Positing and the Idea of God," Kant suggests that "moral-practical reason, if it contains laws of duty (rules of conduct in conformity with the categorical imperative), leads to the concept of God."[122] It is possible to see this "practical self-positing" toward "the idea of God" as Kant's existential theology, which especially comes to bear on the final section of *Opus postumum* discussing "transcendental philosophy"—here, though somewhat fragmented, Kant begins this final section with an understanding of "God and the world," insomuch as, under the caveat *to the limit of all knowledge*,[123] "the totality of beings, God and the world, presented in a synthetic system of the ideas of transcendental

---

116. Kant, *Lectures on Philosophical Theology*, 23.
117. Kant, *Lectures on Philosophical Theology*, 23.
118. Kant, *Lectures on Philosophical Theology*, 23.
119. Kant, *Lectures on Philosophical Theology*, 23.
120. Kant, *Opus postumum*, xvi.
121. Kant, *Opus postumum*, xxviii.
122. This, though abbreviated slightly on my part, is apparently a marginal note made by Kant to the fascicle of the original manuscript. Kant, *Opus postumum*, 200.
123. Kant, *Opus postumum*, 200.

philosophy in relation to each other." This sentiment is carried forward until the end of the *Opus postumum* text, with Kant's following assertion:

> Without transcendental philosophy one can form for oneself no concept as to how, and by what principle, one could design the plan of a system, by which a coherent whole could be established as rational knowledge for reason; yet this must necessarily take place if one would turn rational man into a being who knows himself. What necessarily (originally) forms the existence of things belongs to transcendental philosophy. God, as a holy being, can have no comparative or superlative. There can be only one. Transcendental philosophy precedes the assertion of things that are thought, as their archetype, [the place] in which they must be set.[124]

Johann Fichte

Influenced predominantly by Kant and considered as the impetus for German Idealism, Fichte is believed to have chiefly written his first major work, *Attempt at a Critique of All Revelation* (1792), to get Kant's attention, after Fichte had immersed himself in Kant's work—in particular, Fichte's study of Kantian philosophy focused on the three *Critiques*, the last of which (*Critique of Judgment*) had been published just two years prior to the publication of Fichte's *Attempt at a Critique of All Revelation*. In it, generally speaking, Fichte sought to synthesize the meaning of divine revelation with Kant's critical philosophy—this, of course, expanded upon Kant's critical project and, in a certain sense, extended Kant's argument about "true revelation" and "the system of knowledge of God" in *Lectures on Philosophical Theology*.

The close proximity of the publication of Fichte's *Attempt at a Critique of All Revelation* with the publication of Kant's *Critique of Judgment*, with the inadvertent or intentional omission of Fichte's name from the first edition of *Attempt at a Critique of All Revelation* set the stage for Kant being erroneously assigned as the author of *Attempt at a Critique of All Revelation*. At the time, it was thought, too, that only Kant could have written a book such as *Attempt at a Critique of All Revelation* and that it appeared to be a natural successor to Kant's *Critique of Judgment*. While this eventually proved to be problematic for Kant and his reputation, he greatly helped Fichte, his own reputation, and the critical acceptance of *Attempt at a Critique of All Revelation* itself—essentially, it is with *Attempt at a Critique of All Revelation* and its Kantianism that it is possible to find that Kant's existential theology, if we may call it that, is infused into Fichte's *Attempt at a Critique of All Revelation*, such that the work presents a kind of theologizing about God that becomes ultimately Kant's primary preoccupation in *Opus postumum*.

---

124. Kant, *Opus postumum*, 256.

As noted in the introduction to Cambridge edition of *Attempt at a Critique of All Revelation*, Allen Wood points out that

> the opening of *Attempt at a Critique of All Revelation* certainly follows earlier Kantian treatments of the relation of morality to religion (in the first and second Critiques, for instance) by focusing on the idea that faith in God is needed to guarantee the proportionality of happiness to morality (or worthiness to be happy).[125]

Because of this, the first edition of *Attempt at a Critique of All Revelation* is described as "[an] account [that] follows Kant especially closely"—Wood surmises that this was "largely responsible" for the earliest readership of *Attempt at a Critique of All Revelation* believing it had been written by Kant.[126] More than that, Wood additionally points out that "Fichte also follows Kantian formalism by regularly expounding concepts in accordance with the four headings of the categories (quantity, quality, relation, and modality)."[127] The second edition of *Attempt at a Critique of All Revelation* (1793) does not follow Kant as closely as the first edition and, instead, according to Wood, "interpolates a long and elaborate new [second section], where the relation of happiness and morality is derived from a development of the concept of *volition* or practical self-activity."[128] Wood considers this "from the standpoint of Fichte's philosophy as a whole, [as] the most interesting part of the *Attempt at a Critique of All Revelation*."[129]

As important as "the concept of *volition* or practical self-activity," as Wood identifies, is to Fichte's "philosophy as a whole," Wood speaks of this in isolation from Kant. That is to say, Wood looks at Fichte's innovation as altogether disassociated from Kant. This may not be entirely true, given that Kant articulates something similar to Fichte's "the concept of *volition* or practical self-activity" with the discussion of "practical self-positing" in *Opus postumum*. Though both Fichte and Kant are undoubtedly—though perhaps arguably—working through something conceptually synonymous, it remains unclear if Fichte was aware of what Kant says about "practical self-positing" in *Opus postumum*. It would seem that the most likely answer to this would be no. For that matter, if a definitive date can be ascribed to the section of *Opus postumum* where "practical self-positing" appears, it may be even more difficult to say whether Kant was influenced by Fichte's use of "practical self-activity"—Fichte's influence on Kant, on this specific point, may be too complicated to completely dismiss.

What must also not completely be dismissed is Fichte's reference to "self-positing" in three other major works, written sequentially: *The Science of Knowledge* (1794–1795), *Foundations of Natural Right* (1796–1797) and *Foundations of Transcendental Philosophy*

125. Fichte, *Attempt at a Critique*, xiv.
126. Fichte, *Attempt at a Critique*, xiv.
127. Fichte, *Attempt at a Critique*, xiv.
128. Fichte, *Attempt at a Critique*, xiv.
129. Fichte, *Attempt at a Critique*, xiv.

(1796–1799). While the first text frequently uses "self-positing," and the second text uses "self-positing" as well as "self-preservation," and the third text uses both "self-positing" and "self-activity," it is clear that, in all three, Fichte is not just carrying forward Kant's "idea of God," but is also presenting Fichte's existential theology predicated on an epistemological understanding of God in *The Science of Knowledge*, God in relation to "natural right" in *Foundations of Natural Right*, and God as "the transcendental" in *Foundations of Transcendental Philosophy*. Across these three texts, especially as they stand with respect to *Attempt at a Critique of All Revelation*, is the role that the self-consciousness plays in Fichte's existential theology—it is the sense that the development of "the I" is crucial to Fichte's conceptualization of Kant's "idea of God."

Friedrich Schelling

While Fichte is often considered both historically and philosophically as the beginning point of German Idealism, Schelling is often positioned—in reference to Fichte—as in the middle of the movement of German Idealism. Because of this, Schelling is influenced by Fichte and, as a contemporary, influences Hegel—accordingly, if it is possible to define the aim and scope of Schelling's existential theology, his positioning between Fichte and Hegel significantly shapes how Schelling theologizes about God's existence in relation to his philosophical understanding of human existence.

Three of Schelling's texts that can constitute how his existential theology—if you will—functions are: *System of Transcendental Idealism* (1800), *Philosophy and Religion* (1804) and *Philosophical Inquiries into the Nature of Human Freedom* (1809). In the first text, as a means of exploring a Kantian epistemological project based on denoting a ground to it, Schelling's use of "self-determination" seems to be a stand-in for "self-positing" as it appears in Kant and Fichte—though Schelling similarly locates "self-determination" in reference to a similar understanding of self-consciousness seen in Kant and Fichte, Schelling's first true mention of God—and perhaps the most noteworthy—in *System of Transcendental Idealism* comes through an explication of "absolute synthesis," with which, for the "purposes of this deduction," Schelling finds that "self-consciousness is the absolute act, through which everything is posited for the self."[130] To this end, Schelling concludes that "absolute freedom is identical with absolute necessity."[131] By concluding this, Schelling points to the following example, setting aside the patriarchal language: "if we could imagine an action in God, for example, it would have to be absolutely free, since in God we can think of no law or action that does not spring from the inner necessity of [God's] nature."[132] By theologizing this way, from a philosophical standpoint, Schelling continues with asserting that "such an act is the original act of self-consciousness; absolutely free, since it is

---

130. Schelling, *System of Transcendental Idealism*, 47.
131. Schelling, *System of Transcendental Idealism*, 47.
132. Schelling, *System of Transcendental Idealism*, 47.

determined by nothing outside the self; absolutely necessary, since it proceeds from the inner necessity of the nature of the self."[133] This example, as such, carried forward into *Philosophical Inquiries into the Nature of Human Freedom*, when Schelling notes the following, with a similar use of patriarchal language:

> As there is nothing before or outside of God[,] he must contain within himself the ground of his existence. All philosophies say this, but they speak of this ground as a mere concept without making it something real and actual. This ground of his existence, which God, contains [within himself], is not God viewed as absolute, that is insofar as he exists. For it is only the basis of his existence, it is *nature*—in God, inseparable from him, to be sure, but nevertheless distinguishable from him.[134]

Here, as a connection to what Schelling speaks of in *System of Transcendental Idealism*, the key to Schelling's existential theology—if we may call it that—is the notion that "there is nothing before or outside of God," to the extent that, as Schelling says, "no law or action that does not spring from the inner necessity of [God's] nature." God's nature, for Schelling, is God's ground, insomuch as "nature" and "ground" serve as "the basis for [God's] existence" itself.

Even in speaking this way, Schelling is careful to note that such language is more than just pointing to God's "ground as a mere concept." For Schelling, this conceptualization cannot be made "without making it something real and actual." In other words, as Schelling proclaims in *Philosophy and Religion* (1804), theologizing about God requires recognizing God as "the idea of the Absolute"—if noting Schelling's emphasis through capitalization, and further noting the relationship between "the Absolute" and "absoluteness,"[135] it is clear that "the Absolute" is also meant to conceptualize God, in light of what he articulates in *System of Transcendental Idealism*, as the "ground of his existence."

Clearly, when Schelling believes that "all philosophies say" that "[God] must contain within himself the ground of his existence," he is undoubtedly thinking of Kant and Fichte, and the manner in which neither go a step further toward suggesting how God can be theologized in reference to "something real and actual."

While this may be more of a critique of Kant than Fichte—since the latter figure does, in fact, consider "something real and actual" in, for example, his *Foundations of Natural Right*—there is concerted effort on Schelling's part to distinguish himself from the two. What becomes "real and actual" for Schelling is in the aim and scope of *Philosophical Inquiries into the Nature of Human Freedom* itself, which is devote

---

133. Schelling, *System of Transcendental Idealism*, 47.
134. Schelling, *System of Transcendental Idealism*, 32.
135. Schelling, *Philosophy and Religion*, 11.

largely to "the real and vital conception of freedom itself [such that] it is a possibility of good and evil."[136]

Georg W. F. Hegel

Just as seminal a figure in the development of the German school of thought as Kant, and positioned at the height of the German Idealism movement, Hegel is often considered as a divisive figure, perhaps more so than Kant. I say this recognizing that, even though Hegel is inarguably divisive—not just during his lifetime, but also subsequently historically—Hegel inarguably remains an unavoidable figure, both from a philosophizing and a theologizing standpoint. Because of this, and how Hegel stands in reference to Kant, Fichte, Schelling and anticipates Marx, Nietzsche, and even Schopenhauer (to an extent), if we are to further define the meaning of existential theology to the German school, as such, Hegel becomes all the more a critical figure on how such a thing is to be conceived of, understood, and explained—and, in even speaking about Hegel, it means, at minimum, acknowledging Hegel's most famous (and infamous) work, *Phenomenology of Spirit* (1807), which, on occasion (though problematically) is translated as *Phenomenology of Mind*.

Given that there has been an inordinate amount of scholarship exploring the meaning of Hegel's *Phenomenology of Spirit*—which need not be necessarily recapitulated here—it is without question that the work serves as not just an influence on existentialism (as it comes to fruition in Kierkegaard), but provides a framework for Marx and the underlining movement of Marxism, and Nietzsche's "God is dead" proposition (as the initiation of the death of God theology). In particular, as it pertains to Nietzsche, the "God is dead" proposition, in itself, first occurs in *Phenomenology of Spirit*. Beyond this, speaking theologically, there arises an immense difficulty in pinpointing what kind of theologizing *Phenomenology of Spirit* is engaging in, if any—this is due to the challenge inherent in nature of the philosophizing in the text, and, as it has been a subject of frequent scholarly debate, if *Phenomenology of Spirit* is a work of historical significance (as argued by Jean Hyppolite) or a work of allegorical significance (as argued by Alexandre Kojève). I will not adjudicate this here. For the purposes of denoting Hegel's existential theology, as such, *Phenomenology of Spirit* will not prove to be central to that definition, but, instead, it will merely be peripheral to Hegel's *Lectures on the Philosophy of Religion*, with various iterations dated to 1821, 1824, 1827, and 1831.

In a lecture dated 1824, in a section entitled "The Position of the Philosophy of Religion vis-à-vis the Needs of Our Time," Hegel lays the foundation for "consider[ing] philosophy of religion as the treatment of the concrete idea of the divine in rational

---

136. Schelling, *Philosophy and Religion*, 26.

form, as the conceptualizing [or] cognition of God."[137] It is from this point that Hegel argues the following:

> If we call the cognition or knowledge of God "theology" generally, whether we approach it from the standpoint of philosophy or from that of theology in the narrower sense, we seem at first to be treading the same path as the theology that used to be called rational theology. It is the universal highroad or the universal mode in which what is known of God is said of God.[138]

What Hegel attempts to do, here, is make a differentiation from what he calls "the cognition or knowledge of God" and "rational theology," which is a fundamental difference between forms of theologizing about God. The former, for Hegel, seems focused on what can be considered as an existential theology, while the latter—from which he is distancing himself—is a kind of theology build on reason and "the rational." In this way, this latter sense of theology is a theologizing that the German Idealism movement positions itself against, which Hegel explains in the following manner:

> This rational theology has on the whole been called the theology of the Enlightenment. Pertinent here, however, is not merely this kind of theology but also the kind that leaves reason aside and expressly rejects philosophy, and then erects a religious doctrine from the plentitude of its own argumentative power. Though biblical words lie at its basis, to be sure, *private opinion* and *feeling* still remain the controlling factor.[139]

Hegel goes on to say that

> it very often happens that philosophy is set aside in the process, that philosophy is represented as something ghostlike that must be ignored because it is uncanny. Philosophy, however, is nothing other than cognition through reason, the common feature in the cognition of all human beings.[140]

This "rational theology," or "the theology of the Enlightenment," is a theologizing that, as Hegel claims, allows for "philosophy [to be] set aside in the process" of its very theologizing. Hegel's sense of theologizing as "the cognition or knowledge of God" is one where philosophy is not "set aside" but integral to what can only be described, in my belief, as an existential theology. This seems all the more possible if differentiating existential theology with what Hegel understands to be "modern theology"—if, for that matter, Hegel understands "modern theology" as "the theology of the Enlightenment," particularly as a kind of theologizing that does not make an account for what it means to theologize about "the cognition or knowledge of God." Considering this lapse in

---

137. Hegel, *Lectures on the Philosophy of Religion*, 121.
138. Hegel, *Lectures on the Philosophy of Religion*, 121.
139. Hegel, *Lectures on the Philosophy of Religion*, 125.
140. Hegel, *Lectures on the Philosophy of Religion*, 125–26.

"modern theology" or "the theology of the Enlightenment," Hegel makes the following case, which, in itself, points to Hegel's own existential theology:

> But when modern theology says that we cannot have cognition of God or that God has no further determinations within himself, it knows only that God is as something abstract without content, and in this way God is reduced to this hollow abstraction. It is all the same whether we say we cannot have cognition of God, or that God is only a supreme being. Insomuch as we know [only] *that* God is, God is the *abstractum*. To cognize God means to have a definite, concrete concept of God. As merely having being, God is something abstract; when [God is] cognized, however, we have a representation with a content.[141]

Arthur Schopenhauer

To say that Schopenhauer espouses a certain kind of existential theology can certainly be debated, especially when standing his philosophizing and theologizing against Kant, Fichte, Schelling, and Hegel. Part of the problem is with Schopenhauer's influences, with respect to delineating these influences in terms of the positive and the negative—while Schopenhauer was positively influenced by Kant, he was, at the same time, negatively influenced by Fichte, Schelling, and Hegel. That is to say, even though Schopenhauer found some redeeming qualities in Kant's thought (and, generally speaking, Kantianism) and, to an extent, he unfortunately did not find anything remotely redeeming in the thought of Fichte, Schelling and Hegel (as representatives of German Idealism and Post-Kantianism). For Schopenhauer, Fichte, Schelling, and Hegel were not philosophizing in a serious way and, for that matter, none of them reached a philosophizing that could be called (as I have offered) theologizing, even though Schopenhauer did think that Schelling was "the most talented" of the group—these reflections and critiques are offered in "Sketch of a History of the Doctrine of the Ideal and the Real" as it appears in the collection *Parerga and Paralipomena* (1851).

Schopenhauer's reverence for Kant over Schopenhauer's contemporaries (Fichte, Schelling, and Hegel) is explicit in his best-known, major work, *The World as Will and Representation* (1818–1819 as a first edition), which is often considered as holding more fidelity to Kant's transcendental idealism than Fichte, Schelling, Hegel, or any of the other figures generally grouped into German Idealism (or a post-Kantian idealism). Setting aside the fact that Schopenhauer expanded *The World as Will and Representation* into a second edition (1844) and a third edition (1859), and a second volume to the work that expands upon topics covered in the first volume and includes explicit attacks on Fichte, Schelling, and Hegel, Schopenhauer refers to Kant's understanding of "the idea of God" in terms of "cosmological proof" and "physico-theological proof"—this is especially noted in Schopenhauer's following claim:

---

141. Hegel, *Lectures on the Philosophy of Religion*, 127.

> After Kant has proven that the path of earlier dogmatism, honestly proceeding from the world to a God, does not lead there after all—these gentlemen now think they have found a fine alternative route, and did it up in style.[142]

If, as Schopenhauer claims, the need to proceed "from the world to a God" is a path that Kant reconceptualizes in contrast to "earlier dogmatism," Kant's own dogmatism, as understood by Schopenhauer, suggests that the path "from the world to a God" does not arrive at "a God" at all. Likewise, the "gentlemen"—presumably those of German Idealism—take what they assume to be "a fine alternative route," which, in itself, "does not lead [to a God]" either. Schopenhauer points to "the inner experience"—as that which he finds missing in Kant and as what the German Idealists intend to "[do] it up in style." This "inner experience" for Schopenhauer is predicated on the will—Schopenhauer's understanding of "the will" is analogous to Kant's "thing-in-itself," such that Schopenhauer's "will" becomes an object that, like Kant's "thing-in-itself," is independent of observation. As with Kant's "thing-in-itself," Schopenhauer's "will" allows for human existence to connect to all that exists in the world by way of how the world presents (or represents) itself. Included in this, is "the idea of God,"—in this way, in light of Schopenhauer's "will," it is possible to locate Schopenhauer's existential theology (if you will) within the ability of "the will" to connect to "the idea of God" as God presents (or represents) God-self to human existence as a transcendental representation of God's Being, with respect to how "time and space attach to the *subject*."[143]

Karl Marx

Though Marx is well known mostly for *The Communist Manifesto* (1848, coauthored with Friedrich Engels) and the seminal three-volume work *Capital: A Critique of Political Economy* (1867, 1885, and 1894)—the first serving as an influential text for the 1917 Vladimir Lenin–led Bolshevik Revolution in Russia, and the second serving as a foundational text for materialist philosophy—any discussion of Marx's contribution to the German school of existential theology requires focusing more closely on Marx's early career, which would be prior to the publication of *The Communist Manifesto*.

This early period in Marx's career is when, as Saul K. Padover notes in the introduction to *On Religion* (1974)—a collection of Marx's religious and theological writings—"[Marx] concerned himself with [the subject of religion] in his early years, when he was interested in philosophy, which then included theology, or vice versa, as the Christian theologians would have it."[144] It was during this time, in particular, as Padover points out, that Marx wrote two philosophical-theological texts, *Difference between the Democritean and Epicurean Philosophy of Nature* (1841) and *On the*

---

142. Schopenhauer, *World as Will and Representation*, 399.
143. Schopenhauer, *World as Will and Representation*, 37.
144. Marx, *On Religion*, ix.

Jewish Question (1844)—while the former, as Marx's doctoral thesis, "deal[t] with classic Greek philosophy, [and] also examined theological questions, such as the gods, the heavens, etc.[,] [the latter] was a philosophical-political essay ranging through a particular theology: Judaism, the religion of the Jews."[145] Padover continues with the point: "Thereafter Marx lingered but intermittently on questions of theology, and then only as religion affected politics and economics."[146] Be that as it may, if we are to define Marx's religious views not just as they are expressed across his career into the extent to which "religion affected politics and economics," Padover makes it clear that "Marx's religious position was in line with that of contemporary German theological radicals, notably Ludwig Feuerbach and Bruno Bauer."[147] What Padover fails to mention—but, nevertheless, must be mentioned—is that what Marx's "religious position was in line with" was a group of German intellectuals that became known as the "Young Hegelians"—these "theological radicals" expanded upon Hegel's legacy following Hegel's death in 1831. This group included Feuerbach and Bauer, but also David Strauss, Carl Nauwerck, Arnold Ruge, Max Stiner, all as main members of the group, with its younger members consisting of August Cieszkowski, Karl Schmidt, and Edgar Bauer. As one of the younger members of the "Young Hegelians," Marx's "religious position was in line with," more generally, criticized Christianity in order to criticize the Prussian government. By the time Marx writes *The German Ideology* (written in 1846, and coauthored with Engels), he has broken with the "Young Hegelians" altogether—as a collection of texts, *The German Ideology* sharply criticized Bruno Bauer, Feuerbach, Stirner, as well as others from the group.

How Marx distances himself from the "Young Hegelians" is particularly notable in the "Theses on Feuerbach," as it appears in *The German Ideology*—among the series of eleven notes to Feuerbach's *The Essence of Christianity* (1841), the seventh note, in which Marx argues that Feuerbach "does not see that the 'religious sentiment' is itself a social product, and that the abstract individual whom he analyses belong to a particular form of society,"[148] presents one dimension of Marx's theologizing. For Marx, religion—and, therefore, theologizing itself—is connected inextricably to society. Another dimension of Marx's theologizing—also in purview of the connection between theologizing and society—can be found in his *A Contribution to the Critique of Hegel's Philosophy of Right* (written in 1843), which, though directly criticizing Hegel's *Elements of the Philosophy of Right* (1820), was not published until after Marx's death. In its introduction, published in 1844, Marx proclaims that

> the basis of irreligious criticism is: *Man makes religion*, religion does not make man. And indeed, religion is the self-awareness and self-regard of man who

---

145. Marx, *On Religion*, ix.
146. Marx, *On Religion*, ix.
147. Marx, *On Religion*, ix.
148. *Karl Marx and Friedrich Engels*, 1:13–15.

either has not yet found or has already lost himself again. But man is not an abstract being, crouching outside the world. Man is the *world of men*, the state, society. This state, this society, produce religion, which is an inverted world consciousness because they are an inverted world.[149]

The extent to which, as Marx believes, "man makes religion," he considers "religion"—and by extension, theologizing itself—as serving a practical societal function. In effect, this can be thought of as a structural-functionalist view of religion and theologizing, such that, as Marx proposes, "religion is the self-awareness and self-regard" of the meaning of human existence. If Marx's existential theology can be defined, it is in reference to a structural-functionalist theologizing about God—it is based on the notion that "the idea of God," if returning to Hegel, is regulated by the practical needs of society: for Marx, theologizing is not about theologizing only about God but, more importantly, it is about theologizing the grounding "self-awareness and self-regard" to society. With this in mind, Marx makes the following series of analogies about religion and, in turn, what it means to theologize about God:

> Religious misery is in one way the expression of real misery, and in another a protest against real misery. Religion is the sign of the afflicted creature, the soul of a heartless world, as it is also the spirit of spiritless conditions. It is the opium of the people.[150]

Here, if, as Marx concludes, "[religion] is the opium of the people"—and, as I have suggested synonymously, "[theologizing] is the opium of the people"—Marx's existential theology, as such, is about theologizing about God as a means to pacify rather than sustain. What this means, then, is that Marx's existential theology is rooted fundamentally on a theological facade, or illusion that does not provide true sustenance to human existence. To this end, we might ask: what kind of existential theology can be located in Marx if it is, at its most fundamental, focused on articulating theologizing itself as an "opium" that does not authentically anchor human existence to God's existence? Is it, in fact, more atheistic than theistic, more philosophical than theological? It is certainly too harsh to say that any atheistic strand exists in what can be called Marx's existential theology—rather, his is more philosophical and, in that respect, it can be aligned more closely with Sartre's meaning of "the existential," as best articulated in Sartre's *Critique of Dialectical Reason* (1960).

Friedrich Nietzsche

By 1933, with Hitler's rise to power, the development of positive Christianity as what can be considered as Nazism's existential theology undoubtedly—and explicitly—incorporates Nietzsche's philosophical thought into the overall aim and scope of

---
149. Marx, "Criticism of Religion," 35.
150. Marx, "Criticism of Religion," 35–36.

National Socialism. While Nietzsche is certainly not the only thinker to have had their thought explicitly affiliated with Nazi ideology, no more than Nietzsche is the only figure to have had this happen posthumously, Nietzsche's relationship with National Socialism is extremely and uniquely complicated. Not only are there complications with the handling of Nietzsche's philosophical legacy by Nietzsche's sister, Elizabeth Förster-Nietzsche, with her establishment of the Nietzsche Archive in 1894 and the coediting of Nietzsche's unpublished posthumous manuscript *Nachlass* in 1901, but these complications became exploited by the Nazi Party in a way that misused and abused Nietzsche's thought for certain ideological ends.

Given that Elizabeth Förster-Nietzsche's editorial work on *Nachlass*—which would later become translated as *The Will to Power* (1901, originally translated in English in 1910)—sought to rework Nietzsche's fragments into her own ideology, this reworking across various editions of Nietzsche's work throughout the 1910s–1930s became eventually associated with German militarism and anti-Semitism. As early as the 1930, as Elizabeth Förster-Nietzsche began to openly support the National Socialist movement, and by 1933, when she would officially become a member of the Nazi Party, the Nietzsche Archive began to receive financial support from the German government—her alignment with the National Socialism also aligned Nietzsche's legacy with the movement, so that Nietzsche's philosophizing became injected into Nazi ideology and further reified, for example, by Alfred Baeumler (1887–1968), most notably with Baeumler's *Nietzsche, der Philosoph und Politiker* (1931).

Despite National Socialism's use of Nietzsche's philosophizing and Förster-Nietzsche's role in standing Nietzsche's legacy alongside Nazi ideology, three philosophers introduced immensely important studies of Nietzsche's thought that more broadly sought to separate Nietzsche from Nazi: Löwith (1935), Jaspers (1936), and Heidegger's lectures on Nietzsche beginning in the Winter 1936/1937 semester at Freiburg—as with Baeumler's work, Löwith, Jaspers, and Heidegger all attempted to understand, to varying degrees, the meaning of Nietzsche's oft-discussed (and controversial) proposition of "God is dead," as it appears in Nietzsche's *The Gay Science* (1882) and later in *Thus Spoke Zarathustra* (1883). While Baeumler's work interpreted and propagandized Nietzsche's "God is dead" into an anti-Christianity and an atheism that contributed to the development of Nazi ideology, Baeumler's brand of theologizing about God does not explicitly appear in Löwith's, Jaspers's, nor Heidegger's approaches to Nietzsche—for Löwith, Jaspers, and Heidegger alike, "God is dead" is philosophized, in order to more generally make sense of the landscape of Western philosophy.

Heidegger's philosophizing about Nietzsche's "God is dead" has been thoroughly-discussed in the history of Heidegger scholarship and need not be elaborated here—just as Heidegger recognized the philosophical significance in "God is dead," Tillich, influenced by Heidegger, recognized the theological significance in the statement. Throughout Heidegger's reading of Nietzsche, Heidegger frequently considers the meaning of "God is dead" in terms of "we have killed him" and the implications of this philosophically—yet, Heidegger's understanding of these implications are not necessarily theological in nature. It is Tillich that theologizes "God is dead" and the implications of "we have killed him" to what it means to theologize about God, insomuch as Tillich's theologizing about God, through Heidegger's "Nietzsche," brings Tillich to conclude, in *The Courage to Be* (1952), that "the courage to be is rooted in the God who appears when God has disappeared in the anxiety of doubt."[151]

In the years following Tillich's theologizing about God through Nietzsche's "God is dead"—taking into account, quite possibly, Heidegger's influence on Tillich's reading of Nietzsche, in light of Heidegger's direct influence on Tillich's theologizing—a larger "Death of God" movement developed, sparked by Gabriel Vahanian's *The Death of God* (1961) and further critiqued in Thomas W. Ogletree's edited collection *The Death of God Controversy* (1966). What becomes apparent about the "Death of God" movement, if placing Tillich's *The Courage to Be* as a precursor to the movement and, in turn, a proto-text, Nietzsche's "God is dead" sentiment undeniably has ramifications to what it means to theologize about God—to theologize about God from the standpoint of "God is dead" means doing a kind of existential theology that fundamentally questions the very meaning of being in the human imagination.

Dietrich Bonhoeffer

As one of the leading opponents of the development of positive Christianity and the Nazi-led government's desire to unify all German Protestant churches into a Nazi-sanctioned "Reich Church" or what is also known as the "German Evangelical Church," Bonhoeffer was involved in an anti-Nazi movement that became known as the "Confessing Church"—this was sparked by the "Barmen Declaration of Faith" (chiefly authored by Karl Barth), which not only rejected the "German Evangelical Church," but also believed that the "Confessing Church," as such, rightfully constituted the authentic Evangelical Church of Germany.

Bonhoeffer's role in the Confessing Church movement can be viewed as a kind of existential theology, given that it opposed the existential theology developed from and espoused by the "German Evangelical Church." Thinking of Bonhoeffer's existential theology this way—as just as concerned with what it means to theologize about God as that of the Nazi's existential theology—his *The Cost of Discipleship* (1937) and the unfinished *Ethics* (posthumously published in 1949) generally stand out as seminal examples of Bonhoeffer's theology. Yet, another text that is "far less well known and read . . . that come[s] from the first half of Bonhoeffer's adult life"[152] will prove to be a more significant example of what Bonhoeffer's existential theology looks like: *Act and Being: Transcendental Philosophy and Ontology in Systematic Theology*, which was accepted

---

151. Tillich, *Courage to Be*, 190.
152. Bonhoeffer, *Act and Being*, 1.

in 1930 as Bonhoeffer's qualifying thesis. Published in 1931, *Act and Being*, as noted by Wayne W. Floyd's editor's introduction to the 2009 edition of the work, "evidences Bonhoeffer's emerging practical concern to find for theology a methodology adequate and proper to its unique subject matter—and to the challenging terrain of its cultural and historical location."[153] Floyd goes on to find that "despite its seemingly abstract philosophical cast, [*Act and Being*] begs to be interpreted within the concrete, historical context of the cultural crisis in Germany between the world wars, which eventuated in the National Socialist rise to power in 1933."[154] This is certainly true, given that *Act and Being* predates or anticipates the significant benchmark year of 1933—what is also true, more importantly, is that *Act and Being* provides a beginning point for Bonhoeffer's participation in the *Confessing Church* movement and his overall antipathy toward National Socialism in general. The very nature and existence of the German Evangelical Church and Hitler's role in it further contextualizes *Act and Being*, as an explication, as Floyd argues, of the fact that "Bonhoeffer wished theology to speak with all the resources of modern thought, yet with its own distinctive voice, including the prophetic tone of the critique of idolatry."[155] It is "the prophetic tone of the critique of idolatry," as cited by Floyd, which points to Bonhoeffer's critique of National Socialism itself and, perhaps, Hitler's idolized role in it.

To a great extent, with all of this in our purview, Floyd is correct to assert that "Bonhoeffer therefore approached his chosen topic for *Act and Being*, a theology of consciousness, from within the perspective of the Reformation tradition's insights about the origins of human sinfulness in the *cor curvum in se*—the heart turned in upon itself and thus open neither to the revelation of God, nor to the encounter with the neighbor."[156] Though such an argument certainly predates the rise of the German Evangelical Church, it is still possible to see how well the sentiment of "the heart turn[ing] upon itself" resonating with what Bonhoeffer's allies in the Confessing Church experienced by 1933—for Bonhoeffer, the National Socialist movement itself would be "neither open to the revelation of God, nor to the encounter with the neighbor," and the same can be said about the German Evangelical Church by its definition.

By further contextualizing *Act and Being*—though I am projecting its context upon what Bonhoeffer had not yet confronted during the writing of this work—Floyd comes to the following understanding:

> Throughout *Act and Being*, Bonhoeffer is arguing that what is needed is a form of theological thinking that takes seriously both philosophy's own repeated attempts to surmount its intrinsic tendency towards system, towards totality, and the reasons they must be judged a failure. He wished to clarify the extent to which theology can or cannot affirm transcendental epistemology's

---

153. Bonhoeffer, *Act and Being*, 7.
154. Bonhoeffer, *Act and Being*, 7.
155. Bonhoeffer, *Act and Being*, 7.
156. Bonhoeffer, *Act and Being*, 7.

subject-object paradigm as appropriate for theological thinking that remembers the sociality of the Other, the ethics of difference—between humanity and God, as between one human being and another.[157]

What is all the more apparent, here, is how *Act and Being* speaks not just to what Bonhoeffer confronted in 1933 and what led him to align himself with the Confessing Church movement, but also what he experienced after having been accused of having an affiliation with the plot to assassinate Hitler on July 20, 1944, and his eventual execution on April 9, 1945. The very trajectory of Bonhoeffer's life, then, is ultimately predicated on National Socialism's refusal to consider "the sociality of the Other, the ethics of difference" as much as the German Evangelical Church would not engage in theological thinking that occurs "between humanity and God, [and] between one human being and another."

It is precisely this problem that underscores the outset of *Act and Being*, which Bonhoeffer articulates in the following manner:

> At the heart of the problem is the struggle with the formulation of the question that Kant and idealism have posed for theology. It is a matter of the formulation of genuine theological concepts, the decision one comes to between a transcendental-philosophical and an ontological interpretation of theological concepts. It is a question of the "objectivity" of the concept of God and an adequate concept of cognition, the issue of determining the relationship between "the being of God" and the mental act which grasps that being.[158]

Here, in particular, at "the heart of the problem," for Bonhoeffer, is the question of the meaning of existential theology, which Bonhoeffer defines as "[a] struggle with the formulation of the question that Kant and idealism." Bonhoeffer seemingly pinpoints that "struggle" in relation to the theologizing of Fichte, Schelling, Hegel, and German Idealism more broadly—it is a "struggle" which, in itself, "posed for theology," such that theologizing itself cannot be fully accomplished with reckoning with the struggle of "the formulation of genuine theological concepts." As Bonhoeffer sees it, the problem and struggle inherent in the problem is constituted "between a transcendental-philosophical and an ontological interpretation of theological concepts"—at this intersection, Bonhoeffer chooses to mitigate "the problem" and "the struggle" in terms of "determining the relationship between 'the being of God' and the mental act which grasps that being," which becomes the means by which he engages in an existential theology.

157. Bonhoeffer, *Act and Being*, 11.
158. Bonhoeffer, *Act and Being*, 27.

The Russian School

The Russian school of existential theology is comprised of three key writers and thinkers: Fyodor Dostoyevsky (1821–1881), Leo Tolstoy (1828–1910), and Nikolai Berdyaev (1874–1948). To be sure, while Dostoyevsky and Tolstoy are generally considered as novelists operating mainly within the realist literary movement, and Berdyaev is generally thought of as existentialist religious thinker, all three figures are largely influenced by Russian Orthodox Christianity—this can be especially said about Dostoyevsky and Berdyaev, though Tolstoy would become excommunicated from the Russian Orthodox Church in 1901. Together, each of the figures uniquely philosophize what must be theologized, to the extent that each of them espouses an existential theology that is either expressed through narratives (Dostoyevsky and Tolstoy) or treatises (Berdyaev)—what makes each of their philosophizing from a theological standpoint expressions of existential theology is that, in each figure, there is a devotion to the relationship between humanity's existence and God's existence. This seems especially so, when considering that the existential theologies of Dostoyevsky, Tolstoy, and Berdyaev, as I wish to define them, stand outside the Russian Orthodox Christian tradition by way of their own respective existentialist proclivities.

There is an undeniable tension between what has been referred to as the existential theologies of Dostoyevsky, Tolstoy, and Berdyaev and the general idea of modern Russian theology. Indeed, the thought of Dostoyevsky, Tolstoy, and Berdyaev belong to the same modernized understanding of Russian theology, though, as I have presented the philosophical leanings inherent in them, how the three figures respectively theologize tend to do so largely outside, in confrontation, or in contrast with the kind of modern Russian theology that falls within established orthodoxy.

In a recent study, *Modern Russian Theology: Bukharev, Soloviev, Bulgakov; Orthodox Theology in a New Key* (2000), Paul Valliere makes a case for the theological contributions of Aleksandr Bukharev, Vladimir Soloviev, and Sergei Bulgakov, which, admittedly, is focused "on the theology itself, that is to say, on what Russian-school thinkers actually believed and taught as the Orthodox faith."[159] Also, Valliere admits that "while a history of the Russian school is needed, this book is not it."[160] Nevertheless, at the very outset of his introduction to *Modern Russian Theology*, Valliere asserts that "the material presented in this book is drawn from a stream of Orthodox Christian thought which arose in nineteenth-century Russia, flourished in the early twentieth century and figured prominently on the Orthodox theological scene as late as the 1930s."[161] The term "Russian school," which refers to this period and "the stream of thought" that belongs to it, as it is used by Valliere, is drawn from Alexander Schmemann's "Role of Honour" (1954), which Schmemann further applies to a later survey

---

159. Valliere, *Modern Russian Theology*, 8.
160. Valliere, *Modern Russian Theology*, 8.
161. Valliere, *Modern Russian Theology*, 1.

entitled "Russian Theology: 1920–1972" (1972).[162] Influenced by Schmemann's work, Valliere's use of "Russian school" points to a theology that

> grew out of the need to relate the Orthodox faith to what is usually called a modern free society, that is to say, a society consisting of relatively autonomous, unharmonized spheres of activity operating outside the tutelage of church and state.[163]

The manner with which Valliere positions the "Russian school" theologically is more than just in terms of historical or even social contexts, but it is also in terms of another context altogether, by drawing from Michael Meerson (labeled as "a present-day Orthodox theologian"), having "reviv[ed] the project of the Russian school, and describing the 'Russian school' as fundamentally grounded theologically to an 'anthropological paradigm shift' in modern theology."[164] Though Valliere makes use of the historical, social, and anthropological contexts that shapes the theological preoccupations of the Russian school, Valliere writes that, on the whole, the "historical background is supplied only to the extent necessary for appreciating the theology."[165] With this in mind, Valliere's selection of Bukharev, Soloviev, and Bulgakov attempts to "represent the beginning, middle and end of the Russian school respectively."[166] While Bukharev, as "Russian Orthodoxy's first modern theologian,"[167] and Soloviev, as "the crucial mediator between home-grown Orthodoxy and modern critical thought,"[168] both are contemporaneous to Dostoyevsky and Tolstoy. Valliere's third figure ascribed to his definition of the "Russian school," Bulgakov, "belong[s] to the first generation of Russian intellectuals inspired by Soloviev,"[169] which is contemporaneous to Berdyaev.

Even though Valliere's characterization of the modern theologies of Bukharev, Soloviev, and Bulgakov, as Valliere's version of a Russian school, is broadly concerned with sustaining a relationship with Russian Orthodox Christianity, the existential theologies of Dostoyevsky, Tolstoy, and Berdyaev, as another Russian school, is not as concerned with a theological relationship with the Russian Orthodox Church—rather, unlike the interests of Bukharev, Soloviev, and Bulgakov, the interests of Dostoyevsky, Tolstoy, and Berdyaev lie with sustaining a philosophical relationship with existentialism that largely has its roots in Nietzsche, as well as the thought of Kant, Hegel, and Schopenhauer.

---

162. See first note. Valliere, *Modern Russian Theology*, 1.
163. Valliere, *Modern Russian Theology*, 2.
164. Valliere, *Modern Russian Theology*, 3.
165. Valliere, *Modern Russian Theology*, 8.
166. Valliere, *Modern Russian Theology*, 8.
167. Valliere, *Modern Russian Theology*, 8.
168. Valliere, *Modern Russian Theology*, 9.
169. Valliere, *Modern Russian Theology*, 10.

EXISTENTIAL THEOLOGY

Fyodor Dostoyevsky

Throughout his body of work, it has been generally noted that Dostoyevsky employs philosophical, religious, and even psychological ideas—these ideas are now often cited as "existential" and Dostoyevsky himself has been increasingly thought of as an existentialist thinker. Yet, Dostoyevsky's status as an existentialist has been directly questioned in Walter Kaufmann's *Existentialism from Dostoyevsky to Sartre* (1956) and viewed as irrationalism in William Barrett's *Irrational Man* (1958). While Barrett ties Dostoyevsky to Nietzsche, proposing that Dostoyevsky's "existentialism" in *Crime and Punishment* (1866) exerted an influence on Nietzsche's "will to power," as a concept, as it initially emerged in the 1880s, insomuch as Barrett can label Dostoyevsky an "existentialist,"[170] Kaufmann does not agree with this. Kaufmann writes, "I can see no reason for calling Dostoyevsky an existentialist, but I do think that Part One of *Notes from Underground* is the best overture for existentialism ever written."[171] Not only does Kaufmann seemingly challenge Barrett's take on Dostoyevsky's "existentialism" in general, but Kaufmann views *Notes from Underground* (1864) as the best example of what existentialism looks like, to the extent that "the major themes," Kaufmann posits, "are stated here that we can recognize when reading all the other so-called existentialists from Kierkegaard to Camus."[172] In this manner, it is obvious that Kaufmann thinks of Dostoyevsky as a "so-called existentialist"—perhaps what makes Dostoyevsky a "so-called existentialist" is not so much about the major themes routinely cited in Dostoyevsky's novels, particularly *Crime and Punishment* and *Notes from Underground* respectively highlighted by Barrett and Kaufmann, but more about the mode of realism in which Dostoyevsky's work predominantly operates. As a realist novelist, Dostoyevsky's "existentialism" becomes all the more debatable and difficult to define, when measuring that "existentialism" against that of Camus, who, also as a novelist, employed what has been described as absurdism. If the use of absurdism makes Camus a "so-called existentialist"—with *The Stranger* (1942), *The Plague* (1947), *The Fall* (1956), and the short-story collection *Exile and the Kingdom* (1957) as representations of Camus's form of existentialist novelization—we have to question what is it about absurdism and realism that make them both merely "so-called" existentialist fiction.

The issue, here, is that Camus's absurdist work and Dostoyevsky's realist work eventually become absorbed into the very meaning of existentialist literature. Indeed, as existentialism, in itself, was further defined in the 1960s, after the 1950s surveys of Barrett and Kaufmann, while Camus's work became aligned with modern existentialism, Dostoyevsky's *Notes from Underground* became considered as an early example of existentialist literature. It is *Notes from Underground*, in particular, that is included

---

170. Barrett, *Irrational Man*, 133–234.
171. See Kaufmann, *Existentialism from Dostoyevsky to Sartre*.
172. Kaufmann, *Existentialism from Dostoyevsky to Sartre*.

in two of the earliest anthologized readers devoted to existentialism: Maurice Friedman's *The Worlds of Existentialism* (1964) and William Y. Spanos's *A Casebook on Existentialism* (1966). To Dostoyevsky's contributions to existentialism with *Notes from Underground*, Friedman includes *The Possessed* (1872, which is alternatively titled *Demons*) and *The Brothers Karamazov* (1880), with Spanos including only *The Brothers Karamazov*. What remains in agreement between Friedman and Spanos is the foundational importance of *Notes from Underground* to Dostoyevsky's "existentialism," as it especially comes to bear through Dostoyevsky's articulation of his understanding of the relationship between philosophy and Russian Orthodox Christianity.

Notes from Underground consists of two main parts, with the first of these embodying Dostoyevsky's "existentialism." With what can be described as either a monologue or a diary, the unnamed narrator—referred to in scholarship as the "Underground Man"—is a retired civil servant living in St. Petersburg. The narrative begins in the following manner:

> I'm a sick man ... I'm an evil man. I'm an unattractive man. I think my liver is sick: it hurts. But I really don't understand squat about my sickness, and I'm not sure what hurts inside me.... I know better than anyone that all this is hurting only me, nobody else. Nevertheless, if I'm not seeking treatment, it's because I'm evil and angry. My liver is sick and it hurts—well, let it hurt even more.[173]

From this, the unnamed narrator is presented as harboring an internal conflict that, on one level, seems merely physiological but, on another and more important level, it is philosophical and even theological. The references to being "sick" and "evil" point to a necessary comparison being drawn between the two, so that they act synonymously. This relationship between "sick" and "evil" is furthered by comparing them to "angry." All three together denote a tension within the unnamed narrator that—through the initial and enduring reference to sickness—seemingly points to an understanding of sickness drawing from Kierkegaard's *The Sickness unto Death*. Viewed this way, "sickness," for the unnamed narrator, is most certainly a theological understanding of the term, just as "evil" is—the notion of "angry," then, can be read as an angriness toward God, which, in itself, ventures into an atheism that is expounded upon in Dostoyevsky's *The Possessed*.

Setting aside the accuracy in the English translation as *The Possessed* (in 1914 and 1962) or *Demons*, or even *The Devils* (in 1953) with respect to the original Russian title of *Bésy*, what has been most recently translated as *Devils* (in 2018) is structured as a first-person narrative much like the perspective of *Notes from Underground*. From the point of view of a secondary character, Anton—a local civil servant, though not retired as the one in *Notes from Underground*—*Devils* follows Anton's chronicling of a series of abnormal events that have happened in his town. Even though Anton's voice is important to the manner with which the narrative of *Devils* is presented,

---

173. Dostoyevsky, *Notes from the Underground*, 1.

particularly given that Anton's voice expresses far-reaching and, at times, unrealistic intimate knowledge of the entire world of the novel, Anton's voice does not remain dominant and eventually disappears from the narrative. Because of this, the narrative of *Devils* is presented dialogically, by way of interactions between characters, a single character's internal dialogue, or varying degrees of the two—in *Problems of Dostoyevsky's Poetics* (1929), Mikhail Bakhtin terms the technique that Dostoyevsky employs as "polyphonic," to the extent that there is a proliferation of "voice-ideas" that challenge one another, so that Anton, as the initial narrator, adjudicates and synchronizes the multiplicity of perspective in the narrative.[174] Through this "polyphonic" approach, *Devils* offers not just a notable tension between belief and nonbelief, and even, respectively speaking, between theism and atheism. Friedman notes this tension in the selection from a well-noted conversation in *Devils* included in *Worlds of Existentialism*, in the following passage, which I have expanded from Friedman's use and added names to the dialogue for clarity:

> "If there is no God, then I am God." [Alexei]
>
> "There, I could never understand that point of yours: why are you God?" [Pyotr]
>
> "If God exists, all is His will and from His will I cannot escape. If not, it's all my will and I am bound to show self-will."
>
> "Self-will? But why are you bound?"
>
> "Because all will has become mine. Can it be that no one in the whole planet, after making an end of God and believing in his own will, will dare to express his self-will on the most vital point? It's like a beggar inheriting a fortune and being afraid of it and not daring to approach the bag of god, thinking himself too weak to own it. I want to manifest my self-will. I may be the only one, but I'll do it."[175]

Here, in this conversation between Alexei and Pyotr, Dostoyevsky depicts a theological tension between the two, which is undoubtedly centered on Alexei's nonbelief and atheism. However, what Alexei further represents is a tension between humanity's existence and God's existence, such that, though Alexei exhibits a nonbelief and atheism, there remains a need to define Alexei's understanding of either in terms of belief and even theism—it is the sense that, even though Alexei is intent on "making an end of God," the existence of God is still at the very ideological core of Alexei's description and espousal of "self-will."

The existence of God reemerges in *The Brothers Karamazov*, in an often-examined section of the novel entitled "The Grand Inquisitor," which occurs in chapter 5 of book 5. The section includes a tale told by Ivan Karamazov to his younger brother

---

174. Bakhtin, *Problems of Dostoyevsky's Poetics*, 90–95.
175. Dostoyevsky, *Possessed*, 580.

Alexei (Alyosha) Karamazov, a monastery novice—through recounting this tale, Ivan, as noted by William V. Spanos in the introductory remarks offered before its inclusion in *A Casebook on Existentialism*, "attempts to reveal his true self to his sanity brother."[176] Ivan's tale only further explains what Ivan has begun to divulge to Alexei earlier in the novel in chapter 3 in book 5, entitled "The Brothers Get Acquainted." In this earlier section, Ivan states the following:

> I, my dear, have come to the conclusion that if I cannot understand even [Euclidean geometry], then it is not for me to understand about God. I humbly confess that it do not have any ability to resolve such questions, I have a Euclidean mind, an earthly mind, and therefore it is not for us to resolve things that are not of this world. And I advise you never think about it, Alyosha my friend, and most especially about whether God exists or not. All such questions are completely unsuitable to a mind created with a concept of only three dimensions. And so, I accept God, not only willingly. . . . And now imagine that in the final outcome I do not accept this world of God's, I do not admit it at all, though I know it exists. It's not God that I do not accept, you understand, it is this world of God's, created by God, that I do not accept and cannot agree to accept.[177]

What is illustrated through Ivan is, indeed, a tension between belief and nonbelief, as it is similarly expressed in *Devils*, but it also further extrapolates a point of view about human existence, which is similarly provided in *Notes from Underground*. All three novels explore the complexity of the relationship between human existence and God's existence, while additionally offering three examples of Dostoyevsky's version of existential theology—for Dostoyevsky, the meaning of existential theology occurs at the connectedness of the philosophical, the theological, and the psychological.

Leo Tolstoy

Leo Tolstoy's *The Death of Ivan Ilyich* (1886), as an essential realist text, is chiefly concerned with exploring the details of a fictionalized life in such a way that mirrors the essence of a real life. These details within *The Death of Ivan Ilyich*, include the mundane and the ordinary, the trivial and the cerebral, and the events and habits that shape the main protagonist Ivan's personality, psychological tendencies, and emotional infrastructure. But, more importantly, rather than strictly being a realist text following in the same literary ideological vein of Tolstoy's masterworks *Anna Karenina* (1869) and *War and Peace* (1877)—albeit, a historical novel functioning within the realist mode—*The Death of Ivan Ilyich*, breaks the standard boundaries of realism by comporting itself theologically.

---

176. Spanos, *Casebook on Existentialism*, 116.
177. Dostoyevsky, *Brothers Karamazov*, 235.

As the first major work of fiction Tolstoy published following his conversion to Protestant Christianity from Russian Orthodox Christianity, what is ultimately evidenced in *The Death of Ivan Ilyich* is Tolstoy's critical shift in faith. In effect, there is the transformational representation of this shift through the awakening of Tolstoy's new religious identity. In turn, this shift is forged into Tolstoy's chief literary concerns during the last thirty years of his life, whereby the publishing of *The Death of Ivan Ilyich* marks the inauguration of this period. This shift, as a result, is systematically extrapolated through *The Death of Ivan Ilyich*, which, though grounded on a realist footing as a kind of orthodoxy, displays undeniably transcendent qualities that consciously venture from realism into more of a religious-naturalistic construct.

The Death of Ivan Ilyich, as Vladimir Nabokov suggests, "was written in March 1886, at a time when Tolstoy was nearly sixty and had firmly established the Tolstoyan fact that writing masterpieces of fiction was a sin." To refer to writing panoramic literary works, like those he had been known for, Nabokov notes, as "a sin" seems to suggest that Tolstoy hoped to narrow his vision of the human condition and, in turn, greatly streamline what he deemed as sinful into something more visceral, righting what Tolstoy perceived wrong with his previous work. Nabokov furthers this argument with the belief that

> [Tolstoy] had firmly made up his mind that if he would write anything after the great sins of his middle years, *War and Peace* and *Anna Karenin[a]*, it would be only in the way of simple tales for the people, for peasants, for school children, pious educational fables, moralistic fairy tales, that kind of thing.[178]

What, in essence, Nabokov addresses here—and quite astutely, indeed—is that *The Death of Ivan Ilyich* represents a drastic shift in Tolstoy's outlook on life and the purpose of his fiction, particularly within the conceptual framework of the Tolstoyan realist novel. Perhaps, the "Tolstoyan fact," as Nabokov describes it, occurs theologically in reference to Tolstoy's Christian conversion, where Tolstoy found himself wanting to write simpler tales of extreme moralistic and educational value by significantly paring down the artistic indulgences inarguably apparent in *Anna Karenina* and *War and Peace*.

These indulgences are, of course, the "great sins" that Nabokov speaks of and, more precisely, they embody Tolstoy's rejection of realist fundamentals in order to advocate principles building on religious thought and morality. Not only was this necessary to reach the peasants and school children rather than focusing on the limited readership of the highly educated in the uppermost rungs of the Russian social hierarchy, who would have adhered to the very Russian orthodoxy Tolstoy had philosophically broken with, but it also stands in reverberation to an idea Tolstoy would eventually set forth in *What Is Art?*

---

178. Nabokov, *Lectures on Russian Literature*, 238.

In *What Is Art?* (1897), Tolstoy finds that "God expresses himself in two ways: in the object and in the subject, in nature and in spirit."[179] It is this essential understanding, as Tolstoy would relate further in the aforementioned philosophical work—as well as later instill in the philosophical infrastructure of *Resurrection* (1899)—in relation to art and literature being creatively analogous endeavors, from which he surmises the following:

> Art is thus the production of this appearance of this Idea, and is a means, together with religion and philosophy, of bringing to consciousness and of expressing the deepest problems of humanity and the highest truth of the spirit.[180]

Summoning words in the dichotomous pairs of "truth" with "spirit" and "religion" with "philosophy" as parts of a canvas upon which the writer, as an artist, works out the "deepest problems of humanity" through depictions that exalt the "highest truth of the spirit," Tolstoy implies that the realist canvas is inadequate and limiting. In order to present what Nabokov calls "moralistic fairy tales," Tolstoy suggests the notion that realism provides a rather one-dimensional canvas for his multidimensional ambitions and, as a result, with *The Death of Ivan Ilyich*, Tolstoy transcends functional realism toward a hyper-functioning form of naturalism.

Yet, there is a distinguishable connection between naturalism and realism, where "naturalism is another form of realism—a sterner realism."[181] While naturalism is defined as "a mode of representation that is detailed, detached, and objective" depicting humans as being "subject to their instincts, passions, and surroundings,"[182] it encompasses the same goals, concepts, objectives, and aspirations of realism. In other words, naturalism is born out of realism and they are, in essence, kindred ideologies, even though "naturalists not only elaborated on and intensified the basic tendencies of realism; they also added important new elements which turned naturalism into a recognizable doctrine such as realism had never been."[183] As Furst and Skrine ascertain further, "naturalism is therefore more concrete and at the same time more limited than realism" as much as it is based on "distinct theories, groups, and practices."[184] To extend Furst and Skrine a little further, not only do "distinct theories" and "recognizable doctrines" make realism naturalistic but, when considering *The Death of Ivan Ilyich*, it is evident that the undercurrent of its religious philosophy provides a naturalistic perspective arising from the core of its realist essence.

From the outset, what becomes evident about *The Death of Ivan Ilyich* is that it is not the stock realist novel, particularly in terms of depicting the gradual progression of

---

179. Tolstoy, *What Is Art?*, 24.
180. Tolstoy, *What Is Art?*, 24.
181. Lehan, *Realism and Naturalism*, 35.
182. Martin and Ray, *Bedford Glossary*, 329–30.
183. Furst and Skrine, *Naturalism*, 8.
184. Furst and Skrine, *Naturalism*, 9.

a life through some form of physical, emotional, or spiritual decadence. This decadence, of course, has already occurred prior to the first sentence of the narrative. Rather than the course of Ivan's life advancing from the beginnings of its decadence to an ending that is a by-product of that decadence, the first chapter abruptly reports this decadence in retrospect. Though this first chapter employs an "in medias res" technique for Ivan's funeral in the opening chapter, it contains no conventional details of Ivan's life that can be displayed through Ivan's point of view with Ivan in the present. Instead, Ivan's life, after death, becomes fodder for his funeral attendants, who are more concerned with their still being alive. The details of Ivan's life are, essentially, presented in a condensed and controlled narrative mode in the second chapter: over roughly seven pages, Ivan's life is referred to in the past tense, littered with words like "was" and "had." All the events of Ivan's life—such as his career as a judge, his school experiences, his being socially matched with a woman rather than falling in love with her, his wedding, his marriage, his children—are listed rather than embellished, itemized as if they are simple objects within the ordinary machinery of a life, and compressed within a handful of pages rather than elaborated. But, perhaps by inventorying aspects of Ivan's life as a normal life, this leads Tolstoy to perceive this: "Ivan Ilyich's life had been most simple and most ordinary and therefore most terrible."[185]

As aforementioned, the narrative is stripped of all realist indulgences, particularly in terms of it focusing on a single character's life within a single plot—not the multiple plots of Anna Karenina following multiple characters with intertwined lives—where a life is presented in terms of a death. The fact that Ivan is dead does not change the notion that, as Nabokov describes, "this is really the story not of Ivan's Death but the story of Ivan's Life. The physical death described in the story is part of mortal Life, it is merely the last phase of mortality."[186] So, to amplify Nabokov's assertion with Tolstoy's own opinion in his *My Confessions*, "death was much better than life, and life's burden must be got rid of."[187] While, on the surface, Tolstoy's opinions seem to conflict with Nabokov's assertion, in actuality, both are approaching the same ideological premise from different ends of the same ideological spectrum. The link between them is in the concept of Ivan experiencing a kind of dying life as well as a living death, where there are, essentially, two kinds of deaths and two kinds of lives. Nabokov defines this premise as the "Tolstoyan formula" by pointing out that "Ivan lived a bad life and since a bad life is nothing but the death of the soul, then Ivan lived a living death; and since beyond death is God's living light, then Ivan died into new Life—Life with a capital L."[188]

Taking the aforementioned idea pragmatically—that is, to say, by developing the concept of life into a kind of duality, both of which can be examined separately—what becomes evident is that not only is there "life," but there is a kind of "Life."

185. See the opening of *The Death of Ivan Illyich*.
186. Nabokov, *Lectures on Russian Literature*, 237.
187. Tolstoy, *My Confessions*, 61.
188. Nabokov, *Lectures on Russian Literature*, 237.

Specifically, in terms of realism and naturalism, the concept of life is exemplified respectively through "Life," with a capital *L*, and "life" with a lowercase *L*. This is, fundamentally, the calculus of Nabokov's Tolstoyan formula. Not only is this rather blatantly apparent in Tolstoy's belief that Ivan's life "had been most simple and most ordinary" and was "therefore most terrible," but the naturalistic ideology fundamentally provides a means to depict "nature, in the disguise of physical disintegration, [which] enters the picture and destroys the automatism of conventional life."[189] It is this "automatism of conventional life," as Nabokov ascertains it to be, which makes Ivan's normal, rudimentary, ordinary life a terrible life, which is vulnerable to disintegration. This "automatism," in fact, makes Ivan's life a "life" rather than a "Life" to the point that disintegration is inevitable.

According to Nabokov, "[Ivan's life] is terrible because it had been automatic, trite, hypocritical—animal survival and childish contentment."[190] Perhaps, more importantly, to embellish on Nabokov, there is, in Tolstoy's Ivan, a belief in a physical death and a spiritual death. From this, it is safe to assume that, when a life is lived superficially, it becomes the impetus for a spiritual death. On the other hand, when considering Ivan's mysterious illness as the impetus for his physical death, the fact that he has already experienced a kind of spiritual death before his physical one is of the utmost importance. As a result, it is easier to understand Nabokov believing, in terms of the role nature plays for Ivan, that "one of the props of Ivan's conventional life was property, superficial decency, elegant and neat surfaces of life, decorum."[191] In light of this, Nabokov further postulates that,

> according to Tolstoy, mortal man, personal man, individual man, *physical* man, goes his physical way to nature's garbage can; according to Tolstoy, spiritual man returns to the cloudless region of universal God-Love, an abode of neutral bliss so dear to Oriental mystics.[192]

This seems to suggest, frankly, that the self contains a physical self as well as a spiritual self, both of which provide complementary halves or hemispheres to the "mortal man, personal man, individual man" trifecta represented in Ivan Ilyich.

It is precisely this ideology that makes *The Death of Ivan Ilyich* not just a naturalist novel launched from the launching pad of realist fundamentals, but, to a larger extent, is much more than a conventional naturalist novel. In other words, rather than representing a kind of naturalism espoused by Emile Zola, it embodies a distinctly Tolstoyan brand of naturalism—Tolstoy's form is known as religious naturalism, which involves exploring the theological meaning of life.

---

189. Nabokov, *Lectures on Russian Literature*, 241.
190. Nabokov, *Lectures on Russian Literature*, 241.
191. Nabokov, *Lectures on Russian Literature*, 241.
192. Nabokov, *Lectures on Russian Literature*, 241.

What makes *The Death of Ivan Ilyich* the Tolstoyan-naturalism of religious naturalism rather than Emile Zola's naturalism can be best illuminated through the notion that naturalism is divided into two philosophical concepts: methodological or scientific naturalism, and metaphysical or ontological naturalism. The Tolstoyan-naturalism, as a religious naturalism, is defined in terms of the latter of the aforementioned two. Since Tolstoy employs a conscious distinction between physical life and spiritual life, Ivan's dilemma—if one can call it, truly, a dilemma—is a philosophical problem. Therefore, it is problem that can only be approached through a religious ideology enacted through religious naturalism.

This ideology, through religious naturalism, is particularly apparent in the last scene of *The Death of Ivan Ilyich* through obvious religious symbolism. First, this becomes evident in the notion that "suddenly, some force struck [Ivan] in the chest and side," which seems to refer to Jesus being speared in the side by a Roman soldier and the difficultly Jesus would have had with breathing. Though Jesus hung on a cross and Ivan is bedridden, both embody settings for significant discomfort and suffering. To explore this religious symbolism a little further, when considering Ivan's bedridden status in that final scene, there is something rather symbolic in the interactions between Ivan and his wife and son. Consider the following:

> He felt that someone was kissing his hand. He opened his eyes, looked at his son, and felt sorry for him. His wife came up to him and he glanced at her. She was gazing at him open-mouthed, with undried tears on her nose and cheek and a despairing look on her face. He felt sorry for her too.[193]

All of this provides an analogous culmination of Jesus's interactions with Mary the mother and Mary Magdalene—while Ivan's wife is, perhaps, Mary the mother and wedded to Ivan through the Mary-Jesus mother-son relationship, Ivan's son is, as a result, Mary Magdalene and the begotten representation of Jesus's ministerial influence. Furthermore, Ivan saying "It is finished" before dying points to Jesus's final words, according to the Synoptic Gospels, before allowing himself to expire.

Subsequently, what becomes evident about *The Death of Ivan Ilyich* is that, rather than adhering to the realist mold, it becomes philosophically charged with a unique Tolstoyan form of religious naturalism, and ultimately, as a result, becomes a precursor to what would eventually become Russian modernism. In essence, if "naturalism as a kind of realism," it does so by relying on nature as the central category of analysis—in this way, naturalism will inevitably take the view that there are aspects of nature that are real and significantly independent of our realistic interpretation of them.

In terms of naturalism, *The Death of Ivan Ilyich* espouses a human character shaped by the inescapable force of the social condition—in this case, the social condition at work, above all, is the nature of death and illness, and how both are involved in the molding of Ivan Ilyich. This notion of death and illness as being social conditioning

---

193. See Tolstoy, *Death of Ivan Illyich*.

structures are unquestionably presented from the outset of the narrative, where instead of using the realist approach of progressing chronologically through a life, Tolstoy begins with Ivan's death, which breaks from the realist ideology.

As a result, Ivan's death is presented as a force—a force of nature, perhaps—that has not only affected Ivan but others around him, an inescapable force that lends psychological insight into the influence one person's death has on others around them. Ivan's death, when deconstructed through the narrative as a kind of literary flashback, is due to an unknown illness and this illness, though not described in any certain scientific terms or any irrefutable biological fact, becomes the inescapable force working against the integrity of Ivan's mortality. Even though the source of Ivan's illness is represented as an invading phantom, Tolstoy presents variations on explaining it. Nothing, of course, is clearly defined and the only thing that becomes clearer is how Ivan feels in reaction to this illness and, eventually, how this illness, whatever it may be, is grave enough to march Ivan ceaselessly toward his demise, a physical death. This demise—not just a physical, but a spiritual death—in terms of Ivan's mortality, as well as the notion of looking at life in retrospect rather than within the fluidity of existence, is at the core of Tolstoy's naturalist approach and embarks toward a Russian modernism.

Nabokov believed this to be the case, particularly in light of the differences between *Anna Karenina* as an integral brand of realism and *The Death of Ivan Ilyich* as a kind of religious naturalism with tendencies toward modernism. This seems certainly so, when he points out that

> nobody in the [eighteen] eighties in Russia wrote like that. The story was a forerunner of Russian modernism just before the dull and conventional Soviet era. . . . There is too a tender, poetical intonation here and there, and there is the tense mental monologue, the stream of consciousness technique that he had already invented for the description of Anna's last journey.[194]

Perhaps, to truly understand how *The Death of Ivan Ilyich* becomes a naturalist novel and, in turn, represents a kind of Russian premodernist novel can be best surmised in the notion that "while the naturalist writer emphasized the sequential plot, the modernist writer tried to conceal it."[195] If we understand how *The Death of Ivan Ilyich* is situated after Tolstoy's religious conversion, it is precisely this conversion that converts Tolstoy from a naturalist writer to a modernist writer. For this reason, *The Death of Ivan Ilyich*, in itself, is an acknowledgment that "while naturalism exploited causal connection, modernism questions the process of causality."[196]

While the realistic qualities of *The Death of Ivan Ilyich* inarguably personify the structural framework of the novel, they undeniably do so strictly by way of forming

---

194. Nabokov, *Lectures on Russian Literature*, 238–39.
195. Nabokov, *Lectures on Russian Literature*, 238–39.
196. Lehan, *Realism and Naturalism*, 207.

a rudimentary skeleton around which Tolstoy operates on higher frequencies. As a result, the novel is fully fleshed out with the employment of distinct naturalistic elements that provide a multidimensional structure directly in line with Tolstoy's religious concerns and literary goals.

The only way to logically explain Tolstoy's religious concerns unilaterally with his literary goals is through the concept of religious naturalism, where *The Death of Ivan Ilyich* epitomizes the newfound philosophical duality Tolstoy wished to express in the novel, particularly on the heels of his religious conversion. But, more importantly, *The Death of Ivan Ilyich*, as a hybrid of realism and religious naturalism, represents, through Tolstoy's own rejection of realism and his desire to tell moralistic tales in the religious naturalistic paradigm, a significant literary advancement into the foundational applications of modernism.

Nikolai Berdyaev

Influenced by Kant, Hegel, Nietzsche, and Dostoyevsky,[197] Berdyaev has been characterized as not just a Christian religious philosopher but also a Russian political figure, which both converge in Berdyaev's membership in the Russian Orthodox Church. Because Berdyaev staunchly believed that Russian Orthodox Christianity, as a religious tradition, is the closest to early Christianity of "Apostle Paul, the martyrs, the saints and the whole Christian world," which he argues in "The Truth of Orthodoxy" (1952), Berdyaev comes to the conclusion that "in tradition," as he continues to write, "my knowledge is not only personal but superpersonal and I live not in isolation but within the Body of Christ, within a single spiritual organism with all my brothers in Christ."[198] Here, more than anything, Berdyaev distances the theologizing of Russian Orthodox Christianity from both Catholicism and Protestantism, by recognizing that the Russian Orthodox Church, as Berdyaev describes, "is primarily the Church of tradition, in contrast to the Catholic Church, which is the Church of authority, and to the Protestant churches which are essentially churches of individual faith."[199] By distancing the theologizing of Russian Orthodoxy from all the theologizing of other Christian traditions, this view directly informs Berdyaev's conceptualization of the meaning of Russian culture and identity as a Russian Nationalism, which Berdyaev directly espouses in *The Russian Idea* (1947). Though Russian Nationalism, in itself, originated in an imperial form, within the relationship between the Russian Orthodox Church, the autocracy of the House of Romanov, and the meaning of Russian nationality, by Berdyaev's time, after Russian revolution of 1917, the fall of the Romanov dynasty, and the rise of the Soviet

---

197. Berdyaev wrote a book on Dostoyevsky, entitled *Dostoyevsky: An Interpretation* (1923).
198. Berdyaev, "Truth of Orthodoxy," 1.
199. Berdyaev, "Truth of Orthodoxy," 1.

State, "Russian Nationalism," as a term, for Berdyaev's political views, was especially shaped by World War II and the defeat of Nazi Germany.

Indeed, Berdyaev's political stance on what it meant to be Russian in a postwar world directly figures into how Berdyaev philosophizes and theologizes more generally, which David B. Richardson cites, in "Existentialism: A Personalist Philosophy of History" (1968), as "personalism" and "Christian Existentialism." As Richardson writes, "Berdyaev's Existentialism fulfills a need in his philosophy of history,"[200] such that this fulfillment, in my view, is tied to Berdyaev's political perspective by the 1840s. Given that, for Richardson, Berdyaev presents "a Personalist doctrine which is inspired by religious thought and stems from certain philosophical currents," the same personalism can be found in Marcel. While Marcel is inspired by Catholic thought and Berdyaev is inspired by Russian Orthodoxy, the personalism in both leads to a "Christian existentialism" that, on one hand, Marcel refuses to accept and, on the other hand, Berdyaev openly accepts, though posthumously.

To even describe Berdyaev as a "Christian existentialist"—so that we can say that he is operating through a "Christian existentialism"—comes with the help of Donald A. Lowrie, first with what is considered as the most definitive biography on Berdyaev, *Religious Prophet: A Life of Nicolai Berdyaev* (1960), and Lowrie's editorial work on *Christian Existentialism: A Berdyaev Anthology* (1965). In the first review of Lowrie's anthology of Berdyaev's work, J. Heywood Thomas notes that the anthology is "a most valuable book not only because some of [its] material appears in English for the first time but also because it is a fresh translation even of what had been translated."[201] Being that, as pointed out by Thomas, "the anthology itself is divided into twelve chapters dealing with epistemology, metaphysics, the relation of philosophy to theology, the nature of man, the God-man relationship, society and history."[202] As brief as Thomas's review of Lowrie's edited *Christian Existentialism*, and the degree to which it is an "anthology" of Berdyaev's work, what Thomas does not make clear is that, though Lowrie's anthology is "selected" and "edited" from Berdyaev's body of work, Lowrie makes an intentional effort to include all of Berdyaev's works, from the earliest, *Subjectivism and Individualism in Social Philosophy* (1901), to three posthumous texts, *Dream and Reality* (1949), *The Realm of Spirit and the Realm of Caesar* (1949), and *Truth and Revelation* (1953).

Though, if taking a cue from Lowrie, the whole of Berdyaev's body of work can be described as "Christian existentialism" and, by extension, it can be comprehensively thought of as Berdyaev's existential theology, there are specific texts within Berdyaev's oeuvre that best illustrate how Berdyaev does his form of existential theology. These texts, as each originally appeared in Russian, are: *The Meaning of the Creative Act* (1916), *The Destiny of Man* (1931), and *The Divine and the Human* (1947).

200. Richardson, "Existentialism," 90.
201. Thomas, "Christian," 91.
202. Thomas, "Christian," 91.

In *The Meaning of the Creative Act*, Berdyaev is chiefly concerned with the meaning of human existence and how that existence is construed and allows itself to be construed in terms of a "creative act." The meaning of the creative act, then, as Berdyaev explains: "always presupposes self-being, independence and freedom of personality, which is unknown to the pantheistic consciousness."[203] From here, Berdyaev goes on to say that "the creative act presupposes a mono-pluralism, that is the existence of a multitude of free and independent beings; in other words, a concrete all-oneness."[204] This notion of "all-oneness" is a continuation of an idea that is perpetuated through earlier works—with common threads found in *Subjectivism and Individualism in Social Philosophy* (1901) and *The New Religious Consciousness and Sociality* (1907)—while "the existence of a multitude of free and independent beings," in itself, also becomes a rearticulation of a concept that appears in an earlier work—this can be found in *The Philosophy of Freedom* (1911). Yet, here, as these terms come to bear on the meaning of "the creative act," Berdyaev finds that

> the creative act is a free and independent force, immanently inherent only in a person, a personality.... Only a personalist doctrine of the world, for which every being is personal and original, can give meaning to creativity. Such a personalist doctrine recognizes the originality of personality, derived from nothing outside or general, from no other means.[205]

As much as Berdyaev's personalism is intent on "recogiz[ing] the originality of personality" and viewing that originality as being "derived from nothing outside or general, from no other means," the latter point requires further explication. It may seem that this latter point ventures into the territory of an atheistic existentialism, such that, if personality is "derived from nothing outside or general, from no other means," the implications of this is that all that personality needs resides within it. This is not entirely the case. Rather, for Berdyaev, even if this is part and parcel of the meaning of personalism as an emphasis on human freedom and subjectivity, the meaning of creative act, as Berdyaev defines it, suggests that this freedom and subjectivity is developed in relation to that which is indeed "outside" and, in fact, must come from "other means"—what comes from "outside" and from "other means" exerts a creative force on the "originality of personality," as an existential expansion of what lies within human subjectivity. What Berdyaev is seemingly addressing, more generally, is a reconceptualization of Tolstoy's *The Kingdom of God Is Within You* (1893). With such a possible influence on Berdyaev, the manner with which the meaning of the creative act "creates" within the human personality and allows for human subjectivity makes the following all the more relevant:

---

203. Berdyaev, *Meaning of the Creative Act*, 133.
204. Berdyaev, *Meaning of the Creative Act*, 133.
205. Berdyaev, *Meaning of the Creative Act*, 135.

> To know the creative activity of the person means being a creatively active person.... The inner relationship between the subject of knowing and the object of knowing is a necessary condition of true knowing.... To know anything in the world is to have this in oneself. Knowing is a creative act and we cannot expect to have knowledge of freedom from a slavish submission to necessity.[206]

In this, through Berdyaev's notion of "creative activity," we find another important term to Berdyaev's overall existential theology: "freedom." The term appears as a dominating concept in the already mentioned *The Philosophy of Freedom*, as well as *Freedom and Spirit* (1927), *Slavery and Freedom* (1939), and *The Realm of Spirit and the Realm of Caesar* (1949). That sense of "freedom," for Berdyaev, is what calibrates the meaning of the creative act, so that creative activity steers us toward meaning, by way of Berdyaev's understanding of "spirit." It is through this understanding that Berdyaev arrives at the following conclusion:

> Truth is revealed only by the creative activity of the spirit; outside this, truth is incomprehensible and unattainable.... Truth is not that which is, that which is forced upon us as a given condition, as necessity. Truth is not the duplication, the repetition of being in the knower. Truth is comprehension and liberation of being, it presupposes the creative act of the knower within being; truth is meaning and may not deny meaning. To deny meaning in the world means to deny truth, to recognize nothing but darkness. Truth makes us free.[207]

Even though "truth makes us free," Berdyaev later finds a problem with human freedom, which he expresses more thoroughly in *The Destiny of Man* as a "tragedy."[208] Along these lines, in *The Destiny of Man*, Berdyaev suggests that "the tragedy of freedom shows that there is a struggle between the conflicting principles which lie deeper than the distinction between good and evil."[209] All of this is, indeed, comprised in Berdyaev's understanding of human destiny, insomuch as that destiny is grounded on "the tragedy of freedom" and an overarching "struggle" between good and evil.

Still, as much as "truth makes us free," Berdyaev seems to propose that this truth comes with a consequence. It is the sense that, as Berdyaev continues in *The Destiny of Man*, "fate is the child of freedom—this means that freedom itself is fatal."[210] More than anything, what this means is that truth itself, as a derivative of freedom, is also fatal—in other words, truth becomes the foundation for human fatality. The degree to which humans are fatal and that this fatality is predicated on our "struggle" between good and evil puts forth another truth: "that God is 'beyond good and evil,' for on

---

206. Berdyaev, *Meaning of the Creative Act*, 155.
207. Berdyaev, *Meaning of the Creative Act*, 43.
208. Berdyaev, *Destiny of Man*, 31.
209. Berdyaev, *Destiny of Man*, 31.
210. Berdyaev, *Destiny of Man*, 31.

this side of it is our fallen world and certainly not God."[211] Because of this, "God certainly is not bound by the moral good and is not dependent upon it," Berdyaev writes, "[God] is the Good as an absolute force."[212]

As an "absolute force" which mitigates the being of good and the nonbeing of evil, Berdyaev is clearly pointing to the problem of being. This problem is made more explicit in *The Beginning and the End* (1947), which is outlined as a "problem of knowledge" comported to "the problem of being and existence" oriented toward the problem inherent in "being and creativity" and "the mystery of newness," in order to arrive at "the problem of history and eschatology."

With all of this in tow from *The Beginning and the End*, in *The Divine and the Human* (1947)—if the two texts can be thought of as companion texts—Berdyaev further recognizes these problems that are currently baked into human existence, human freedom, human destiny, and the extent to which truth actually reveals itself in the following:

> In this world of ours not only God acts; but fate, necessity, chance, also act. Fate continues to operate when the world abandons God or when God abandons the world. Moments and times of God-forsakeness are fateful in human life. Man and the world are subject to inevitable necessity as a result of falsely directed freedom.[213]

In this, Berdyaev presents what can be described as his own version of existential theology—it is an approach that attempts to employ both a philosophical understanding of human existence and a theological understanding of God's existence, but does so in a way that both understandings communicate from a decidedly personalist standpoint, rather than simply as a synthesis of the philosophical and theological. Berdyaev's existential theology, which substantiates Berdyaev's inclusion in Herberg's *Four Existentialist Theologians* (1958), can be summarized as:

> The belief that everything which happens to me has a meaning, cannot be expressed in the cosmological system after the manner of theological rationalism. It must always be remembered that God is Spirit, not nature, not substance, not force, not power. God is Spirit; that is to say freedom. God is Spirit, and that means that [God] must be thought of apophatically in relation to the realities of the natural and social world.[214]

---

211. Berdyaev, *Destiny of Man*, 43.
212. Berdyaev, *Destiny of Man*, 43.
213. Berdyaev, *The Divine and the Human*, 9.
214. Berdyaev, *The Divine and the Human*, 9–10.

CHAPTER 3

Countertraditions of Existential Theology

Liberation Approach

Power, Liberation, and the Black Theological-Political Selfhood

IF POWER RELATIONS BETWEEN the powerless and the powerful is essential to understanding the task of political theology, Black theological-political selfhood, as I define it, is shaped in reference to power. I would go so far as to conclude that a Black theological-political self is specifically construed in relation to power. In fact, I would argue that a Black theological-political self is developed from knowing that, within the power paradigm, it is among the powerless. This is so, since, as James Evans Jr. asserts, "power is necessary for human existence."[1] Blackness, in this regard, is a mode of human existence that is keenly aware of the role that power plays in the powerlessness of Blackness.

Evans would agree with this, particularly when considering that he supposes that "in order to describe what is essential in human existence from an African-American perspective, it is necessary to move from a consideration of the virtue of black folk to a consideration of their power."[2] I find that what Evans is suggesting is that, when existence is extrapolated from an African American perspective, that existence is a unique one. Its uniqueness is in a certain set of circumstances that, in their totality, provide for a relative powerlessness in a world where power is essential to authentic existence—if it is possible to say that power authenticates existence. In other words, "Blackness" is an existence that manifests from a specific existential situation: the limitations placed on Blackness within social power structures define Blackness as a state of powerlessness. Perhaps, this can best be illustrated further with Evans arguing the following: "Power is the animus of human existence because people need the ability to individuate—that is, to exercise freedom—and the ability to relate—that is,

---

1. Evans, *We Have Been Believers*, 110.
2. Evans, *We Have Been Believers*, 110.

to exercise love. If power is essential to authentic human existence, then the question with which early black theologians were faced was the function of that power."[3] So, if I may extend the argument that Evans makes, the facticity of power that functions against the facticity of Blackness dictates the need for theologizing about God in a way that arises from the Black experience.

In my view, when the facticity of Blackness yields the facticity of an existential situation governed by powerlessness, the Black theological-political self theologizes from the predicament of their experience. Essentially, this kind of theologizing is Black political theology. To that end, as M. Shawn Copeland correctly ascertains, "black political theology esteems ordinary people's critical consciousness of their own predicament."[4] The predicament, in other words, is the totality of facts, which, as Ludwig Wittgenstein describes, becomes "the case."[5] I view this as a collective understanding of the following facts: the facticity of existence, the facticity of Blackness, the facticity of the existential situation, and the facticity of the predicament of powerlessness. This is "the case." But, recognizing "the case" as such is not possible without some form of inward reflection about the outward manifestation of Blackness, and how that Blackness shapes a specialized being-in-the-world that is problematic. There is a great degree of self-reflection occurring here. As such, Black political theology, as Copeland argues, "takes self-criticism seriously, and grasps theory as passionate, communal, collaborative intellectual engagement aimed to understand, interpret, and transform the culture through creative and healing social praxis grounded in the Gospel."[6] What Copeland calls "creative and healing social praxis" is what Black theology is all about: using hermeneutical skills to read and apply scripture to the Black experience.

To define oneself as a Black theological-political self means to not only be cognizant of their Black experience, but be in search of a contingent truth[7] about it. That is, that the Black experience "is" what it is, and cannot be construed as something else. This contingent truth is undeniable and an essential starting point in Black theology. James H. Cone, who first systematized Black theology as a synthesis of the thought of Martin Luther King Jr. and Malcolm X, asserts that "there is no truth for and about black people that does not emerge out of the context of their experience [and] truth in this sense is black truth, a truth disclosed in the history and culture of black people."[8] I would argue that this contingent truth—or what Cone calls a "black truth"—is what a Black theological-political self uses to negotiate Black theology with political theology into a "Black Political Theology." In doing this, the Black theological-political

---

3. Evans, *We Have Been Believers*, 110.
4. Copeland, "Black Political Theologies," 271.
5. Wittgenstein, *Tractatus Logico-Philosophicus*, 29.
6. Copeland, "Black Political Theologies," 271–72.
7. This is a term used by Leibniz to imply, in brief, that a contingent truth shows that there is more reason for that which has been done than there is for its opposite. Leibniz, *Philosophical Essays*, 101.
8. Cone, *God of the Oppressed*, 17.

self acknowledges that the contingent truth of their Black experience and the relative powerlessness inherent in it must be reappropriated into an empowering and meaningful sense of selfhood. Cone would certainly refer to this as "Black Power," which he defines as "an attitude, an inward affirmation of the essential worth of blackness."[9] The importance in such a statement is in the term "affirmation." Black theological-political selfhood is constructed on that kind of "affirmation," particularly with respect to Black Power, which J. Deotis Roberts argues in *A Black Political Theology* (1974), "affirms a self-understanding that asserts [a Black theological-political self's] humanity."[10] Moreover, Roberts goes on to surmise that this kind of affirmation, or Black Power, or what I would call empowering Blackness, "suggest[s] that blacks as a people must unite and take the appropriate steps to win their liberation from white oppression."[11] I am not sure if I would agree completely with Roberts about winning "liberation from white oppression," since I am more inclined to argue that it is about winning liberation from the oppressive actions of anyone in a position of power.

A Black theological-political self, who is situated in a position of powerlessness against the oppressive actions of anyone in a position of power, does, as Roberts accurately ascertains, "seek a balance between the quest for meaning and protest against injustices."[12] However, I would add that this balance is also sought between the Black theological-political self's adherence to their faith, their relationship with God, their roles in the Black Church, and the fact that the predicament of their being-in-the-world is as much existential[13] as it is due to the political arrangements of the power-structured society in which they live and hope to change.

James H. Cone and Theologizing "The Cross"

For James Cone (1936–2018), as the original and most important proponent of this form of theologizing about God, "Black theology" is a theological perspective that contextualizes Christianity in an attempt to theologize about the meaning of Blackness through the fundamental questions of oppression and injustice, as they are grounded in the Civil Rights movement, the thought of both Martin Luther King Jr. and Malcolm X, and brought to bear by the Black Power movement (peaking in the early 1970s) and the Black Consciousness movement (emerging in the mid-1960s)—the former emphasizes racial pride, economic empowerment, and the creation of political and cultural institutions, while the latter arose by way of grassroots, anti-Apartheid activism in South Africa. All things considered, Cone's development of Black theology arises from the

9. Cone, *Black Theology and Black Power*, 8.
10. Roberts, *Black Political Theology*, 72.
11. Roberts, *Black Political Theology*, 72.
12. Roberts, *Black Political Theology*, 58.
13. What I mean here is the existential situation of Blackness, or, as I have mentioned earlier, the facticity of Blackness.

contingent theological needs of Blackness as that which must be theologized and from which uniquely theologizes God—this situatedness of Blackness is "existential," insofar as the meaning that must be made from "Blackness" is oriented toward a meaning that is made from the theologizing about God existentially.

By theologizing about the meaning of Blackness, Black theology, more broadly, seeks to liberate "Blackness" from various forms of political, social, economic, and religious subjugation, such that Christian theology, itself, becomes "a theology of liberation" or a "liberation theology," such that, as Cone writes, it is "a rational study of the being of God in the world in light of the existential situation of an oppressed community, relating the forces of liberation to the essence of the Gospel, which is Jesus Christ."[14]

As it is founded by Cone, the following texts are foundational to "Black theology" and what is ostensibly referred to as "Black liberation theology": *Black Theology and Black Power* (1969), *A Black Theology of Liberation* (1970), and *God of the Oppressed* (1975)—though these three major texts embody a trilogy for "Black theology," providing a foundational framework for Cone's form of theologizing, Cone's final major text, *The Cross and the Lynching Tree* (2011), is, in one sense, a culmination of the trilogy, and, in another sense, presents a theologizing that ventures further afield from the trilogy.

When defining what it means to theologize from the standpoint of "Black theology," what must be considered is the roles that hermeneutics, methodology, contextualization and the task of the Black theologian play in this form of theologizing about God. To theologize from the siutatedness of Blackness means to take a hermeneutical approach—that is to say, injecting an interpretive lens—that begins with the experience of African Americans and from the point of view of "Blackness." From this perspective, to do Black theology does not necessarily mean overlaying a "Blackness" to the traditional meaning of theologizing, if we can say, by definition, that there is a normative theologizing to how theology itself is handled, but rather, it means situating a specific experience at the very heart and as the impetus of doing a kind of theology that does not align with normative theologizing. What it means is theologizing about God from a place that is often marginalized, oppressed, and separated, insomuch as that marginalization, oppression, and separation comes to bear on a belongingness in the very act of theologizing about God—it is the sense of, as Cone offers, theologizing at the margins, while recognizing that there is, in fact, liberation at the margins. More importantly, when theologizing from this kind of positionality—from a marginalized, oppressed, and separated state of existence—it is about raising theological questions that are not asked by traditional Western theology. These questions not only become essential to conceptualizing what it means "to be Black," but they also shape what it means to theologize about God. Because these theological questions, as they arise from a position of Blackness, go unanswered by traditional Western theology, there arises a need—one might even say a contingent need, a need to substantiate oneself at the point

14. Cone, *Black Theology of Liberation*, 1.

of existence—to locate a kind of theologizing that gives an account for Blackness and what Blackness itself means. In effect, this is carried forward into the development of the role of the Black church, as an institution capable of explicating the very meaning of Blackness through defining identity, community, culture, and society—it is the extent to which all of these dimensions orient "Blackness" existentially toward a theologizing that ponders the meaning of Black existence while it ponders what it takes to theologize about God through that Black existence.

If we can say that theologizing about God from the standpoint of Black existence is about engaging in hermeneutics, we can certainly say, then, that "Black theology," as a means of theologizing about God, is undoubtedly presenting a kind of existential theology—to do "Black theology" at all means confirming and actualizing Black existence as a unique question of the meaning of being and simultaneously theologizing about God as that which reconfirms and reactualizes the meaning of "Blackness." Yet, the manner in which "Blackness" is confirmed and reconfirmed, and actualized and reactualized is through an underlying (or overarching) methodology. In other words, in order to theologize about God through "Black theology," when taking into account what the meaning of Blackness holds for this kind of theologizing, there are methodological considerations. These involve, if further connecting Black theology to existential theology, answering *the question of the meaning of being*, particularly for the African American experience as a specific kind of "being-in-the world," translated into Blackness and couched in a certain degree of "thrownness"—it is the notion of *what* the meaning of Blackness is, *how* that meaning uniquely expresses or articulates itself within American society (i.e., historically, sociologically politically, culturally, ethically, and economically), and *why* "Blackness," as a "meaning of being," is fundamental, substantive, and significant to what it means to be one kind of American.

Because Cone's "Black theology" tends to the theological needs and concerns of what it means to hold "Blackness" and be "American," the tension between these two states of existence must not be overlooked or minimized. To be "Black" and be an "American" means, at the very heart of this existence, recognizing that there is also an inherent tension in act of theologizing itself: theologizing in Black and theologizing from an Americanism. It is a tension that adds a complexity to "Blackness" itself, when the meaning of being is grounded in Scripture, but it is also grounded in slave spirituals, the blues, and the writings of key thinkers such as W. E. B. Du Bois (i.e., *The Souls of Black Folk* and the notion of "double-consciousness"). This tension is apparent pedagogically in "Black theology," when taking into account all of Cone's influences, most notably Martin Luther King Jr. and Malcolm X, who fundamentally disagreed on how theologizing about God could further define the role of "Blackness" in America. But also, in Cone, there is a tension between the traditional and the radical, between theologizing about God through Barth and Tillich or theologizing about God by deconstructing Barth and Tillich.

Barth and Tillich are important theological figures in Cone's theologizing "Black theology." While Cone's dissertation on Barth's "Doctrine of Man" (1965) provides a foundation for Cone's own reach into theological anthropology, Tillich's philosophically influenced notion that theology is not universal positions Cone's impulses toward a contextual theology. Together, though to differing degrees, Barth and Tillich compel Cone's development of the methodological demands of "Black theology" to hone in to a stance that is against the Western theological tradition of abstract theologizing, in order to examine the social context in which this kind of theologizing presents and sustains itself.

Because neither Barth and Tillich are concerned with what it means to theologize about God from a standpoint of Blackness, Cone further distinguishes the meaning of "Black theology" by focusing on the Black experience of oppression in particular, with respect to Jesus' identification with the poor and oppressed (i.e., Christology), whereby the resurrection (i.e., eschatology) becomes an act of liberation. This is the contextualization of Black theology, but it is also the delineation of meaning, and how meaning in its varied forms contribute to what Cone conceptualizes as the meaning of "Blackness."

For Cone, the task of the Black theologian, when defined as such, essentializes what it means to theologize about God from a standpoint of "Blackness." In *A Black Theology of Liberation*, Cone asserts the following:

> The black theologian must reject any conception of God which stifles black self-determination by picturing God as a God of all peoples. Either God is identified with the oppressed to the point that their experience becomes God's, or God is a God of racism. . . . The blackness of God means that God has made the oppressed condition God's own condition. This is the essence of the Biblical revelation . . . by becoming the Oppressed One in Jesus Christ, the human race is made to understand that God is known where human beings experience humiliation and suffering. . . . Liberation is not an afterthought, but the very essence of divine activity.[15]

When "the black theologian," as defined by Cone, "rejects any conception of God which stifles black self-determination," this is a rejection of traditional Western theology. To avoid "picturing God as a God of all peoples" is about avoiding a traditional theologizing that assumes that there is only one way to theologize about God—it becomes "picturing God" in a way that speaks to and sustains "the Black theologian" and best positions "the Black theologian" toward theologizing from the existential state of Blackness. For Cone, to find that "either God is identified with the oppressed to the point that their experience becomes God's, or God is a God of racism" suggests how theologizing about God directly affects the very meaning of Black existence. But, more importantly, the existentializing of Black existence orients itself to an existentializing of

---

15. Cone, *Black Theology of Liberation*, 67.

God at the point of God's existence, so that it is not enough to simply theologize about God from the meaning of Blackness—as Cone proposes, "the blackness of God means that God has made the oppressed condition God's own condition," insomuch as "God's own condition" speaks existentially to humanity's condition and that "the blackness of God" speaks existentially to the Blackness of human existence.

In exploring how Black theology, through Cone, occurs at the intersection of hermeneutics, methodology, contextualization, and task of the theologian, I will focus on Cone's last major text, *The Cross and the Lynching Tree*, which is a culmination of his first three major texts on Black theology. Though the text is ultimately concerned with drawing a connection between "the cross" and the "lynching tree," such that the former is a source of divine power and life, while the latter is a source of oppressive power and death, the liberating power of the cross over the dehumanizing power of the lynching tree is oriented toward a conception of God. Being that, as Cone argues, "the black theologian must reject any conception of God which stifles black self-determination by picturing God as a God of all peoples," there arises, as it seems to me, the need to conceptualize God beyond the Western theological tradition, insomuch as God is conceived beyond humanism, beyond metaphysics, and beyond anthropo-logocentrism.

Viewed this way, there are important, but philosophical underpinnings to Cone's *The Cross and the Lynching Tree*, so that, in light of what ties "the cross" and "the lynching tree" together being predicated on murder and dehumanization, and the extent to which "the cross" literally liberates us from what "the lynching tree" does to the Black body, "the cross," in itself, is hermeneutically predicated on the murder and dehumanization of *the meaning of being*. Note that both of these—what happens to the Black body on the lynching tree and what happens to the meaning of being on the cross—occurs, by necessity, in the public sphere. Because the public sphere in which the lynching tree is used purposefully wields humanism, metaphysics, and anthropo-logocentrism in a way that murders and dehumanizes the Black body, the *meaning of being* is never truly addressed in its authenticity.

What has been murdered, what has been dehumanized, continues to fundamentally live beyond the experience of the murder itself and the dehumanization itself—two things that are constituents of what it means to be human. And yet, because the public sphere in which the cross is used does not utilize humanism, metaphysics, nor anthropo-logocentrism, what has been "murdered" and "dehumanized" only allows the meaning of being to become all the more unconcealed in the clearing of divine power and life itself (without the distinction of Blackness), such that the liberation of "Blackness" is a liberation of the meaning of being, with a directedness toward an existential theology that, ultimately, theologizes beyond what it means to be human.

James Cone's Black Liberation Theology, Black Power, and the Black Hero/Heroine: Trinitarianism in Blaxploitation Film

Having primarily emerged in the United States in the early 1970s as an ethnic sub-genre, blaxploitation film, more broadly, focused on Black heroic figures and were set in economically disadvantaged urban communities, to the extent that the depiction of Black heroism often used violence to overcome the oppressive acts of "The Man" as monolithic embodiment of the white majority. In doing so, blaxploitation films such as *They Call Me Mister Tibbs* (1970), *Shaft* (1971), *Coffy* (1973), *Foxy Brown* (1974) were unavoidably influenced by the "Black Power Movement" that can be traced to as early as 1965, but, from this movement, the term itself, "Black Power," was popularized by the Student Nonviolent Coordinating Committee (SNCC).

Just as "Black Power," as a sociological and racialized slogan, challenged "The Man" in American society, it grounds the Black hero's quest in a centralized purpose, which occurs at the intersection of activism, religiosity, and the public sphere. At that intersection, "Black Power," in the world of the typical blaxploitation film, functions pneumatologically—to this end, "Black Power" is the Holy Ghost. The blaxploitation film, itself, in light of the pneumatological "Black Power," can be viewed christologically, not just as a negotiation of the divinity and humanity of the Black hero/heroine, but as a negotiation between the exploitation of a Christ-like figure that becomes crucified in the blaxploitation narrative, by way of subversive, political activism that mirrors the broader subversion and political activism of the narrative itself. Yet, as a Jesus-like figure, through "Black Power," the Black hero/heroine directly challenges the patriarchal structure upon which "The Man" sits over and above what can be called "Black subalternity," by affirming that, if reconsidering Gayatri Spivak's famous 1988 essay, the subaltern *can* speak.

Not only is "Black subalternity," as I have called it, a means of liberation for the Black hero/heroine, but it also calls for a specific kind of liberation through theologizing about the Black hero/heroine's existence in the film narrative and beyond, as a "Black subaltern" liberated in the *imago Dei*. To theologize about the meaning of the existence of the Black hero/heroine, within the world of the blaxploitation film, is structured around an existentializes of "Blackness" translated through God's existence and by way of how God's existence comes to bear on the hero/heroine's worlds. The manner in which the "Black subaltern" speaks is through an underlying theology in the term "Black Power," such that the Black hero/heroine theologizes about the meaning of Blackness in relation to—and often confronting, or being an affront to—that which intends to demean the meaning of that Blackness.

In this way, the Black theology of the hero/heroine—that is to say, the way that the Black hero theologizes about God—is focused on developing a theological meaning of an unforgivable Blackness as it is unashamedly expressed in the blaxploitation film. How the Black hero/heroine embarks on their heroic quest is, at is very core, a theological project, which intends to empower through the power placed in the theologizing about God from a position of Blackness. This empowerment, then, is one that hinges on "liberation"—the Black hero/heroine liberates themselves through theologizing about God as a "Black Liberation Theology," fundamentally predicated on James H. Cone's *Black Theology and Black Power*, *Black Theology of Liberation*, and *God of the Oppressed*—the publication of these texts appear contemporaneously to the Black Power movement and the beginning of the blaxploitation era. Because of this, Black theology, Black power, and the Black hero/heroine operate in a Trinitarianism in the blaxploitation film.

J. Deotis Roberts and the Politicizing of Blackness

Published just a year prior to Cone's *God of the Oppressed*, J. Deotis Roberts's *A Black Political Theology* (1974) is the earliest, most important, and most significant explication of Black theology outside of Cone's groundbreaking work in the field. What allows *A Black Political Theology* to noticeably stand out in early scholarship devoted to Black theology is that it brings together "Blackness" and "the political" into an expansion of Cone's concerns in *Black Theology of Liberation*, while it provides an anticipatory direction for Black theology ahead of what Cone would eventually argue in *God of the Oppressed*. More than that, *A Black Political Theology*, as the first full-length examination of Black theology that had not been authored by Cone himself, becomes an early interpretation of Cone's "Black theology," particularly in terms of what is expected of the Black theologian, what is the task of Black theology itself, and what "Blackness" yields existentially from a kind of theologizing that resists traditional Western theology.

Though E. Franklin Frazier's *The Black Church in America* (1964), Joseph R. Washington Jr.'s *Black Religion: The Negro and Christianity in the United States* (1964), and Gayraud Wilmore's *Black Religion and Black Radicalism* (1973) had been previously published, each serving as influences on Cone's own work, Roberts's recognition of "Blackness" and "the political" undoubtedly carves a decidedly theological path toward understanding of the meaning of Blackness in America, while Frazier's and Wilmore's respective works remain rooted in sociological and historical studies. Like Cone, Roberts is concerned with the task of the Black theologian and the extent to which theologizing as a Black theologian requires not just a more specialized understanding of God and God's existence, but also on a specialized understanding of how God's existence shapes and sustains human existence. More broadly speaking, rather than thinking strictly about human existence, like Cone, Roberts finds that "Blackness," or what we might call the meaning of being human from a position of "Blackness" presents unique problems that must be theologized through the role that oppression and marginalization play in the subalternity of "Blackness."

To a certain extent, given that Roberts writes in such a close proximity to Cone's *God of the Oppressed*, it is possible to view Roberts's effort as either a companion to

Cone's or a stand-alone study—to this latter possibility, if viewing Cone's first three major works on Black theology as a theological trilogy, *A Black Political Theology* can be seen as a fourth installment. More importantly, in maintaining that Cone's Black theology, as it is expressed across *Black Theology and Black Power*, *Black Theology of Liberation*, and *God of the Oppressed*, is a kind of existential theology, such that it is preoccupied with the question of the meaning of being, and how "Blackness" translates that meaning in a unique way, and how the uniqueness of that translation orients "Blackness" differently toward what it means to theologize about God, Roberts's *A Black Political Theology* situates "the political" at the heart of his own existential theology, insomuch as how "Blackness" handles and is handled by "the political" influences the theological meaning of "Blackness."

The manner by which "Blackness" handles and is handled by "the political" as a means of theologically understanding "Blackness" means, first and foremost, acknowledging a definition of theology—that is to say, defining what it means to theologize about God—which Roberts provides in the following way:

> Theology is "God-talk," "logos" about "theos," or talking and reasoning about God. . . . Theology has to do with divine revelation. It is not based upon a human quest for God. . . . Theology involves our reflection upon the divine-human personal encounter. Theology interprets a redemptive drama in which God and man are involved on the plane of history.[16]

This definition of theology is not only aligned with Cone's, but it is also in alignment, generally speaking, with traditional Western theology—what Roberts offers, through an understanding of theology as "God-talk," is the relationship between theologizing and language. John Macquarrie makes this explicit connection in *God-Talk: An Examination of the Language and Logic of Theology* (1967). Given that Macquarrie's study predates Roberts, it is impossible to know, with any degree of certainty, if Roberts read or was familiar with Macquarrie's *God-Talk*. To the best of my knowledge, there is no study that draws any comparison between Macquarrie and Roberts on this point. Nonetheless, Roberts recognizes, as Macquarrie does, that "God-Talk" is the means by which theologizing truly and authentically happens, particularly at the intersection of "logos" and "theos." Not only is it possible to surmise from Roberts's handling of "logos" and "theos" as "talking and reasoning about God" as Macquarrie's reference to the "logic of theology," but Roberts similarly understands that the relationship between language and theology gives rise to the notion that "theology has to do with divine revelation." Macquarrie certainly agrees with this, and the same can be found in Tillich's and Barth's respective theologizing—Roberts follows suit with acknowledging the "human quest for God" and how that quest, in itself, is grounded in "our reflection upon the divine-human encounter." Such a description, like Macquarrie, Tillich, and even (arguably) Barth, ventures into existentializing

---

16. Roberts, *Black Political Theology*, 19.

what it means to be human through the linguistic act of theologizing about God. This act is dependent on language and the extent to which language allows us—from the standpoint of human existence—to make sense out of God's existence, so that God's existence theologically speaks to our existence.

This is especially so when existence is expressed in "Black." When existence is an existence in "Black," the underlining "Blackness" of existence contains a meaning that is fundamental to what it means to do Black theology. What this means is that, though the term "Black" in Black theology refers to the theologizing of Blackness and what it means to theologize from a position of Blackness, Roberts notes, too, that "'black' [in black theology] is a symbol of self-affirmation."[17] Accordingly, when considering what the meaning of Blackness itself means to theologizing about God, Roberts writes, "'Black,' therefore, in the reconception of Black theology, is a meaningful symbol of our new self-understanding as persons in black skin who are equal in nature and grace with all humans."[18]

Where Roberts differs from Macquarrie, Tillich, and Barth—as we see Cone differing from Tillich and Barth (and possibly Macquarrie as well)—is with formulating an understanding of theology that incorporates the Black experience. Because that experience requires, as Roberts points out, "a meaningful symbol" explicated by "a new self-understanding as persons in black skin," the Black theologian theologizes "Blackness" as that which is "equal in nature and grace with all humans." The Black theologian utilizes "God-talk" in a way that is altogether foreign from Macquarrie, Tillich, and Barth—though Macquarrie, Tillich, and Barth theologize nature and grace for human existence, Black skin complicates the meanings of nature and grace, so that Blackness itself remains conceptually outside of the theological purview of what Macquarrie, Tillich, and Barth respectively theologize. For Roberts and Cone alike, they are more concerned with the theology and the theologizing of the Black theologian, of which Roberts writes in the following way:

> The black theologian . . . knows what it means to bear the "mark of Cain" for a lifetime. There is even a very important experiential difference between those black theologians who speak from the ivory towers of white academic centers in the North and those who identify with the poverty and insecurity of struggling black academic institutions in the South.[19]

Here, we see Roberts drawing an interesting distinction between two kinds of Black theologians, both situated in different existential situations and, in turn, positioned in a way that both theologize about God through Blackness differently. This difference is a political difference—it is a difference based on the role that institutions, as political entities, mitigate how a Black theologian theologizes about God. For Roberts,

---

17. Roberts, *Black Political Theology*, 21.
18. Roberts, *Black Political Theology*, 24.
19. Roberts, *Black Political Theology*, 26–27.

this difference is not merely superficial but substantive. In effect, it is Roberts's way of purifying what it means to do Black theology, by citing that Black theology, itself, as an existential theology, can only be true to itself when it clearly defines what authenticity looks like in relation to inauthenticity—this idea that, for Roberts, there is a way of doing Black theology in a manner that is either distanced from or working among "Blackness" and theologizing from the outside or theologizing from the inside speaks to the state of Black theology at the time. We must be not forget that "Black theology" was less than a decade old and, given that there were only a small handful of "Black theologians," we might ask to whom is Roberts referring. Who are the "Black theologians" that can be categorized as those "speak from the ivory towers of white academic centers in the North and those who identify with the poverty and insecurity of struggling black academic institutions in the South"? We might even inevitably ask: Into what group does Roberts place Cone, as a "Black theologian"? Unfortunately, Roberts does not answer this—and any answer to this, if there is one, is rather complicated. What is clear, however, is that Cone, at the time of Roberts writing this, was, indeed, "speak[ing] from the ivory towers of white academic centers in the North" at Union Theological Seminary in New York, and yet, he was, indeed, "identify[ing] with the poverty and insecurity of struggling black academic institutions in the South."

Be that as it may, Roberts's definition of the "Black theologian" attempts to more firmly root the relationship between "Blackness" and theologizing about God. The very meaning of the "Black theologian," through his/her awareness of what that role entails existentially, must be regulated by a direct, authentic, and personal connection to the meaning of "Blackness" as a uniquely existential state fundamentally shaping what it means to theologize. Roberts considers this, by writing:

> The oppressed feel themselves to be objects owned by someone else, emotionally dependent upon the "boss," the one who imposes values upon them. This leads to a self-depreciation that becomes a pattern of hopelessness about doing anything to change their condition. The oppressor is characterized by a will to dominate or to subject everyone and everything to his purchasing power, and he is determined to use technology as a means of manipulating the oppressed.[20]

With this in mind, Roberts goes on to say:

> Black theology is existential, but it is also political. It is a theology of survival, of meaning, of protest against injustice. It deals with the issue of life and death. . . . The black theologian must deal with the hard questions and the problems of an oppressed people who seek liberation in the here and now rather than in the afterlife, though the one does not, indeed must not, exclude the other.[21]

---

20. Roberts, *Black Political Theology*, 27–28.
21. Roberts, *Black Political Theology*, 41.

What Roberts defines, here, is his sense that "Black theology," as such, is simultaneously "existential" and "political," and, when articulated this way, "Black theology" has a kinship with the concerns of both existential theology and political theology. As with "the existential" and "the political," Black theology is, as Roberts claims, "a theology of survival, of meaning, of protest against injustice." Yet, as Roberts defines it, the fact that Black theology "deals with the issue of life and death" places it closer to existential theology than political theology—that is to say, to do "Black theology" means that, first, existential theology has already been worked out, which ultimately paves the way for a political theology. It is only when "Blackness" is reckoned with through existential theology that Black theology is even possible—once Black theology, in itself, has been existentialized by existential theology, there arises, by the necessity of finding out how "Blackness" handles and is handled by community and society, the need to do political theology to reaffirm what Black theology has "said" about "Blackness."

To move from existential theology to Black theology to political theology as what Roberts notes as "black political theology," Roberts finds the following to be true:

> We have had all along in black religious experience the raw materials for a political theology. Theologies of hope and liberation emerge from a different set of experiences. In black religious experience we have the basis of a theology of a living hope which has been tempered in the heat of black suffering. Black political theology is based upon an understanding of the gospel of Jesus Christ as the power of God to do far more than we ask or think. It is a theology of meaning, protest, and liberation. It is a theology that merges the secular and the sacred. It is a theology that combines the priestly and the prophetic—pietism and activism.[22]

JAMES H. EVANS JR.: BETWEEN THE UNGIVEN GOD AND THE VISION OF GOD

In chapter 3 of *We Have Been Believers: An African-American Systematic Theology* (1992), James H. Evans Jr. argues that God is "ungiven" for African Americans on what I find to be two essential fronts: the idea of God and language about God. The former, as Evans proposes, "is rooted in concrete human experience,"[23] while the latter "is experiential, metaphorical, analogical, and functional"[24]—in Evans's view, the African American experience provides for a unique idea of God which is articulated through specialized language about God. Though I am initially compelled to believe that Evans is overgeneralizing and making the African American experience a monolithic one, there is, in fact, merit in his argument. What Evans is arguing is that the African American vision of God is developed from a uniquely problematic experience—an experience that

---

22. Roberts, *Black Political Theology*, 152–53.
23. Evans, *We Have Been Believers*, 53.
24. Evans, *We Have Been Believers*, 53.

W. E. B. Du Bois characterizes as a double-consciousness[25]—and shaped by a specific mode of existence. From that mode of existence, which Evans discusses more in-depth in chapter 5,[26] there is a need to create a vision of God that directly relates to the Du Boisian "two-ness"[27] of the African American experience.

To say that the African American experience presents a vision of God as an "ungiven God" suggests, in my view, a reconstitution of the idea of God in order to reappropriate that idea by what I would describe as meaning based on the subjective objectification of what is deemed as true.[28] In other words, rather than passively accepting the traditional Christian notion of God, the African American experience dictates the necessity to actively grope for and find a subjective vision of God that is meaningfully objectified in reference to what God is to and what God does for the African American. This is my best extrapolation of Evans's argument. In this respect, the African American "vision of God" is a way of theologizing a "God" that, instead of maintaining the status quo, intends to push against that status quo—instead of perpetuating the problem with a "given" God, the "ungiven God" symbolizes a means of solving, then transcending the problem.

The "ungiven God" as a "vision of God" is based on an individualized encounter with God, which Gilles Deleuze would regard as an immanent event, one that is "actualized in a state of things and of the lived that make it happen."[29] The "state of things" for the African American, as I am sure Evans would agree, is construed through a living experience shaped by racism, oppression, and marginalization. What these problems have done is made the African American keenly aware of the differences that defer them to places of inferiority by way of a process that Jacques Derrida refers to as "*différance*."[30]

---

25. The suggestion, here, is that African Americans share a double-consciousness with both their Blackness and their Americanism to the point that they do not truly belong to either. I would argue further that this is critical to what Evans is arguing, because it is through this experience of double-consciousness that the African American vision of God is construed. I find this to be particularly relevant when considering that Du Bois feels that this double-consciousness provides a "sense of always looking at one's self through the eyes of others, of measuring one's soul by the tape of a world that looks on in amused contempt and pity." Du Bois, *Souls of Black Folk*, 3.

26. In this chapter that is entitled "On Being Black," Evans discusses the African American experience in terms of social, political, historical, and cultural contexts which all, more or less, come to bear on what it means to be Black as what I would call a "mode of being" or "mode of existence" in American society.

27. Du Bois, *Souls of Black Folk*, 3.

28. Here, I am referring to Soren Kierkegaard's "subjectivity is truth." My point, in short, is that the definition of truth, as Kierkegaard suggests, "must include an expression of the antithesis to objectivity . . . this expression will at the same time serve as an indication of the tension of inwardness." Kierkegaard, *Concluding Unscientific Postscript*, 171.

29. Deleuze, *Pure Immanence*, 31.

30. Derrida describes "différance" as an economic concept designating the production of differing/deferring. Derrida, *Of Grammatology*, 23.

Consequently, what *différance* yields, in my view, is a kind of being that is, essentially, what Emmanuel Levinas proposes as "otherwise than being" or "being's other."[31] In effect, this is very important in understanding the African American experience as a sense of being which, just as Evans contends, is relegated "in a world where African-Americans [are] defined primarily in terms of their 'otherness' [so that] their identification with the God who created them required that God be seen as embodying that otherness."[32] Here, what Evans is suggesting, I would argue, is something more than just the relatedness between the otherness that African Americans experience in American society and the Otherness of God that transcends all humanity.

In Evans's otherness-Otherness relation, which he asserts is foundational to the African American "vision of God," I find it possible to, then, draw a more important connection between African Americans' "being" and God's "Being." That is, developing a vision of God that is not longitudinal, but lateral—a vision that is, respectively, not concerned with the Heideggerian being-in-the-world as it is filtered through the Christian notion of God, but, rather, with God's transcendent Being and the possibility of ontotheology.

This is what I believe is at the heart of Evans's argument about the African American "vision of God." It is a "vision" that is ontotheological, where it is just as much ontological as it is theological. For Martin Heidegger, anything "ontotheological" is concerned with "the metaphysical concept of God [and the] metaphysics must think in the direction of the deity because the matter of thinking is Being."[33] So, I propose that any "vision of God" is preoccupied with God's Being as the Being of beings. And, as Heidegger would likely agree, God as the Being of beings involves "the separateness and mutual relatedness of grounding and of accounting for [so that] Being grounds beings, and beings, as what is most of all, account for Being."[34] To that end, is it possible to suggest that "the ungiven God" is not created exclusively out of the African American experience, but arises from the universal need to develop a sense of Being that grounds and accounts for being? In other words, if any "vision of God," as I would argue, is systematically ontotheological, then is it safe to say that the "ungiven God" is the ideological creation of a given set of experiences that are not race-centric?

From James Evans to Justo Gonzalez

When considering the respective stances of Evans and Gonzalez, I would like to focus particularly on how both are ultimately concerned with theological anthropology in their respective pieces entitled "On Being Black" and "On Being Human."

---

31. "Otherwise than being" is, for Levinas, transcendence that is passing over to being's other. Levinas, *Otherwise than Being*, 3.

32. Evans, *We Have Been Believers*, 57.

33. Heidegger, *Identity and Difference*, 60.

34. Heidegger, *Identity and Difference*, 69.

What Evans and Gonzalez are doing, then, through their approaches to theological anthropology, is centering their respective arguments on the idea of race which defines and influences what it means to exist, or have human "being." So, when considering Evans and Gonzalez, I would like this response paper to, first, address Evans's view of what it means to be Black, but also engage Gonzalez's assertion that "the notion of what it means to be human—in traditional terms, the doctrine of 'man[kind]'—has been used in oppressive ways"[35]—I would contend that there is an important connection to be made between the two.

In my view, Evans's and Gonzalez's views on human existence and racial identity can be synthesized in the following manner: what it means to be a particular race or have a specific racial identity often transcends what it means to be human. What Evans and Gonzalez are asserting is that racial identity supersedes human identity. Not only would I agree with this, but I find that, when we speak of humanity's "being," we are not speaking of, as Gonzalez would likely agree, the traditional doctrine of mankind. Perhaps, it is safe to contend, then, that there is truly no such thing as a "traditional doctrine of humanity" as long as society becomes the arena in which humanity, as an object of understanding, is defined, interpreted, and pursued. This is because humanity is stratified into racial forms of humanity through the ideology of racism, where, as Evans rightly argues, "racism assumes black people to be defective in their essential being."[36] There is no doubt in my mind that Gonzalez would agree with Evans, undoubtedly inserting "Hispanic people" in place of Evans's "black people." But, more importantly, what underscores Evans's argument is that, somehow, certain racial identities are discerned as lower or lesser forms of "being." In other words, to have a Black or a Hispanic racial identity means being existentially distanced from some essential "being-ness." Again, this goes back to the stratification of humanity along racial categories, where society utilizes the "concept of race" to suggest that one race is functionally, cognitively, and biologically superior to another race and, as a result, decidedly creates a power paradigm between those races. However, I would additionally assert that any such stratification along positions of power shaped through theological anthropology is linked to suggesting that race represents tangible degrees of estrangement from God.

This notion of "estrangement" is best illustrated by Paul Tillich in a selection from his *Systematic Theology*, vol. 2, *Existence and the Christ*, that we previously read entitled "The Marks of Man's Estrangement and the Concept of Sin." In that selection, Tillich makes a great analysis of human existence in relation to God's existence by arguing that "the state of existence is the state of estrangement [because] man[kind] is estranged from the ground of his being, from other beings, and from himself."[37] Tillich equates this "state of estrangement" to the fall, and the fact that human existence

---

35. Gonzalez, *Manana*, 125.
36. Evans, *We Have Been Believers*, 105.
37. Tillich, *Systematic Theology*, 2:44.

comes into "being" as a result of the sin of that fall. In this regard, Evans makes a very important gesture in this direction as a means of understanding the concept of race, where he proposes that "black people are supposedly the victims of a 'double Fall,' first into the human predicament of sin, and second into the peculiar plight of blackness."[38] What makes this assertion particularly powerful is that Evans is drawing a distinction between the "concept of race" and the "physicality of race." Not only are these two very different objects of understanding, but the former is elevated over the latter, since human existence and humanity's "being" are frequently situated within the situatedness of the "concept of race."

The concept of race, as I am sure both Evans and Gonzalez would agree, is always bracketed through a kind of Husserlian phenomenological reduction, where the "concept," as an idea, is appropriated through physical acts of oppression, marginalization, and racism. Such acts are often based on rationalizing the "concept of race" as differences in the power relations between the powerful and powerless and, filtering racism through theological anthropology. Not only does this mean that theological anthropology is about "being" in relation to other "beings," but the extent to which "being," physically encapsulated in a racial identity, somehow informs a certain kind of being-Being dialectic with God. To that end, the ability "to be" becomes inextricably linked to race as a form of anthropological existence, and, in turn, the degree to which the "concept of race" is contextualized in order to inform theological existence.

For Evans and Gonzalez, what it means to exist as a human being is fundamentally skewed in terms of the "concept of race" and oppressive societal norms. In this respect, while Evans's is an African American perspective and Gonzalez's is a Hispanic perspective, I would argue that both are dealing with the same problematic issue: what it means to exist, or have "being," in this world is construed through what it means to be human but, in the end, becomes overwhelmingly predicated by what it means to belong to a particular race of people.

So, the question I would offer is this: is there a difference between what it means to exist in relation to one's racial identity and what it means to exist as a human?

Brian Blount and New Testament Ethics

In *Then the Whisper Put on Flesh: New Testament Ethics in an African-American Context* (2001), Brian Blount argues not only against the conventional interpretation of the New Testament writings through a Euro-American perspective as an all-inclusive representation of the American experience but, more importantly, explicitly argues for a cultural-specific interpretation employed through a decidedly African American lens as the only accurate method of extrapolating the African American experience from the ideology evident in the New Testament.

38. Evans, *We Have Been Believers*, 105.

By what he proposes in his preface as "an attempt to help readers who live outside of an oppressed circumstance read the New Testament through the circumstance of oppressed others,"[39] Blount invokes liberation theology as a lens through which to read New Testament theology. This, undoubtedly, is the "thematic window" Blount describes, whereby he proceeds to "detail exactly how such a reading influences an understanding of New Testament ethics from an African-American perspective,"[40] as well as, quite frankly, incorporates the themes associated with New Testament theology to what can only be defined as a liberation theological approach to the understanding New Testament. Liberation theology, then, for Blount, is, perhaps, at the intersection of cultural interpretation of the New Testament, biblical ethics, and African American Christianity, as his three areas of research interest.[41] These three elements, according to the argument Blount postulates, function in a three-prong effect through "the questions that have been the most formative and frequent in the recent history of African-American Christians [that] have operated from the theme of liberation."[42]

This theme of liberation as seen through a liberating lens is not founded in the modern-day African American experience any more than it is built upon the African American experience of the Civil Rights era but, instead, accordingly to Blount, harkens to the enslaved African American experience, which is "a window into understanding the ethical perspective of the New Testament materials."[43] It is from this supposition that Blount begins a general discussion of New Testament ethics as the prerequisite to considering how New Testament ethics operate through an African American lens. Within that discussion, therefore, Blount categorizes ethics as being "the rationale, the philosophical structure of reasoning behind the moral exhortation"[44] in order to surmise, then, that ethics are "oriented toward and structured around the event of Jesus' life, death, and resurrection."[45]

According to Blount, the event of Jesus' life, death, and resurrection as they are recounted in the New Testament becomes the lens through which New Testament ethics are founded.[46] This event, while residing at the core of New Testament ethics, is, through Blount's extrapolation, something we can tangibly engage with through a means of drawing a certain degree of moral reasoning from it. In other words, the event of Jesus' life, death, and resurrection engages us first as a significant historical event then, subsequently, engages us on a deeper level that procures how we deduce the morality in it in a further effort to, as Blount believes, see ourselves in it. For

---

39. Blount, *Then the Whisper Put on Flesh*, 9.
40. Blount, *Then the Whisper Put on Flesh*, 10.
41. Blount, *Then the Whisper Put on Flesh*, 9.
42. Blount, *Then the Whisper Put on Flesh*, 10.
43. Blount, *Then the Whisper Put on Flesh*, 16.
44. Blount, *Then the Whisper Put on Flesh*, 17.
45. Blount, *Then the Whisper Put on Flesh*, 17.
46. Blount, *Then the Whisper Put on Flesh*, 19.

Blount, this is what New Testament ethics is all about: the interaction between space, the Jesus event, and the text[47]—in effect, it is the act of reading the Jesus event, the ability of holding a reader's dialogue with the text describing the Jesus event, and the development of moral resonance that occurs in the space the reader occupies. This is what Blount proposes as operating from in front of the text, where the reader "[allows] their cultural and methodological space to influence their interpretative process [because] they read into (eisegesis) rather than out of (exegesis) the text."[48] In saying this, not only does Blount suggest that African American slaves perceived the Jesus event through the oppressive reality of their horrific space but, then, by extension, encouraged within them a particular kind of interpretative constancy, through which, as a result, Jesus embodied freedom.[49]

This is the liberating lens, whereby the antebellum African American slave "could see into and interact with a part of the New Testament that other communities, because of their space implications (limitations), could not."[50] It is the notion that, by operating from in front of the text, it was possible for the African American slave to draw a meaning from the Jesus event relative to their specific social and political circumstances, indicative of how they perceive their degree of oppression in relation to the agencies of oppressor, and communicative to the moral undercurrent that understands the necessities of freedom.

What this is, as Blount terms it, is the reconfiguration of ethics through a "compositional process," that involved African American slaves "fusing biblical material with their own life situation and concerns, their space, [in order to compose] a biblical witness that was uniquely their own and spoke to their uniquely tragic circumstances."[51] To accomplish this, African American slaves composed slave narratives as a way of communicating their experiences through the liberating lens to, perhaps, bring into focus and bring to bear their thoughts about the world, their places in that world, the roles of their oppressors in relation to theirs as the oppressed, and their ultimate desire to transcend their sufferings under oppression by way of liberation. In Jesus and, specifically, the Jesus event, Blount is able to, then, argue that the African American slave not only reconfigured the evidence of Jesus' resurrection to align with their circumstances but created a version of Jesus that became "an even closer companion to the slave believer because Jesus suffered as the slave suffers; Jesus can understand the pain, the tragedy, the hopelessness, the sorrow, and, most important, the hope."[52]

Therefore, when comparing the Jesus seen through the liberating lens of the African American slave and the Jesus of the slave owner, in juxtaposition, there are

47. Blount, *Then the Whisper Put on Flesh*, 19.
48. Blount, *Then the Whisper Put on Flesh*, 20.
49. Blount, *Then the Whisper Put on Flesh*, 20.
50. Blount, *Then the Whisper Put on Flesh*, 20.
51. Blount, *Then the Whisper Put on Flesh*, 24.
52. Blount, *Then the Whisper Put on Flesh*, 33.

obvious differences in how to interpret the Jesus event, the role of Jesus in the New Testament texts, and the ensuing message, or theme, embodied in the theology of the writings. The interpretation personified with the liberating lens of the African American slave is a result of their doing it:

> By being critical, by focusing on their liberating God and God's liberating message in the biblical story[,] this allowed them to critique not only the slave owners' biblical interpretations, but even, and more important, the Bible from which they crafted them.[53]

As a result, the interpretation of God as a liberating God is not only a reconfiguration of message, as Blount describes, but, undoubtedly, is a kind of reinterpretation. It is, at its fundamental level, an application of message to a certain circumstance, the defining of theme to how the African American slaves perceive, realize, and comprehend themselves in political, cultural and social contexts in reference to powerlessness and hopelessness.

For me, the issues Blount raises about interpreting the New Testament is the incomplete, albeit inaccurate, conventional interpretation of the New Testament as it has been commonly interpreted through a Euro-American lens. At the core of this issue is the notion that there is no one complete, all-inclusive interpretation of the New Testament that universally speaks to all people regardless of their cultural or societal experiences. There are, instead, a plethora of interpretations that can be derived, whereby, though there is no universal interpretation for all, there is a relative universality through the elasticity within the message or themes of the New Testament, from which Blount is able to interpret through a liberating lens.

But, nevertheless, there are significant challenges evident in this—the idea that multiple interpretations can be achieved in the reading of the New Testament writings. The challenges, as I see them, specifically involve misapplication, misappropriation, and abuse. Though Blount has been able to read the New Testament through a liberating lens as seen through the interpretative decisions African American slaves made during their antebellum dialogue with the texts, it becomes likely, however, that a proliferation of lenses can be incorporated to, perhaps, sometimes, see certain things—or truths, as defined by the one defining the term "truth"—in the texts that, though supported word for word and verse for verse, bastardizes the prevailing wisdom through what can be described as a cherry-picking process.

In a sense, when supposing this in terms of ministry and leadership as well as academically and theologically, multiplicity in interpretation through various lenses molded by different experiences creates the frightening possibility that the New Testament writings and the Jesus event can be subjugated into something illogical and malicious, something that, in effect, does little to positively enlighten and educate, but, frankly, methodically negatively enrages and incites for the sake of a corrupting doctrine.

---

53. Blount, *Then the Whisper Put on Flesh*, 37.

COUNTERTRADITIONS OF EXISTENTIAL THEOLOGY
Theodore Walker Jr.'s "Black Atlantic"

In the preface to *Mothership Connections: A Black Atlantic Synthesis of Neoclassical Metaphysics and Black Theology* (2004), Theodore Walker Jr. defines the term "Black Atlantic" as "refer[ring] to postslavery black populations and settlements on continents and islands up and down both sides of the Atlantic Ocean, and to their various black and colored relations across the whole globe."[54] Walker conceptualizes this definition by way of Paul Gilroy's *The Black Atlantic: Modernity and Double Consciousness* (1993)—similarly to Gilroy, Walker not only makes it clear, through defining the "Black Atlantic" as such, the various explications of hyphenated Blackness as they all come to bear on the very meaning of "African American," but also how these hyphenated aspects of Blackness are more broadly regulated by modernity and, in turn, problematized by postmodernity.

With this in mind, it brings Walker to "offer a black Atlantic contribution to constructive postmodern efforts to understand and transcend modern worldviews and modern world orders." To do this, Walker first reckons with "constructive postmodern views of modernity," then "black Atlantic views of modernity," in an effort to "introduce black Atlantic scholarship to postmodern scholars."[55] This dialogue is necessary, according to Walker, "because any adequate account of modernity and its possible transcendence must include sustained analysis of our various connections to transatlantic slavery and black Atlantic experiences."[56] Walker emphasizes "our" here from "our various connections," as a means of "refer[ring] to all modern humans."[57] Yet, this emphasis on "our" also points to a theologizing about God, which becomes, in itself, the very point by which "our various connections" are drawn. To theologize in this way means to recognize, as Walker does, that "all humans shaped by modernity are connected to transatlantic slavery and black Atlantic experiences."[58] The entire conceptualization of "black Atlantic" becomes, to a certain extent, about theologizing about God by theologizing about the meaning of Blackness itself, if Blackness is to be explained both philosophically and theologically in terms of the connectedness of "transatlantic slavery and black Atlantic experiences." Through this kind of theologizing, Walker brings Black Atlantic scholars "instructed by W. E. B. Du Bois" into philosophical-theological conversation with "black and womanist theologians instructed by black Atlantic thought."[59] The manner with which philosophizing about Black Atlantic thought speaks to the theologizing of Black Atlantic thought is predicated a framework of constructive postmodernity

---

54. Walker, *Mothership Connections*, vii.
55. Walker, *Mothership Connections*, vii.
56. Walker, *Mothership Connections*, vii.
57. Walker, *Mothership Connections*, vii.
58. Walker, *Mothership Connections*, vii.
59. Walker, *Mothership Connections*, viii.

from which the question of the meaning of God to the question of the meaning of Blackness—both of these questions, if understanding Walker's approach, are rooted in the meaning of existence, so that, for Walker, the appropriation of the "Black Atlantic" informs a kind of existential theology.

By theologizing about God through his use of the "Black Atlantic," Walker is "equally concerned to introduce constructive postmodern metaphysics of the neoclassical and process-relational varieties to black and other liberation theologians."[60] This concern, for Walker, is grounded on the extent that "no theology or theological ethic can be fully adequate until its metaphysical and metaethical presuppositions are rendered fully explicit, and because . . . classical metaphysics yields nonliberating visions of God."[61] To this end, Walker's handling of "black and other liberation theologians," as undoubtedly theologizing liberating "visions of God," views "the neoclassical and process-relational varieties" to what they do as constructive. The question, then, is how do these constructive theologies, as Walker finds them, theologize about God from the standpoint of neoclassical metaphysics oriented toward Black, liberation, and womanist theological perspectives? It is clear that, for Walker, what forges the relationship between neoclassical metaphysics and Black (and liberation and womanist) theology is Walker's understanding of the "Black Atlantic." Indeed, though Walker seemingly conflates liberation and womanist theologies into an all-encompassing "Black theology," he, nevertheless, speaks to three dimensions that pedagogically inform his meanings of "neoclassical metaphysics," "Black theology," and the "Black Atlantic," which are: "metaphysics of struggle," "metaphysics of power," and "metaphysics of ethics." What these dimensions further illustrate is an underlining existential theology to what synthesizes neoclassical metaphysics and "Black theology" through the "Black Atlantic"—to theologize about God, through philosophizing about the "Black Atlantic" means ultimately engaging in an existential theology predicated on "struggle," "power," and "ethics."

Anthony Bradley, Liberating Black Theology and Black Victimology

In *Liberating Black Theology* (2010), Anthony Bradley, as the title aptly suggests, wishes to "liberate Black theology"—such a call for liberation is not strictly about reconceptualizing how Black theology theologizes about God, but is more about "liberating" the very meaning of being with which Black theology is fundamentally engaged. For Bradley, to "liberate" Black theology means decentering it from the meaning of Blackness. That is to say that, though the very meaning of Blackness is the impetus for doing Black theology at all, it becomes all the more important to define "Blackness" more narrowly, in an effort to more narrowly understand what Blackness contributes to the

---

60. Walker, *Mothership Connections*, viii.
61. Walker, *Mothership Connections*, viii.

theologizing of God—even though the meaning of Blackness is always-already at the core of what it means to do Black theology, Bradley's chief concern is with how "Blackness" is addressed in a more substantially postmodern way, particularly in a manner that redefines "what Blackness is" since the original conception of James Cone's Black theology in the late 1960s and the 1970s.

How Bradley intends to "liberate" Black theology from what it has become is by taking an "interdisciplinary" approach, focused on, as Bradley argues, "engaging theology, sociology, anthropology, and economics."[62] To be sure, Bradley is careful to explain how he uses the term "Black theology" itself, if the intent is to liberate it. Bradley defines "Black theology," then, "to broadly encompass writings on Christianity in religious studies by a wide spectrum of black authors including theologians, authors of biblical studies, ethicists, and the like."[63] In defining "Black theology" this way, Bradley does not consider "Black theology" as a systematic theology, since, as he defines it, theologians are not alone in theologizing in the vein of "Black theology." Even so, Bradley's rooting of "Black theology" in religious studies seems to suggest that he views "Black theology" as not solely about theologizing about God, but more about understanding the meaning of Blackness through the various experiences that make "Blackness" so—these various experiences are not just explained by theologians, but are, as Bradley notes in his definition, also explained by "authors of biblical studies [and] ethicists."

Though Bradley certainly suggests that "theologians, authors of biblical studies, ethicists, and the like" all engage in Black theology by definition, the fact that he seeks to define "Black theology" as "Black liberation theology" attempts to carve a division between the role theologians play in favor of the roles of "authors of biblical studies [and] ethicists." It is this latter group to which Bradley focuses, if we recognize that his intent on "liberating" Black theology requires—by necessity, it would seem—that Black theology comes to terms with the extent to which "authors of biblical studies [and] ethicists" have caused a paradigm shift in what it means to Black (liberation) theology now. That shift is at the intersection of sociology, anthropology, and economics. Because of this, Bradley "primarily focus[es] on the role that victimology has played in the rise and fall of black liberation theology."[64] This victimology that Bradley points out in Black liberation theology is most certainly a by-product of the work of "authors of biblical studies [and] ethicists" in response to the work of theologians—theologizing God through what "Blackness" offers to the meaning of human existence becomes, in the hands of certain "authors of biblical studies [and] ethicists," a view of victimized Blackness, such that grounding the meaning of human existence to that victimology and any theologizing about God is mediated by that victimology.

---

62. Bradley, *Liberating Black Theology*, 14.
63. Bradley, *Liberating Black Theology*, 14.
64. Bradley, *Liberating Black Theology*, 14.

For Bradley, "the major flaw of black liberation theology is that it views people perpetually as victims."[65] This "major flaw" is what Bradley believes to be "the rise and fall of black liberation theology" as such—it is the fact that there arises a tendency to theologize about God in terms of the meaning of Blackness as that which is, by nature, after-Cone, victimized to the extent that theologizing from a position of Blackness influences what it means to theologize about God. Rather than follow the way of victimology, Bradley "suggest[s] an alternate strategy for developing a redemptive-historical approach for understanding the black experience in America while remaining faithful to Scripture and orthodox Christianity."[66] From here, Bradley continues, by concluding that

> the thesis is that James Cone's presupposition of black consciousness construed as victim supplies a fundamentally flawed theological anthropology for later developments in black liberation theology, leading to the demise of black liberation theology. In other words, reducing black identity primarily to that of victim, albeit at times inadvertent, contributed to the decline of black liberation theology to obscurity.[67]

Among these "later developments in black liberation theology," as Bradley points out, include, namely, J. Deotis Roberts—in Bradley's view, in purview of Black theology's "fundamentally flawed theological anthropology," he finds that "black theologians like [Roberts] clearly pointed out core weaknesses [in black liberation theology] but, like most other critics, simply did not go deep enough to the presuppositional level."[68] For that matter, Bradley writes, "victimology also wove its way through the social ethics of black liberation theologians and set the stage for the adoption of Marxism as an ethical framework for black liberation theology after Cone."[69]

Cornel West: On Structural Sin, Marxist Thought, and the "Prophetic"

As a means of continuing to explain what he refers to as "the victimologist vision" in black liberation theology, Bradley turns to social structures and the degree that "Cone and others focus much attention on the racism inherent in social structures, including those in the church."[70] In turning here, and eventually arriving at notions of institutional racism that has "continued after the civil rights movement as the next great evil to be tackled,"[71] Bradley introduces his first specific reference to Cornel

---

65. Bradley, *Liberating Black Theology*, 14.
66. Bradley, *Liberating Black Theology*, 14.
67. Bradley, *Liberating Black Theology*, 14–15.
68. Bradley, *Liberating Black Theology*, 15.
69. Bradley, *Liberating Black Theology*, 15.
70. Bradley, *Liberating Black Theology*, 48.
71. Bradley, *Liberating Black Theology*, 49.

West with respect to "structural sin," which provides an excellent foray into what West contributes to what it means to do Black theology more generally and West's kind of theologizing reaches into "the existential" when theologizing about God.

Consider, first, Bradley's characterization of West's relationship with Black theology. It must be noted that, in Bradley's first specific reference to West, as it appears in *Liberating Black Theology*, Bradley notably uses "black theology" and not "black liberation theology." Be that as it may, Bradley presents an immensely important discussion of West in the following manner, which situates West firmly within Bradley's own call for "liberating" Black theology:

> Cornel West maintains that black theology has not gone far enough in addressing structural sin. Early conceptions of black theology, according to West, had severe limitations in this area. West understands that the early limitations of black theology when addressing structural issues are to be found in [a lack of systematic social analysis].[72]

These "structural issues," for West, as cited by Bradley, are expressed in West's "Black Theology of Liberation as Critique of Capitalist Civilization," which appears in *Black Theology: A Documentary History*, vol. 2, *1980–1992* (1993). As Bradley recognizes, one of the "structural issues" in Black theology is West's understanding of "structural sin" and how Black theology does not provide an adequate "systematic social analysis" of it, particularly within institutional racism and the extent to which this, in itself, upholds Bradley's own "victimologist vision" in Black theology.

To provide a "systematic social analysis" of "structural sin" requires a Marxist approach. In particular, what is required is a conversation between Black theology and Marxist thought, as a means to address "structural issues" in a general sense, how these issues affect what it means to understand Blackness within social structures, and how Blackness, when assessed in terms of a systematic social analysis, affects theologizing about God. The conversation that must be had between Black theology and Marxist thought is, in fact, presented by Cone himself in the slim book *The Black Church and Marxism: What Do They Have to Say to Each Other?* (1980). As Cone notes, it was originally "written for the Democratic Socialist Organizing Committee's seminar on 'Religion, Socialism, and the Black Experience,' held at Asbury United Methodist Church, Washington, D.C., April 9, 1980."[73] What Cone also notes is that "an earlier version of this paper was presented in a 'Black Theology and Marxist Thought' seminar at Union Theological Seminary, jointly taught by Professor Cornel West and me."[74] This latter note is immensely important, since it, on one sense, brings Cone to the forefront of a development of the relationship between Black theology and Marxist thought and, in another sense, places Cone and West in dialogue—where Cone leaves

---

72. Bradley, *Liberating Black Theology*, 49–50.
73. Cone, *Black Church and Marxism*, 1.
74. Cone, *Black Church and Marxism*, 1.

off pedagogically in order to lean into the theoretical is where, perhaps, West continues theoretically in order to venture into "the philosophical" and "the theological." As much as Cone certainly recognized that Black theology needed to productively converse with Marxist thought, so that Black theology could more effectively address what Blackness means within social structures and how the institutional aspects of these social structures influence what it means to theologize God from a positionality of Blackness, West's "Black Theology and Marxist Thought" makes the necessary dialogue more explicit. This is not just with the undated seminar "jointly taught" by Cone and West, but also with West's essay on the subject, which, as West admits, is influenced by the undated seminar.

In the essay "Black Theology and Marxist Thought" (1979), as it appears in *Black Theology: A Documentary History*, vol. 1, 1966–1979 (1979), West makes it clear that "both focus on the plight of the exploited, oppressed and degraded peoples of the world, their relative powerlessness and possible empowerment."[75] For West, "this common focus warrants a serious dialogue between Black theologians and Marxist thinkers."[76] The "serious dialogue," then, becomes a meaningful encounter between the two, such that

> the aim of this encounter is to change the world, not each other's faith; to put both groups on the offensive for structural social change, not put Black Christians on the defensive; and to enhance the quality of life of the dispossessed, not expose the empty Marxist meaning of death. In short, Black theologians and Marxist thinkers must preserve their own existential and intellectual integrity and explore the possibility of promoting fundamental social amelioration together.[77]

In explaining it this way, I find that, when the relationship between Black theologians and Marxist thinkers, in West's words, "preserve their own existential and intellectual integrity," Black theology itself ventures into an existential theology translated through a philosophical Marxism. To this end, the mere ability for Black theologians and Marxist thinkers to "explore the possibility of promoting fundamental social amelioration together" seems to acknowledge that Black theology, as an existential theology, becomes naturally and inevitably disposed to philosophical Marxism in much the same manner as Sartre's existentialism sought to "explore the possibility of promoting [a] fundamental social amelioration" with Marxism. Here, too, for West, just as Roberts's *A Black Political Theology* similarly articulates (in 1974) and Cone more explicitly describes (by 1980), Marxism reifies and reconceptualizes "Blackness," as it is defined by Black theology and as it stands as "the existential" in existential

---

75. West, "Black Theology and Marxist Thought," 552.
76. West, "Black Theology and Marxist Thought," 552.
77. West, "Black Theology and Marxist Thought," 552.

theology, so that, in order to theologize from a position of Blackness, theologizing about God existentializes the meaning of Blackness.

In *Prophesy Deliverance! An Afro-American Revolutionary Christianity* (1982), West considers the "sources and tasks" of what he refers to as Afro-American critical thought, which, as he defines it, "is the past and the present, the doings and the sufferings of African people in the United States."[78] One source of Afro-American critical thought is "prophetic Christian thought"—what makes this "prophetic," according to West, is that it highlights the idea that "every individual regardless of class, country, caste, race, or sex should have the opportunity to fulfill his or her potentialities."[79] It is on this point, in particular, that West's conceptualization of "the prophetic'" aligns to "the existential," insomuch as both are concerned with the question of the meaning of being and how that meaning makes human existence measurably meaningful. As West notes, "the opportunity to fulfill his or her potentialities" is "the first and fundamental norm [at] the core of the prophetic Christian gospel."[80] The extent to which the "prophetic" is realized is through "a transcendent God before whom all persons are equal," as it comes to bear on "endow[ing] the well-being and ultimate salvation of each with equal value and significance."[81] Not only is that "value and significance" crucial for the very meaning of human existence as that which is grounded to being, but it also becomes essential for how human existence, at that point of grounding, is able to theologize about God as the grounding for human existence. The "prophetic" aspect of this, if understanding West's use of the word, is theologizing about God in a way that substantializes the meaning of human existence—the "prophetic" becomes "the existential" and, in turn, "the existential," through West's "prophetic," becomes a kind of existential theology.

West's "prophetic," as it is synonymous with "the existential," brings West to argue that a "quite similar fundamental thrust of Marxism, despite the numerous brutalities perpetuated by Marxist regimes, is the self-fulfillment, self-development, and self-realization of harmonious personalities."[82] Because of this, and in an effort to more authentically align the "prophetic" to Marxist thought, West considers a more progressive version of Marxism, which, in itself, aligns more congruently with a more progressive version of Christianity in the "prophetic." To this end, West finds that, even though "Christianity and Marxism are the most vulgarized, distorted traditions in the modern world, yet I believe the alliance of prophetic Christianity and progressive Marxism provides a last humane hope for humankind."[83]

---

78. West, *Prophesy Deliverance*, 15.
79. West, *Prophesy Deliverance*, 16.
80. West, *Prophesy Deliverance*, 16.
81. West, *Prophesy Deliverance*, 16.
82. West, *Prophesy Deliverance*, 16.
83. West, *Prophesy Deliverance*, 95.

This "alliance," as West calls it, is further narrowed into two subsequent collections: *Prophetic Fragments: Illuminations of the Crisis in American Religion and Culture* (1988) and *Prophetic Reflections: Notes on Race and Power in America* (1993), as the second volume of *Beyond Eurocentrism and Multiculturalism*. From these two collections that both follow the broader "prophetic" theme, two texts provide a further explication of West's understanding of the relationship between "prophetic Christianity" and Marxist thought: the first from *Prophetic Fragments* is "Dispensing with Metaphysics in Religious Thought" (1986) and the second from *Prophetic Reflections* is "Prophetic Theology" (1988)—while the former substantiates the relationship philosophically, the latter does so theologically, which, on the whole, presents an "existential" framework by which West's form of existential theology permeates.

While "Dispensing with Metaphysics in Religious Thought" acknowledges that "metaphysical or ontological reflections are never free of a particular set of presuppositions, prejudices, and prejudgments," West suggests that "metaphysics and ontology in the grand mode or in the old sense are anachronistic, antiquated, and most important, unwarranted."[84] To this end, West concludes that "the Age of Metaphysics is over, yet inescapable metaphysical reflections will and must go on."[85]

All said, if tending to West's form of existential theology, as it is filtered and shaped through how he locates the relationship between Black theology and Marxist thought, "the existential" must resist traditional metaphysics, even if, to a certain extent, it must allow itself to be explained and defined through "metaphysical reflections." That is to say, in order to theologize about God to ground the meaning of human existence, the question of the meaning of being, as such, must escape traditional metaphysics in an effort to draw closer to God's existence, even if our mere ability to understand God's existence requires our own metaphysical reflections. Similarly, when keeping our own problematic relationship with metaphysics in mind, in "Prophetic Theology," West defines "three basic components in Prophetic Theology," if we are to define it, through West, as that which extrapolates "the existential"—the three are: (1) "a religious conception of what it is to be human, of how we are to act, of what we are to hope for," (2) "historical and social analysis," and (3) "action, [insomuch as] what will we do?"[86]

Feminist Approach

What Is Feminist Theology?

Generally speaking, "feminist theology" is chiefly concerned with theologizing about God from a feminist perspective, or from the standpoint of femaleness, femininity, and womanhood, such that the mere engagement with feminist theological thinking

---

84. West, "Dispensing with Metaphysics," 267.
85. West, "Dispensing with Metaphysics," 267.
86. West, "Prophetic Theology," 224.

is meant to counter patriarchy as an institution, history of ideas, and system that prevents women from theologizing from the groundness of being a woman. The meaning of doing feminist theology seeks to redefine and reconceptualize the role of women in traditional theologizing, by developing a theological understanding of femaleness, femininity, and womanhood outside of traditional, patriarchal, phallocentric definitions.

Even in setting aside the larger relationship between feminist theology and the feminist movement, and the ideological kinship arising between feminist theologizing and existentialism, there are many ways of doing feminist theology. The variants of feminist theology that exist in various methodologies cannot be fully accounted for here—even if contextualizing feminist theology within the existential framework of selfhood, otherness, difference, subjection, objectification, oppression, and marginalization, by its very nature, feminist theology embarks on an existential theology predicated on what it means to theologize about God from a feminine perspective and how a theologized God actualizes and existentializes womanhood. Because of this, aligning "feminist theology" to existential theology requires attending to more than just a modern series of intersecting themes or a postmodern network of ideas, but it necessitates a historical account of femaleness, femininity, and womanhood collected into a feminist perspective that theologizes about God. When historicizing the meaning of feminist theology to *the question of the meaning of existential theology*, theologizing about God from a woman's perspective must consider the following "existential" dimensions: women depicted by early Christianity, the roles of medieval Christian women, womanhood during the Reformation, the relationship between women and liberal theology, the theologizing of Evelyn Underhill, the dialectical feminism of Simone Beauvoir and Betty Friedan, the subalternity of Gayatri Spivak, Luce Irigaray's feminism, and the philosophical feminism of Judith Butler.

PRAISEWORTHY WOMEN IN EARLY CHRISTIAN LITERATURE

According to early Christian literature, "praiseworthy women" were depicted, most notably, in terms of their roles in the Christian family and by their roles in the Christian church. In the Christian family, "praiseworthy women" exemplified virtuosity by way of their relationships with their husbands, where their familial role was considered virtuous through how they adhered to the societal parameters of being a wife and a mother within the construct of subservience. On the other hand, rather than strictly through societal subservience, "praiseworthy women" in the Christian church were spiritually defined by the christological notion of the *"theios aner,"* such that their worthiness is judged by their aptness at manifesting divine power.

The Virtuous, Virtuousness, and Virtuosity

The idea of subservience for "praiseworthy women" in the Christian family becomes placed strictly within the dynamics between husbands and wives. By this, it is evident in early Christian literature, such as the letters of Paul, that "female subjection has meaning only in the context of marital roles [where] Paul's [writings] pertain strictly to his conception of the ideal Christian housewife behaving herself quietly and unobtrusively, yielding gracefully to her husband as head of the family."[87] In effect, then, when considering Paul's writings, what makes a woman "ideal" or, in other words, "praiseworthy," is based on how well that woman adheres to her subordinate role as wife in the husband-wife construct, which, by extension, is related in terms of God, Christ, man, and woman. Paul's "praiseworthy woman" doctrine, perhaps, is reflected in the belief that "[man] is the image and reflection of God; but woman is the reflection of man. Indeed, man was not made from woman, but woman from man. Neither was man created for the sake of woman, but woman for the sake of man."[88] Here, what Paul is suggesting is not particularly a division of class between men and women,[89] but instead the notion of a hierarchy in relation to the respective relationships between God and man, God and woman, and man and woman in Christ. This hierarchy, specifically, is with "the use of the term 'head' [personifying] the hierarchy of God, Christ, man, and woman."[90] Paul's injection of "head" comes by way of an ancient belief that the head was the center of thought, motivation, and physical coordination and, as a result, the chief governing faculty of the body—the way Paul uses this concept with the husband-wife construct supposes that "when one imposes his will upon another, or holds a position of authority over another, the second party can be thought of as subordinate to the first as 'his head.'"[91] Paul, then, describes this head-hierarchal concept in his First Epistle to the Corinthians with "Christ is the head of every man, and the husband is the head of his wife, and God is the head of Christ."[92] What can be further gleaned from this is that women were placed at the bottom of Paul's head-hierarchal concept of family, where "Paul advocates a triple subordination for women."[93]

To venture beyond Paul's head-hierarchal concept of family in his 1 Corinthians epistle, the same evidence of the subordination of women to men with "subjection" language can be found in the ideology of 1 Timothy. As a letter written in the Pauline tradition, it historically represents "some kind of tension [that] seems to have risen

---

87. Massey, *Women and the New Testament*, 100.

88. Refer to 1 Cor 11:7–9.

89. In terms of early Christian literature, "one would be hard pressed to find anything in the New Testament to suggest that women as a class are to be subject to men as a class." Massey, *Women and the New Testament*, 100.

90. Massey, *Women and the New Testament*, 101.

91. Massey, *Women and the New Testament*, 101.

92. Refer to 1 Cor 11:3.

93. Malone, *Women and Christianity*, 1:76.

which necessitated an authoritative reminder concerning the respect and reverence which a married woman owes her husband."[94] This was, then, explained with the use of "subjection," as in a woman's duty to be submissive to the authority of a man. In 1 Timothy the subjective nature of a woman's role as a submissive wife to her authority-wielding husband is approached through the utilization of the Adam and Eve story, where "[a] woman [should] learn in silence with full submission . . . or to have authority over a man; she is to keep silent. For Adam was formed first, then Eve; and Adam was not deceived, but the woman was deceived and became the transgressor."[95] What seems to be suggested, accordingly, is that not only is Eve an example of a woman that was not "praiseworthy," who did not adhere to Paul's head-hierarchal concept of the relationship between husbands and wives as they are related to God and Christ, but that Eve's inability to be subject to Adam—the notion that Eve was not virtuous—brought about the fall of mankind. Moreover, what 1 Timothy points out in the Genesis account of the fall "was not so much [an emphasis on] the deception of Eve [but] the failure on the part of Adam to exercise his authority over her in light of her apparent imperception."[96]

Passages in the Letter to the Ephesians,[97] the Letter to the Colossians,[98] and 1 Peter[99] offer other explicit examples in early Christian literature not just on the subservience of women as wives to the authority of husbands but, also, on the ideal characteristics of a virtuous woman. First, in the Letter to the Ephesians, it is apparent that the household is defined in terms of a church, or, more poignantly, as a "house-church," through the use of bridal imagery, such that, though 5:22–24 "goes on to quote Genesis about the male and female 'becoming one flesh' . . . no matter how gloriously this union is described, there is no doubt that this is not a union of equals."[100] Next, when considering both Col 3:18 and 1 Pet 3:1, this inequality is defined within a household code as "an attempt . . . to find a compromise between the Christian vision of equality and the absolute demands of a patriarchal household."[101]

94. Massey, *Women and the New Testament*, 102.

95. Refer to 1 Tim 2:11, 12b–14.

96. Massey, *Women and the New Testament*, 103.

97. Through Eph 5:22–24, saying, "Wives, be subject to your husbands as you are to the Lord. For the husband is the head of the wife just as Christ is the head of the church, the body of which he is the Savior. Just as the church is subject to Christ, so also wives ought to be, in everything, to their husbands," the concept of head-hierarchy is connected to the importance of women being "subject" or submissive.

98. Col 3:18 states, "Wives, be subject to your husbands, as is fitting in the Lord."

99. By 1 Pet 3:1 declaring, "Wives . . . accept the authority of your husbands," and later proposing, "Husbands . . . show consideration for your wives in life together, paying honor to the woman as the weaker sex," the subservience of women in relation to men is not just defined in terms of authority ordained in the head-hierarchy but through the injection of an ideology about women being the "weaker sex" and men being the "stronger sex."

100. Malone, *Women and Christianity*, 1:81.

101. Malone, *Women and Christianity*, 1:78.

The "Theios Aner"

In addition to virtue, another way that early Christian literature depicts "praiseworthy women" is with the christological *"theios aner,"* which is based on "a doctrine [coming] from Hellenism [that] strongly influenced the Hellenistic Jews of the Diaspora who later became Christians."[102] The Christian belief in *"theios aner,"* then, is distinctly aretalogical,[103] having originated in the Christian interpretation of Jesus as being "a 'divine miracle-man' demonstrating his divine character by acts of power."[104]

For those that believed in the *"theios aner,"* divine character and acts of power weren't limited to Jesus as interpreted in early Christian literature, but, instead, Christian tradition "proclaim[ed] that [because] a divine power was operative in Jesus of Nazareth [it was] consequently [evident] in those who followed him [so that] through faith in him, his admirers too acquire[d] the same power to exorcize, perform cures and so forth."[105] What this means is that, when "praiseworthy women," as admirers and followers of Jesus, had faith in Jesus as Christ, early Christian literature represented them as vehicles of divine power. This, of course, was similar to the Judaic tradition of the spirituality of women,[106] but in early Christian literature, the spirituality of women had more divine resonance, where they become more than just the spiritual influences in the Judaic home, but become spiritually-divine representations of Jesus as Christ in the Christian community.

Two examples of the *"theios aner"* in early Christian literature are in "The Gospel of Mary" of ca. 100s CE and "Acts of Paul and Thecla" of ca. 150–200 CE. "The Gospel of Mary," as supposedly authored by Mary Magdalene, dates from the second century and seeks to "convey a closeness between Mary [Magdalene] and Jesus that some of the other disciples may have found enviable."[107] This closeness, then, is perpetuated through the notion that "Christ [came] to her in a vision to impart special knowledge and honor"[108] not afforded to the disciples. More importantly, this special knowledge and honor can be construed as the embodiment of the *"theios aner"* in Mary Magdalene, by which she "claims [in the text] to have a continuing experience

---

102. Schillebeeckx, *Jesus*, 424.

103. The concept of aretalogy is a recitation of the virtues of a hero, deity, or holy man in Hellenistic literature. Refer to Liefeld, "Hellenistic 'Divine Man,'" 196.

104. Schillebeeckx, *Jesus*, 425.

105. Schillebeeckx, *Jesus*, 426.

106. Women in Judaism embodied an atoning force stronger than the traditional altar especially when they were wives within the domestic seclusion of their families. This same spiritual influence was not only within the woman as mother in the home, where rabbis considered a child a Jew only if the child's mother was a Jewess, but for the woman in relation to a man, where "if a pious man marries a wicked woman he will become wicked, but if a wicked man marries a pious woman, she will make him pious." Witherington, *Women and the Genesis of Christianity*, 6.

107. Oden, *In Her Words*, 17.

108. Oden, *In Her Words*, 17.

of Christ."[109] The potency of Mary's experience of Christ, as imparted in the text, solicits conflict from Peter and, in the end, allows for another disciple named Levi to postulate, in reference to the ineffable *"theios aner"* in Mary, "if the Saviour made her worthy, who are you to reject her."[110] The worthiness of Mary as a "praiseworthy woman" is, then, also evidenced in Thecla from the "Acts of Paul and Thecla," which was written in Greek in the latter half of the second century. In this text, as with Mary Magdalene in "The Gospel of Mary," Thecla is transformed by her experience in Christ but as it is translated through the teachings of Paul. In response to Paul's teachings of chastity as part of the role of a Christian in order to receive salvation, Thecla is "convinced to renounce her impending marriage and commit herself to a life of witness."[111] By making this choice, Thecla is condemned by her fiancé and her mother to be "burned as an example to other women who follow Paul."[112] What ensues, however, is evidence of something miraculous occurring within Thecla due to "her fierce commitment to purity and faithfulness"[113] that can only be described as the *"theios aner."* As a result, Thecla has become deified as a patron saint of the early church and Mary Magdalene, though her reputation as being likewise has been disputed throughout tradition,[114] the *"theios aner"* motif in early Christian literature represents a means of propaganda[115] to advance the New Testament church message about the recognition of women as prophetic figures.[116]

Medieval Christian Women

When considering the medieval Christianity, it must be, first, placed in context as, above all, being a significant era in history between the years of the birth of Christianity and the rise of the early church and and our modern-day church. To approach it this way means to understand that this period involved many changes and upheavals in the church, not to mention a very important transitional period that consolidated the early church from many of the splintered religious sects such as Marcionism,[117]

---

109. Oden, *In Her Words*, 17.
110. Oden, *In Her Words*, 20.
111. Oden, *In Her Words*, 21.
112. Oden, *In Her Words*, 21.
113. Oden, *In Her Words*, 21.
114. Western tradition mistakenly identifying her with the repentant sinner spoken of yet left unnamed in Luke 7:37–50. Oden, *In Her Words*, 21.
115. Liefeld, "Hellenistic 'Divine Man,'" 203.
116. Urban, *Short History of Christian Thought*, 377.
117. The name is given to the religious movement led by Marcion, who supported the separation of salvation from creation and of the church from its Old Testament heritage. This movement accelerated the early church's recognition of the New Testament canon and sharpened its emphasis on certain doctrines in the rule of faith. Ferguson and Wright, *New Dictionary of Theology*, 412.

Montanism,[118] and Gnosticism[119] into a centralized, unilateral church that developed a systematic way of approaching the Christian faith through the utilization of church practices and the relevance of tradition. Though many of these practices and traditions were controversial[120] and, subsequently, became the catalyst for the Reformation movement led by Martin Luther in 1517,[121] nevertheless, the era of medieval Christianity—the years that have come to be called the "Middle Ages"—is still a stage in the development of modern Christianity necessary for study, examination, and reflection. This is, specifically, the case with respect to the state of women during this time as representations of medieval Christian womanhood. Needless to say, then, that medieval Christian women were afforded more opportunities in the medieval church than the women of the early church. But, still, limitations and challenges remained evident. To understand this, particularly in relation to our current understandings and interpretations of the Christian faith and relative Protestantism, there are five things that every Protestant needs to know about medieval Christian women in order to not just understand the ideologies and beliefs of the period that were espoused and enacted by the medieval church before the sweeping theological reform[122] of the Reformation movement, but how those practices and traditions directly affected the medieval Christian women of the time—these five things are included under the following headings: The Monastic Life of the Nun, The Life of Women as Monastic Missionaries, A Life of Virginity, The Married Life, and Life as a Widow.

The Monastic Life of the Nun

Monasticism, in general, involved the "special and real calling of the Christian, [and] the ideals most beset for every Christian, that he free himself from the world and dedicate himself alone, in a monastic life, to God and Christ."[123] This monastic life,

---

118. The name given to a second-century movement which, along with Gnosticism, provided the early church with is greatest challenge. The movement, initially led by Montanus before falling under the control of Tertullian, was otherworldly, stressed the importance of martyrdom, and awaited the coming of the Lord. Reese, *Dictionary of Philosophy and Religion*, 367.

119. A movement committed to the increase of genuine knowledge, but also a philosophic-religious movement related to the mystery religions and directed toward personal salvation. Ferguson and Wright, *New Dictionary of Theology*, 192.

120. These include iconoclastic, filioque, predestination, and transubstantiation controversies. Ennis, *Moody Handbook of Theology*, 433–35.

121. On October 31, 1517, Martin Luther affixed to the door of the Schlosskirche at Wittenberg a set of ninety-five theses assertive of his position on such matters as penitential exercises and other "good works," with more particular reference to the doctrine of indulgences as it was being presented by Tetzel in Tetzel's preaching in Germany. MacGregor, *Dictionary of Religion and Philosophy*, 390.

122. The Protestant Reformation produced a theology that was a massive reassertion of the centrality of God, the glory of his sovereignty, and he primacy of his grace in the salvation of humanity through Jesus Christ. Ferguson and Wright, *New Dictionary of Theology*, 565.

123. Sohm, *History of Christianity*, 154.

then, was not only steeped in an engagement in continually renewed struggles to realize [one's] own spiritual ideals, [and] the ideals of Roman Catholic Christianity,[124] but included the "wish to give all [of one's] goods to the poor, and preach to all [people] the gospel of repentance and love."[125] It is precisely in this ideological framework that those committing a life to monasticism did so out of seeking a practical Christianity, which was, in effect, the monastic-ascetic that came to bear through the power of God's irresistible love.[126] Subsequently, this was the goal of monastic life: to seek God's love through adherence to a strict Christian lifestyle ordered and structured around the ultimate crucifixion of the flesh and all of its affections and lusts.[127] This monastic message spoke not just to men, but to women who sought, above all, spiritual freedom and entirely new social relationships.[128] With that, in mind, monastic life for the medieval woman was one of relative equality with that of the medieval man, specifically through their chastity and virginity, where their virginal bodies "offered to the world of the fourth century a powerful image of the advent of a new kind of woman."[129] What this new kind of woman, as a result, exemplified was an "intent on achieving a new kind of egalitarian living" that, sometimes, involved wealthy women disposing of their wealth in favor of living and practicing a more evangelical life.[130]

The Life of Women as Monastic Missionaries

Though partaking in the same brand of monastic life, the life of women as monastic missionaries had a much different monastic experience than those of the monastery or, in the case of all-women monasteries, nunneries. This experience was shaped, in part, throughout the ninth and tenth centuries by intense ecclesiastical reform.[131] Reform movements, of these kinds, were "usually greet[ed] with enthusiasm and relief as bringing only benefit to the Christian church."[132] Nevertheless, when it came to women, these reform movements were rarely a good thing and, generally, "official ecclesiastical reform tend[ed] to sweep women aside."[133] With that in mind, unfortunately, the role of women changed from the preceding centuries as reaching the highest point of partnership and shared authority[134] to roles, by the ninth century, that

---

124. Sohm, *History of Christianity*, 151.
125. Sohm, *History of Christianity*, 154.
126. Sohm, *History of Christianity*, 154.
127. Sohm, *History of Christianity*, 154.
128. Malone, *Women and Christianity*, 1:134.
129. Malone, *Women and Christianity*, 1:140.
130. Malone, *Women and Christianity*, 1:140.
131. Malone, *Women and Christianity*, 1:198.
132. Malone, *Women and Christianity*, 1:198.
133. Malone, *Women and Christianity*, 1:198.
134. Malone, *Women and Christianity*, 1:199.

drew a "deepening of the great male weariness with women's ecclesial partnership"[135] to the degree that monastic women were "reduced to virtual invisibility through the imposition of cloister."[136] Eventually, just as mid-ninth-century legislation with regard to women began to focus on the aims of separating women and men into their respective monasteries and subject all of them to Episcopal authority,[137] women perhaps rediscovered their lost monastic equality through the service of others outside of their monasteries and nunneries by embarking on travels to preach and evangelize the Christian faith to pagans.

A Life of Virginity

Rather than living monastic lives, medieval Christian women also were subject to the doctrine of virginity, which was based "on a series of formulae, some arising from the experience of the writers [of the doctrine] rather than the practitioners, and some rooted in the scriptures."[138] The idea of the virgin goes beyond the nature of women and, essentially, represents the notion of leading an angelic life.[139] In that, not only was there both astonishment and fear evident in the writing describing the phenomenon of the virgin-angel, but virgins, by extension, became "the glory of the church, the new aristocracy of faith."[140] What that meant, then, was virginity was prized, exalted, and, when women chose to practice virginity, it "raised them to the level of men [while it] helped them to attain to the transformation offered to the perfect."[141]

The Married Life

For the married woman, there was a doctrine of marriage, where women had no choice or say in whom they marred but, rather, had their marriages arranged for the benefit of both families involved, and "the young woman [was] passed from the authority of her father to the authority of her husband."[142] Not only was a woman's role in this doctrine an extrapolation of her sole reason for existence, but brought about the dominance of the male in marriage.[143] This dominance was, in effect, based on the male in the marriage having control over the wife. Due to this emphasis on control, giving in to pleasure

---

135. Malone, *Women and Christianity*, 1:199.
136. Malone, *Women and Christianity*, 1:199.
137. Malone, *Women and Christianity*, 1:218.
138. Malone, *Women and Christianity*, 1:149.
139. Malone, *Women and Christianity*, 1:149.
140. Malone, *Women and Christianity*, 1:149.
141. Malone, *Women and Christianity*, 1:150.
142. Malone, *Women and Christianity*, 1:153.
143. Malone, *Women and Christianity*, 1:153.

was suppressed with the "conscious control of sexual urges"[144] especially since the married household was the basis of the Christian community[145] as a representative structure for the Christian relationship between men and women.

Life as a Widow

If for any reason a medieval Christian woman became a widow, it was definitely not a beneficial thing, since widows were categorized as those who are completely alone and destitute and therefore deserving of assistance, those who still have families to care for them, and those who are enrolled on the church's official list of widows.[146] These categorizations were defined under the Order of Widows.[147] This doctrine with regards to the widowed Christian woman was one that clearly involved defining what she was not allowed to do.[148] Among these restrictions were that they could not teach or baptize and, without the authority of the bishop, they were not allowed to visit other houses for the purposes of eating, drinking, fasting, receiving gifts, laying on hands, or praying.[149] As a result, it suggests that widows were meant to be out of society and away from any normal societal interactions within the medieval Christian community.

Faithful Women to the Reformation

As the back cover of Amy Oden's *In Her Words: Women's Writings in the History of Christian Thought* (1994) book suggests, the overall picture of the Christian faith is one that tends to exclude the contribution of women, particularly when considering that women "have played a central—and usually—unacknowledged role in the development of Christian thought throughout history." To not include these faithful women who, as female theologians, expressed a specific perspective of the faith from a woman's point of view, is to fail to understand that the development of the Christian faith and its underlying theologies is not male-centric. To put it more aptly, the experiences of Christian men do not fully encompass what it means to be a Christian, what it means to abide by the Christian faith, and what it means to implement Christian values into a life stewarded by that Christian faith. Instead, it is a shaping, molding, creating, and defining of a Christian doctrine based on the experiences of both men and women. While the contributions of men to the faith are well known and well documented by a wide-ranging collection of male authors, the contributions of women are just as important. This is particularly the case when considering contributions of

---

144. Malone, *Women and Christianity*, 1:153.
145. Malone, *Women and Christianity*, 1:153.
146. Malone, *Women and Christianity*, 1:128.
147. Malone, *Women and Christianity*, 1:128–29.
148 Malone, *Women and Christianity*, 1:129.
149. Malone, *Women and Christianity*, 1:129.

women to the Reformation movement: in Oden's selections included in *In Her Words*, chapters 22–27 illustrates, supplements, and diverges from or perhaps disagrees with the experiences of faithful women of the Reformation.

* * *

In chapters 22–27, what Oden illustrates with six very different female writings from the period of 1500 to 1800 CE is six reactions to the Reformation in the form of confessional writing. Each of these confessional writings—to varying degrees of execution and dimensions of confession—illustrates the female authors' understanding of what it means to be a Christian woman during the Reformation. In the first selection, the poetry of Vittoria Colonna (1492–1547) "address[es] the most pressing issues of her day, secular and religious, where she illustrates, through sonnet form, the internal dialogue of someone negotiating their faith in reference to how that faith might be perceived in the world." The same can be said, therefore, about the following selection by Teresa of Ávila (1515–1582), entitled *The Interior Castle* (1577), which, as Oden notes in its introduction, is a "text [that] provides an exposition of the soul's progression toward God, through the many rooms of the castle until [the soul] reaches the very center, where union with God and full human being are found."[150] What Teresa of Avila illustrates is the way that faith transforms the soul into a seeker of truth, something that can only find solace in union with God. The "interior castle," then, is undoubtedly an illustration of searching into the innermost recesses of the soul, navigating the corridors and channels of the human heart in order to understand the fundamentality of the God-human relationship and the necessity of Christian faith as an anchor to Christian spirituality. This is similarly illustrated in the third selection from the letters of Jane Frances de Chantal (1572–1641) on spiritual devotion, which "reveal the heart of her theology and devotion."[151] Jane de Chantal's letters, as Oden notes, places at its center Jesus and illustrates the notion that Christian life revolves around Christ, where Christ becomes the embodiment of Christian knowledge. Knowledge, of course, is also illustrated in the fourth selection from Juana Inés de la Cruz (1648–1695), which "addresses the character of human knowing and the persecution often attendant upon those seeking knowledge."[152] What follows, then, in the fifth selection, from Madame Jeanne Guyon (1648–1717), is a further extrapolation of knowledge and, specifically, thought, with an illustration of "[Guyon's] basic notions about the nature of the human soul and the avenues, differentiated in details, through which God leads it."[153] Finally, in the last selection of the Reformation section, the letters and writings of Susanna

---

150. Oden, *In Her Words*, 223–24.
151. Oden, *In Her Words*, 231.
152. Oden, *In Her Words*, 240.
153. Oden, *In Her Words*, 245–46.

Wesley "demonstrate Wesley's own theological insights on the nature of human being, predestination, the nature of God, and salvation."[154]

* * *

Each of the writings selected by Oden for the Reformation section of *In Her Words*, essentially, serve as supplements to what might be considered as the canonized writings of Christian faith, Christian thought, and Christian theology. These canonized writings are not just customarily those written by men enacting an explanation of what it means to be a Christian man during the Reformation but, more importantly, are a collection of writings that are deemed as the best scholarly and theological articulations of the Reformed movement. It is, in a way, analogous to the canonization of the Bible, where only certain voices—in this case, strictly male voices—are considered the most accurate embodiment of the Christian experience, the most profound illustration of the Christian faith, and the most noteworthy theologizing of Christianity. The selections that Oden offers in her Reformation section are examples of apocryphal writings that, unlike the extra-canonical texts of the Bible, do not present anything particularly gnostic. In other words, the premises, concepts, and ideas brought forth by the six Christian women through their different writings are meant to extend the Christian conversation of its day rather than oppose it, replace it, and subjugate it. They are, in effect, interjecting the feelings, sentiments, and reactions of faithful Christian women to the same doctrinal reforms that their male counterparts addressed in their own writings. What becomes different here, other than these writings strictly being authored by Christian women, is that they suggest that women did have a more active role in the development of the Reformed church. In this, then, they provide a supplement to what little is known about Christian women of the Reformation period, while they also become a supplement to the theological arguments already being made about controversial subjects in the church.

* * *

What Oden's selections specifically diverge from or perhaps disagree with is the stereotypical representations of women and their roles in the Reformation movement. Particularly, what Oden's selections are is an affront to the "traditional understandings of subordination of women and their confinement to the private sphere."[155] Each of the Christian female writers that Oden selects for her Reformation section are female theologians in their own rights, where they respectively show that women were just as engaged in the Reformation movement as their male counterparts. Frankly speaking, then, they were thinkers that contemplated the ramifications of the Christian faith,

---

154. Oden, *In Her Words*, 251.
155. Malone, *Women and Christianity*, 3:8.

and wrestled with articulating the very theological issues that made the Reformation movement such a revolutionary reinterpretation of the faith. Like the faithful men of the Reformed Church, these Christian women thinkers were involved in the intellectual discourse of the time, steeped in the process of redefining what it means to be a Christian, and plugged into the reconstitution of the roles of the Bible, tradition, and the church. Not only do Oden's selections "demonstrate that Christian women were continuing to create new opportunities for themselves despite all the continuing prescriptions on their lives,"[156] but they exemplify the notion that Christian women wanted to have active roles in the Reformation movement. Rather than accepting the status quo and being relegated to relative obscurity and subordination, the faithful Christian women whose writings Oden selects are among those that wanted to be respected as Christian thinkers and theologians instead of strictly women—what they wanted was to be put on an equal social footing with their male counterparts with the hopes, perhaps, that all the sweeping changes being made in the church would directly result in their having a greater, more public role in the Reformed church. This is precisely in disagreement with how the average Reformation-era woman is depicted—this depiction being one of subtraction from the Reformation movement on the whole. In the writings of chapters 22–27, Oden not only presents seven composites of faithful Reformation-era women searching for themselves by way of their faiths, but, more importantly, provides an avenue for seven female Christian theologians to express their preoccupations with understanding the complexities of the Christian faith.

Women and Liberal Theology

Pietism, enlightenment, liberal theologies, and alternatives to liberalism, as the four chief terms that have been highlighted in this course, provide a means to sketch large movements of changing conceptions of "what is Christianity" from the eighteenth century forward. Nevertheless, women were influential in and influenced by one of these movements in particular: liberal theologies. In other words, liberalism, which developed from "an outlook [that served the purpose of being] favorable to all [by way of] foster[ing] freedom of the human spirit,"[157] influenced the ways in which women viewed themselves and their roles in society at large. Since, in this respect, liberalism "arose as a result of the rationalism and experimentalism of the philosophers and scientists,"[158] women living in the post-eighteenth century sought to use rationalism to question some of the assumptions, opinions, and beliefs about women by men and bring a change to some of the traditional understandings of women in relation to men.

What women did, during this period, by applying liberalism to theology, was seek to allow "an openness [in] culture, a willingness to adapt theological expression to

---

156. Malone, *Women and Christianity*, 3:8.
157. MacGregor, *Dictionary of Religion and Philosophy*, 384.
158. Ennis, *Moody Handbook of Theology*, 349.

cultural norms, and [a]continuing flexibility in interpreting the sacred texts and practices of its tradition."[159] In effect, particularly when considering the role the Bible played in everyday religious life, under the banner of liberal Protestantism,[160] women ascribed to the "view of the Bible as [being] a fallible human record of religious thought and experience rather than divine revelation of truth and reality."[161]

This kind of fallibility, here, from women's standpoint, became extrapolated through the feminist movement's issue with the subjection of women to men. An influential early feminist, Elizabeth Cady Stanton (1815–1902), in this regard, according to Mary Malone, "set out to discover what exactly the Bible said about the subjection of women beyond the readily accepted belief that all anti-women texts were the results of male intransigence."[162] What Cady Stanton discovered was that "the Bible itself was androcentric [whereby it was] written wholly from a male perspective and, having been officially interpreted for centuries only by men . . . [became] a political tool in the hands of male churchmen to impose their will."[163] Hence, Cady Stanton reasoned that the Bible was essentially a "man-made book"[164] and the means with which men interpreted the scriptures and used those scriptures to subordinate women could not be blamed on God.

From here, issues with subjection extended, then, to the abolition movement, where abolitionists such as Sarah Grimké (1792–1873) were involved in "emphasizing the totally destructive aspects of slavery for all [since] it corrupted the owners, the slaves and the whole society and was utterly inconsistent with the moral responsibility of Christians."[165] In relation to the "obedience and hardship suffered cheerfully by slaves [as something that] would aid [in] their salvation, both Sarah and [her sister] Angelina despised such arguments, and replied that moral responsibilities entailed moral rights."[166] It was in thinking about moral rights and how those rights should be incorporated into the Christian life that Grimke found "connections between the slavery of slaves and the slavery of women,"[167] and published *Equality of the Sexes* (1838) to examine the subject more in full, in order to teach women strategies that would be necessary to end women's oppression.

159. Musser and Price, *New Handbook of Christian Theology*, 285.

160. Liberal Protestantism is characterized by the following: an eagerness to discard old orthodox forms if they were judged to be irrational in the light of modern knowledge or irrelevant to what was regarded as the central core of religious experience, a confidence in the power of humanity's reason when guided by experience, a belief in freedom, and a belief in the social nature of human existence. Harvey, *Handbook of Theological Terms*, 144.

161. Ferguson and Wright, *New Dictionary of Theology*, 385.

162. Malone, *Women and Christianity*, 3:216.

163. Malone, *Women and Christianity*, 3:216.

164. Malone, *Women and Christianity*, 3:216.

165. Malone, *Women and Christianity*, 3:210.

166. Malone, *Women and Christianity*, 3:210.

167. Malone, *Women and Christianity*, 3:210.

The notion of women's oppression, therefore, brought about a different kind of feminist movement by Maude Petre (1863–1942). As Malone notes, "it would be difficult to call [Petre] a feminist [since] she wrote against the 'suffragettes' and accused them of trying to be men."[168] Still, what makes Petre an influential figure in the feminist movement was that she wrote about "real feminism," which "had more to do with the acceptance of femininity as the defining characteristic of all women."[169] Because of this, Petre was mostly interested in the private sphere rather than the public sphere. What Petre was concerned with was "look[ing] on women as having a 'humanizing' influence on men and thought that, if women had to work outside the home, they should bring these feminine gifts to humanize the workplace."[170]

As a part of this feminist movement, it is important to consider, also, the contributions made by women in the history of Christian thought. In *In Her Words*, Oden outlines in the book's section 4 the theological work of female theologians such as Ann Lee (1736–1784) with Quakerism,[171] Jarena Lee (1783–1864) as the first female preacher in the African Methodist Episcopal Church,[172] Phoebe Palmer (1807–1874) founding the Five Points Mission in the slums of New York in 1850,[173] and Lucretia Mott (1793–1880) serving as president of the American Equal Rights Association from 1866 to 1868.[174]

Theologizing without Calling It Theology: Evelyn Underhill

Based on the preface to *Life of the Spirit and the Life of Today* (1922), what Evelyn Underhill (1875–1941) is chiefly concerned with, admittedly in the author's own words, is "indicating first the characteristic experiences which justify or are fundamental to the spiritual life, and the way in which these experiences may be accommodated to the world view of the modern man [then] the nature of that spiritual life as it appears in human history."[175] But, the work is operating on larger, philosophical themes, where it can be considered as working from the center toward the edges. In other words, what becomes more at play in the work is Underhill's examination of the "normal life of the Spirit,"[176] as being presumably at the ideological—albeit, theological, to put it more aptly—core of religious or spiritual existence. It is from the centralizing of existence, as it is pitted in the human soul, that all other things that

---

168. Malone, *Women and Christianity*, 3:224.
169. Malone, *Women and Christianity*, 3:224.
170. Malone, *Women and Christianity*, 3:224.
171. Oden, *In Her Words*, 267.
172. Oden, *In Her Words*, 276.
173. Oden, *In Her Words*, 282.
174. Oden, *In Her Words*, 292.
175. Underhill, *Life of the Spirit*, viii–ix.
176. Underhill, *Life of the Spirit*, viii.

harbor along the periphery can be objectified through purposeful objectification.[177] If the argument that Underhill hopes to make about spiritual existence is construed through "describ[ing] the character and [the] meaning of life in the ordinary terms of present day thought,"[178] then it can be surmised that she is, in actuality, utilizing a distinctly existential language. In effect, by appropriating terms such as "character" and "the meaning of life," it becomes evident that Underhill is injecting the concept of subject-object relationship—the existential notion that subjects define themselves through the ways and manners by which they interact, understand, and perceive their objective reality,[179] or life. This life, as Underhill argues in chapter 1, is best perceived without its history, since "that history will only be valuable to us in so far as we keep tight hold on its direct connection with the present, its immediate bearing on our own lives."[180] What can be gleaned from this, then, is that when a life is defined as a spiritual life it should only be concerned with communicating with its most readily accessible sense of reality. Underhill refers to this as living Reality.[181] Furthermore, in order to ascertain that what it experienced from this reality is "as real within its own system of reference as anything else," what is being approached is a version of the truth. This is more than just the truth, but, as Underhill would agree, it is an existential Truth, something that tries to reconcile with "our inevitably limited way of laying hold on the stuff of existence."[182] In light of this claim that Underhill makes, if taking Underhill's aforementioned proposition about "character" and "the meaning of life" at their most implicit philosophical posturing, then the possibility of existing in a "living Reality" is constructed around defining spiritual existence in two epistemic veins: consciousness and knowledge. Both, as Underhill would undoubtedly argue, "allow for man's communion with an independent objective Reality."[183] To, therefore, appropriate consciousness and knowledge as epistemic veins for the sake of arguing for spiritual existence, Underhill is assuming that the Life of the Spirit takes on both an existential phenomenological[184] stance as well as an existential epistemological[185] perspective. This is precisely where Underhill evokes the "life of Spirit" that makes it

---

177. By this, I am referring to the human subject's ability to understand that something other than itself is an object through projecting, or objectifying the object's status from the subject's point of reference.

178. Underhill, *Life of the Spirit*, viii.

179. This refers to a reality in which a subject lives, or a reality that exists in an objectified manner beyond the understood or perceived existence of the subject.

180. Underhill, *Life of the Spirit*, 1.

181. Underhill, *Life of the Spirit*, 3.

182. Underhill, *Life of the Spirit*, 4.

183. Underhill, *Life of the Spirit*, 6.

184. What I am referring to is defining existence, or the concept of being, through a self that is centered strictly in a conscious awareness of the world.

185. Here, I am defining existence, or the concept of being by way of the acquisition and utilization of knowledge as it is found in the world.

possible for "beauty and fragrance [to] surround us."[186] To push Underhill's argument here just a bit further and extrapolate what she is unquestionably pursuing is this: while beauty is only understood epistemologically in terms of what it is and what it is not, fragrance, on other hand, interacts with certain phenomenological processes to the point that it might manifest into a consciousness-specific awareness of something greater than the physical. In this respect, when "beauty and fragrance surround us," spiritual existence, as the Life of the Spirit, is always connected to what it perceived as life through what Underhill postulates as "an experience [that] is more real and concrete, [and] therefore more important, than any of the systems by which theology seeks to explain it."[187] It is, perhaps, from this that Underhill advances her argument in an unknowingly theological fashion even though she does so through an attempt at representing an anti-theological view. More specifically, Underhill's concept of the Life of the Spirit is a theology, even if such a theology is christened as "an experience." Here, though Underhill seems unaware, she is representing a system of thinking about spiritual existence, where, for it to be "real and concrete," it must be explained systematically. She does this, of course, as she proceeds throughout the remainder of the book, going from "The Character of Spiritual Life" to "History and the Life of the Spirit" to the two parts entitled "Psychology and the Life of the Spirit" and so on, where she defines the Life of the Spirit in the contexts of the individual, education, and social order. Each of these aforementioned sections systematically examines the Life of the Spirit in what can only be described as Underhill's theology of spiritual existence, even if how she believes she is not theologizing it.

From Beauvoir to Friedan: The Problem of Dialectics

Here, I will look at Betty Friedan's *The Feminine Mystique* (1963), in order to shed more light on what I believe to be the limitations and problems inherent in the second-wave feminism movement. Friedan's *The Feminine Mystique* arises out of "a response" to Simone de Beauvoir's *The Second Sex* (1949) with the purposeful intent of "fill[ing] in the ideological gaps left behind by De Beauvoir." I still believe this to be true. To that end, I referred to these gaps as being "related to the framework of womanhood's existence in reference to men"—the fact that, as I wrote in that response paper, "everything a woman is and everything femininity can be is linked to teasing out that definition from the definition of a man or masculinity." I still maintain that this is the case, if comparing Beauvoir to Friedan. In my view, both Beauvoir and Friedan's response to Beauvoir fail to escape the need to define women in reference to how they define men.

More specifically, I find this to be the most important issue with connecting Beauvoir to Friedan and, in the end, connecting their respective ideologies to the

---

186. Underhill, *Life of the Spirit*, 24.
187. Underhill, *Life of the Spirit*, 6.

second-wave feminist movement as influential texts of that movement.[188] I am referring to what I would call the Beauvoir-Friedan dialectical problem. This is the problem that neither seems to deal with in either text and, thusly, becomes, perhaps, "the problem with no name" that Friedan invokes. With respect to the conclusion I made in my previous response paper, I will continue to argue it in this paper. That is, Friedan extends Beauvoir's idea of woman-ness as "the Other" to the point that, within the man-woman dialectic, there is no real solution to how women can transcend "The Other" distinction. In other words, by suggesting that womanhood is always linked to manhood, wives to husbands, mothers to children, and so forth, the dialectical problem inherent in this undermines the purposes and goals of the second-wave feminism movement, which I would argue is about "being for self." In fact, it is a conundrum. As I have previously mentioned in my response paper, it is the "conundrum of dialectics." How is it possible to define "being for self" without defining that definition, first, in relation to "being for others"?[189] This is because "being for self" is inextricably linked with Martin Heidegger's concept of "being-in-the-world."[190] It is based on the Heideggerian notion that the world is made up of selves and others, those that embody either sameness or otherness. I believe that this "sameness" is what the second-wave movement equates to maleness, while "otherness" is femaleness.

The "Other" and "Otherness" as Femaleness

To flesh this out just a bit more, I assert that sameness-otherness as maleness-femaleness is manifested from normative values, where maleness has a "sameness" with what can be considered "the norm." From this, femaleness has an "otherness" quality to it. This is so, particularly under the ideology of the second-wave movement which contends, if I may paraphrase, that men control everything and our society and culture is so male-centric and male dominated that women are pushed to the periphery and become, therefore, an "Other." It is possible to since, if we may apply something particularly relevant from Plato in *The Sophist*, men do affect the "being" of women by imposing power over them.[191] However, to say that men impose power over women

---

188. I would go so far as to say that Simone de Beauvoir's *The Second Sex* and Betty Friedan's *The Feminine Mystique* are more than just influential texts of the movement—they are, I contend, the two founding documents of the movement.

189. The terms "being for self" and "being for others" is Hegelian in the fields of phenomenology, but also Heideggerian in the existentialism.

190. Haim Gordon defines Martin Heidegger's "being-in-the-world" in the following way: "The immersed character of human existence insofar as it relates to being, in opening up the clearing in which beings can be encountered in meaningful relations." Gordon outlines "being-in-the-world" into the following three constituent elements: (1) in the world, (2) the being that is in the way of being-in-the-world, and (3) being-in as such. For Heidegger, "dasein," which is the German word for existence, is the being that is in-the-world. Gordon, *Dictionary of Existentialism*, 37; 100.

191. In the *Sophist* dialogue, Plato explains "being" as anything which possesses any sort of power to affect another, or to be affected by another, if only for a single moment, however trifling the cause

means to suggest a link between the two, confirming a dialectical construction. In such a construction, women become "the Other" and, through what Jacques Derrida calls "différance," become deferred to a position of inferiority based on certain tangible and verifiable differences.[192] These differences are what the second-wave feminist movement are most concerned with, since these differences culminate in and are indicative of womanhood's "Otherness."

I would argue that transcending that "Otherness" is the purpose and goal of the second-wave feminism movement so women and womanhood can be standalone, self-identifiable entities similar to a Kantian "thing-in-itself."[193] I do, of course, believe that, while Beauvoir makes a good first step in identifying this reality as "the situation,"[194] Friedan also does a good job in meaningfully articulating Beauvoir's "situation" as "the problem with no name." Though Friedan does articulate what I believe to be the problem of "Otherness" and the man-woman dialectic by arguing, "I want something more than my husband and my children and my home,"[195] I still feel that Friedan falls into the same semantic traps that Beauvoir has fallen into. By saying that she "want[s] something more than my husband and my children and my home," Friedan is unwittingly playing a dialectic game of self-identification through identification. What I mean is that Friedan is self-identifying herself as a wife, a mother, and a homemaker, which can only be identified in reference to a husband, children, and a home. In other words, it is safe to say that a woman cannot have a husband without first being a wife of that husband, and a woman cannot have children without first being a mother to those children, and so on. The point here is that, in order to truly "want something more," there must be a way to look beyond the dialectical construct of what is already there. This, in fact, is an impossible task. Not only is it impossible in terms of dialectics, but impossible existentially, since, as Heidegger suggests, human existence is about "being-there."[196] In effect, to exist as a woman who is a wife, a mother,

---

and however slight the effect. To that end, it has real existence. The definition of being, then, is simply power. Hamilton and Cairns, *Collected Dialogues of Plato*, 957–1017.

192 For Derrida, différance as the following: "The différance of the other, the other as differed from the sensible, as sensible differed; the concept as differed-differing intuition, the life as differed-differing matter, mind as differed-differing life, culture as differed-differing nature." Derrida, *Of Grammatology*, xxix.

193. To say that something is a "thing-in-itself" supposes, as Immanuel Kant describes, that it is something that is "completely determined." This means, of course, that what we see is literally what we see, and that "what is seen" is nothing more than a universal set of elements that can "be seen" by all. I think this is important for womanhood as it is argued for in the second-wave feminist movement, since, I would contend, that the "they" of the movement want to have their femaleness be considered as a "thing-in-itself" rather than just something that is related and reverent to maleness. Kant, *Critique of Pure Reason*, 490.

194. I contend that what Simone de Beauvoir calls "the situation" is the existential situation. This arises, obviously, from existential philosophy. But, more importantly, is something that she picks up from her relationship with Jean-Paul Sartre during the composition of *The Second Sex*.

195. Friedan, *Feminine Mystique*, 78.

196. "Being-there" is the English translation of Heidegger's "Dasein." Heidegger refers to "dasein"

and a homemaker means to exist in a "being-there" that is among all those elements of life. There is a multiplicity of immanent events that occur between a woman and those elements of life. For Gilles Deleuze, each immanent event is a correlation between a lived experience and the actualization of a state of things.[197]

The Problem That Does Have a Name

Let me address the nature of the problem in the following manner: once a woman is a wife, she remains a wife. Even if she gets divorced, she is still referenced as an ex-wife. And, once a woman has children, she remains a mother, even if those children were to suffer untimely deaths. In a way, this stands to suggest, I would argue, that dialectics are inescapable constructs once they have been constructed. These inescapable constructs link women to roles and those roles attribute to facts of their existence. Despite what some third-wave feminists might want to believe, a woman cannot kill her husband and children as a way of escaping the reality that that husband and those children once existed. Having a husband, having some children, and being a homemaker are all, as Ludwig Wittgenstein proposes, facts that, in their totality, present the notion that the world is encased by the totality of those facts.[198]

To take this point just a bit further, with the hope that I am not taking myself too far afield, when third-wave feminists assert that, in killing all men and chopping off all men's penises, they intend to regain some lost sense of humanity, they fail to realize that being a woman is a facticity of femaleness. There is, if I may, a facticity in gender. It is impossible to consider femaleness and womanhood without denoting the obvious fact that there must be a facticity of maleness. This is so, too, when looking at this thing from the other way around: maleness is not maleness without being related to femaleness. So, to a certain extent, even though third-wave feminists—who, I believe, are to second-wave feminists in much the same manner as the Republican Party is to the Tea Party—believe that killing all men and chopping off those dead men's penises somehow empowers them, they are wrong. There is no empowerment in such a thing: there is only a kind of futile barbarism. Women are still women and men are still men, even if murderous women stand over the bodies of murdered and mutilated male corpses. This is because there is no possibility in changing gender, or assuming a neutered state, if that is what the third-wave feminists hope to achieve by committing what they believe to be empowering acts of "being for self."

---

as human existence. Heidegger uses this term when explaining how a being uses existence to establish selfhood. For Heidegger, this occurs only when the basic structures of human existence, or what he calls "Dasein," has been adequately worked out with explicit orientation toward the problem of "being" itself. Heidegger, *Being and Time*, 37.

197. Deleuze, *Pure Immanence*, 31.
198. Wittgenstein, *Tractatus Logico-Philosophicus*, 29.

Though I do not pretend to know the logic that fuels third-wave feminist thought, I do not intend to psychoanalyze them, either. I only invoke them to make a point, and that is the following: I believe, however, that their ideology does not solve the problem, if, in fact, they were created as counterculture against the second-wavers. In my view, such ideology is only infused with hate and insanity, and extremely counterproductive. Not only does it do little to transform the second-wave feminist movement and develop a more militant agenda, but it fails to confront or truly handle the problem: the problem that arises from certain undeniable facts. If anything can be considered, it is that the third-wavers are just as aware of the problem of dialectics as the second-wavers are—hence, the reason why the third-wavers believe that women can find some kind of satisfaction or self-actualization in killing men and chopping of men's penises.

As I have previously mentioned, if following Wittgenstein's quite poignant supposition, the world is "a totality of facts." That is, these facts make life a "life." That life is one capable of immanence, where an existing entity that realizes that they exist and understand that state of things and of their lived experience.[199] That life begins with the facticity of existence. From there, setting aside the facticity of race for the sake of argument, there is the facticity of maleness and the facticity of femaleness. These two facts are indelible once they manifest themselves in the world. What is also an indelible fact is the need for femaleness and maleness to procreate and organize families, and how such organizations are generally deemed authorized and normative if they occur within the context of marriage. At that point, there are certain notions of what a family should be and what criteria can be used to define marriage as a "real marriage." Then, there are notions of what it means to be a parent and how a parent should treat their children. In saying all of this, I am not attempting to take sides in the marriage debate of today. I only mean to show that there are facts of life that are inescapable.

So, what I argue is that the second-wave feminist movement cannot escape the following facts: the facticity of maleness, the facticity of marriage, and the facticity of motherhood. I am referring to these facts as Friedan presents them in *The Feminine Mystique*, the notion that it is possible to "want something more than my husband and my children and my home" once those dialectics have already been established. It is not, in actuality. Of course, I do concede the fact that some women never get married, never have children, and never become homemakers. Also, there are women that do have children, but do not get married to the man with whom they have had a child. In addition, there are women that do get married, but never have children. But, when I consider not getting married and not having children, I am very much aware that there are women that are very capable of defining their selfhoods without marriage, without children, and without the need to keep house and spend the day baking cookies like June Cleaver.

---

199. Deleuze, *Pure Immanence*, 31.

But, my problem with Friedan's dialectical ideology is that it is built on a relatively archaic, neoconservative foundation, something apparent in the fact that *The Feminine Mystique* was published in 1963. To put it more frankly: that *The Feminine Mystique* was produced at a time in America when there were still a great many June Cleavers, and plenty of households where respective Ward Cleavers were the sole breadwinners, and many instances where those representative June Cleavers constructed their entire sense of selves on keeping up with what their Ward Cleavers were doing at work and what recurring shenanigans their Theodores and Wallys were getting into. In such a world that remains, now, in black-and-white in rerun syndication, women were not "being for self," they were, rather, "being for others."

Not only do I find that Friedan is basically espousing a way of life that has become unmistakably antiquated, but, in a sense, has injected such antiquated notions of femaleness, womanhood, and what it means to be a woman into the second-wave feminist movement at large. Even though Friedan rightly conceives of "want[ing] more," I would argue that she is still connecting gender to normative values and socioeconomic hierarchical structures. I do contend that "want[ing] more" does denote that she believes that there should be a selfhood for women that transcends the "otherness" with which they exist in a male-centric and male-dominated society that places normative value in patriarchy. And, even though she is very much aware of "the problem"—one that I would assert is existential in nature—suggesting that "the problem has no name," I believe that the problem is dialectical, and has the task of doing feminism in the second-wave feminist movement immensely difficult.

In my view, I consider the dialectical problems that Beauvoir and Friedan have injected into the ideology of the second-wave feminist movement occur on three essential fronts: woman-man, wife-husband, and mother-child.

Woman-Man and the Kantian Dialectic

First, I would like to consider the woman-man dialectic, which is not just based on a biological difference, as Beauvoir notes, but is a Kantian dialectic between antithesis and thesis. For all practical purposes, since I am discussing this from a feminist point of view, a woman is the "thesis" and a man is the "antithesis." In this regard, being a woman is one representation and being a man is another representation. To consider what it means to be a woman alongside what it means to be a man, the Kantian dialectic, as Immanuel Kant describes, "is the act of putting together different representations, and of grasping what is manifold in them in one act of knowledge."[200] I take Kant to mean that, if I am putting together what it means to be a woman with what it means to be a man—the concept of a woman and that of a man—which are two very different representations, I am doing so dialectically, in order to discover

---

200. Kant, *Critique of Pure Reason*, 111.

something from their combination. This combination has epistemological value inherent in it. I would argue that, within the woman-man dialectic, a woman better understand what she is by understanding what she is not. In effect, the knowledge a woman gains is not just that she is a woman, but that she is not a man. Though Kant would admit that this kind of knowledge is "crude and confused,"[201] what is gathered are "the elements knowledge [where the process of synthesis] unites them to form a certain content."[202] The content, I would argue, is, from the point of view of a woman, being a woman is "this" and being a man is "that."

When a woman understands she is a woman and, by extension, understands that a man is not a woman, a woman develops the facticity of femaleness. Such a facticity cannot be negated or refuted once it is so. It is constituted, of course, in the facticity of gender—this means coming to the realization that there are two possible genders and a human person can only be one.[203] It is by way of this facticity being so, a woman must reconcile with the fact that she can no more be a man than a man can be a woman. I do not mean to become repetitive here, but I hope this allows me to set the stage for a particular point I want to make with regards to how the facticity of femaleness, and the degree to which the facticity of femaleness functions in society. That point is this: second-wave feminists fail to effectively confront the problem of the facticity of femaleness and how that facticity functions in society. In my view, their failure is in laying blame on men and the plight of their existential situation as women, rather than confronting the fact that society is male-dominated and male-centric. That is, I would argue that the second-wave feminists seek equality with men, which is based too much on referencing that equality in relation to men. They believe that women should have the same opportunities as men: the same income, the same ability to work in comparable fields, and the same opportunities at advancement—I feel that seeking equality in this manner only promotes and perpetuates the woman-man dialectic, rather than truly getting to the heart of the problem as it exists in society. What I mean to say is this: the power structure within the male-dominated society must be changed first before true "equality" can be attained.

Wife-Husband and the Hegelian Dialectic

Next, I would like to discuss the wife-husband dialectic and how such a dialectic is Hegelian in nature, instead of Kantian. I do admit, however, that it is possible to conceive the wife-husband dialectic as Kantian, but I think a much better way

---

201. Kant, *Critique of Pure Reason*, 111.

202. Kant, *Critique of Pure Reason*, 111.

203. Of course, I would like to note two things: (1) the possibility of persons being born with both forms of genitalia and, therefore, having gender confusion, and (2) the possibility of persons feeling that they have been born in the wrong body and with the wrong gender, and seek gender reassignment surgery.

to conceptualize the problems that feminism faces is through the Hegelian model. Now, that I have said that, I will say this to further that point: Hegel contends that "the relationship of husband and wife is in the first place the one in which one consciousness immediately recognizes itself in another."[204] When Hegel invokes the term "consciousness," he is speaking of self-consciousness—the possibility of being conscious of another and self-conscious of oneself. What arises from self-consciousness, as Hegel goes on to propose, is a kind of "knowledge of this mutual recognition."[205] In my view this "mutual recognition" not just best describes a man knowing he is a man and knowing that a woman is a woman, but also describes a husband knowing he is a husband and knowing that his wife is his wife. More importantly, it is about a woman recognizing she is a woman and a wife. In a sense, it is about a woman knowing that she cannot be a husband.[206] The "knowledge," in turn, that comes from this kind of recognition, particularly on the part of the woman in the dialectic, is steeped in the existential nature of her inferior position.[207] Here, Derrida would label this "recognition" as "différance," understanding that differences defer. Since I have already mentioned this earlier in this paper, I will only offer this nuance: when a woman recognizes the differences between herself and another (a man, in this case), she immediately grasps the epistemological value of being deferred to a position of inferiority within the two-person family construct of marriage.

I would argue, then, that second-wave feminists fail to consider the wife-husband dialectic in any meaningful way, particularly with respect to the traditional marriage construct. I do not feel this is all Friedan's fault, even if Friedan falls into the trap, as I have mentioned, of defining herself as a wife. But, I do believe that being a wife is a traditionalized role that is meant to conform to normative values of the facticity of marriage. What I mean to say is that when women call themselves a wife, they do so implicitly addressing the existence of a husband and, furthermore, explicitly wearing a wedding ring that advertises the facticity of marriage. This links them to the man as husband. So, when the second-wavers call for equality in society, they do so without truly taking into account the relative inequality within marriages. There are many examples I can give, but I will give only one, since I believe it is immensely helpful in illustrating my point: when women marry men, they take their husband's last name. I am not trying to advocate that women need not carry their husband's last name any more than I am suggesting that women not marry at all. What I am asserting, however, is that the facticity of marriage holds with it too many traditionalized elements, all of which have been carried forward from Friedan's *The Feminine Mystique* of the 1960s and, by

---

204. Hegel, *Phenomenology of Spirit*, 273.
205. Hegel, *Phenomenology of Spirit*, 273.
206. I would like, of course, to allow for the possibility that, in same-sex marriages between women, there is no traditional role of husband.
207. Hegel mentions this in another very important dialectic: the lordship-bondsman. Or, to use more contemporary terminology: the master and the slave. Hegel, *Phenomenology of Spirit*, 111–19.

correlation, from Beauvoir's *The Second Sex* in a Europe only four years removed from the end of World War II. Among these elements is the old-fashioned belief that women need husbands, and women need to be wives, and women need to have marriages in order to bring "legitimate" children into the world.

Mother-Child and the Marxist Dialectic

This leads me directly into examining the third dialectic that I would like to submit is a particularly challenging dialectic that feminists have to consider if they want to truly implement change through the feminism movement. The third dialectic structure I want to mention is the mother-child, which I would argue is Marxist in nature. I say this to mean that, when women have children, those children are commodities, and are, as Marx suggests of a commodity, "an object outside us, a thing that by its properties satisfies human wants of some sort or another."[208] In this regard, becoming a mother "satisf[ies] human wants," since the ability to procreate is something that is arguably important to most women. The ability to become pregnant, I would contend, is also another kind of commodity. Motherhood, for women, is something that validates their sense of being female and what it means to be a woman—the idea of becoming pregnant, in general, can be viewed as a self-actualizing event, since motherhood has an inherent monetary-like value[209] that allows women to engage in a kind of capitalist marketplace that men cannot. Such an engagement is a dialectical materialism, where there is an exchange of goods for services rendered. I know this sounds a bit unrefined when discussing the nature of motherhood, but I will maintain it in the following way: when women give birth to children, they become bestowed with the commodity of motherhood and, in turn, their children are bestowed with a mother to nurture them through the various crucial stages of human developmental actualization.

I believe that the second-wave feminists, and especially the third-wavers, fail to realize that motherhood is a divine gift. I do not mean to go on too long of a theological tangent here, but motherhood is inextricably linked to what it means to be a woman. Frankly speaking, men cannot become pregnant nor go through childbirth. There is an inequality in this, of course. But, more importantly, in my view, feminists tend to either extremely play down this facticity of motherhood or frequently make reference to it. Regardless of the extreme, when feminists seek equality, they should never use the facticity of motherhood in their arguments.

---

208. This is from Marx's *Capital*, vol. 1. See Tucker, *Marx-Engels Reader*, 303.
209. Marx refers to this as an exchange value. See Tucker, *Marx-Engels Reader*, 312.

GAYATRI SPIVAK'S SUBALTERNITY, THE SUBALTERN, AND POST-COLONIALITY

In the version of "Can the Subaltern Speak? Speculations on Widow Sacrifice" (1988), as it is included in *Critical Theory* (2012), Gayatri Spivak begins by asserting an inextricable relationship between learning and speaking—not only does the former inform the latter, but the latter validates the former, particularly with respect to how the "subaltern" exists as being-in-the-world. To be a "subaltern" means, I would argue, recognizing a stratification of being-in-the-world—if I may use Heidegger's terminology again—while conceptualizing that this stratification attempts to confine what being is and what being can be, through the situatedness of power and the purposeful separation of the powerful from the powerless.

For Spivak, the "subaltern" is someone in a position of powerlessness—it is a mode of being that is regulated by the ideology of a specific power structure. This positionality, then, places the "subaltern" at the margins of a given ideological state apparatus (in an Althusserian way), but also represses the extent to which the subaltern's "subalternity" can reach psychologically beyond a Hegelian lordship-bondsman dynamic. In one sense, when placing *the subaltern* at the margins, any ability to speak is quite literally pushed away from where power resides. That distance, therefore, represses what *the subaltern* is capable of learning, since any learning accomplished at the margins is a kind of learning contaminated by a psychoanalytic point of view rooted in powerlessness. Learning—not just in terms of the fundamental capacity or possibility to learn, but what can be meaningfully learned at all—becomes the means by which *the subaltern* conceives of, grasps, and "speaks to" their *subalternity*. I use this term to denote two things about *the subaltern*: the limitations that are placed upon positionality in a state apparatus, on one hand, and, on the other, the ramifications that this positionality becomes as a repressive ideology.

Taken together, these limitations and ramifications embody *subalternity*, and connects it to Spivak's understanding of the relationship between learning and speaking. Spivak assesses this relationship—and what can be referred to as *subalternity*—in the following way:

> In seeking to learn to speak to (rather than listen to or speak of) the historically muted subject of the non-elite ("subaltern") woman in the imperialist theater, the post-colonial intellectual *systematically* "unlearns" her privilege.[210]

In beginning here, Spivak makes a clear distinction between "speak to" and the lesser derivatives of "listen to" and "speak of." What makes the latter two "lesser" is related to the functionality of *subalternity*—when engaging in "listen[ing] to" and "speak[ing] of," the positionality and repressiveness of *subalternity* is perpetuated and sustained. In other words, when *the subaltern* "listen[s] to" and "speak[s] of," a physical and psychological distancing occurs. Consequently, if learning and speaking are to be

---

210. Spivak, "Can the Subaltern Speak?," 676.

prized, existential acts for *the subaltern*, as Spivak seems to suggest, "listen[ing] to" and "speak[ing] of" do not liberate learning and speaking, but, rather, subjugate them to *subalternity*. It is only "in seeking to learn to speak," as Spivak argues, that *subalternity* can both physically and psychologically bridge the divide between the Powerful and the Powerless. "Listen[ing] to" and "speak[ing] to" further codify and commodify *subalternity* itself, since both ratify *the subaltern* as a "historically muted subject of the non-elite," which must "learn to speak to" the "elite."

As evidenced in the above passage, Spivak's notion of "seeking to learn to speak to" envisions *the subaltern* and *subalternity* specifically in terms of a "woman in the imperialist theater." This is particularly significant not just with respect to Spivak's own *subalternity*, but to the extent that there is an essentialized "woman in the imperialist theater" that is a "post-colonial intellectual [that] systematically 'unlearns' her privilege." What exactly does this mean, if we read what Spivak calls *the subaltern*? Though it may be possible to read *the subaltern* autobiographically, such a reading becomes a misreading, since Spivak's "her" functions similarly to Irigaray's in "This Sex Which Is Not One" (1977)—any traces of autobiography are not as important as a theoretical "she," "her," or "woman" capable of representing "is-ness" in singularity. This singular "is-ness" points to a universal audience of rhetorical resonance—an audience in which Spivak is inevitably included—that embodies a universal "post-colonial intellectual [that] systematically 'unlearns' her privilege." Not only must this universal audience of *subalternity* focus on "seeking to learn to speak to" what Spivak describes as "the imperialist theater," but the prerequisite of this focus is the act of "unlearning"—that is to say, the only way to "speak to" any *imperialist theater* is through "unlearning" what *subalternity* "systematically" does to *the subaltern*. With this in mind, according to Spivak:

> This systematic unlearning involves her in learning to critique post-colonial discourse with the best tools that it can itself provide and not simply to substitute the lost figure of the colonized.[211]

In effect, Spivak proposes that any "systematic unlearning" is connected to any "seeking to learn to speak to" the "imperialist theater." But, what exactly does this "unlearning" look like in the *imperialist theater*? Perhaps, the better question is this: What kind of learning is accomplished through "unlearning," when the *imperialist theater* dictates what learning is? To be sure, "unlearning" is a deconstructive kind of learning, so that the means by which *the subaltern* "learns to critique post-colonial discourse" is by "seeking to learn to speak" to the *imperialist theater* that subjugates *subalternity*. The act of "unlearning" systematically deconstructs what "privilege" is in the *imperialist theater* and, as a result, steps in a "post-" direction—though there is a "post-" direction that can be called "postcolonial," Spivak is concerned with what kind of epistemology such a direction presents to *subalternity*, specifically when

---

211. Spivak, "Can the Subaltern Speak?," 676.

the goal is "not simply to substitute the lost figure of the colonized." In fact, this is precisely what postcoloniality intends to do: it is concerned with what it takes to "unlearn" the ideology of the *imperialist theater*, while recognizing the historical baggage that the *imperialist theater* has placed on *subalternity* through *the subaltern*. To be a *subaltern* means being mindful of the history personified in the "figure of the colonized," even if that figure is lost in a "post-" sense. Spivak considers "unlearning" as a way to confront "the lost figure of the colonized," so that *subalternity* can develop an epistemology deconstructed from the *imperialist theater* that originally created *the subaltern* as a specific mode of privilege and being, in the first place. What this means, then, is when *subalternity* hopes to "unlearn" privilege as it gets defined in *the imperialist theater*, there remains the "problem of the muted subject of the subaltern woman."[212] What kind of problem arises from "the muted subject" of *subalternity*? If Spivak's efforts are toward "seeking to learn to speak to" *subalternity* as it is represented in the *imperialist theater*, what necessary utterances are available? To this end, Spivak confronts the "problem" as one rooted in "the consciousness of the woman as subaltern," which she considers "tactically" in terms of

> reinventing the problem in a sentence and transforming it into the object of a simple semiosis: What does this sentence mean?[213]

The "sentence" in which Spivak "reinvent[s] the problem" is: "The subaltern cannot speak."[214] Not only does this "sentence" seem emphatic, but it underscores Spivak's sentiments of what post-coloniality for *subalternity* means and must ultimately become. It is, *prima facie*, liberating evidence of what *subalternity* must go "seeking to learn to speak to"—yet, in another sense, this evidence is limiting. Granted, Spivak notes that "the post-colonial intellectual—as intellectual—has a circumscribed task of recording this evidence, which she must not disown with a flourish,"[215] but, if we are left with "the subaltern cannot speak," what does post-coloniality look like?

In an updated version of "Can the Subaltern Speak?," Spivak concedes that the "the subaltern cannot speak" assertion was a "failure of communication" as much as it was "an inadvisable remark."[216] Rather than maintaining that *subalternity* "cannot speak," Spivak poses a question that, I would argue, points back to the notion of "seeking to learn to speak to . . . the historically muted subject of the non-elite ('sub-altern') woman in the imperialist theater." That new question for Spivak is: "What is at stake when we insist that the subaltern speaks?"[217] Spivak's question leads me to pose the following: Is Spivak, indeed, "insisting" that *subalternity* speaks? To put it another

---

212. Spivak, "Can the Subaltern Speak?," 677.
213. Spivak, "Can the Subaltern Speak?," 677.
214. Spivak, "Can the Subaltern Speak?," 690.
215. Spivak, "Can the Subaltern Speak?," 690.
216. See Leitch and Cain, *Norton Anthology of Theory and Criticism*, 2206.
217. Leitch and Cain, *Norton Anthology of Theory and Criticism*, 2207.

way, if there is a need to "insist," and there is something "at stake" when *subalternity* is given a voice in the *imperialist theater*, what does this precisely mean for *the subaltern*, post-coloniality, and coloniality itself?

Any means of answering either Spivak's question or any of mine require a post-colonial thinking that works within the *imperialist theater*, even if the intent, at least epistemologically, is to provide a "post-colonial critique." In effect, a "post-colonial critique" is still a critique from within the ideological state apparatus of coloniality, even if we "insist" that *subalternity* must speak—to be clear, my use of the term "post-colonial" does place me in a "post-" direction from coloniality, but that direction still has, as its teleological origin, coloniality. Even if we follow Spivak and maintain that *subalternity* must "unlearn" her privilege (or lack thereof) as it is has been defined in coloniality, this kind of deconstructive thinking is ultimately epistemologically wired to the very thinking that *subalternity* wishes to deconstruct. In other words, though post-coloniality for *subalternity* embarks on deconstructive thinking, such a post-colonial approach, in itself, has just as many limits as it has benefits. When these limitations manifest themselves after "unlearning," *the subaltern* epistemologically remains within the *imperialist theater*—everything that *subalternity* knows (or will ever know through "unlearning") is trapped in the imperialist ideological state apparatus, particularly when *the subaltern* "speaks." Essentially, what *the subaltern* speaks comes from, as Walter Mignolo contends, "a web of imperial knowledge." In light of this, Mignolo argues for "de-colonial thinking" which "presupposes de-linking (epistemologically and politically) from the web of imperial knowledge (theo- and ego-politically grounded) from disciplinary management."[218]

Luce Irigaray's Feminism: Moving beyond "the Phallic Function" and "Woman's Destiny"

In Luce Irigaray's "This Sex Which Is Not One" (1977), not only does Irigaray specifically reject Freudian-Lacanian psychoanalysis as part and parcel of a deconstructive stance—that is to say, she rejects psychanalytic understandings of "woman," "femaleness," and "femininity" by deconstructing phallocentrism and phallogocentrism—but, to a larger extent, she also participates in a French theoretical movement influenced by Simone de Beauvoir's *The Second Sex* (1949). I would like to begin with the latter first.

By doing so, I will situate Irigaray contextually as a theoretical extension of Beauvoir's anti-phallocentric, contra-Freud position and demonstrate how, as a result, Irigaray contributes to a "second-wave" feminist movement—not just contra-Freud, but contra-Lacan—which can be assessed in terms of its benefits and limitations. While the benefits of Irigaray's feminism can be specifically enumerated

---

218. Mignolo, "Epistemic Disobedience," 20.

in reference to the limitations of Freudian-Lacanian psychoanalysis, these same benefits present more theoretical limitations that are addressed by Black feminism and Womanism, both of which attempt to not only attempt to move beyond phallocentricism and phallogocentrism, but both also move beyond Irigaray's logocentric interpretation of "woman's destiny."

Before considering Irigaray, it is, again, important to place her in the context of *The Second Sex*—in anticipation of Irigaray, Beauvoir recognizes that Freudian psychoanalysis creates a "psychoanalytic point of view" that manipulates biological data in order to shape conceptualizations of "woman's destiny" and "history." To be clear, when *woman's destiny* is filtered through a *Freudian psychoanalytic point of view*, Beauvoir highlights two underlying ramifications of this point of view toward *history*: (1) it ignores biological data that denotes, more empirically, that "males and females are two types of individuals who are differentiated within one species for the purposes of reproduction; they can be defined only correlatively,"[219] and (2) it perpetuates a "history" grounded on "[a] world [that] has always belonged to males, and none of the reasons given for this have ever seemed sufficient."[220] Through these ramifications, Beauvoir's definitions of *woman's destiny* and *history*, then, are connected to her critique of the *Freudian psychoanalytic point of view*—for Beauvoir, this connection, on one hand, promotes "myths" of patriarchy while, on the other hand, attempts to suppress the "lived experience" of women. Because the former is promoted and the latter is oppressed. What Beauvoir calls for, at least theoretically, is a fundamental reconceptualization of the *myths* of patriarchy and the *lived experience* of women, so that the former can be suppressed and the latter will be liberated. But, what exactly does this mean theoretically for Beauvoir? In other words, what does a suppression of the *myths* of patriarchy and a liberation of the *lived experience* of women look like in theory? For Beauvoir, it certainly begins with critiquing Freud, but, more broadly, it reassesses *history* for the distinct purposes of rearticulating *woman's destiny*—that is to say, Beauvoir's theory is rooted in critiquing the *Freudian psychoanalytic point of view* as a means to critique a *history* of assumptions within the very structure of patriarchal thinking that makes Freud possible in the first place. In terms of Beauvoir's theory, Freud is Beauvoir's ideological foil, not just as a way to deconstruct (in a pre-Derridean way) the *Freudian psychoanalytic point of view* and the *history* from which Freud draws his point of view, but to reconstruct—albeit, through a Sartrean-existential,[221] deconstructive method—what *woman's destiny* should be contra Freud. To this end, Beauvoir concludes that "Freud was not very concerned with woman's destiny; it is clear that he modeled his description of it on that of masculine destiny, merely modifying some of the traits."[222] Beauvoir is, in fact, "very

---

219. Beauvoir, *Second Sex*, 21.

220. Beauvoir, *Second Sex*, 71.

221. Beauvoir was philosophically influenced by Jean-Paul Sartre's form of existentialism, just as much as Beauvoir influenced Sartre's understanding of ethics.

222. Beauvoir, *Second Sex*, 50.

concerned" with *woman's destiny* and intends to deconstruct "[Freud's] description of it on that of masculine destiny" by reconstructing woman's destiny as something more than just a modification of "some of [masculine destiny's] traits." This requires a sort of deconstructive-reconstructive effort and a direct engagement with a problem inherent in Freud's psychoanalytic thinking. What is this "problem" and how can it be governed/engaged/solved? Unfortunately, *The Second Sex* only presents the "problem" in a poetic way, but offers very little prose toward how that "problem" is governed/engaged/solved. Betty Friedan's *The Feminine Mystique* (1963) acknowledges that Beauvoir's recognition of the "problem" only goes so far, even if assessing the "problem" from Friedan's American, Civil Rights situation, rather than in Beauvoir's French, post-World War II context—this is particularly evidenced in Friedan's assertion that this is a "problem that has no name."[223] Nevertheless, though Friedan takes an Americentric pathmark from Beauvoir, Irigaray's Eurocentric pathmark is equally haunted by the mystique[224] of "the problem that has no name"—it is not until Lacan's seminars from 1954–1973, particularly in reaction to Lacan's "Encore" seminar, when Irigaray carries Beauvoir's notion of *woman's destiny* and the underlying Friedan's "problem" further.

In "Encore—on Feminine Sexuality, the Limits of Love and Knowledge" (1972–1973), Lacan argues that woman "is excluded by the nature of things."[225] For Lacan, what makes woman excluded is due to "being not-whole [since] she has a supplementary jouissance compared to what the phallic function designates by way of jouissance."[226] This phallic function, then, becomes the "nature of things"—because of how the phallic function denotes a "nature of things" and the degree to which woman is "not whole," Lacan concludes that "there's no such thing as Woman, Woman with a capital W indicating the universal."[227] To this end, Lacan's conceptualization of the "nature of things" is grounded in the law of the father through "the phallic function," which, in "The Signification of the Phallus," Lacan suggests, "indicate[s] the structures that will govern the relations between the sexes."[228] Lacan defines "structure" in terms of desire as the vehicle by which "the relations between the sexes" are governed—in a Freudian way, Lacan contends that "the phallus is the privileged signifier . . . in which the role of the logos is joined with the advent of desire."[229] If the phallus is a "privileged signifier," it enacts, as Lacan proposes, *the phallic function*—this function is elucidated in Lacan's reading of Freud's interpretation of

---

223. Friedan describes this "problem" along two fronts. First, she considers it in terms of it having intensified for over fifteen years, since Beauvoir's *The Second Sex*. But, second, it has been perpetuated "in [the] voices of tradition and of Freudian sophistication," to the point that women "could desire no greater destiny than to glory in their own femininity." See Betty Friedan, *Feminine Mystique*.

224. I use Friedan's term here, but qualify it further in terms of Derrida's term "specter."

225. Miller, *On Feminine Sexuality*, 73.

226. Miller, *On Feminine Sexuality*, 73.

227. Miller, *On Feminine Sexuality*, 72.

228. Lacan, "Signification of the Phallus," 279.

229. Lacan, "Signification of the Phallus," 277.

female sexuality and desire. To be clear, *the phallic function* creates the structure and the ideology by which "the relations between the sexes" are governed—this Freudian ideology about female sexuality encapsulates Beauvoir's *woman's destiny*, but, more importantly, through the Lacanian sense that "there's no such thing as Woman," the phallic function is at the core of Friedan's identification of "the problem that has no name." In a very literal sense, if taking Lacan at his word, the extent to which *woman's destiny* is defined through *the phallic function* and the overarching ideology that the function produces in the structure of "the relation between the sexes," the problem, truly, does not have a name—*woman's destiny* and female sexuality itself, as Lacan appropriates from Freud, is so inextricably linked to the phallic function that woman becomes "[a] problem that has no name."

Irigaray's "This Sex Which Is Not One" not only attempts to wrestle with "the problem that has no name," but does so by connecting the problem itself to Beauvoir's *woman's destiny* and the theoretical consequences that can be traced to *the phallic function*. In effect, the benefits of Irigaray's feminist theory—which represents one of many feminist theories—arises from the limitations in the Freudian-Lacanian interpretations of *woman's destiny* and *the phallic function*. To this end, in light of the limitations, Irigarary begins by conceding that "female sexuality has always been conceptualized on the basis of masculine parameters."[230] These parameters, as noted by Irigaray, make it possible for Lacan to tease out, by way of Freud, the notion that female sexuality is based on the following:

> "Woman" (*la*) is a signifier, the crucial property (*propre*) of which is that it is the only one that cannot signify anything, and this is simply because it grounds woman's status in the fact that she is not-whole. This means we can't talk about Woman (*La femme*).[231]

Here, what Lacan has articulated, especially for Friedan and Irigaray alike, is "the problem that has no name." The "problem" is situated in what "not whole" means. But, how does "woman's status in the fact that she is not-whole" mean that we cannot "talk about Woman (*La femme*)"? Does this mean, too, that, because of this "not-whole" status, we cannot talk about female sexuality either? That is to say, can we actually talk about female sexuality without talking about it in relation to "masculine parameters"? Lacan and Freud certainty hold the view that we cannot talk about female sexuality or "Woman" without referring to an ideological conceptualization, as Irigaray points out, that is ultimately construed "on the basis of masculine parameters." What this comes to mean, for Irigaray, is that "[female] sexuality offers nothing but imperatives dictated by male rivalry."[232] I would argue that this "rivalry" is between the roles of men and women within a patriarchal, phallic-defined state apparatus—the perpetuating ideology is

---

230. See Parker, *Critical Theory*, 258.
231. Miller, *On Feminine Sexuality*, 73.
232. See Parker, *Critical Theory*, 258.

constructed around "imperatives" about *the phallic function*, and how *the phallic function* dictates *woman's destiny* toward desire and pleasure. The fact that Irigaray points out that there are "imperatives dictated by male rivalry" suggests that she perceives these "imperatives" as Freudian-Lacanian limitations, which compartmentalize feminine desire and pleasure. Moreover, as Irigaray observes, "woman lives her own desire only as the expectation that she may at last come to possess an equivalent of the male organ."[233] If *the phallic function* holds true with "woman's status in the fact that she is not-whole," possession of the phallus is meant to overcome being "not-whole." Even if woman expects "to possess an equivalent of the male organ" in order to define the parameters of her desire and pleasure, such an expectation does not escape *the phallic function*. Irigaray agrees with this, particularly as a Freudian-Lacanian limitation, since it means that female desire and pleasure remain "within the dominant phallic economy"—if desire and pleasure are aligned teleologically with *the phallic function*, issues "about woman and her pleasure" become based on, as Irigaray argues, "the penis being the only sexual organ of recognized value."[234]

In turning from this "recognized value"—that is, in deconstructing the Freudian-Lacanian "imperatives" of what *the phallic function* means to do to/for *woman's destiny*—Irigaray believes that *woman's destiny* is not bound to *the phallic function*, when deconstructing phallocentrism and phallogocentrism. In other words, female sexuality should not be defined as "not-whole," female pleasure should not be given an exchange value, and female sex organs should not be assigned a use-value "within the dominant phallic economy." Instead, Irigaray proposes that (with her emphasis added)

> woman *has sex organs more or less everywhere*. She finds pleasure almost everywhere. Even if we refrain from invoking the hystericization of her entire body, the geography of her pleasure is far more diversified, more multiple in its differences, more complex, more subtle, than is commonly imagined—in an imaginary rather too narrowly focused on sameness.[235]

Irigaray's recognition of "sameness" highlights the problems inherent in both phallocentric and phallogocentric thinking (of the Freudian-Lacanian *psychoanalytic point of view*)—there lies the assumption that, "within the dominant phallic economy," the only means for "woman" to define desire/pleasure is by locating "the geography of her pleasure" in a "sameness" regulated by *the phallic function*. How does this "sameness" affect *woman's destiny*? Ultimately, *woman's destiny* becomes, just as Irigaray argues, "an imaginary rather too narrowly focused on sameness." But, more importantly, I would argue that Irigaray suggests that this "sameness" suppresses and oppresses *woman's destiny* through the repressive ideology of *the phallic function* itself. What this necessitates, then, is a path outside and beyond *the phallic function*, so that *woman's destiny*

---

233. Parker, *Critical Theory*, 258.
234. Parker, *Critical Theory*, 258.
235. Parker, *Critical Theory*, 261.

is not strictly "an imaginary rather narrowly focused on sameness," but is, instead, grounded on Irigaray's sentiment that "woman *has sex organs more or less everywhere.*" Consequently, Irigaray seemingly offers the notion that *woman's destiny* is contingent on "find[ing] pleasure almost everywhere," and not in a desire/pleasure "too narrowly focused on sameness" constructed and expressed by *the phallic function.*

Essentially, Irigaray opposes this "sameness" on two levels, with her opposition to *the phallic function* representing only on one level. That is to say, any assessment of *woman's destiny* through deconstructing *the phallic function* means taking only a first step—*woman's destiny* cannot just be construed by delinking it historically from *the phallic function*, but by guiding *woman's destiny* itself in a post-*phallic function* direction that reconstructs what *woman's destiny* can be, particularly with respect to desire/pleasure. Granted, Irigaray recognizes this in the following:

> In order for a woman to reach the place where she takes pleasure as woman, a long detour by way of the analysis of the various systems of oppression brought to bear upon her is assuredly necessary.[236]

Here, Irigaray's assertion that there is a "place where [woman] takes pleasure as woman" suggests, in my view, that *woman's destiny* is possible in a post-*phallic function* direction. This direction, as such, does require "a long detour." When considering what *the phallic function* does to *woman's destiny*, taking "a long detour" is, as Irigaray notes, "assuredly necessary." Yet, if this "long detour" is taken "by way of the analysis of the various systems of oppression brought to bear upon [woman]," is Irigaray purposefully limiting herself? To put it another way, if it can be argued that the first step Irigaray takes is to construct *woman's destiny* by deconstructing *the phallic function*, can a second, more important step be taken to delink *woman's destiny* from *the phallic function* altogether, if such a "detour" purposefully utilizes "[an] analysis of the various systems brought to bear upon [woman]"?

While the answer to the latter question is no, the answer to the former must be yes. In other words, not only does "[an] analysis of the various systems brought to bear upon [woman]" greatly limit Irigaray's understanding of *woman's destiny*, but it makes any step moving in a post-*phallic function* direction equally limited to essentialist language about "woman." Though there are theoretical benefits to Irigaray's deconstruction of *the phallic function* for the sake of delinking *woman's destiny* from a Freudian-Lacanian *psychoanalytic point of view*, in order to reconstruct the meaning of *woman's destiny*, using the term "woman" in *woman's destiny* presents unavoidable limitations. As a result, just as making a post-*phallic function* move does not completely delink anything from *the phallic function* itself, any notion of a *woman's destiny* assumes, in a general way, that all women share a common "destiny." By this, there is only a single *woman's destiny*—a "destiny" that is binary opposition to the "destiny" of "The Other."

236. Parker, *Critical Theory*, 262.

Admittedly, Irigarary does not use the term *woman's destiny*—a term I have appropriated from Friedan, and applied to Irigaray—but she does, however, provide a monolithic, logocentric vision of "woman" through her repetitive use of the word. For this reason, I have put Freidan's *woman's destiny* and Irigaray's "woman" not in juxtaposition with one another, but to situate them as one sign. Along with *woman's destiny* and *woman*, the terms "female," "femininity," "female sexuality," and "feminine" all contribute to the same logocentrism, so that each is a different signifier pointing to a singular signified—for Irigaray, it would appear that each of these terms are interchangeable signs expressing the same "logos." Comparatively, Irigaray's interpretations of desire and pleasure are also logocentric, since they are employed as a means of embodying a generalization about "female sexuality" and all other signs alike, which, I would argue, contradicts Irigaray's idea that "the geography of [woman's] pleasure is far more diversified." If, as Irigaray continues, "[desire and pleasure are] more multiple in its differences, more complex, more subtle than is commonly imagined," are these complexities, differences, multiplicities, and diversification theoretically undermined by monolithic terms such as "woman," "she," and "her"? Does the theoretical upshot of these complexities, differences, multiplicities, and diversification in "the geography of [woman's] pleasure" unearth larger contradictions for Irigaray's terms such as *female, femininity, female sexuality, feminine, woman*, and, by extension, and the overarching *woman's destiny*?

What these questions illustrate, then, are theoretical limitations to Irigaray's brand of feminism—these limitations stem from an undergirding set of benefits that, in turn, are derived from the limitations Irigaray finds inherent in the Freudian-Lacanian *psychoanalytic point of view* about female sexuality. Nevertheless, the specific limitations in Irigaray's brand of feminism open gaps in her theory, through which one noteworthy theory positions itself: Black feminism or Womanism.

Just as Irigaray's feminism situates itself against the Freudian-Lacanian *psychoanalytic point of view* that presents an essentialist understanding of female sexuality in reference to *the phallic function*, Black feminism or Womanism also situates itself against Irigaray's essentialist understanding of "woman" in reference to *woman's destiny*. For Black feminism or Womanism—despite the fact that there are subtle difference between the two, the most notable being in the former's use the term "feminism" as a pivot point for the Black experience, and the latter completely rejecting "feminism" altogether—there is a "Black feminist thought" that conceives of *woman's destiny* differently from Irigaray's, particularly since Irigaray is limited to a Eurocentric perspective of gender oppression. To this end, "Black feminist thought" adds racial oppression, and perceives an intersectionality between race and gender by way of oppression. According to Patricia H. Collins in *Black Feminist Thought*, "Black women's experiences with both racial and gender oppression result in needs and problems distinct from white women and Black men, and that Black women must struggle for equality both as women and as African-American."[237]

Judith Butler's *Giving an Account of Oneself*

When further contextualizing the theoretical limitations of Irigaray's brand of feminism against the existential situatedness of Black women's experiences, what allows "Black feminist thought" to arise from feminist thought is the extent to which "Blackness" gives an account for itself outside the traditional feminist normative account. This normative account does not account for the role and meaning of "Blackness"—to be "Black" and be a woman means existing, by the very fact of that "Blackness," beyond the feminist normative through the development of an "I" that is uniquely existential and stands altogether separately from the existential feminist normative.

In *Giving an Account of Oneself* (2003), Judith Butler explains these existential circumstances in the following way: "When the 'I' seeks to give an account of itself, an account that must include the conditions of its own emergence, it must, as a matter of necessity, become a social theorist."[238] Indeed, "the I," as the very center of any existential experience of the meaning of being, is what "gives an account of itself"—it is this "I" that captures the dimensions of existence.

Just as the feminist movement defined and expressed its own "I" in relation to the patriarchal demands made upon the development of what I will refer to as the "feminist-I," the experience of Black women becomes an experience that cannot be fully expressed within the "feminist-I," as this expression of this "I" grew increasingly normative to the white experience and, in turn, developed into a new patriarchal structure that marginalized and oppressed the unique experience of Black women. It is not only that Black women fundamentally view their own experience—their own "I"—as excluded in every conceivable way from the "feminist-I" (i.e., historically, psychologically, sociologically, and politically), but it was also that, by way of sustaining the meaning of their existence, there arose a contingent need to define themselves. That definition of self—or what Foucault describes as the hermeneutics of the subject—"must include the conditions of its own emergence," which are delineated, "as a matter of necessity," for Black women, through unique historical, psychological, sociological, and political experiences intersecting at an "I." In doing so, as Butler suggests, "[the I] become[s] a social theorist." That is to say, in order for Black women to separate themselves substantively from the "feminist-I," Black women do so by acting as a "social theorist," theorizing the meaning of the "feminist-I" and theorizing the meaning of their own experience outside of it.

The movement that arises from becoming a social theorist is one that provides commentary "on the conditions of its own emergence," such that, in the development

237. Collins, *Black Feminist Thought*, 19–20.
238. Butler, *Giving an Account of Oneself*, 8.

of a "new-I," an "I" that is not reflected by the meaning of the "feminist-I," Butler notes that any "new-I" must lay a normative foundation for itself as it gives an account of itself. The normative foundation of any "new-I" is grounded on how this "new-I" handles and is handled by unique historical, psychological, sociological, and political experiences and how, as a whole, all of these dimensions inform "the existential" for that "new-I." To give an account of oneself means negotiating "the existential" and, though not made explicit by Butler, aligning oneself to "the theological," so that "the theological" explicates "the existential" and "the existential" explicates the uniqueness of "the historical," "the psychological," "the sociological," and "the political" experiences. All of these dimensions are regulated by "the theological," and the extent to which theologizing about God functions differently between the "feminist-I" and the "I" expressed by Black women. Setting aside "the theological" and "the existential," Butler considers the normative development of the "I" in the following way:

> It is one thing to say that a subject must be able to appropriate norms, but another to say that there must be norms that prepare a place within the ontological field for a subject. In the first instance, norms are there, at an exterior distance, and the task is to find a way of appropriating them, taking them on, establishing a living relation to them. The epistemological frame is presupposed in this encounter, one in which a subject encounters moral norms and must find his way with them.[239]

Normative development, as "be[ing] able to appropriate norms," is only part of a larger "existential" process in the development of an "I"—for Butler, what is also at stake is "prepar[ing] a place within the ontological field for a subject."

On this point, through Butler, in the development of an "I" for Black women, not only do Black women need to appropriate the norms of the "feminist-I," but they must also "tak[e] them on, establishing a living relation to them." In doing so, the "I" of Black women assume the anti-patriarchal stance of the "feminist-I," while "establishing a living relation" that is different from the feminist perspective. This means, too, that the theologizing of Black women assumes a theological stance similar to the "feminist-I," while carving out a theologizing about God that utilizes a different "epistemological frame" than that of the "feminist-I." Because of this "epistemological frame," the development of Black women's "I," as a subject unique from the "feminist-I," as Butler writes, "encounters moral norms and must find [her] way with them." To "find [her] way," it requires, in Butler's words:

> Giving an account [that] takes a narrative form, which not only depends upon the ability to relay a set of sequential events with plausible transitions but also draws upon narrative voice and authority, being directed toward an audience with the aim of persuasion. The narrative must then establish that the self

---

239. Butler, *Giving an Account of Oneself*, 9.

either was or was not the cause of that suffering, and so supply a persuasive medium through which to understand the causal agency of the self.[240]

Not only is the development of Black women's "I" a narrative that, in form, becomes different from the "feminist-I," but the "I" of Black women also "draws upon narrative voice and authority" that grounds Black women to an existence that is more "existential" to their own narrative than the "feminist-I." It is a narrative—once predicated on theologizing about God—that is existentially "directed toward an audience with the aim of persuasion." In giving an account of herself, the development of Black women's "I" grounds her existentially to her existence through an existence that persuades her away from the "feminist-I," persuades her to present an existential narrative, and persuades her to uniquely theologize about God.

Womanist Approach

Womanist Ethics, the Tripartite Self and "Being-Womanist"

In my view, Womanist ethics, as it is grounded on a tripartite self, can be described as the following dimensions of selfhood: the moral-communal, the theological-political, and the ontological-existential. These three selves are predicated on what I will refer to as "being-Womanist"—a collective sense of "being" and "being-in-the-world" through the facticities of Blackness and femininity. As such, "being-Womanist" is translated through interactions with moral and communal being, an engagement with the "theological" with "the political" spheres of society, and the meaning-making process of merging the existential Blackness with the ontological Blackness.

As I intend to use it, "being-Womanist" has certain ethical obligations to itself and to others, particularly all existing things construed through a Husserlian "life-world" that revolves around the notion of living together and how that "living together" is an apparent commonality between all "beings."[241] When "being-Womanist" is oriented toward "self" and toward "others," it becomes possible to explain them, then, as what Jean-Paul Sartre describes as being-for-self and being-for-others.[242] In this "being-for-self" and "being-for-others," as part and parcel of "being-Womanist," is the sense of the possibility of becoming "dialogic."

I consider the term "dialogic" precisely as Mikhail Bakhtin does, where it is embodied in "forces that serve to unify and centralize the verbal-ideological world."[243] For "being-Womanist," these "forces" that Bakhtin proposes are particularly extrapolated through the relatedness between intersubjective beings in a Husserlian "life-world." As such, especially for Womanist's moral self, there are "forces" that come

---

240. Butler, *Giving an Account of Oneself*, 12.
241. Husserl, *Crisis of European Sciences*, 108–10.
242. Sartre, *Being and Nothingness*, 548.
243. Bakhtin, *Dialogic Imagination*, 270.

to bear in a moral community predicated on a "verbal-ideological world." When "being-Womanist" encounters these "forces," it positions itself as an intersubjective being, an entity of intentionality similar to what Edmund Husserl argues for in *The Crisis of European Sciences and Transcendental Phenomenology: An Introduction to Phenomenological Philosophy* (1936).[244]

So, in a decidedly Husserlian way, I think that, through intentionality, "being-Womanist" as an intersubjective being recognizes their "intented-ness" to the point that one "being" becomes the epistemological ultimacy of the other "being," and vice versa. This is the moral community, where "being-Womanist" is relational and connected through a sense of epistemological ultimacy. In light of this epistemological ultimacy, Womanists' moral selves become "dialogic" with one another, conceiving not just on their own individual subjectivity, but extending that subjectivity transitively toward a relational-connectedness shared with others in the "life-world" of a moral community.

In this kind of "life-world" community, the ethical obligation one "being" has toward another "being" is linked dialectically by what Aristotle calls, in his *Nicomachean Ethics*, the "highest good."[245] This "highest good," I would like to argue, is what the Womanist's moral self is oriented toward—there is an inevitable orientation toward, as I have mentioned, an epistemological ultimacy, or "telos" in the "highest good." This is particularly the case when situating Womanist's moral self as one that is predicated on an ascetic life, which, in turn, is construed through having the right faith, the right knowledge, and the right conduct,[246] all as a way of reaching "truth." But, more importantly, "truth" is a state of being—it is a decidedly existential existence where meaning is made through "truth" and "freedom." In other words, meaning-making for Womanist's moral self comes by "how well" the well-lived life is lived and, then, the trajectory that that well-lived life has toward "truth." At the point of "truth," Womanist's moral self becomes something other than human and becomes, in the end, aligned with "Right."

What I take this to mean, therefore, is that Womanist's moral self has an ethical obligation toward the "highest good" and "Right." As Aristotle would likely agree, Womanist's moral self collectively—as a communal being—and individually has a dialectic with the "highest good" and the ultimate actualization of "being-Right." I use this term "being-Right" as critical to the relationship between "being-Womanist" and Womanist's moral self—both have "being-Right" as a point of intentionality. So, allow me to argue what I mean by "being-Right" in the following manner: not only is the "highest good" something that Womanist's moral self existentially strives for as a personal aim, but it is also a communal aim and, since a communal aim is involved, there is an alignment present with "Right."

244. Husserl, *Crisis of European Sciences*, 85.
245. In terms of Bekker numbers, this occurs in 1094a. See Aristotle, *Nicomachean Ethics*, 1–2.
246. Iannone, *Dictionary of World Philosophy*, 274.

If I may extend Aristotle a bit further, the "highest good" can be viewed as the centralizing component that validates relatedness, becomes the Platonic mathematical number inherent in the "forces" that Bakhtin offers about "dialogism," and, like gravity, holds together the Husserlian "life-world" as a moral community of selves and others.

In my view, a Husserlian "life world" is analogous to a moral community, where "Right" holds together that community. Moral community is oriented toward the "highest good," and structured around the dialogic relationship between "being" and "Right"—the moral obligation of "being" is to, ultimately, become "Right," which is not just critical to what I have argued for "being-Womanist" but also for Womanist's moral selfhood. I would argue, then, that Womanist's moral self is not strictly an individual enterprise, but one that is inextricably linked to the community as a communal self—in this regard, I would offer that "being-Womanist" is a moral-communal self. Be that as it may, "being-Womanist" is linked to what Hegel describes as "world-history"—I take this mean, then, that there is an inevitable historicity to what it means to be "Womanist," where historicality is embodied in "being-Womanist." But, more specifically, a combination of moral-communal selfhood and "being-Right" as an agent of history make up what "being-Womanist" is all about, particularly if situating that sense of self politically and theologically.

Nevertheless, "being-Womanist," as a theological-political self, is focused on liberation, freedom, and empowerment. A Womanist's theological-political self, who is situated in a position of powerlessness against the oppressive actions of anyone in a position of power. However, I would add that this balance is also sought between Womanist's theological-political self's adherence to their faith, their relationship with God, their roles in the Black Church, and the fact that the predicament of their being-in-the-world—of course, as "being-Womanist"—is more than just due to the political arrangements of the power-structured society in which they live and hope to change, but is existential.[247]

Womanist's existential-ontological selfhood is inextricably linked to the question of being, since "being" is conceptually related to the premise of human being. In this, selfhood means to, by extension, have Paul Tillich's idea of courage[248] and the ability to enact Nietzsche's power through sheer will[249] over other things, either in the larger context of the world in which that being subsists or through the manipulation of other beings or nonbeings, in the effort of defining self "for self." In order to do this, "being-Womanist" must exist temporally within the scope of time, analyzing

247. What I mean here is the existential situation of Blackness, or, as I have mentioned earlier, the facticity of Blackness.

248. Tillich, *Courage to Be*, 3.

249. Power brought to bear by will is a concept of Friedrich Nietzsche. It is used to express the motivation of a "being" to define self as a means of acquiring knowledge about itself. To have "will" is to have freedom. To have "power" is to have the ability to use that freedom and the desire to not recede into nonbeing. Kaufmann, *Will to Power*, 44.

the authenticity of that existence in reference to the past, the present, and the future and the contingency of freedom available to an authentic self.[250] Utilizing this anxiety-laden freedom to choose itself,[251] an authentic self is constructed to address its authenticity and subsequent selfhood in light of its prevailing ontology. This is precisely how I intend to define a Womanist's ontological-existential self—a selfhood that systematically defines what it means exist in theory and, then, bring forth an emerging existence ontologically.

Michelle Wallace's "A Black Feminist's Search for Selfhood"

What Michele Wallace articulates in her essay entitled "A Black Feminist's Search for Selfhood" (1975), in the collection *All the Woman Are White and All the Blacks Are Men, but Some of Us Are Brave: Black Women Studies* (1982), is not just a sociological problem confronted by the African American woman relegated to the lower strata of the American society, but the unquestionably existential problem of what it means to be Black and be a woman in relation to being human. These sociological and existential issues are at the core of Wallace's search for selfhood. More importantly, when seeking that selfhood, Wallace is also seeking a Blackness that stands in recognition of the history of slavery and her African roots. But, this Blackness, as Wallace realizes, is a different form of Blackness than that of males or that which exhibits an innate masculinity—hers is female and feminine.

The problem for Wallace, then, is finding how Blackness can be reconciled with femininity, how both can inhabit the same existence through a Du Boisian double-consciousness, and the means by which female Blackness relates to male Blackness and female whiteness simultaneously. Black femininity is in constant conversation with Black masculinity and White femininity due largely to the sense of "otherness" that such an identity inevitably holds within both respective paradigms—the former is relative to Marxist-like power struggle within the male-female social relationship while the latter is always in reference to the Black family as a communal-social construct. What Wallace learns, by one turn after another, is that Blackness is often described in reference to Black masculinity as much as femininity assumes, chiefly, the interests of white females. To that end, then, Wallace approaches the realization that

---

250. Authentic existence is resolute and makes choices in the present in light of the past and open to the future. The authentic self is a unitary, stable, and relatively abiding structure, in which the polarities of existence are held in balance and its potentialities are brought to fulfillment. Ferguson and Wright, *New Dictionary of Theology*, 243–44.

251. Anxiety, according to Heidegger, is at the core of a "being" that is coming into existence. This anxiety is fueled by the freedom of choice and, in turn, is embodied in a "being" choosing between actualization of its existence or descending into nothingness. When a being uses its "being-free for" it chooses to authenticate its existence and, therefore, becomes a being-in-the-world. Heidegger, *Being and Time*, 232.

her "otherness" is no more in line with the message of Blackness than it is with that of femininity and, thusly, must embody a unique voice.

This unique voice is what Wallace is searching for. It is the search for a sociologically, existentially relevant perspective that embodies both what it means to be Black and what it means to be a woman. The two, when combined, exemplify a singular American experience, an experience that is combined with a dehumanization at the hands of Black masculinity and a marginalization at the hands of white femininity. At the heart of Wallace's argument is not so much a case for subjectivity—since it can be argued that her search for selfhood in terms of her Black femininity underscores her awareness of it as such—but it is a longing for objectification. Wallace wants to be seen just as she sees—she wants to receive relevance just as she projects relevance upon others, the sense of self and the sense of selves.

Within Wallace's argument about the objectification of Black feminism is M. Shawn Copeland's body ideology: the objectification of Black women's bodies. Here, just as Copeland, Wallace understands that her being is not necessarily a spiritual and psychological being-in-the-world but an existence—if it can be called that—centered on the physical. It is this physicality that Wallace points to when she describes the relationships between Black males and females as well as that of Black females and White females through the vein of physical victimization. This is unquestionably the central issue that Wallace come to terms with over the course of her bemusement: the fact that the physical representation of her Black femininity as it comes to bear in society through societal roles must be transcended in order to have a true existence in the world—transcending the physical in order to assume something much more existential is the focal point of her brand of Black feminism: the appropriation of an objectification that is not relative to the Black feminine body. At the heart of Copeland's concerns, too, is this desire to "enflesh freedom," the possibility of incorporating a body theology that is liberating.

In terms of theology, there are blatant implications involved in Wallace evoking the "otherness" of Black femininity, the belief that their Blackness and femininity completely marginalizes African American women in a unique way. This stands to suggest that, through Copeland's body theology, there is a chance for liberation, and it is only through this liberation that that "otherness" is transformed into a sense of belonging. But, more importantly, it is through something else that Copeland points to in her book *Enfleshing Freedom* (2010) that proves to be much more liberating, framing a more complete degree of belonging: the theological affirmation of salvation through Christology, where Black femininity assumes a form of humanity through the body of Christ. In this, then, the way through which Black femininity approaches humanity and what it means to be human is through a theological anthropological understanding of being-in-the-world. Being-in-the-world is about time and space, about temporality and reality, and about potentiality and existence—all of these elements taken on the whole formulate selfhood.

Patricia H. Collins's *Black Feminist Thought*

In the preface to *Black Feminist Thought: Knowledge, Consciousness, and the Politics of Empowerment* (1990), Collins begins with a personal narrative, which, if understanding the meaning of narrative through Judith Butler, gives an account of herself. Collins's account, in its brief narrative form, describes, in Collins's words, how "my personal odyssey forms the catalyst for [*Black Feminist Thought*]."[252] Not only does Collins recognize that giving an account of herself allows her personal narrative to give rise to the development of her selfhood into an existential awareness of her meaning of existence, but it also allows her to, as Collins writes, "know that [her] experiences are far from unique."[253] In fact, Collins finds that, "like African-American women, many others who occupy societally denigrated categories have been similarly silenced."[254] To be "silenced," and belong to "societally denigrated categories," means being marginalized from what is deemed as normative. In Collins's case, as the title "Black Feminist Thought" suggests, Collins views the extent to which she gives an account of herself as being "silenced" by the feminist normative—in being "silenced" this way, "Black feminist thought" provides a space in which those that belong to "societally denigrated categories" can align to a different narrative by a different voice capable of speaking to and about a different experience.

When considering the concerns of her narrative, voice, and experience, Collins writes:

> So the voice that I now seek is both individual and collective, personal and political, one reflecting the intersection of my unique biography with the larger meaning of my historical times.[255]

Because of Collins's concern with her "unique biography" and how that narrative represents "the larger meaning of [her] historical times," what Collins seeks is to make sure that "Black women's experiences and ideas [are] at the center of analysis."[256] With Collins's focus on that center, she makes it clear that "I have deliberately chosen not to begin with feminist tenets developed from the experiences of white, middle-class, Western women." More specifically, Collins did not wish to "insert the ideas and experiences of African-American women"[257] into the former's experiences. By not "insert[ing] the ideas and experiences of African-American women" into the "ideas and experiences" of the feminist normative and, in doing so, creating a space from which the "ideas and experiences" that more broadly conceptualize Collins's personal narrative, Collins maintains that

---

252. Collins, *Black Feminist Thought*, xii.
253. Collins, *Black Feminist Thought*, xii.
254. Collins, *Black Feminist Thought*, xii.
255. Collins, *Black Feminist Thought*, xii.
256. Collins, *Black Feminist Thought*, xii.
257. Collins, *Black Feminist Thought*, xii.

> [*Black Feminist Thought*] is not a book about what Black women think of white feminist ideas or how Black women's ideas compare with those of prominent white feminist theories. . . . In order to capture the interconnections of race, gender, and social class in Black women's lives and their effect on Black feminist thought, I explicitly rejected grounding my analysis in any single theoretical tradition.[258]

The fact that Collins "explicitly reject[s] grounding [her] analysis" on a feminist normative as a "single theoretical tradition" speaks to a lack of belonging on that "theoretical tradition." Indeed, for Collins, her narrative, her voice, and her experience are so far removed from "any single theoretical tradition" that it forces her, existentially speaking, to pool her "ideas and experiences" into another tradition, particularly a tradition which situates Black women "at the center of analysis." That tradition, as Collins intends to define it, is a tradition that hails from the very meaning and necessity of "Black feminist thought," and how the meaning of being a "Black feminist" is, by its own existentiality, explicitly grounds itself and its analysis on its own theoretical tradition.

As a means of developing a theoretical tradition for "Black feminist thought," Collins outlines the existential need for a social construction of the meaning of Black feminist thought itself, beginning with "the politics of Black feminist thought." Collins's sense of the social constructive needs of Black feminist thought becomes situated on an intellectual tradition by African American women intellectuals of the nineteenth and twentieth centuries, insomuch as these "Black women intellectuals have laid a vital analytical foundation for a distinctive standpoint on self, community, and society and, in doing so, created a Black women's intellectual tradition."[259] In noting this, Collins also points to Maria W. Stewart as the originator of this tradition, whereby, Collins writes, "one striking dimension of the ideas of [Stewart] and her successors is the thematic consistency of their work."[260] With respect to this, Collins questions why this intellectual tradition has "remained virtually invisible until now"—this question leads Collins to see this invisibility as linked to a broader suppression traced to economic and political dimensions, to the extent that, as Collins notes, "ironically, feminist theory has also suppressed Black women's ideas."[261] Collins goes on to find that, "even though Black women intellectuals have long expressed a unique feminist consciousness about the intersection of race and class in structuring gender, historically we have not been full participants in white feminist organization."[262] Because of this, Collins concludes that

258. Collins, *Black Feminist Thought*, xiii.
259. Collins, *Black Feminist Thought*, 5.
260. Collins, *Black Feminist Thought*, 5.
261. Collins, *Black Feminist Thought*, 7.
262. Collins, *Black Feminist Thought*, 7.

> this historical suppression of Black women's ideas has had a pronounced influence on feminist theory. Theories advanced as being universally applicable to women as a group on closer examination appear greatly limited by the white, middle-class origins of their proportions.[263]

The "historical suppression of Black women's ideas," as argued by Collins, must be reclaimed, through the reclaiming of the Black feminist tradition through the means of activism. It is through this mode of activism that "African-American women's position in the economic, political, and ideological terrain," Collins writes, "[as] bounding intellectual discourse has fostered a distinctive Black feminist tradition."[264] The discourse that is derived from the Black feminist tradition, given that activism existentializes and even theologizes the meaning of "Black feminist thought" in spite of historical suppression, to the point that "Black feminist thought" outlines itself more fundamentally. For Collins, there are "two basic components of Black feminist thought," which are "its thematic content and its epistemological approach." When we speak about the meaning of Black feminist thought, as that which is "existential" and must theologize about God, what is expressed thematically and how it is expressed epistemologically, in Collins's view, "have been shaped by Black women's outsider-within stance and by our embeddedness in traditional African American culture.[265]

"My overall goal in this book," accordingly to Collins, "is to describe, analyze, explain the significance of, and generally further the development of Black feminist thought."[266] In "further[ing] the development of Black feminist thought," Collins details the following:

> In addressing this general goal, I have specific objectives. First, I summarize some of the essential themes in Black feminist thought by surveying their historical and contemporary expression. . . . My second objective is to explore selected neglected themes currently lacking a comprehensive Black feminist analysis. . . . My third objective is to develop an epistemological framework that can be used both to assess existing Black feminist thought and to clarify some of the underlying assumptions that impede the development of Black feminist thought.[267]

With respect to its "essential themes," the "neglected themes," and the development of an "epistemological framework," Collins eventually ponders the question: "What constitutes black feminism?"[268] Collins partly answers this question by finding that "the

---

263. Collins, *Black Feminist Thought*, 7.
264. Collins, *Black Feminist Thought*, 16.
265. Collins, *Black Feminist Thought*, 16.
266. Collins, *Black Feminist Thought*, 16.
267. Collins, *Black Feminist Thought*, 16–17.
268. Collins, *Black Feminist Thought*, 37.

primary guiding principle of Black feminism is a recurring humanist vision."[269] More specifically, to address the meaning of being a Black feminist, Collins turns to defining Black feminism as "womanism," which, as Collins argues, "addresses [the] notion of the solidarity of humanity."[270] In fact, what Collins seems to recognize is that the term "Black feminism," though constructing to distance itself from feminist thought in the same manner as Cone's Black theology sought to distance itself from traditional Western theology, inserting "Black" to the broader notion of feminist thought does not fully give an account for the unique existential needs and concerns of those that must philosophize about their existence and even theologize about God from a position at the intersection of "Blackness" and "womanhood." Though Collins recognizes that "womanism" more aptly gives an account for Black women in a way that the term "Black feminism" remains largely inadequate, Collins's single reference to "womanism" is notable and does not seem to completely address how the epistemology and consciousness of Black women, at the point of a unique existential experience and a unique kind of theologizing, become a "politics of empowerment."

KATIE CANNON'S *BLACK WOMANIST ETHICS*

Published just two years prior to Collins's *Black Feminist Thought*, Katie G. Cannon's *Black Womanist Ethics* (1988) begins with a personal narrative, in which Cannon explains the "origins of [her] study."[271] These "origins" are described by Cannon as grounded on how she "first began pondering the relationship between faith and ethics."[272] Not only does Cannon's approach mirror the personal narrative found in Collins's *Black Feminist Thought*, it becomes all the more apparent that, like Collins, Cannon is also attempting to locate her voice—Cannon's personal narrative contains her voice and that voice dictates a unique experience which is different from what Collins expresses. For Cannon, her personal narrative, her voice, and her experience is rooted in "the relationship between faith and ethics," such that, unlike Collins, Cannon recognizes that theologizing about God works at the intersection of narrative, voice, and experience. While Collins resists—or perhaps omits the role that theologizing plays in how she develops "Black feminist thought"—connecting faith to ethics, insomuch as Collins leans more toward extrapolating an ethics to her meaning of the "politics of empowerment," Cannon relies on "the relationship between faith and ethics" to existentially inform Cannon's own "politics of empowerment."

The connection that Cannon makes between "faith" and "ethics" brings Cannon further on the theological spectrum from Collins's efforts—this becomes essential to Collins's limited perspective of Black women to "Black feminism" and Cannon's more

269. Collins, *Black Feminist Thought*, 37.
270. Collins, *Black Feminist Thought*, 37–38.
271. Cannon, *Black Womanist Ethics*, 1.
272. Cannon, *Black Womanist Ethics*, 1.

expansive and deliberate embrace of "womanism." Though Cannon is also addressing the connection between epistemology and consciousness as they come to bear on the politics of empowerment, Cannon's alignment with womanism becomes, in itself, a way for Cannon to theologize about God in a way that Collins is unable or unwilling to do. This difference is, in one sense, regulated by Cannon's awareness of how faith and ethics both speak to "epistemology," "consciousness," and the "politics of empowerment," but, in another sense, regulated by a more "existential" and a more "theological" understanding of what it means to be a Black woman. Cannon captures this by ascertaining that "my community of faith taught me the principles of God's universal parenthood which engendered a social, intellectual and cultural ethos, embracing the equal humanity of all people."[273]

What we find, here, is that, while Collins seeks a "parenthood" for Black feminism that lies outside and beyond what is suppressed and marginalized by feminist thought, Cannon seeks a parenthood in God's universality. On this point alone, we see that Cannon's articulation of womanism—which Collins only mentions in passing—becomes not just an alignment to a closer horizontal experience of community than what could ever be drawn from feminist thought, but also to a closer vertical experience with God predicated on a "community of faith."

This community of faith, as Cannon defines it, is the means by which theologizing about God is possible and, in turn, it is the means by which epistemology, consciousness, and the politics of empowerment, as Collins defines them, becomes actualized. For Cannon, it is not enough to create a community that, as Collins writes, "addresses [the] notion of the solidarity of humanity"—only a community of faith allows that "solidarity of humanity" to happen, through theologizing the experience of what it means to be human and, from that standpoint, theologizing about God anchored to a "solidarity of humanity." With a "community of faith" and the necessity of the solidarity of humanity in mind, Cannon develops an ethics that exceeds Collins's ethics—for Collins, ethics only goes as far as the connection between epistemology, consciousness, and politics of empowerment, when Black women locate an ethos to the very meaning of "Blackness" and "womanhood" as too far afield from feminist thought. What Collins's ethics seems to suggest is a philosophical or theoretical ethics that does not venture far enough into a theological understanding of what makes the experience of Black women existentially removed from what feminist thought outlines. Cannon's handling of ethics is theological, in the sense that she expands upon the philosophical or theoretical, in order to more thoroughly explain the existential situation in which Black women find themselves morally speaking.

Cannon's focus for *Black Womanist Ethics* is, in her words, "to show how Black women live out a moral wisdom in their real-lived context that does not appeal to the fixed rules or absolute principles of the white-oriented, male-structured society."[274]

273. Cannon, *Black Womanist Ethics*, 1.
274. Cannon, *Black Womanist Ethics*, 4.

This becomes the pitfall in Collins's "Black feminist thought" project. And yet, Cannon claims that "[her] goal is not to arrive at my own prescriptive or normative ethic."[275] Not only is this precisely what Collins attempt to do with "Black feminist thought," but it also speaks to Cannon's understanding that "womanism," as it is predicated on a "community of faith" that theologizes about God, cannot be presented in a prescriptive or normative way. In avoiding any prescriptivizing or normativizing of "womanism," Cannon intends to "pursu[e] an investigation" that adheres to two goals: (1) "help Black women, and others who care, to understand and to appreciate the richness of their own moral struggle through the life of the common people and the oral tradition,"[276] and (2) "further understandings of some of the differences between ethics of life under oppression and established moral approaches which take for granted freedom and a wide range of choices."[277]

Though Cannon concedes that her study is "a partisan one"—which certainly mirrors what can be ascertained from Collins's own study—Cannon qualifies this admission by offering that "[her study] is not merely a glorification of the Black female community, but an attempt to add to the far too few positive records concerning the Black woman as a moral agent."[278] Cannon links this moral agency existentially to what she refers to as "the black woman's moral situation," relegated to the period of 1619–1900.[279] In order to quantify what Cannon refers to as the Black woman's "moral situation" between 1619 to the Civil War era, she lists the following: (1) the Black woman as "property," (2) the Black woman as "brood-sow," (3) the Black woman as "work-ox," (4) the slave-owner's "total control" over the slave-woman, (5) sexual exploitation, (6) racial discrimination, and (7) the denial of "social bonds" for the Black woman. In the eighteenth century, the "moral situation" after the Civil War, according to Cannon, includes: (1) Black women as sharecroppers, (2) Black women as educators, and (3) Black women as "victims of racial segregation, defamation and discrimination."[280]

While Collins's view of "Black feminist thought" also treads the same territory as Cannon when conceptualizing the experiences of Black women during the Civil War era and post-World War II, Cannon's encapsulating of these experiences as indicative of a moral situation speaks more explicitly to the necessity of ethics than Collins does. In fact, in tying the moral situation of Black women to being "victims of the aggravated inequalities of the tridimensional phenomenon of [race, class, and gender oppression],"[281] it becomes clear that Cannon employs an understanding of

275. Cannon, *Black Womanist Ethics*, 5.
276. Cannon, *Black Womanist Ethics*, 5.
277. Cannon, *Black Womanist Ethics*, 5–6.
278. Cannon, *Black Womanist Ethics*, 6.
279. Cannon, *Black Womanist Ethics*, 31.
280. Cannon, *Black Womanist Ethics*, 31–51.
281. Cannon, *Black Womanist Ethics*, 68.

victimology, which becomes voiced in Bradley's *Liberating Black Theology* as a counter to Cone. In this same manner, Cannon's recognition of victimology is voiced in a way that is challenged by Collins's "politics of empowerment"—while Collins points to an ethic of personal accountability, Cannon subscribes to what can be referred to as an ethic of theological accountability, which must be made "existential" through theologizing about God.

The Theologizing of "bell hooks"

In "Between Activism, Religiosity, and the Public Sphere: The Intellectual Insurgency of bell hooks" (2019), I suggest that the thought of bell hooks operates as an insurgent intellectualism, predicated on the relationship between activism, religiosity, and the public sphere—the very meaningfulness of that relationship is calibrated by a Black feminism that attunes itself existentially toward a Womanist approach. This approach, as I argue in the article, "pits her status as a Black woman more accurately against a general patriarchy and, more importantly, against a twofold marginalization from both patriarchy and matriarchy."[282] Not only, by way of its attunement, does Womanism locate a twofold lack of belongingness to the general structure of patriarchy and the more specific patriarchy established by Black theology, but it also locates another twofold lack of belongingness to the general structure of matriarchy of feminism and the more specific matriarchism construed by Black feminism—the insurgency of bell hooks's intellectualism confronts this lack of belongingness with a "rage" similar to James Baldwin's that, as I propose, "provides the foundation for an insurgent Black intellectual life that is more insurgent than Baldwin's."[283] In doing so, in order to, as I write, "[channel] the meaning of [her] *being* into the meaning of insurgent intellectual life,"[284] hooks's ability to theologize about God from the standpoint of Womanism orients itself into a selfhood that translates itself through acts of activism, approaches to religiosity, and an engagement in the public sphere.

To say that hooks operates as "bell hooks" means, as I offer in the article, recognizing that her pseudonym existentializes *the meaning of being* for bell hooks. By this, we find that the *nom de plume* accomplishes more than just "mask the identity of the literary authorship of all the texts ascribed to 'bell hooks.'"[285] To even think of it in this rather simple way means only thinking about the literary or perhaps the philosophical comportment of bell hooks to "bell hooks"—thinking of her thought this way does not address "the theological," even if we must begin here, for the sake of laying a foundation for further reflection. However, in beginning here as I do in the article—in what is, in fact, the article's opening sentence—I wished to make a clear distinction between bell

---

282. Woodson, "Between Activism, Religiosity, and the Public Sphere," 7.
283. Woodson, "Between Activism, Religiosity, and the Public Sphere," 7.
284. Woodson, "Between Activism, Religiosity, and the Public Sphere," 6.
285. Woodson, "Between Activism, Religiosity, and the Public Sphere," 1.

hooks the person and "bell hooks" the thinker. That distinction is a critical first move to make when understanding how hooks theologizes about God and, in turn, allows the very meaning of "bell hooks" to become theologized itself—what is at stake, here, is a dialectical distinction for the purposes of theologizing.

It is a kind of theologizing that occurs through "bell hooks," insomuch as "bell hooks" is existentialized at the intersection of activism, religiosity, and the public sphere. In other words, the very meaning of "bell hooks" is existentially tied to the meaningfulness of activism, religiosity, and the public sphere. The notion of "bell hooks," as such, becomes a relation of the relatedness of activism, religiosity, and the public sphere, which individually relate to "bell hooks." I use these terms "relation," "relatedness," and the implicit "relate" as Kierkegaard does in *Sickness unto Death*, through the explication of "the self is a relation that relates itself to itself."[286] The same construction applies to "bell hooks." That is to say, *the meaning of being* for "bell hooks" is delineated in the relation of the activism of "bell hooks," the religiosity of "bell hooks," and "bell hooks" in the public sphere—each individually theologizes the other two at its own level, while individually theologizing "bell hooks."

The theologizing of "bell hooks" becomes, in itself, a theologizing that results from the relation. In other words, the relation informs what is theologized and how theologizing happens. But, more importantly, when theologizing "bell hooks," there is an existential distance placed between what is theologized and what does the theologizing: "bell hooks" as that which is theologized, and bell hooks as that which does theologizing. In this way, for the theologizing of "bell hooks" to even become possible, it means that bell hooks does a kind of theologizing that, by necessity, existentializes itself in the role of the activist, in the role of religiousness, and in the role of the public sphere. All three come to fruition through hooks's Womanism—this is what allows "bell hooks" to be theologized as much as it allows bell hooks to do theology, particularly when what is theologized and doing theology itself theologizes "bell hooks" beyond any theologizing that can be had within Black feminism.

If following the proposition that, as I write in "Between Activism," "hooks does not operate in the same space as Black feminism, no more than she does within the space of Black intellectualism,"[287] I am speaking, here, of the extent to which the theologizing of bell hooks exceeds the bounds of both Black feminism and even Black intellectualism. This is not to say that neither hold significance to the meaning of being "bell hooks"—rather, "bell hooks," as that which is theologized and does the theologizing from bell hooks, is attuned by Black feminism and Black intellectualism. This does not minimize what bell hooks means to the Black feminist movement or even the Black intellectual tradition—to even theologize at all means that bell hooks does so in acknowledgment, on the one hand, of Black feminism and, on the other hand, of Black intellectualism. Yet, to theologize at all means theologizing beyond the two and into a

---

286. Kierkegaard, *Sickness unto Death*, 1.
287. Woodson, "Between Activism, Religiosity, and the Public Sphere," 12.

Womanist thought, which, as I suggest, "is contingently, by necessity, an *insurgent* Black intellectualism."[288] What this means is the theologizing of "bell hooks"—once bell hooks does the theologizing—is a Womanist theologizing that grounds itself in an insurgent Black intellectualism. It is this insurgency that existentializes how bell hooks theologizes about God and, in turn, allows for a theologizing of "bell hooks." This insurgent spirit is what existentially holds bell hooks to "bell hooks" dialectically, such that the two have a spiritual unity predicated on a Womanism that, in itself, engages in a kind of theologizing about God as a form of existential theology.

Delores S. Williams's *Sisters in the Wilderness*

In her preface to *Sisters in the Wilderness: The Challenge of Womanist God-Talk* (1993), Delores S. Williams argues that "[her] female faith seeking understanding asks questions." These questions are contextualized against, as she suggests, "what looks like genocidal impulses in American culture directed toward black people (male and female)," such her first question in this regard asks: "What kind of 'works' can stem from black women's belief in God who helps them 'make a way out of no way'?"[289] Such a question, as a starting point into how Williams theologizes God from a Black female perspective, is grounded on the problematized situational experience—it addresses what it means to be a Black woman and how being a Black woman requires a kind of theologizing that must make an account for the "kind of works" that can possibly "stem from black women's belief in God."

From this initial question, which situates the question of the meaning of Black women in relation to the question of the meaning of God, Williams's next question is this:

> How do [black women] shape a theology that is at once committed to black women's issues and life-struggles and simultaneously addresses the black community's historic struggle to survive and develop a positive, productive quality of life in the face if death?

This question is an "existential" one, insomuch as it is concerned with mitigating meaningfulness and meaninglessness to the unique dimensions of Black womanhood, or what we might call Black femaleness, or even Black femininity. With these unique dimensions in mind, Williams is right to ask: "How do I design theological language and devise theological methods that not only speak in the academy but also speak to African-American women and the African-American community in a language they can understand?"[290] Not only is theological language an essential aspect of "the existential" position that Black women must explicate, it also becomes, as noted in

---

288. Woodson, "Between Activism, Religiosity, and the Public Sphere," 12.
289. Williams, *Sisters in the Wilderness*, xii.
290. Williams, *Sisters in the Wilderness*, xii.

Williams's own shift from "Black women" to "African-American women," important to define terms and remain faithful to this terminology. As Williams points out, how we term the unique dimensions of "Black women" within a broader understanding of human existence necessitates "design[ing] theological language"—this must be a kind of language that, in one sense, allows "Black women" to speak about God and, in another sense, allows this theologizing about God to be meaningful to what is ultimately conceptualized by the term "Black women."

This brings Williams to another question that must be asked, particularly if the uniqueness of the Black female theological voice is capable of articulating a meaningfulness of theologizing about God—Williams asks this question, in a two-part manner, as the following:

> How does my black female theological voice join the chorus of non-black women's voices and male voices in theology without compromising black women's faith? How do we black female theologians speak with all our strength when some white female and some black male scholars work together to crowd out our voices or take control of our words?[291]

The notion of a "theological voice" and the ability to "speak" are, together, part and parcel of what means to theologize about God, when theologizing itself is predicated on existence and how that existence expresses itself as a precursor to the act of theologizing.

The very positionality of theologizing about God with a "Black female theological voice" seeks to carve an "existential" point of view, which is not just altogether removed from the space that "white female" theologians occupy, but also from the space occupied by male-normative Black theology. It is a positionality that arises from what Williams points out as a "theological corrective," which, as she writes, "is developing [with] considerable potential for bringing black women's experience into theology so that black women will see the need to transform the sexist character of the churches and their theology."[292] This "sexist character" is not just espoused from the male-normative aims and tasks of Black theology, but it also, if we take Williams a bit further, is certainly espoused by "white female" theology that, in itself, becomes patriarchal enough to marginalize white-normative views of womanhood. Both, in light of what Williams acknowledges, frame a "sexist character" to what it means to theologize about God within feminist theology and Black theology.

Accordingly, Williams navigates the marginalization of feminist theology and that of Black theology into a womanist theology, which "emerge[s] from what many of us saw as characteristic of black women's experiences of relation, loss, gain, faith, hope, celebration, and defiance."[293] All of these concerns—or issues that either benefit

---

291. Williams, *Sisters in the Wilderness*, xii.
292. Williams, *Sisters in the Wilderness*, xiii.
293. Williams, *Sisters in the Wilderness*, xiv.

or limit the meaning of human existence more generally—are "existential," providing a framework by which "Black women" are able to theologize about God. Though Williams suggests that "like black male liberation theology, womanist theology assumes the necessity of responsible freedom for all human beings[,] but womanist theology especially concerns itself with the faith, survival and freedom-struggle of African-American women."[294]

Kelly B. Douglas and the Existentiality of Sexuality

In *Sexuality and the Black Church: A Womanist Perspective* (1999), Kelly Brown Douglass introduces a phenomenon that existentially comports the meaning of being a Black woman to her community, which ultimately mitigates how she theologizes about God and how her womanism stands before God: sexuality. For Douglas, in order to address the meaning of Black sexuality as it is represented by Black womanhood requires "untangl[ing] the complex reality of Black sexuality as well as [discerning] a theology in regard to the same."[295] Douglas finds that, in entering this discussion about what can be described as the existentiality of sexuality, woman religious scholars, including herself, "[have not] given any sustained consideration to issues of homophobia/heterosexism or any other issue related to Black sexuality."[296] Not only does Douglas contemplate why womanist theology is "silent on sexuality," but she also locates an inadequacy or a contradiction in womanist theology, given that womanist theology is, by definition, as Douglas defines it, "a theology recognized by some as providing one of the most holistic visions for human life and freedom."[297] Without addressing the existentiality of sexuality, Douglas seems to suggest that womanist theology is not as "holistic" a "vision" as it could be, particularly if the existentiality of sexuality is something that adds complexity and authenticity to human life and, in turn, becomes the means by which freedom takes place.

> Why were we womanist theologians, who so aptly criticize Black and feminist theologians for their failure to comprehend the complexity of Black women's oppression, so disinclined to confront the oppression of lesbians or broadly the presence of homophobia/heterosexism within the Black community?[298]

With this fundamental question in mind, Douglas devotes the first of three parts of *Sexuality and the Black Church* with "seek[ing] to determine why Black churches and the Black theological community in particular have been so reluctant to discuss

---

294. Williams, *Sisters in the Wilderness*, xiv.
295. Douglas, *Sexuality and the Black Church*, 1.
296. Douglas, *Sexuality and the Black Church*, 1.
297. Douglas, *Sexuality and the Black Church*, 1.
298. Douglas, *Sexuality and the Black Church*, 1.

matters of sexuality."²⁹⁹ For Douglas, "the essential function of Black sexuality" is developed and influenced in relation to White culture, insomuch as, in Douglas's words, "the exploitation and manipulation of Black sexuality are crucial to the maintenance of White patriarchal hegemony in America."³⁰⁰

Douglas proceeds further on this point by presenting, in a second part, an examination of "Black people's responses to the White cultural assault upon their sexuality." This part, along with the first, seem to suggest a direct critique of the blaxploitation movement predominant in the 1970s, in which, under the guise of existential empowerment, there arose an existential exploitation of the meaning of Blackness, particularly in terms of, if reminded of Douglas's words, "the exploitation and manipulation of Black sexuality." Not only was this "crucial to the maintenance of White patriarchal hegemony in America," but there also seemed to be something in it, through Black existential empowerment, a desire to provide a means for maintaining a reconceptualized "patriarchal hegemony."

Yet, as much as Black theology, and even womanist theology, intends to capture and express this reconceptualized "patriarchal hegemony," Black sexuality goes unaddressed from the standpoint of Black womanhood, since that sexuality, in itself, is articulated by "White patriarchal hegemony in America." In light of this, and in thinking of the meaning that sexuality holds when theologizing about God, Douglas develops "a theology of black sexuality," which, in a part three to the text, "examines the responses of the Black Church and Black theologians to Black sexuality."³⁰¹ From this, Douglas constructs an existential theology rooted in the existentiality of sexuality to Black womanhood, such that sexuality, at its most existential, translates and is translated by a theologizing about God.

Emilie M. Townes and the "Womanist Dancing Mind"

From the outset of *Womanist Ethics and the Cultural Production of Evil* (2006), Emile Townes draws on the concept of "the dancing mind" as it is presented by Toni Morrison, and as Townes notes, in "Morrison's acceptance speech for the National Book Foundation's Medal for Distinguished Contribution to American Letters in 1996."³⁰² From this speech, Townes references Morrison's focus "on the dangers, the necessities, and the pleasures of the reading/writing life in the late twentieth century."³⁰³ The dangers that Townes cites from Morrison are, through how "they are captured in two anecdotes," existential, in the sense that they are defined by and define what Morrison calls, "the dance of an open mind." Through the dancing and the openness of

---

299. Douglas, *Sexuality and the Black Church*, 6.
300. Douglas, *Sexuality and the Black Church*, 7.
301. Douglas, *Sexuality and the Black Church*, 7.
302. Townes, *Womanist Ethics*, 1.
303. Townes, *Womanist Ethics*, 1.

this mind, Morrison finds that the "activity that occurs most naturally" is one that existentially positions a unique meaning of existence toward "the communal," "the psychological," "the cultural," and "the historical." For Townes, Morrison's notion of "the dance of an open mind" turns into the following understanding:

> It is in the dancing mind that many of us meet each other more often than not. ... It is this dancing mind—where we tease through the possibilities and the realities, the hopes, the dreams, the nightmares, the terrors, the critique, the analysis, the plea, the witness—that womanist work is done in the academy, in the classroom, in the religious gatherings of our various communities, in those quiet and no so quiet times in which we try to reflect on the ways in which we know and see and feel and do.[304]

The "dancing mind," as Townes presents it, is that which existentializes the question of the meaning of being, such that, when operating at the intersection of "the communal," "the psychological," "the cultural," and "the historical," the very openness of this mind attunes existence to a grounding point. The openness anchors human existence to centrality, around which all the dimensions of the meaning of being a Black woman—as it is comprised of, in Townes's words, "the possibilities and the realities, the hopes, the dreams, the nightmares, the terrors, the critique, the analysis, the plea, the witness"—impose an "existential" weight of meaning upon the Black woman. It is only through "womanist work," rather than that of feminist work or even the work of Black theology proper, that the Black woman grounds the meaning of her being to the "existential" demands made "in the academy, in the classroom, in the religious gatherings of our various communities." In these spaces, "the dancing mind" of the Black woman attunes and is attuned by the meaning of her existence, so that, from her unique experience, through a unique voice, with the use of a unique narrative is able to speak "in those quiet and not so quiet times." The dancing mind, then, is the "techne" by which the Black woman resists subalternity and the degree to which, as Spivak argues, her existence is grounded on the inability of the subaltern to speak. The speaking is in "womanist work," which partly involves "try[ing] to reflect on the ways in which we know and see and feel and do." Not only does this mean that the dancing mind grounds "womanist work," it also means that "womanist work" becomes a ground, in itself, for the dancing mind—the relationship between two, as inextricable as they are, allow the Black woman to "know and see and feel and do," so that, in grounding themselves in the meaning of their existence, they are, likewise, grounding themselves to the broader world. Townes further explains this connectedness in the following way:

> This womanist dancing mind is more than my attempt to make sense of the worlds surrounding us—sometimes enveloping us, sometimes smothering us, sometimes holding us, sometimes birthing us. It is more than my desire

---

304. Townes, *Womanist Ethics*, 1.

to reconfigure the world and then invite others to come and inspect the textures, the colors, the patterns, the shapes, the sizes of this new order, this new set of promises.

Townes finds that the task of the "womanist dancing mind," as that which calibrates "the existential" between the grounding of existence and grounding to worldhood, is oriented toward the worldliness of the meaning of being human and the "existential" threat that evil poses to human existence. This "threat" is not just something that must be overcome as a means of ensuring that the meaning of human existence is optimized, it also becomes an essential aspect of what it means, by nature, to be human—this meaning, for Townes, becomes explicated into the extent to which the "womanist dancing mind" optimizes what it means to be a Black woman and how "evil" is handled and handles Black womanhood. Townes describes the relationship between "evil" and what it means to be a Black woman in the following sentiment:

> Exploring evil as a cultural production highlights the systematic construction of truncated narratives designed to support and perpetuate structural inequities and forms of social oppression. Thus, this interdisciplinary study of dismantling evil as a cultural production seeks to understand the interior material life of evil through these narratives.[305]

Because evil, as Townes defines it, is a "cultural production," it means that evil is created out of the very meaning of being a Black woman, when that meaning is grounded, first and foremost, on a unique narrative, a unique voice, and a unique experience. Narrative, voice, and experience, then, as a collective perspective, point to a "systematic construction" that, in itself, is "designed to support and perpetuate structural inequities and forms of social oppression." It is in this way that evil becomes embedded in not just the meaning of being human, but interwoven into the very fabric of the "structural inequities and forms of social oppression" that place Black women in a unique position in the world—when speaking from this situatedness, the presence of evil directly affects the manner in which Black women speak, and the manner in which Black women narrate and conceptualize their experience. Dismantling evil is a necessity in defining what is "existential" about being a Black woman—this dismantling not only confronts an issue of theodicy, but it also confronts a broader sense of theologizing. The "womanist dancing mind," by itself, does not allow for or present the conditions for the dismantling of evil for the "existential" sake of Black womanhood—it is a theologizing about God with a kind of existential theology that situates Black womanhood within the "womanist dancing mind" and extends that "womanist dancing mind" toward a God as a point of reactualization.

---

305. Townes, *Womanist Ethics*, 4.

Monica Coleman's *Making a Way out of No Way*

In *Making a Way out of No Way* (2008), Monica Coleman does not make a direct or even an indirect reference to Emilie Townes's *Womanist Ethics and the Cultural Production of Evil*, published just two years before Coleman's work. What makes this notable is that Coleman's text, in standing so close to Townes's text, carries forward the close connection Townes makes between Black women, culture, and evil—the companionship between Coleman's and Townes's respective texts place Coleman's womanism in theological and literary context against Townes on Coleman's notion of evil. Like Townes, Coleman views evil as exerting an existential threat on the meaning of human existence and "existential" to the relationship between Black women and culture (i.e., community, society, womanhood, etc.), insomuch as it must be, as Townes argues, "dismantled" for the sake of existentializing Black womanhood's approach to theologizing about God. Also, as Townes does, Coleman considers the meaning of Black womanhood at the intersection of narrative, voice, and experience—and like Townes, Coleman begins with a specific narrative, outlining a specific voice and presenting a specific experience.

After presenting a narrative about "Lisa" couched in a voice that expresses "Lisa's" experience, Coleman arrives at the conclusion:

> I wanted to connect the specificity of [Lisa's] story with a worldview that acknowledges the reality of evil and loss and finds opportunities for life in each new moment without either waiting on God to make it happen or making Lisa do it all herself.[306]

In order to approach the narrative, voice, and experience of "Lisa," Coleman finds that "[she] needed a postmodern womanist theology."[307] If we understand that the story of "Lisa," in itself, is an explication of womanism and womanism, in itself, must be articulated theologically, we must ask about Coleman's need for a "postmodern" womanist theology. From this call—if we view Coleman "need" as a call to action—we might wonder what Coleman wishes to express that has not been expressed in the womanist theologizing of, for example, Townes. To this end, we are positioned to contemplate if Townes and the "dancing womanist mind" is rooted in a modern theologizing that becomes inadequate for Coleman—the limits of Townes's womanism, as far as Coleman is concerned, limits the very meaning of being a Black woman, even at the intersection of narrative, voice, and experience. The question is, then, does Coleman locate something "existential" in the narrative, voice, and experience of "Lisa" that is not captured in Townes or the broadening tradition of womanist theology, or is it that the kind of theologizing that best expresses the existential needs and concerns of "Lisa" grounded in a postmodernity that Coleman does not find in Townes?

---

306. Coleman, *Making a Way*, 3.
307. Coleman, *Making a Way*, 3.

Perhaps, answering these questions requires revisiting Coleman's desire "to connect the specificity of [Lisa's] story with a worldview." Coleman believes that Townes's notion of the cultural production of evil is not sufficiently "acknowledg[ing] the reality of evil and loss." If this is so, it seems to me that Coleman is also contending that Townes—as Coleman's most immediate womanist contemporary working explicitly within the context of evil—is not fundamentally intent on "find[ing] opportunities for life in each new moment without either waiting on God to make it happen," or asking that "Lisa" takes personal "existential" ownership in the meaning of her Black womanhood. In short, Coleman is pointing out the omission of the role of salvation in the encounter with evil. Even if we can suggest that Coleman agrees with Townes about the cultural production of evil, Coleman recognizes that it is not enough to simply—or even fundamentally—dismantle evil. It is more important to be saved from evil. If adhering to theodicy, it would seem that "dismantling" does not eradicate evil altogether. Rather, to dismantle means to break down or even deconstruct what evil is and what evil does, but it does not more forthrightly address our situatedness to evil, and the extent to which a dismantled evil becomes constructed elsewhere in another form. Coleman seems to follow this train of thought, finding that salvation more existentially addresses how human existence handles and is handled by evil than Townes's dismantling—to be saved from evil is to be saved from evil everywhere, insomuch as the necessity for salvation allows us to authentically theologize about God in a way that is not fully possible in the mere dismantling of evil.

Coleman's need for a "postmodern womanist theology" as that which provides a salvific "existential" framework to counter the problem of evil, does not overlook the notion that "womanist theology is a response to sexism in Black theology and racism in feminist theology."[308] As a womanist theologian, Coleman "want[s] to maintain [her] connection to black men and remain faithful to the church tradition from which [she] come[s]."[309] To "remain faithful to the church tradition" means adhering to the traditional understandings of the relationship between evil and salvation, especially as a theological construction of the meaning of human existence, which is actualized by the social construction of Black womanhood. It is this theological construction that brings Coleman to agree that "womanist theology examines the social construction of black womanhood in relation to the African American community and religious concepts."[310] To this end, Coleman writes, "womanist theology is known for its analysis of religion and society in light of the triple oppression of racism, sexism and classism that characterizes the experience of black women."[311] This characterization, as Coleman notes, is brought to bear by "unearth[ing] the hidden voices in history, scripture, and the experiences of contemporary marginalized African American women to discover

308. Coleman, *Making a Way*, 6.
309. Coleman, *Making a Way*, 6.
310. Coleman, *Making a Way*, 6.
311. Coleman, *Making a Way*, 7.

fragments that can create a narrative for the present and future."[312] The narrative that is created "for the present and future" contains a temporal significance that existentializes "the experiences of contemporary marginalized African American women," situating that womanist perspective between history and scripture—what is unfolded in this "existential" is a perpetual, cyclical relationship with what the meanings of history and scripture have toward "the present and future."

Coleman connects the meanings of history and scripture, and "the present and future" to an ongoing narrative—this connection is not limited to the scope and task of womanist theology, but is expanded into a dialogue Coleman holds between womanist theology and process theology. It is through a womanist-process dialogue that Coleman is able to satisfy her need for a postmodern womanist theology—this postmodernization, through process theology, makes an account for "everything that happens [becoming] a product of the past, what's presently possible, and what we do with those things."[313] For Coleman, what process theology injects into womanist theology and, in doing so, allows it to become a postmodern womanist theology, consider what it means to have Black womanhood as a process, insomuch as:

> This continual process of sorting these three inputs: what you inherit from the world, what's possible in your context, and what you do about it. God is the one who offers the possibilities to the world, urging us to choose the paths that lead to a vision of the common good. While the principles of God's vision do not change, the way it gets played out on the earth depends on what is happening in the world. God takes in, or incorporates, the events of the world into who God is.[314]

Coleman continues, by adding:

> God then relates those events with God's vision for the common good, searching for the best of what has happened in order to offer those aspects back to us in our next instance of living. In short, our experiences in the world influence who we are and what we do. We then go on to influence those around us. What we do also affects God and how God relates to the world.[315]

Described this way, Coleman's explication of a postmodern womanist theology—a theology that theologizes about God in a way that understands how "what we do also affects God and how God relates to the world"—is an existential theology that is predicated on how "our experiences in the world influence who we are and what we do," our worldhood, and God's existence.

---

312. Coleman, *Making a Way*, 7.
313. Coleman, *Making a Way*, 8.
314. Coleman, *Making a Way*, 8.
315. Coleman, *Making a Way*, 8.

Dorothy Akoto's "Women and Health in Ghana and the *Trokosi* Practice"

When considering Dorothy Akoto's article entitled "Women and Health in Ghana and the *Trokosi* Practice," as it is included in *African Women, Religion, and Health* (2006), in the conclusion, Akoto suggests that "this article has attempted to address some of the issues that affect the health of women [since] women's health issues and those of human rights cannot be divorced from each other."[316] I think this is a very important connection that Akoto is making: the relationship between health and human rights and how, through this relationship, African women come to understand their relationship to the world through various, hierarchal iterations. It is in this latter sense that I wish to focus this journal on—the extent to which the relationship between an African woman's health and her human rights is predicated on a foundational conception of an African woman's selfhood. The self, then, is a point of intersectionality, where health issues and human rights issues meet.

Akoto is quite clear in her article to quantify her idea of "health" as being, as she argues, "multi-faceted," containing the physiological, psychological, social, and the economic.[317] All of these "domains,"[318] as Akoto refers to them, are linked to issues of the body. Of course, anything physiological directly denoted the body, but I find that the psychological, the social and the economic, particularly in relation to the African woman's role in a male-dominated, patriarchal society, venture to understand the African woman's body as a psychological body capable of maintaining the patriarchal status quo, as a *social body* capable of producing children and as an *economic body* capable of marrying. In both of these cases—though respectively linked to the institutions of the family and marriage—the social and the economic inform the physiological.

So, though Akoto quantifies the physiological, the psychological, the social, and the economic as four essentialist domains to the issue of African women's health, I would add the *existential*—in this, I mean not only the philosophical or the religious as independent epistemological understandings of the most intrinsic mysteries of human reality, but, rather, combined to describe both the ontological and the metaphysical aspects of what it means to be human and how human existence, as an experience, comes to bear on "being."

When I consider "being," I am thinking about selfhood and the extent to which the role of being "a self" refers to a positional manifestation of "being-human"—that is, a manifestation that is just as much spatial as it is temporal—but also, in light of the uniqueness of the African woman, the situatedness of "being-an-African-woman." In this sense, health, particularly as Akoto describes it—as she begins to address

---

316. Akoto, "Women and Health," 107.
317. Akoto, "Women and Health," 98.
318. Akoto, "Women and Health," 98.

what "health" is by, first, offering a dictionary definition of the word[319]—is a kind of "condition" which, perhaps, is a balance between sickness and well-being. Of course, in a rather obvious manner, good "health" is well-being, while bad "health" is sickness. But, if moving a bit beyond such obligatory binaries, "well-being" and "sickness" influence selfhood—how an individual understands themselves in relation to the world is filtered through whether they have "good health" or "bad health," and, by extension, any ability the individual has to determine if their health is "good" or "bad," is not self-referential, but in reference to others. To this end, the possibility of "good health" or "bad health" is more than just physiological, social, or economic—though they all play very important roles, nonetheless—but is an existential issue that is quantified through human rights.

Denise Ackerman's "From Mere Existence to Tenacious Endurance"

Here, I will focus mainly on Denise Ackerman's article entitled "From Mere Existence to Tenacious Endurance," as it appears in *African Women, Religion, and Health* (2006). In it, Ackerman constructs a dialectic between existence and endurance, which, as she argues, is respectively delineated as "mere existence" and "tenacious endurance." First, in relation to the former term, Ackerman defines "mere existence" in the following manner: "a kind of existence in conditions that rob people of their autonomy, and where the daily struggle to deal with stigma, shame, deteriorating bodily functions, discomfort, pain, and fear is overwhelming."[320] To this end, when considering "tenacious endurance," Ackerman conceives of the ability to "put up"[321] with "mere existence," particularly if encountering "mere existence" as a condition grounded on the situatedness of suffering, but specifically predicated on, as Ackerman denotes, "bearing suffering with fortitude, courage and tenacity without giving way to [suffering]."[322] Here, what Ackerman is setting up is the notion of suffering as an ontological form of human existence—it is something that is graspable, conceivable, and explainable. Suffering, then, is the ontological representation of the metaphysical concepts of "mere existence" and "tenacious endurance"—in this regard, "mere existence" and "tenacious endurance" are idealities that can only concretized through suffering.

If beginning here—that is, with Ackerman's dialectic between "mere existence" and "tenacious endurance"—it is safe to argue that Ackerman considers the aforementioned dialectic that comes to bear on the teleological condition of suffering is something that makes suffering a unifying and centralizing force for the human experience. I am thinking about this in terms of Mikhail Bakhtin's notion of "dialogic,"

---

319. Akoto, "Women and Health," 98.
320. Ackerman, "From Mere Existence," 225.
321. Ackerman, "From Mere Existence," 224.
322. Ackerman, "From Mere Existence," 224.

as a "force that serve[s] to unify and centralize the verbal-ideological world."[323] As a dialectic, "mere existence" and "tenacious endurance" are dialogical, speaking across "suffering" as a plane of understanding. To speak across "suffering" means not just bringing together "mere existence" and "tenacious endurance" from their respective reference points, but, more importantly, using "suffering" as a way to make sense out of the verbal and the ideological.

Suffering, as the unification and centralization of "mere existence" and "tenacious endurance," becomes the primary focus of Ackerman's "feminist theology of praxis." As such, Ackerman is careful to define her use of "feminist theology" in the following way: "[Feminist theology] takes all women's experiences of oppression and discrimination very seriously."[324] What Ackerman is taking "very seriously," first and foremost, is the extent to which "suffering" is an authentic condition of human "being," a very existential state of the human experience of "being-in-the-world," which must be viewed not from a theoretical standpoint but, instead, from a practical point of view. In other words, suffering as a facticity of existence rooted in positivism and empirical study. This is Ackerman's "praxis"—it is, as she argues, "a central interpretative lens for [her] theology."[325] From this interpretative lens, I would argue that Ackerman is not just developing a theology from the "bottom up," but, through her discussion of suffering as the unifying and centralizing force that brings together "mere existence" and "tenacious endurance," is developing what I will call a "low hermeneutic."

Mercy Oduyoye's *Daughters of Anowa*

From Mercy Oduyoye's *Daughters of Anowa* (1995), I want to focus on chapter 4, entitled "Culture's Bondswoman." What struck me as particularly interesting about this chapter is the sense that African women share a relationship with culture, a relationship where they become, in effect, culture's bondswoman. More importantly, if following Oduyoye's argument a bit further, there is a dialectical relationship between culture and the African woman, where culture situates African women in a situatedness predicated on power and authority. From this, I find it possible to consider Oduyoye's use of power and authority to describe the dialectical relationship between culture and African women as distinctly Hegelian—for Hegel, particularly through the "lordship and bondsman" relation across two self-consciousnesses, a dialectical relationships predicated on power and authority develops between the "relation of the self-conscious individuals [where it] is such that they prove themselves and each other through a life-and-death struggle."[326]

---

323. Bakhtin, *Dialogic Imagination*, 270.
324. Ackerman, "From Mere Existence," 226.
325. Ackerman, "From Mere Existence," 226.
326. Hegel, *Phenomenology of Spirit*, 113–14.

Rather than in the literal sense, I find that what Oduyoye describes, through what I would argue is a Hegelian dialectical structure, is a "life-and-death struggle" of African women within a patriarchal society. It is a "struggle" for legitimacy and existential value—and, in effect, a struggle against classism, oppression, marginalization, and sexism. This especially comes to bear when further considering Hegel's contention that "the relationship of husband and wife is in the first place the one in which one consciousness immediately recognizes itself in another."[327] When Hegel invokes the term "consciousness," he is speaking of self-consciousness—the possibility of being conscious of another and self-conscious of oneself. What arises from self-consciousness, as Hegel goes on to propose, is a kind of "knowledge of this mutual recognition."[328] I view this "mutual recognition" not just best describes a man knowing he is a man and knowing that a woman is a woman, but also describes a husband knowing he is a husband and knowing that his wife is his wife. More importantly, it is about a woman recognizing she is a woman and a wife, most notably within the infrastructure of a patriarchal man-woman relationship.

If considering Oduyoye more carefully through a Hegelian model, I find the following becomes true of a patriarchal society constructing on power and authority: it is about a woman knowing that she cannot be a husband. The "knowledge," in turn, that comes from this kind of "recognition," particularly on the part of the woman in the dialectic, is steeped in the existential nature of her inferior position.[329] Here, what arises, through such a "recognition" is what Derrida calls "différance": an understanding that existential differences defer positionalities. In this respect, recognizes the differences between herself and another (a man, in this case), she immediately grasps the epistemological value of being deferred to a position of inferiority. This, of course, is quite problematic, particularly in light of Oduyoye's argument.

* * *

Next, I will focus on chapter 6 from *Daughters of Anowa*, entitled "Marriage and Patriarchy," particularly in light of chapter 4's concept of "culture's bondswoman." As it has been previously mentioned, there is a dialectical relationship between culture and African women, as expressed in Oduyoye's notion of "culture's bondswoman." This especially comes to bear when considering the "culture-bondswoman" dialectic as predicated on power and authority within a patriarchal structure—it is distinctly notable if using the Hegelian dialectic of "lordship and bondsman"[330] as a means of conceptualizing the positionalities of self-consciousness on either side of the power-authority divide. As it

---

327. Hegel, *Phenomenology of Spirit*, 273.
328. Hegel, *Phenomenology of Spirit*, 273.
329. Hegel mentions this in another very important dialectic: the lordship-bondsman. Or, to use more contemporary terminology: the master and the slave. Hegel, *Phenomenology of Spirit*, 111–19.
330. Hegel, *Phenomenology of Spirit*, 111–19.

has been mentioned about chapter 4, it is possible to see the power-authority divide as a "life-and-death" struggle,[331] as Hegel argues in *Phenomenology of Spirit*, where the struggle firmly situates the situatedness of classism, oppression, marginalization, and sexism for the African woman. Here, in Oduyoye's chapter 6, the African woman's situatedness is exemplified in marriage and patriarchy.

What Oduyoye offers in the marriage and patriarchy model is a means to understand the facticity of the African woman's existence. This facticity—once other aspects of "being" have been adequately worked out in a Heideggerian sense of "Dasein"—is grounded on the African woman's "being-in-the-world." To be sure, a Heideggerian approach has its limitations when applying it to Oduyoye's sense of marriage and patriarchy. However, I find it is helpful to denote that the "world" of "being-in-the-world" is one that can be applied to the conceptualization of society and the institutions therein. In this respect, when thinking about Oduyoye's "marriage and patriarchy," I would argue that she is using a Heideggerian perspective, not just to understand how the African woman construes her "being-in-the-world" through the sociality of marriage and the institution of patriarchy, but, more importantly, translates her most fundamental sense of self, or "being," with regard to the roles that she must adhere to socially and institutionally. In either case, marriage and patriarchy exist, as Oduyoye notes, as a way of perpetuating "systemic and normative inequalities and subordination" for the African woman. This means, as I take it, that the infrastructure of both marriage and patriarchy work as two sides of the same coin, acting independently of one another as devices of enforcement but reenforcing and reaffirming through a kind of system of checks and balances. To address what this means is to address, as Oduyoye points out, that "African women's priorities begin and end in relationships." These relationships are social as much as they are institutional—these relationships become the foundations for grounding the positionalities of African women with respect to African men. Not only does this bring me back to what I discussed in the previous journal about Derrida's "différance" as a way to personify how existential differences defer positionalities,[332] but leads me to consider that the role of African women within the sociality of marriage and the institution of patriarchy was one contingent on childbearing, motherhood, wifehood at the expense of existential independence and autonomy.

---

331 Hegel, *Phenomenology of Spirit*, 113–14.

332. For Derrida, "différance" is denoted as the following: "The différance of the other, the other as differed from the sensible, as sensible differed; the concept as differed-differing intuition, the life as differed-differing matter, mind as differed-differing life, culture as differed-differing nature." See Derrida, *Of Grammatology*, xxix.

Kwok Pui-lan's *Asian Feminist Theology*

Here, from Kwok Pui-lan's *Asian Feminist Theology* (2000), I want highlight chapter 5, entitled "Speaking about God," where Pui-lan states the following which will prove to be worthy of further investigation:

> When Asian feminists talk about God, they do not begin with the abstract discussion of the doctrine of the Trinity, the debate on the existence of God, or the affirmation of God as omnipotent, unchanging, and immovable. Rather, they focus on God as the source of life and the creative, sustaining power of the universe.[333]

Here, what Pui-lan makes clear about how Asian feminists do theology is not from a perspective grounded on "abstract discussions" but, instead, is one that places chief importance on the epistemological situation. If the way that Asian feminists do theology comes from, as Pui-lan suggests, a "focus on God as the source of life" in conjunction with recognizing that God is "the creative, sustaining power of the universe,"[334] then it is safe to assume that she is referring to a specific kind of situation—she is referring to an epistemological situation framed by a certain, specialized understanding of the ontology of existence. To say that God is "the source of life" means that Pui-lan is not only concerned with moving beyond "abstract discussions" but is chiefly concerned, then, with the concrete, ontological manifestation of the human existence. That is, she is precisely determined to extrapolate from humanity's ontological existence an understanding about what it means to be human and, therefore, places "abstract discussions" as the foundation upon which to do theology from the bottom up. To be clear, this kind of situation is epistemological, since it uses theology as a τεχηε to develop an existential επιστημη. Pui-lan seems to suggest this through what is clearly a bottom-up approach to theology, an approach that brings to mind the theologies of Paul Tillich, Rudolf Bultmann, and John Macquarrie. However, Pui-lan's theology is much more political in tone and, accordingly, ventures into a political-theological territory that, among the three aforementioned theologians, only Tillich gestures toward. Like Tillich, Pui-lan's bottom-up theology has three tentpoles: love, justice, and power—this triangularity comes to bear on the intersectionality of sociopolitical institutions, systems of knowledge, and being-in-the-world. This kind of bottom-up theology is associated with what I would call a "low hermeneutic" (i.e., a low Christology, a low soteriology, etc) since it is concerned with the concrete ramifications of meaning-making. Pui-lan seems to agree with this, particularly when she takes into account that God is a source of hope and empowerment for "people struggling to acquire basic necessities and human dignity."[335] As Pui-lan argues, "God is often seen as

---

333. Pui-lan, *Introducing Asian Feminist Theology*, 66.
334. Pui-lan, *Introducing Asian Feminist Theology*, 66.
335. Pui-lan, *Introducing Asian Feminist Theology*, 66.

the compassionate one" focused on the epistemological situation in which people live. For Asian feminists doing theology, God is at the center of all existence, capable of "bring[ing] peace amidst ethnic strife, alienation, and oppression." To this end, when Asian feminists embark on theology, they do so through a God-talk that, as Pui-lan asserts, is employed in a religiously pluralistic context.

Ivone Gebara's "Women Doing Theology in Latin America"

In Ivone Gebara's "Women Doing Theology in Latin America," as it appears in *Through Her Eyes: Women's Theology in Latin America* (1989), the expression of "women doing theology" is infused with linguistic empowerment. As Gebara notes, when applying such a proposition to Latina women, there are certain issues that are being directly addressed. She outlines this in the following way: "the fact that women have entered the world of economic production and, more broadly, into politics and culture and the consequences for change in society."[336] In this regard, then, the role that Latina women must embrace is one that deserves, as Gebara suggests, "deeper reflection" particularly in the various churches that become communities that hinge on economic production, politics, a culture. To do theology as a woman in Latina America means situating one's theologizing through intersectionality—the intersectionality of the economy, politics, and culture—and developing a theological self that can successfully navigate through the various spheres of a broad, multipositional society. What this means, I would argue, is understanding that the shared experiences of Latina women are not static, but dynamic—these are experiences that change over time, to the extent that the historicality of what it means to be Latina and do theology comes to bear from an overarching historicity. I would argue that Gebara is also concerned with the relationship between historicity and historicality—a difference that I would call historical experience and historical space, respectively—when she denotes the "shared experience" of Latina women that arises "from the simple fact of sharing life."[337] To be sure, "sharing life" is about sharing a facticity of "being," sharing an existential selfhood that has a specific meaning to a kind of human existence. For Gebara, Latina women doing theology is grounded "from the simple fact of sharing life," but also, I would add, the extent to which that "shared life" provides a unique perspective to what it means to be human. This is particularly important when considering, as Gebara argues, that

> many women are especially gifted with a deep intuition about human life and are able to counsel, to intuit problems, to express them, to give support, to propose solutions, and to confirm the faith of many people.[338]

---

336. Gebara, "Women Doing Theology," 125.
337. Gebara, "Women Doing Theology," 126.
338. Gebara, "Women Doing Theology," 126.

Here, what Gebara has highlighted is what I would call the hermeneutics of existence: one that is generalized and specialized. I am thinking about this kind of hermeneutics as Schleiermacher is, but extending it to Gebara as a way of positioning the self as a Foucaultian hermeneutical subject. In doing so, Gebara is describing two very important components of how Latina women do theology: "specialized" to the individual's unique experiences in the world as a hermeneutical subject, and "generalized" within the community's experiences as hermeneutical objects. I see these two ways of doing theology—that is, both using subjectivity and project that subjectivity as subjective objectification—become critical to essentialist theological discourse used to "confirm the faith of many people."

Maria Pilar Aquino's "Latina Feminist Theology"

Allow me to discuss Maria Pilar Aquino's article on Latina feminist theology, as it appears in *A Reader in Latina Feminist Theology* (2002), in which her main focus, as she states in her article's title, is to provide the central features of Latina feminist theology. In effect, what Aquino is concerned with is outlining the theory and practice of Latina feminist theology, especially as a particular way that Latina women do theology from their situatedness of being Latina and being a woman. One important place in the article that I wanted to extrapolate is her notion that Latina feminist theology is grounded on what she calls the "current context of reality."[339] Aquino highlights this in the following passage: "Latina feminist theology expresses, in religious language, our commitment and vision."[340] She continues with setting up this vision as a "new model of society," one that is uniquely "free of systemic injustice and violence" and constructed not on patriarchal domination but on "sustain[ing] human dignity and the integrity of creation."[341] What lies at the core of Aquino's idea of Latina feminist theology—that is, how Latina women do theology—is the importance of religious language.

As Aquino seems to suggest, religious language is at the very heart of how Latina women do theology. This is particularly important since, as Martin Heidegger argues in *On the Way to Language* (1959), "being is the house of language." Aquino is operating from this very perspective: how Latina women do theology, how they express their being and extend their being-in-the-world is "housed" in the language that they use. Language, in this case, becomes the means by which being is expressed, but also the vehicle through which knowledge moves beyond the conceivable and the graspable.

For Latina feminist theology, with Aquino as a prime example, language as the expressible form of knowledge is construed through speaking to the power structures inherent in society, speaking to the patriarchal domination that is present in such a society, and speaking to the ways in which such a society marginalizes,

339. Aquino, *Reader in Latina Feminist Theology*, 135.
340. Aquino, *Reader in Latina Feminist Theology*, 139.
341. Aquino, *Reader in Latina Feminist Theology*, 139.

oppresses, and relegates Latina women to entities of nonbeing. In this regard, language becomes a way to authenticate "being," something that concretizes being-in-the-world as valid and essential, even in the face of oppressive and marginalizing social structures. Here, especially, when the Latina feminist theologian engages in language as a τεχνε for meaning-making, they specifically employ religious language to express being-in-the-world in relation to God's "Being" and, then, equating God's "Being" as the first cause of all beings.

In order to understand what Aquino calls "the current context of reality," the use of religious language of a Latina feminist theologian seeks to explain the existential situation in which the Latina woman finds herself. This situation is based on a series of facticities, which culminate with a being-in-the-world limited by gender, race, social status, and so forth. What religious language does, if considering the importance Aquino places on it, is that it quantifies the current context of reality. I see this "current context of reality" as the unique existential situation that, as Heidegger and Paul Tillich argue, is predicated on being thrown into the world. When the Latina feminist theologian recognizes that they have been thrown into the world, religious language is used to negotiate their problematic being-in-the-world and, subsequently, arguing that their "being" is as essential, meaningful, and purposeful as other beings in the world.

CHAPTER 4

Postmodern Traditions of Existential Theology

Anthropological Approach

What Is Theological Anthropology?

BY DEFINITION, "THEOLOGICAL ANTHROPOLOGY"—OR what is sometimes, though synonymously termed in the variant of "Christian anthropology"—is broadly concerned with the relationship between human existence and God's existence. It is relationship that allows human existence to become existentialized with respect to God's existence and, in turn, allows human existence to existentialize the meaning of God's existence through how human existence theologizes about God. This relationship attends to a special "existential" relation that human existence has with God fundamentally from a groundedness, to the extent that this relation is predicated on "*imago Dei*," or the meaning of being human, by way of its very creation, as that which is predicated on the image of God. In this sense, human existence is anthropologically-comported to the theologizing of God, through a unique connectedness that human existence has to God.

In the editor's introduction to *Theological Anthropology* from the Sources of Early Christian Thought series, J. Patout Burns makes the assertion that "theological anthropology investigates the resources, the limitations, and the destiny of the human person."[1] Such an assertion promotes the larger implications of theological anthropology on the meaning of human existence, if, as Burns rightly acknowledges, all the dimensions of "the human person" is predicated on "the conviction that humanity's present condition does not correspond to God's ultimate purpose and original intention in its creation."[2] In this way, "humanity's present condition," as that which is based on "the resources, the limitations, and the destiny of the human person," is grounded on the nature of sin, the quest for grace, and the possibility of salvation. Not only, as

---

1. Burns, *Theological Anthropology*, 1.
2. Burns, *Theological Anthropology*, 1.

Burns argues, is the groundedness of humanity to the existential problems inherent with being human "common to all as well is the assurance that human beings are themselves responsible for this disparity."[3] Though "this disparity," generally speaking, is located in human sin, "the consequences of the Fall," the distance that the fall places between human existence and God's existence, and the extent that grace and salvation mitigates that distance, there is another line of thought in theological anthropology relegated precisely to, in Burns's words, "investigat[ing] the resources, the limitations, and the destiny of the human person."

While Burns's conceptualization of theological anthropology is situated on "present[ing] an overview of a variety of theological anthropologies which enjoyed fairly broad acceptance in early Christianity" from the likes of Augustine, Irenaeus of Lyon, and Gregory of Nyssa, I wish to extend and expand this perspective to the existential demands of race and theologizing about God from the existential groundedness of race that distances "Blackness" anthropologically from God. Here, a postmodern understanding of the relationship between human existence and God's existence, through an investigation of "the resources, the limitations, and the destiny of the human person" in what can be considered as variations of the "the theological anthropologies" of W. E. B. Du Bois (1868–1963), Wallace Thurman (1902–1934), Nella Larsen (1891–1964), the two thematically related films *Pinky* (1949) and *Imitation of Life* (1958), Clarence Major, Toni Morrison (1931–2019), Victor Anderson, Lewis Gordon, Dwight N. Hopkins, Arun Saldanha, and M. Shawn Copeland.

Theologizing W. E. B. Du Bois

The Souls of Black Folk, the Veil-Metaphor, and Existential Phenomenology

W. E. B. Du Bois's *The Souls of Black Folk* (1903) consists of fourteen essays examining race in the United States through the exploration of its ramifications on Black people in terms of the distinctly sociological problems and issues evident in racism. Structurally, the fourteen essays are flanked by what Du Bois labels as a "forethought" and "afterthought," which serve to address the reader as would a preface and postscript. However, the forethought and afterthought function as not only a means by which Du Bois provides explanatory matters but presents an informative tone that he wishes for the reader to engage before and after the reader's engagement with the text. This tone, of course, runs through the fourteen essays in reference to Du Bois's own underlining experiences which led him to write them. But, moreover, what Du Bois's tone interjects is that of a voice that relays to the reader what it means to be Black or African American in an American society—this Blackness or this African Americanism ideologically informs Du Bois's sociological concerns with the appropriation of

---

3. Burns, *Theological Anthropology*, 1.

epistemology and Black existential phenomenology[4] in light of what Du Bois refers to as a Negro's life lived within the veil.

From the first chapter, as well as the introductory "forethought," Du Bois utilizes his veil metaphor to suggest that the veil limits and dehumanizes the African American, since "the Negro is born with [it] and gifted with second-sight in this American world."[5] What this veil does, then, as Du Bois furthers, is provides for "a world which yields [the Negro] no true self-consciousness, but only lets him see himself through the revelation of the other world."[6] This suggests, at its face, that the African American experience is always relative to the larger American experience. More importantly, the way in which an African American interprets themselves—or their innate Blackness—is always through the ways and means by which that larger American experience contextualizes, defines, affirms, and disaffirms what that African American experience is and is not, what it can be and will never be. To that end, then, what Du Bois puts forth in his veil metaphor is the description of an American sociological construct that influences African Americans' access to epistemology[7]—it is the purposeful separation of African Americans from the rest of the American society by way of a color line. This issue of epistemology as the resource limited by being "within the veil" appears most noticeably in chapters 3–6, where Du Bois argues for a form of education that uplifts Black communities with the installation of classically educated leaders and educators. It is here, according to Du Bois, where Black communities, once having access to epistemology, specifically through strides in American education reform, will be able to venture beyond the veil, rather than strictly living in the shadow of that veil.

Still, though this veil is a phenomenon that desperately needs to be transcended through the sociological aid of epistemology, Du Bois argues that this veil affords those that live within it a "second-sight in this American world."[8] This "second-sight" imparts of gift to the African American, because it brings to bear a "double-consciousness, this sense of always looking at one's self through the eyes of others, of measuring one's soul by the tape of a world that looks on in amused contempt and pity."[9] To Du Bois, this "sense of always looking at one's self through the eyes of others" denotes a "twoness"[10] that can be extrapolated into a duality: the possibility of being identified as Black and American. This "double-self" raises the possibility of dual existence in an American society for an African American—it brings up two sociological and ideological points of reference that markedly presents the African American with the sense

---

4. The use of the consciousness as the perspective from which to form or shape human existence.
5. Du Bois, *Souls of Black Folk*, 3.
6. Du Bois, *Souls of Black Folk*, 3.
7. This doesn't just refer to the theory of knowledge, but, more aptly, the utilization of education.
8. Du Bois, *Souls of Black Folk*, 3.
9. Du Bois, *Souls of Black Folk*, 3.
10. Du Bois, *Souls of Black Folk*, 3.

of not wanting to "Africanize America"[11] any more than seeking to "bleach his soul with White Americanism."[12] Since this duality of Black selfhood[13] that Du Bois explores is the "two-ness" of existence in double-consciousness, it becomes evident that Du Bois is expressing a concept of Black existential phenomenology.[14]

At its most fundamental, existential phenomenology examines existence in term of how the meaning of that existing being utilizes their sense of self by way of their consciousness or with their conscious faculties. For the Black, then, Blackness is relative to the consciousness as the focal point for awareness of that Blackness as a kind of existence in the world. This being-in-the-world is of the utmost concern for Du Bois, specifically filtered through the possibility of African Americans assuming a double-consciousness.

This double-consciousness, subsequently, is a double-existence, where the African American has a distinctly Black existence in terms of how they are perceived among Black communities and a poignantly American existence in terms of how they are viewed within a predominantly White society. To that end, it becomes necessary to suggest that Du Bois's notion of double-consciousness is existential, since it involves not only what it means to be human in Black skin from within the veil, but how might meaning of that Black skin and Black humanity be derived from the interpretations of the consciousness. How this works theologically, then, is through the hermeneutical practices that must occur on either side of the veil to draw biblical relevance from basic existence and the meaning in that subsequent humanity—this allows for the possibility of the dehumanization, marginalization, and oppression of Black existence in an American society as much as it provides for the veil as the color line.

DARKWATER, SELFHOOD, AND EXISTENTIAL SOCIOLOGY

W. E. B. Du Bois's *Darkwater* (1920) is chiefly comprised of nine essays on race, which are divided by pieces of prose and poetry, concluding with a science fiction story. The nine essays are, undoubtedly, the ideological core of the work since they are, as Du Bois states in the postscript, "sterner flights of logic."[15] While the interspersed pieces of prose and poetry, as well as the science fiction story to some extent, are "some little alightings"[16] that Du Bois admits have appeared in other publications, such as the *Atlantic*, the *Independent*, the *Crisis*, and the *Journal of Race Development*, they encompass "tributes to beauty" in between what can only be described as essays that

---

11. Du Bois, *Souls of Black Folk*, 3.
12. Du Bois, *Souls of Black Folk*, 4.
13. The connection between Blackness and Selfhood in terms of the distinct, Black self.
14. This refers to the possibility of being Black or Blackness by way of its underlying consciousness and how that consciousness might relate, then, to the development of meaning in Black existence.
15. Du Bois, *Darkwater*, 6.
16. Du Bois, *Darkwater*, 6.

address, as Du Bois suggests, "the problems of my people."[17] These problems are of extreme importance to Du Bois and embody the purpose for his writing *Darkwater*—though Du Bois concedes that what he ventures to write are "on themes on which greater souls have already said greater words,"[18] he still understands the necessity of expressing something "newer even if slighter."[19]

To that end, what Du Bois outlines in the nine essays is ideologically presented in his Credo. Here, not only is there a systematic articulation of Du Bois's theological beliefs[20] but, more importantly, the Credo serves to strike a specific multicultural tone for the work with, "I believe that all men, black and brown and white, are brothers, varying through time and opportunity, in form and gift and feature, but differing in no essential particular, and alike in soul and the possibility of infinite development."[21] But, rather than strictly remaining in that multicultural vein, Du Bois narrows his argument into sociological territory. This occurs by interjecting, "I believe in the Negro Race: in the beauty of its genius, the sweetness of its soul, and its strength in that meekness which shall yet inherit this turbulent earth"[22] as a means for advocating a brand of Black sociology.[23] Though Du Bois's use of this language, perhaps, suggests a Black elitism, or even a Black humanism,[24] what Du Bois actually methodizes is a concept of selfhood in terms of Black existential sociology.[25]

The nine essays on race, the interspersed pieces of poetry and prose, and the concluding science fiction piece collectively frame Du Bois's sociological argument about what it means to be Black. To be Black, not just in the US context of slavery[26] and segregation[27] but in the greater global sense of pan-Africanism,[28] then, is to formulate that being—that is, derive a sense of what it means to be human when being human is ontologically[29] represented from the Black perspective—by way of a specific

17. Du Bois, *Darkwater*, 6.

18. Du Bois, *Darkwater*, 6.

19. Du Bois, *Darkwater*, 6.

20. These theological beliefs are outlined from the beginning of Dubois's Credo with, "I believe in God." Du Bois, *Darkwater*, 7.

21. Du Bois, *Darkwater*, 7.

22. Du Bois, *Darkwater*, 7.

23. The notion of sociology explicated from the Black perspective.

24. This is based on the premise that, like a humanist philosopher, a Black humanist philosopher would be keenly interested in the rich variety of human thought and sentiment, and unwilling to ignore the actual facts for the sake of bolstering up the narrow abstractions of some a priori theory of what all men must think and feel under penalty of scientific reprobation. Schiller, *Humanism*, xxii.

25. Existential sociology examines the essential types, ultimate facts, and meaningful wholes in the inner life of social interaction and social groups as a pure description of intersubjective bonds and of the spiritual elements of collective life. Tiryakian, "Existential Phenomenology," 674.

26. Du Bois, *Darkwater*, 62–77.

27. Du Bois, *Darkwater*, 161–80.

28. Du Bois, *Darkwater*, 44–56.

29. Ontology, in this sense, addresses the possibility of essence and existence, which are both

perspective of existence. Existence, though rather implicitly employed, is the chief concern for Du Bois in *Darkwater*, where the sociological aspects of human nature inform the parameters, limitations, and possibilities of human existence. This is specifically the case for Black existence in terms of Black existential sociology—it is based on the notion that existence is derived from certain sociological concerns directly related to the Black experience such as race, racism, slavery, community, and segregation as they are uniquely expressed within the American sociological context as structures that have an adverse effect on equality. All of these components are expressly relative to the African American experience, which becomes a sociological experience and, in turn, becomes indicative of a larger exploration of Black existence.

What this means, subsequently, is that, when considering the ideological dimensions of Du Bois's *Darkwater* and how it might be appropriated theologically, it becomes evident that existence, the notion of being, and Blackness converge in the underlining purposes of the text. These three things, when articulated through existential sociology, illuminate the societal, communal, and cultural influences of Americanism and Americana on persons of African decent and how, to that end, those influences shape Black existence. To that end, what becomes subsequently apparent in Du Bois's implementation of Black existential sociology to explain Black existence—or the existential factors that comprise of Black selfhood—is not only the sociological ramifications of Black existence in reference to human existence as embodying two unequal states of being when applied to the dehumanizing aspects of Americanism and Americana for persons of African decent, but the theological ramifications of the possibility of perceived inequality in reference to an equalizing God.

Theologizing Wallace Thurman's *The Blacker the Berry*: The Possibility of Triple-Consciousness

Wallace Thurman's *The Blacker the Berry* (1929) imparts a narrative of a dark-skinned African American woman named Emma Lou Morgan and recounts her discriminatory interactions with lighter-skinned African Americans. What makes this degree of discrimination all the more troubling and, perhaps ironic, is that it occurs most explicitly in Harlem, which serves as the seat of the African American experience and the progressive ideologies of the Harlem Renaissance movement—this is particularly of note when considering that Emma Lou travels from place to place to escape such discrimination with the hopes of avoiding it in Harlem. Yet, the discrimination that Emma Lou endures, most notably in Harlem, can only be summated as racial on behalf of her racial equivalents. From this Black-on-Black racism throughout the narrative, then, Emma Lou makes an effort to understand how her skin color comes

---

imperative to the notion of being. MacGregor, *Dictionary of Religion and Philosophy*, 61; 226; 235.

to bear not only in the racism of which she is a victim, but on her overall ability to be content with a life defined by her dark skin.

Emma Lou's experience in *The Blacker the Berry* connects her existence to her dark skin. The two become synonymous with her sense of self, the embodiment of her humanity, and how she identifies herself within the American society at large and within the microcosms of her underlying Black culture and community. What occurs, then, when applying W. E. B. Du Bois's concept of double consciousness as "this sense of always looking at one's self through the eyes of others, of measuring one's soul by the tape of a world that looks on in amused contempt and pity,"[30] the consciousness that Emma Lou experiences transcends the double and assumes the triple. Hers, subsequently, is not just the consciousness of being Black and being American,[31] but being darker skinned. As a result, this triple consciousness affords her a third-sight, rather than strictly a second-sight, as defined by Du Bois.[32] It is with this third-sight that Emma Lou negotiates herself within the veil[33] of skin as a sociological marker within the Black community to project a color line between darkness and lightness, between dark-skinned and light-skinned. With that, the racism Emma Lou experiences from lighter-skinned African Americans throughout *The Blacker the Berry* attempts to define her existence—what it means for her to be Black with darker skin when darker skin is deemed to be lesser than lighter skin—in reference to a decidedly more noble existence as perceived by those in positions to be discriminators. What this does is force Emma Lou to develop a meaning of her dark-skinned existence through the existential-phenomenological[34] processes of her triple consciousness: a hermeneutic self.[35]

The perverse negritude[36] of Emma Lou's existential situation[37] is enacted sociologically in a manner that is no functionally different than the subjugation of Blackness as

---

30. Du Bois, *Souls of Black Folk*, 3.

31. This is what Du Bois refers to as "two-ness" for the African American that represents both Black and American identities in American society. Du Bois, *Souls of Black Folk*, 3.

32. Du Bois, *Souls of Black Folk*, 3.

33. To use Du Bois's veil metaphor, the veil, for Emma Lou, is just as dehumanizing and limiting as that of race, because hers is defined by what is perceived as acceptable.

34. The use of the consciousness to develop meaning from existence.

35. This term derives from the ability of defining the self in response to the question "who," where the relationship between answer and question can be explained in terms of philosophy of language, philosophy of action, the question of personal identity, and ethical and moral determinations of action. Ricoeur, *Oneself as Another*, 16–17.

36. The condition of being Black.

37. The existential situation is exemplified through "being-in-the-world." The term "being-in-the-world" is coined by German existentialist Martin Heidegger in *Being and Time*, where he analyzes this original, unitary phenomenon into the following three constituent elements: (1) in the world, (2) the being that is in the way of being-in-the-world, and (3) being-in as such. For Heidegger, "*Dasein*," which is the German word for existence, is the being that is "in-the-world." See Heidegger, *Being and Time*, 87. See Gordon, *Dictionary of Existentialism*, 37; 100.

being inferior to whiteness in an American society. In this African American society, by extension, those that are already discriminated against—those that are the objects of the White oppressor in a society structured to oppress all forms of Blackness—merely assume normative roles. Not only does this revert back to the cyclic nature of racism but it is undoubtedly based on the assumption that Whiteness is superior and that, even in an African American society, Emma Lou is oppressed as being less White than her lighter-skinned counterparts. In other words, Emma Lou's dark-skin is deemed too Black, harboring too much Blackness and too blatant a brand of negritude in an overtly White, Americanized society in reference to those that exhibit a lighter skin that might be deemed more acceptable for purposes of passing. This, of course, is based on those that do the theologizing, whereby "being-in-the-world" for an African American in *The Black the Berry* is not just relegated to inherit Blackness, or Americanism, but clearly stratified within the triple consciousness of what it means to be Black in the Black community.

The specific way in which *The Blacker the Berry* might be used theologically, then, is through applying the supposition that Black-on-Black racism is inherent in the Black community to the sociological functions of the Black Church. The same theological affirmations that subscribe to the notion of the likeness of God in all humanity must be, even through Black theology, appropriated regardless of how that likeness is perceived to be represented in the strata of the Black community. It is through the problems of Emma Lou that it becomes evident that there are no hierarchal strata to what it means to be Black any more than there is truly a sense of one form of Blackness being more authentic or refined than anything.

Theologizing "Passing"

Though anti-miscegenation laws have existed in the United States as early as 1664, it is the raping of enslaved women by white male slaveowners that ground the origins of "passing," with respect to the births of generations of mixed-race children to enslaved Black women since the seventeenth century. From these subsequent generations, the terms "mulatto," "quadroon," "octoroon," and "hexadecaroon" are used to denote the percentage of "white blood" relative to Blackness, in order to determine the meaning of racial identity of any given person of mixed-race heritage. Essentially, the greater percentage of whiteness held in relation to Blackness presented the best existential likelihood of "passing" for white in spite of Blackness—the ability to "pass" for white became a means for economic, social, and cultural uplift, particularly during the Antebellum era when "passing" allowed for mixed-race slaves to escape slavery. As an objective, "passing" became a way of existentializing oneself on one's own terms, particularly by theologizing about God. It is in this theologizing that "passing" is possible, if "passing" itself is a means to existentialize the meaning of one's existence through a specific handling of one's unique *imago Dei*.

Variations of the handling of "passing" can be found in Frank J. Webb's *The Garies and Their Friends* (1857), Kate Chopin's "The Father of Désirée's Baby" (1893), Mark Twain's *The Tragedy of Pudd'nhead Wilson* (1894), Charles W. Chestnutt, *The House Behind the Cedars* (1900), James Weldon Johnson's *The Autobiography of an Ex-Colored Man* (1912), Jessie Redmon Faust's *Plum Bun* (1928), Nella Larsen's *Passing* (1929), Fannie Hurst's *Imitation of Life* (1933)—adapted in two films: the first in 1934 and a remake in 1959—Langston Hughes's "Passing" in the collection *The Ways of White Folks* (1934), and Cid Ricketts Sumner's *Quality* (1946), which was adapted into the film *Pinky* (1949).

Directed by Elia Kazan, *Pinky* depicts the return of a young woman to a small southern town, where she grew up as a child, after being away in the North for some time training to be a nurse. What becomes distinctly clear right away, however, is that this woman is not just an ordinary, seemingly White woman, but is one that returns to the home of her "granny," who is Black. The two embrace at the "granny" shack of a home, and the granny calls the young woman Pinky. From this point in the movie, the audience sees something in this woman that is unexplainable initially, something that unfolds both from the emotional embrace of Pinky and Granny that can only be described as familial, since Pinky is raised by her Granny, and the distinct sense of "otherness" that arises in Pinky that is not strictly linked to a seemingly-Whiteness. The audience is moved to ask: Is Pinky related to Granny? Is Pinky calling Granny her granny for some other purpose other than the communal use of the term? How is it possible for Pinky to be actually related to Granny, when Granny is Black and Pinky is, to the naked eye, seemingly White?

What manages to surface—albeit surface in layers of perceptions of reality that are gradually stripped away and redefined—is that Pinky is not White. When she has been away in the North training to be a nurse she has merely "passed" for White—she has only assumed a role of Whiteness in that Northern society, due to the fairness of her skin, even though she personally identifies herself as being a Negro. This ability to "pass" is apparent upon her return to the community in which she grew up, perhaps because various inhabitants of the community have not seen Pinky in a long time—but, once they become aware of who she really is, attitudes change. This occurs when she is walking and is approached in a car by two area White men, who ask her if she needs a ride, since they believe it is unsafe for her to be White in a Black community. When Pinky tells them she lives there, the two men instantly become aware of her Blackness and that Blackness objectifies Pinky as not a woman in need of chivalrous aid but a woman that must be oppressed through victimization. At other turns, this occurs in much the same way, occurring always through the initial assumption of Pinky's Whiteness, the realization of her inherent Blackness, the prejudiced disgust that arises for her Blackness, and the complete denial of her initial, objectified Whiteness.

There is an unnerving quality to the perception of Pinky and how she is perceived by others that prevails throughout the movie. Specifically, this is troubling when Pinky's boyfriend, Thomas, comes to find her, believes she is simply doing charity work in the community, and becomes completely unraveled by her subjective Blackness and her ability to "pass" with objectification—to this, Pinky's boyfriend, at first, suggests that they can return to the North and keep her Blackness a secret. Many questions, eventually, remain unanswered: the most important of these being the nature of Pinky's relationship to Miss Em, the old woman who lives in a large, extravagant house within walking distance from Pinky's Granny's home. What becomes unclear between Pinky and Miss Em is if Pinky and Miss Em are granddaughter and grandmother or grand-niece and grand-aunt, since what can be gleaned from the relationship between Miss Em and Pinky's Granny is sisterly. This question is at the core of, upon Miss Em's death, Miss Em bequeathing to Pinky the house and land in Miss Em's will. The ensuing legal battle that erupts from the will that is contested by Miss Em's cousin, Melba Wooley, becomes the talk of the area and the news reaches to the North, specifically in the area where Pinky's boyfriend, Thomas, lives. It is then, even after Pinky is awarded Miss Em's house and land upon the belief of the validity of her will that Thomas decides they should sell the house and go to Colorado, where there is a better possibility that people there will not know about Pinky's story.

What is, then, revelatory about the film is through what it commentates on race, the color line, and perception of reality. These three things have distinctly theological ramifications because they each play important roles in how humans see their fellow humanity, how the mind perceives the body, and how perceptions of reality are often relative to how well the social and cognitive maps are navigated. To that end, the fact that Pinky can "pass" becomes the crux of her problems rather than her social salvation. It represents the facts of Blackness and the facts of Whiteness, what it means to be one over another, and how being human is in reference to the perceptions of reality that is made through subjectivity and objectification.

Textualization, Embodiment, and Trans-corpeality in the Discourse of Sexuality: Theologizing Clarence Major's *All-Night Visitors*

In a 1973 interview with John O'Brien for *Interviews with Black Writers*, Clarence Major maintains that *All-Night Visitors* (1969) "was a novel I had to write in order to come to terms with my own body." The manner in which Major accomplishes this is by textualizing the body through readability of sexuality. That is, the body becomes a text that is read through sexuality, and that sexualized reading textualizes the meaning of the body through the meaning of sexuality and the sexual act. Sexuality, in this regard, is one way of contextualizing Major's use of the body, not just as an epistemology by which we know ourselves through sexuality, but as an ontology that allows the body to stand out as being-in-the-world predicated on the sexual act and the validation of bodily gratification. Viewed this way, the novel's main character, Eli Bolton, as Major argues, seeks to "express himself only in this one natural way because he had absolutely nothing else." For Major, Bolton's expression of himself is through the textualization of his body, rather than through Blackness, so that the Black body provides a text of trans-corpeality, crossing the material world of *All-Night Visitors*, transforming the bodies it encounters, and becoming transformed itself. From this, it is clear that, in addition to the textualization of Bolton's body, the text itself, *All-Night Visitors*, is an embodied text of trans-corpeality, since it crosses the material world of the reader, similarly transforming the encountered reader and allowing itself to be transformed in the reader-text sexualized experience. The trans-corpealities of Bolton as a textualized body and *All-Night Visitors* as an embodied text suggests that there is "play" occurring between the signifiers and the signified for Bolton and his material world as much as there is between the signifiers and the signified for *All-Night Visitors* and its reader. When considering Jacques Derrida's "Structure, Sign, and Play in the Human Sciences" (1966 lecture) and the "method" of deconstruction that ensues, this "play" exists in not just the structure of Bolton's textualized body, but also in the structure of the embodied text of *All-Night Visitors*.

Theologizing Toni Morrison's *The Bluest Eye*: Subjective Blackness, Objectified Beauty, and the Ontological Eye

Toni Morrison's *The Bluest Eye* (1970) chiefly tells the story of an eleven-year-old Black girl named Pecola Breedlove as told from the point of view of Claudia MacTeer utilizing both present and retrospective perspectives. Claudia lives in Ohio with her sister Frieda and parents, becoming a familial structure that takes in Pecola, who comes from a relatively unstable household where Pecola's parents not only fight physically and verbally, but constantly tell Pecola that she is an ugly girl with such frequency and veracity that it psychologically scars her into desiring to be white with blue eyes.

Pecola's psyche is developed from the toxicity of the household she comes from. Pecola's parents, of course, have an exceedingly toxic relationship shaped by Pecola's mother Pauline's need to define her selfhood in reference to the rich White family she works for and Pecola's father Cholly's rampant alcoholism. It is as a result of Cholly's alcoholism as well as some perverse mixture of hatred and affection for Pecola that motivates him to rape her, an act that, after its second occurrence, causes Cholly to flee and leaves Pecola pregnant. When Pecola's child is eventually born, it is premature and subsequently dies.

Pecola's experiences prior to living with Claudia's family, undoubtedly, have a significantly adverse effect on how Pecola sees herself and ultimately perceives the necessity of and acquisition of whiteness as being a liberating force from her inherent Blackness. For Pecola, her Blackness is not just rooted in the pain of her childhood as a physical remnant of the verbal and physical abuse she suffered from her parents, but is, more importantly, carried forward into her spiritual, albeit phenomenological, understanding of her Blackness as embodying a distinctly violating kind of existence that rapes her of her humanity, just as her father had of her virginity. It is this, then, that promotes Pecola's desire for whiteness, for blue eyes, and for the liberating quality of a transcendent condition beyond the veil of her own—whiteness, as Pecola comes to interpret it, is not just the physical transcendence of assuming an acceptable identity in a society that perceives Blackness as inhuman, but the phenomenological awareness of what that whiteness means in reference to subjectivity and objectification. What this suggests, moreover, is that Pecola's bluest eye is, on one hand, an emotional state of subjectivity, and, on the other hand, a physical state of objectification—there is, in this bluest eye, the denotation of Pecola's suffering in the subjective state of Blackness while seeking the beauty in the objectification of whiteness.

In a way, Pecola's sense of self through subjective Blackness represents a complete marginalization and a total disembodiment of what it means to be human. To be human, when considering Pecola's reasoning, in turn, is to be beautiful—being human connects one to the existential, epistemological, phenomenological, psychological, sociological veins of a full-fleshed existence, where the ontological eye interprets that humanity as an existential truth. This existential truth is based on the perception of reality, and Pecola's perception of reality is unquestionably molded by the relationship between Blackness and whiteness through the Du Boisian veil. From behind that veil, Pecola's ontological eye views the existential truth of her existential situation as lacking humanity or, to some greater extent, assuming an innate ugliness, an ugliness that places the ugly in a constant victimization and oppression. On the other side of that veil, as Pecola sees it, is excessive beauty, the beautification of a more pristine form of humanity, and the blue-eyed innocence of a virgin humanism.

The blue eyes that Pecola seeks is a perfectly, ontological eye that not just sees but can be seen—this is at the core of Pecola's own liberation theology, where she theologizes a perception of a better, truer, and more humane existence. It is the explication of a Heideggeran being-in-the-world that is founded, substantiated, and structured by a reverent whiteness, the possibility that whiteness and blue-eyed-ness exemplifies giftedness and social-hierarchal levitation. But Pecola's sense of self as it is theologized from her own brand of liberation theology is not socially uplifting for her current state of existence, but, rather further anchors her into the reality and existential truth of that existence as it is: an unforgivable Blackness. Yet, the fact that Pecola can see beyond the veil is important as a means of extrapolating the subjectivity of her Blackness as ugliness, the objectification of whiteness as beautiful, and the intersubjectivity of her dubious reality. To that end, then, the theological ramifications of Pecola's existence are far-reaching. Most notably, one specific theological problem is steeped in not just Pecola's perception of the oppressive forces of her Blackness as being within the Du Boisian veil, but is a decidedly self-oppressive, self-dehumanizing theological stance inasmuch as it is based on the acquisition of a physical state that is unattainable.

Theologizing Elaine Scarry's *On Beauty and Being Just*

Notions of beauty and truth, as they are asserted in Elaine Scarry's *On Beauty and Being Just* (1999), are anthropological conceptualizations that require a kind of existential theologizing, insomuch as the decidedly philosophical meanings of "beauty" and "truth" are always fundamentally attached to a theologizing about God. The claim that Scurry explicitly makes is not about beauty and truth being "allied" to the point that they are "identical," but that beauty, as such, "ignites the desire for truth by giving us, with an electric brightness shared by almost no other uninvited, freely arriving perceptual event, the experience of conviction and the experience, as well, of error."[38] What I find that Scarry is essentially arguing is that beauty cannot, in itself, be equated to truth. I would agree with that, and suggest that this is a very critical part of the argument about beauty and truth.

To some extent, it is easy to propose that beauty "is" truth, since beauty, as some would argue, is meant to represent truth, particularly with respect to who defines those parameters. The problem with this is that there is no one truth. In other words, "truth" never reveals itself as "the truth," but, rather, as a "version of the truth," or as "a truth," or, essentially, as a representation. So, the key word is "representation." As such, beauty is only "a representation" of the truth, something that is subjective and relative to the individualized meaning that any individual places in that representation, in terms of its overall aesthetic value.

When thinking about Scarry's argument, I would go so far as to say this: beauty opens the possibility for us to embrace the truth in all its complexity and, then, illustrate it to the best of our abilities. What I think is very important to understanding the truth is that the "truth" is an idea, a concept that must be bracketed through Husserlian phenomenological reduction. To that end, "beauty" is what we use to bracket the truth. I am sure that Scarry would agree with this, since beauty is, in its essence, a transcendental idea, as Immanuel Kant would propose. As such, "beauty" is a transcendent object, containing the same transcendence as "justice," "equality," and "rights," where, in order to truly contextualize that transcendence, we must concretize it into something tangible. In the same manner that we attempt to represent the ideas of "justice," "equality," and "rights," "beauty" is a Kantian object of understanding that, when we encounter it, we are compelled to discover truth within and from it. This is what Scarry maintains when suggesting that beauty does, in fact, "ignite the desire for truth."

One important way that I can describe the nature of this "ignite[d] desire for truth" is through, as Gilles Deleuze would contend, an immanent event, which Deleuze defines as an "actualized state of things and of the lived that make it happen."[39] Scarry seemingly extends her argument in this direction as well, when she imagines a "freely arriving perceptual event." Said this way, Scarry imparts a kind of existential theology

38. Scarry, *On Beauty and Being Just*, 52.
39. Deleuze, *Pure Immanence*, 31.

grounded on the event, and the existential extent at which experience, either of "conviction" or "error" occur—*the question of the meaning of existential theology*, through Scarry, unfolds as a "freely arriving perceptual event." So, in my view, when we encounter either "beauty," as such, or "truth," as such, and assess the aesthetic value inherent in them, as such, we encapsulate that experience within a theologically-existential event, through which, as we implicitly theologize about God, we make aesthetic judgments about what we see in anthropological notions of beauty and truth.

Victor Anderson's *Beyond Ontological Blackness*

In the introduction to *Beyond Ontological Blackness: An Essay on African American Religious and Cultural Criticism* (1995), Victor Anderson begins by suggesting that "[his book] examines the ways that racial discourse operates rhetorically in African-American cultural and religious thought."[40] As the subtitle makes explicit, Anderson's handling of "racial discourse" becomes part of a larger "criticism," which, as Anderson writes, "disclos[es] the ways that race is reified."[41] This reification of race influences a kind of theologizing about God, insomuch as how God is theologized is predicated on the manner in which "racial discourse operates rhetorically." In a way, to reify race is to attune the meaning of human existence to God's existence, so that human existence can theologize about God. Anderson considers this reification of race to be "treated as if it is objectively exists independent of historically contingent factors and subjective intention."[42] It is the reification of race, as Anderson concludes, that leads to "ontological blackness," which Anderson defines as "a covering term that connotes categorical, essentialist, and representational languages depicting black life and experience."[43]

Anderson's move "beyond ontological blackness" is a move beyond the reification of race, especially as an understanding of the meaning of race "in the writings of historical and contemporary African American cultural and religious thinkers."[44] Moving "beyond" this means moving beyond the "tendency" to ontologize race as a meaning that must be objectified—it is the tendency to engage in an objectification of race, through which the meaning of race is understood in terms of what it is attached to, supported by, and expressed as. For Anderson, to move beyond "ontological blackness" requires separating the meaning of race from "categorical" meanings, "essentialist" meanings, and meanings that can be derived from "representational languages depicting black life and experience," which are dimensions that assist in racial reification—to remain is to merely adhere to the inadequate paradigm of modern Blackness, rather than moving beyond this to a "postmodern blackness."

40. Anderson, *Beyond Ontological Blackness*, 11.
41. Anderson, *Beyond Ontological Blackness*, 11.
42. Anderson, *Beyond Ontological Blackness*, 11.
43. Anderson, *Beyond Ontological Blackness*, 11.
44. Anderson, *Beyond Ontological Blackness*, 11.

Though admittedly assuming the term from bell hooks as functioning "in contrast to ontological blackness," Anderson defines "postmodern blackness" in the following way:

> Postmodern blackness recognizes the permanency of race as an effective category in racial formation. However, it also recognizes that black identities are continually being reconstituted as African Americans inhabit widely differentiated social spaces and communities of moral discourse. . . . In these multiple sites, African Americans are continuously negotiating the various languages of race, class, gender, and sexuality. Explicating these languages requires historical research and analysis of the ways that African Americans constitute and negotiate their identities under changing social conditions.[45]

Here, because Anderson resists defining "postmodern blackness" as "the permanency of race" but defines it as that which "recognizes that black identities are continually being reconstituted," he undoubtedly views racial formation as grounded in "moral discourse" that occurs in "widely differentiated social spaces and communities." That "moral discourse" is a kind of theologizing about God, such that, through the act of theologizing, "black identities," as a racial formation, are "continually being reconstituted" to the meaning of human existence. The fact that "black identities" are "continually being reconstituted" points to the existential nature of Blackness itself, and how Blackness, as such, is not tethered statically to a permanency of race, but is grounded dynamically to an existentialized identity.

Anderson's intent on calling for a "postmodern blackness" rather than an "ontological blackness" attends to the necessity of theologizing about God from an existential standpoint of authenticity. What makes "ontological blackness" inauthentic is due to the fact that, as Anderson points out, it "entails a type of categorical racial reasoning and a black aesthetic—a collective racial consciousness expressive and representational of African American genius."[46] Anderson's conceptualization of this "collective racial consciousness" is a philosophizing that "is governed by dialectical matrices that existentially structure African Americans' self-conscious perceptions of black life."[47] Anderson goes on to say that,

> under ontological blackness, the conscious lives of blacks are experienced as bound by unresolved binary dialectics of slavery and freedom, negro and citizen, insider and outsider, black and white, struggle and survival. However, such binary polarities admit no possibility of transcendence or meditation.[48]

---

45. Anderson, *Beyond Ontological Blackness*, 11–12.
46. Anderson, *Beyond Ontological Blackness*, 14.
47. Anderson, *Beyond Ontological Blackness*, 14.
48. Anderson, *Beyond Ontological Blackness*, 14.

Because of this "under ontological blackness," any theologizing about God is not possible, since ontological Blackness is bounded to and grounded by "binary politaries [that] admit no possibility of transcendence or meditation." In this way, the "possibility of transcendence or meditation" is what allows for a theologizing about God, especially as a means of moving beyond what Anderson refers to as ontological Blackness.

How theologizing about God moves beyond ontological Blackness and toward a postmodern Blackness is with the recognition that the former, according to Anderson, "signifies the totality of black existence, a binding together of black life and experience."[49] Anderson finds that "racial identity is not total . . . from a religious point of view, when race is made total, then ontological blackness is idolatrous."[50] In an effort to avoid the idolatry of ontological Blackness, theologizing about God acknowledges that "racial identity is not total"—by theologizing about God as a way of existentializing human existence from the standpoint of Blackness, so that the meaning of Blackness itself and the interests thereof point to a "fulfilled individuality" viewed through a kind of existential theology.

Theologizing Lewis Gordon's *Existence in Black*

In Lewis Gordon's introduction to the collection *Existence in Black: An Anthology of Black Existential Philosophy* (1997), when setting aside the deeply philosophical aims of the collection, which largely avoids "the theological"—with the exception of one essay in the volume, "Existence, Identity, and Liberation," by Robert Birt, which considers Black theology—any theologizing about God that becomes apparent in Gordon defining the meaning of Black existential philosophy is in his use of specific terms that resonate theologically. The first question that Gordon raises, through his understanding of W. E. B. Du Bois's *Darkwater*, asks: "What is to be understood by black suffering?"[51] Gordon is right to consider this question philosophically, even if there is no explicit theological use of it on his part—nevertheless, when speaking of Black suffering, "the philosophical" does not completely address how "Blackness" overcomes "suffering" without addressing "the theological" through the existential importance of salvation. The justification by grace through faith is what positions "suffering" toward salvation, so that salvation becomes the manner by which "suffering" is mitigated in its worldliness and the worldhood of human existence.

In thinking of "suffering" this way—not altogether philosophically, but implicitly theologically—Gordon suggests that the question of "Black suffering" is "[the] question that animates a great deal of the theoretical dimension of black intellectual production."[52] This is certainly true, particularly with respect to, as Gordon finds, "it is what signals

49. Anderson, *Beyond Ontological Blackness*, 14.
50. Anderson, *Beyond Ontological Blackness*, 15.
51. Gordon, *Existence in Black*, 1.
52. Gordon, *Existence in Black*, 1.

the question of liberation on one level and the critique of traditional, read 'European,' ontological claims on another."[53] When speaking of Black liberation this way, Gordon is undoubtedly pointing to the term in its theological understanding and use within "Black theology" and, to be sure, the idea of "Black liberation theology."

The implications of "Black suffering," for Gordon, become a conceptualization of a philosophy of existence, which are comprised of, as Gordon notes, "philosophical questions premised upon concerns of freedom, anguish, responsibility, embodied agency, solidarity, and liberation."[54] These philosophical questions, when asked from the standpoint of "Black suffering," are oriented toward, as Gordon suggests, "a constant posing of the teleological question of black liberation and the question of black identity in the midst of an antiblack world."[55] To even pose a "teleological" question at all means posing in relation to that which ventures beyond, in Victor Anderson's use, "ontological blackness." If we align Gordon's concerns with Anderson's, we find that both are asking decidedly existential questions about the meaning of human existence—a meaning that is constrained by self-imposed limitations as much as by the limitations placed on that meaning from outside structures—to the extent that "the existential" ramifications of human existence, especially Blackness relegated by "Black suffering," steer the question of the meaning of human existence beyond its worldhood and worldliness. Gordon's reference to the teleological—which can be derived, of course, from Anderson as well—points to "the theological" and what this dimension of meaning holds for the meaning of human existence. The teleological, in Gordon's hands, is most certainly referring to "the theological"—the relationship between "the teleological" and "the theological" contextualize Gordon's reference to Alain Locke's understanding the connectedness between value and identity, which, according to Gordon, "are issues by virtue of the values placed upon what has been interpreted as 'given.'"[56] What is "given," then, is Blackness and the extent to which Blackness has a givenness that gives itself over to "suffering." The problem of givenness to Black suffering and what Gordon writes as "[the] question of continuing to live on"[57] requires theologizing about God through a kind of existential theology that makes meaning out of Blackness, in the theological effort to existentially confront, in Gordon's words, "the question of black suffering and the classical encounter with nihilism—that is, the struggle involved in deciding to go on."[58]

---

53. Gordon, *Existence in Black*, 1.
54. Gordon, *Existence in Black*, 3.
55. Gordon, *Existence in Black*, 4.
56. Gordon, *Existence in Black*, 5.
57. Gordon, *Existence in Black*, 6.
58. Gordon, *Existence in Black*, 6.

Dwight Hopkins's *Being Human*: Constructing Theological Anthropology from Self, Culture, and Race

In the preface to *Being Human: Race, Culture, and Religion* (2005), Dwight N. Hopkins proposes "how religious reflection and discussions about the nature of an individual person—what we call theological anthropology—already assumes definite ideas about the self, culture, and race."[59] Not only is this proposition based on the presumption that notions of self, culture, and race[60] are significant determining factors toward understanding what it means to be human, but, when defining "who we are," there becomes an ideological need to do so with the construction of a theological-anthropological self.[61] This form of selfhood specifically confronts being[62] in terms of how that "being" is tied to "some concern or force greater than the limited self [in light of] considerations of transcendence and materiality."[63] In other words, a theological-anthropological self, when furthering Hopkins's argument, allows for "theology and anthropology [to] merge into conversation about normative claims and cultural location"[64] to the extent that they jointly promote human being—or the parameters of being as it is ontologically[65] defined in humanity—by way of how it is embodied communally[66] through the sociological paradigms of race, culture, and religion. In doing so, rather than utilizing the theological-anthropological self in its traditional sense,[67] Hopkins proceeds to focus explicitly on epistemology.[68] To that end, by Hopkins supposing that "humans, not God, systematize and construct theories about divine dimensions of their [lives],"[69] the underlining epistemological purposes of "being human" comes from the usage of a theology that is limited to direct or indirect human

---

59. Hopkins, *Being Human*, ix.

60. Hopkins, *Being Human*, ix.

61. This term is an adaptation of Hopkins's contention that theological anthropology grows out of culture, and culture arises from particular selves and the self and, in turn, selves or the self automatically involve race of the selves/self who create cultures out of which we construct contemporary theological anthropology. Hopkins, *Being Human*, 4.

62. The concept of being should be explored through the use of ontology, which addressing the relationship between being and existing where the notion of being is linked to a living or existing self's connection to reality. Coffey, *Ontology*, 32.

63. Hopkins, *Being Human*, 1.

64. Hopkins, *Being Human*, 1.

65. Being or existence is often held as the most general property of all reality. Ferguson and Wright, *New Dictionary of Theology*, 243–44.

66. Through the appropriation of all human communities, "communally" refers to the summation of human interaction and social hierarchy, which Hopkins defines in terms of issues of compassion and empowerment as it occurs in social strata, oppression, and victimization. Hopkins, *Being Human*, 7.

67. Hopkins defines the traditional concept of theological anthropology as placing a focus on the mental representation of human nature or the intangible question of what it is to be a person. Hopkins, *Being Human*, 14.

68. The theory of knowledge.

69. Hopkins, *Being Human*, 14.

experiences or "presuppositional lenses that rationally interpret the divine revelations in human collective and individual experiences and in nature."[70]

Here, what Hopkins presents, rather poignantly in his introduction, is how the theological-anthropological self can be constructed from Black theology[71] as perceived within the US context. It is in this context where Hopkins explores what he calls four representative stances from which theological-anthropological selfhood catalogues, creates, and does a necessary theology: progressive liberal,[72] postliberal,[73] feminist,[74] and liberation perspectives in the United States.[75] To Hopkins, then, these four representative stances are "disparate voices advocating their own particular lenses [with] unique contexts [that] share at least one common theme: the use of culture, self, and race."[76] In light of this, culture, self, and race, subsequently, become personified "as subject matter in the spiritual connection to humanity, the elaborate explication of what people have been created to be and called to do."[77] With that in mind, Hopkins believes that culture, self, and race become the framework upon which progressive liberal, postliberal, feminist, and liberation theological anthropologies are built.[78]

In chapters 2 and 3, Hopkins individually investigates culture and self as respectively being comprised of, on one hand, human labor,[79] the aesthetic,[80] and

---

70. Hopkins, *Being Human*, 15.

71. Also known as *Black theology of liberation*, Black theology, as a kind of Christian theology, is centered on Jesus Christ and, to that end, utilizes Christology to affirm the Black condition as being the primary datum of reality to the reckoned with. Cone, *Black Theology of Liberation*, 5.

72. This is based on the assertion of David Tracy that the purpose of human beings is to pursue a common good through an understanding of common interests, which is demonstrated by a dedication to the highest form of critical inquiry, as well as a commitment to conversation with the other, the one different from the self. Hopkins, *Being Human*, 16–17.

73. George A. Lindbeck uses this term to describe an existential self-understanding that results from being taught and exposed to a religious dynamic introduced from outside the individual. Hopkins, *Being Human*, 24.

74. Here, what Hopkins points to is how feminist scholars construe an understanding of the human person that intentionally features the particularity of woman's experiences while embracing the authenticity of man's reality. Hopkins, *Being Human*, 31.

75. This comes from diverse movements of liberation theologies among people of color in the United States, such as Black perspectives, Womanist perspectives, Hispanic/Latino perspectives, Mujerista perspectives, Asian American perspectives, and Native American perspectives. Hopkins, *Being Human*, 35–50.

76. Hopkins, *Being Human*, 51.

77. Hopkins, *Being Human*, 51.

78. Hopkins, *Being Human*, 51.

79. The emergence of culture from human energy, creativity, and struggle exerted by the human person in relation to nature and in relation to various human beings occupying definite societal positions. Hopkins, *Being Human*, 61.

80. The aesthetic or beauty in culture coexists with and accompanies moral attributes, and thus the community offers a norm to ferret out beautiful and non-beautiful character in the human being or the individual self. Hopkins, *Being Human*, 67.

the spiritual,[81] and on the other hand, community,[82] communalism,[83] and gender critiques.[84] But, it is in chapter 4 that Hopkins examines race in terms of nature and nurture, where the reader discovers a section larger than the sections devoted to culture and self. This section, which explores the third leg of Hopkins's idea of the theological anthropology within culture, self, and race, undoubtedly, represents the bulk of Hopkins's theological argument as it is brought to bear in his evocation of Black theology in the introduction. More importantly, however, what seems to be at the core of Hopkins's argument when considering his assertion that "to be black in the United States of America is to realize that one's blackness signifies being created in God's image of high self-love, self-esteem, and self-confidence"[85] is an approach that subjugates Black theology into an exploration of philosophical questions of existence: Black existentialism.

Theologically speaking, then, Black existentialism embodies Hopkins's application of Black theology because his definition of Black theology is "geared to[wards] serving the poor and the brokenhearted."[86] This, by extension, existentially projects a specific notion of being that is, in turn, connected to Blackness, as a physical and spiritual state that "denotes both a sacred natural creation and complex social constructions."[87] Blackness represents a concept of existence. To apply Hopkins's theological anthropology as evidenced in ideas about self, culture, and race to Black existence means to explain the reality of existence in terms of a Black-specific reality—this Black-specific reality is based, as Hopkins supposes, on direct and indirect human experiences as much as it is on the rational interpretation of the divine revelations in human collective and individual experiences and in nature[88] but, also, on cultural and racial theological extrapolations of selfhood.

---

81. Discussions about spirit refer to the creativity that unfolds in culture, a creativity that animates both human labor and the aesthetic. Hopkins, *Being Human*, 71–72.

82. This is based on the belief that the human is not defined by frozen notions of memory, will, soul, or rationality but, rather, the self becomes a self through the introduction into the selves. Hopkins, *Being Human*, 82.

83. The idea of communal defines the historical trajectory and contemporary substance and helps guarantee the conditions for the possibility of the self's and selves' perpetual flourishing. Hopkins, *Being Human*, 85.

84. Gender hierarchy, as Hopkins asserts, subverts the affirmation of community, common values, and common good inasmuch as it denotes the concept of equality, which rewards the overall community when the male gender and the female gender are allowed to play in their unique individuality. Hopkins, *Being Human*, 114.

85. Hopkins, *Being Human*, 8.

86. Hopkins, *Being Human*, 8.

87. Hopkins, *Being Human*, 8.

88. Hopkins, *Being Human*, 15.

Theologizing Arun Saldanha, Reontologising Race, and a Call for Deontology

In "Reontologising Race: The Machine Geography of Phenotype" (2006), Arun Saldanha "seeks to defend a materialist ontology of race," by arguing for a creative materiality of race.[89] As such, Saldanha recognizes that a "creative materiality of race" follows a material turn, which is grounded on providing a "contradistinction to the treatment of race as a problem of epistemology"—what this means, then, is that, for Saldanha, this "problem" occurs in how phenotype is "represented in racial discourse."[90] What is exactly "represented" in "racial discourse," if we can contend that such a representation adheres to "what race is" in a general and narrow sense.

This approach to race is, first and foremost, contingent on deconstructing contemporary theory about race, where "race tends to be conceived as a problem of language." If this is so, what Saldanha is pointing out is the degree to which race, when construed through language, is articulated in terms of otherness—that is, race is based on a categorical imperative of separating centralized self from the Other, of subjectivizing the status quo and objectivizing Otherness. As Saldanha rightly argues, "we read that race is an ideology, a narrative, a discourse,"[91] then race, through contemporary theory—especially through the postcolonialism of the Edward Said variety—is a dialectic between subjectivity and that which must be objectified as something outside subjectivity.

This dialectic is about representation—it is the manner in which race is represented to subjectivity and the extent to which "what is objectified" becomes a representation of race—the construction of race as a representation is voiced in Arthur Schopenhauer's *The World as Will and Representation*, though it must be said that Schopenhauer is concerned with "representation" in a general sense, and not the specificity of racial representation. Yet, if we follow Saldanha's contention that race "refers to the cultural representation of people, not to people themselves," then it becomes possible to propose that race is, indeed, an "epistemological problem."[92]

The problem is with how race is epistemologically construed—or the question that Saldanha offers as "How is race known?"[93] That is, when we speak of what race is, we must speak of what it looks like in the world—any understanding of *what race is*, then, is ultimately grounded on the worldhood of race in terms of how race functions/operates in society and what kind of ethics are applied to it. The functionality and ethics of race, particularly if viewing race through a contemporary-theoretical lens (or even by way of continental-philosophical perspective), provides for the notion

---

89. Saldanha, "Reontologising Race," 1.
90. Saldanha, "Reontologising Race," 1.
91. Saldanha, "Reontologising Race," 1.
92. Saldanha, "Reontologising Race," 1.
93. Saldanha, "Reontologising Race," 1.

of the purposefulness of "othering" and Otherness. In other words, if appropriating Emmanuel Levinas, the purpose of Otherness is constructed around the necessity of proposing that there is "being" and something that is "otherwise than being"—to say anything is "otherwise than being" means applying a specific hermeneutics of race that interprets "being" through categorization.

With respect to Saldanha, I wish to define *what race is* in the general sense as "is-ness," while considering *what race is* in the narrow sense as "there-ness"—if I may appropriate Gottlöb Frege, the former adheres to a "sense" or idea of race as an abstract, and the latter is race's "reference" or referent as a concrete.[94] Both must be couched in "racial discourse," whether that is achieved in a general or narrow sense. Yet, this very discourse, as such, liberates and confines not just the language used to explain *what race is* in its "there-ness," but contaminates how "is-ness" is conceived of and grasped, *prima facie*. As Saldanha would agree, if we can say that there is an "is-ness" and "there-ness" to *what race is*, there is, in fact, a "creative materiality" to race, which is not effectively (or even holistically) exemplified in "racial discourse."

In effect, *racial discourse*—both as the manner in which we use language to "house"[95] *what race is* in the general sense and the narrow sense—concretizes "the materiality of race," and ultimately ignores the "creativity," or Derridean "freeplay" between race's "is-ness" and "there-ness." Like Derrida's *freeplay*, Saldanha's use of the term "creative" recognizes a similar "play" in the structure of *the materiality of race*. This "play" can be considered as flexibility, plasticity, or elasticity to race's "materiality"—all these terms point to addressing *the materiality of race* is more than just a series of signifier-signified binaries, but as, in terms of "creativity," a constantly decentering network of *freeplay* between a series of signifiers and various signified elements all encased in the openness-closeness of race's *materiality* toward *what race is*. By assuming this deconstructive stance toward *what race is*, in a fashion similar to Derrida's conceptualization of "what structure is," *the materiality of race* is not just dependent on how race "stands out" as "being-in-the-world" in *racial discourse*, but the degree to which what "stands out" can enact a "creativity" that can be traced to something hidden, something fundamentally ineffable about *what race is*.

The problem, as I have outlined it so far, is based on a grounding question: *What is race?* As a grounding question—a question that allows us to construct a foundation upon which we can built further investigations—I am simply asking about race as *is-ness* and *there-ness*, as *sense* and *reference*, and as it is in the general sense as "what is hidden" and in the narrow sense as "what stands out." This grounding question, then, leads me to pose another question—a guiding question: "How do we know what race is?" By this question—a question guiding us toward further investigations into the grounding question—there is the presumption/assumption that it is possible

---

94. Frege's relationship is between sense and reference.

95. I am thinking, here, of Heidegger's assertion that language is the house of being, in *On the Way to Language*.

to "know" race in terms of its *is-ness* and *there-ness*, and that "knowing" either can be explained through *racial discourse*, in order to justify what has been previously perceived.[96] In thinking through this guiding question, the means by which *racial discourse* "represents" *what race is*, in an effective way, uncovers the problem of language, particularly within contemporary theory about *what race is*. Saldanha agrees with this, suggesting that,

> in contemporary theory, race tends to be conceived as a problem of language. We read race is an ideology, a narrative, a discourse. Race then refers to the cultural representation of people, not to people themselves. It could be said that race tends to be approached as an epistemological problem: how is race known? Why was it invented? Some argue that we should simply stop thinking in terms of race.[97]

Here, if, as Saldanha notes, "race tends to be conceived as a problem of language," the conceptualization of race becomes limited by the language necessary to explain *what race is*, and, by extension, *what race is* becomes read as "an ideology, a narrative, a discourse." Indeed, language about *what race is* does, in fact, limit *what race* is to "[a] cultural representation of people, [and] not to people themselves." To consider what race is strictly "as a problem of language" means misinterpreting where the problem is. Language is only part of the problem, since language itself is subject to "an ideology, a narrative, a discourse," and, taken together, language is a structure that delimits what race is to assertions, claims, and propositions. To this end, if we are dependent on language to express *what race is*, it becomes difficult to "know" *what race is*. The ontological restraints of language prevent us ever "knowing" *what race is* beyond constraints of cultural representation. And if we are concerned, as Saldanha is, with figuring out "how is race known," what we know about *what race is* cannot be reduced to "the cultural representation" of it in discourse.

To be clear, when focused on discourse in this manner, Saldanha is taking a decidedly linguistic turn in terms of rethinking about the effectiveness of language as an accurate representation of race's "there-ness" is in the world, on one hand, while, on the other, assuming a material turn in terms of rethinking the "is-ness" of race itself. Saldanha's *material turn*, in particular, is essential to his "reontologising" project, which I would argue concedes two very fundamental things: first, the "is-ness" of race is couched in the limitations of "racial discourse," and second, there are epistemological problems underlying that "racial discourse" to the extent that any discourse fails to capture the "creative materiality of race." In other words, Saldanha's notion of race is situated in both creativity and materiality, and comes to bear through his assertion that

---

96. This is an adaptation of Socrates's argument about the nature of knowledge in Plato's *Theaetetus*.
97. Saldanha, "Reontologising Race," 1.

race is shown to be an embodied and material event, a "machine assemblage" with different spatiality than the self/other scheme of Hegel.[98]

Here, by resisting "the self/other scheme of Hegel," Saldanha, in turn, resists what I would like to call the Hegelian dialectic of representation—that is, the Lordship and Bondsman (Master and Slave) dialectic of Hegel's *Phenomenology of Spirit*. In that dialectic—just as Saldanha seemingly interprets—the relationship between the personages of the Lordship and the Bondsman are linked to a dialectical understanding of one another, which is phenomenologically rooted in how each is mutually represented to its other. I am not just speaking out this dialectic in terms of spatiality (which Saldanha notes), but in temporality. Though it is certainly possible to interpret race as a dynamic between Lordship and Bondsman—literally, respectively between one person of recognized value and another of dependent value—the "event" of this dialectic of representation is, again, all about representation. The manner through which a Lordship understands the Bondsman is through the "othering" of the Bondsman—when race is added to this "othering," spatiality becomes the means for the former differentiate themselves from "the Other." However, for Saldanha, creativity and materiality of race allows it to exist in a "different spatiality" than Hegelian dialectic permits. Not only does this invite Saldanha's sentiment that "race is shown to be an embodied and material event, a 'machine assemblage,'" but the embodied, materiality of race is more than just a reontologising project. Even when we grant Saldanha's contention that race "refers to the cultural representation of people, not to people themselves,"[99] we must recognize that the embodied, materiality of race is more than just an "epistemological problem." Certainly, the problem is with how race is epistemologically-construed—or the question that Saldanha offers as "how is race known?"—but this is only part of a larger issue, particularly when evoking *the materiality of race*. That is, when we speak of *what race is*, we must speak of what it looks like in the world, and we must use language to express *is-ness* as referent *there-ness*, and we must apply something other than epistemology to understand *what race is*—any understanding of *what race is*, then, is ultimately grounded on the worldhood of race in terms of how race functions/operates in society and what kind of ethics are applied to it. The functionality and ethics of race, particularly if viewing race through a contemporary-theoretical lens (or even by way of continental-philosophical perspective), provides for the ethical notion of the purposefulness of "othering" and "Otherness." In other words, if appropriating Emmanuel Levinas, the purpose of "Otherness" is constructed around the ethical necessity of proposing that there is "being" and something that is "otherwise than being"—to say anything is "otherwise than being" means applying a specific hermeneutics of race that interprets "being" through deontology, or ethical commitments.

98. Saldanha, "Reontologising Race," 1.
99. Saldanha, "Reontologising Race," 1.

If race is more than an "epistemological problem," it is also more than a reontological problem—rather than strictly "reontologising race," as Saldanha argues for, race should be, instead, "deontologized." To put it another way, though Saldanha suggests that, through his "reontologising" project, "race will be approached ontologically, as a real process demanding particular concepts and commitments,"[100] the degree to which that project "demand[s] particular concepts and commitments must take precedent." It is only through deontology that Saldanha's reontology of race is possible.

Like Saldanha, Victor Anderson's *Beyond Ontological Blackness* attempts to work outside race as an ideology, narrative, and discourse—Anderson considers race as an ontological structure, particularly "Blackness," because it is reified, categorized, and representational. Though Anderson and Saldanha share a similar conceptualization of "what race is," Anderson is more invested in what Blackness is, as a category of race. Anderson argues that Blackness has become too ontological, suggesting that "ontological blackness," in light of how Anderson uses the term, is only a superficial understanding of human existence and *what Blackness is*. For Anderson, when we speak of Blackness, we are only speaking of existence in the general sense—that is, generalizing and making sweeping statements, which demand "particular concepts and commitments," as Saldanha argues, about *what Blackness is*. But, such generalizations never authentically get at *what being is*—or "being" as it is outside its racialized, ontological structure. To simply propose that race is ontological fundamentally misreads *what race is*, especially if we must take into consideration *what being is* too. Aside from the ethical messiness, is this not the crux of Heidegger's argument in *Being and Time*: the need to trace "being" by *what being is*, and not simply as *what being is* "in the world"?[101] Can the same be said of Anderson and Saldanha alike?

Reading race simply within the ontological structure of an Aristotlean kind of categorization only reads race as an idea, particularly couched in the Hegelian *grundlage* of self-consciousness through Lordship-Bondsman dialectic in *Phenomenology of Spirit*—race becomes an idea that is representational tied phenomenologically to self-consciousness, selfhood, and identity. Saldanha counters this definition of "what race is," proposing that race is "not so much [about] representations, but bodies and physical events."[102]

If we follow Saldanha by reading "what race is" through the phenotype of humans, which "can be shown to play an active part in the event called race," then race is "an immanent process."[103] Race is a transcorporeal experience—it is an experience

---

100. Saldanha, "Reontologising Race," 1.

101. I am thinking about this in the strict philosophical sense of "being," without ascribing any ethics to Heidegger's argument. Strictly speaking, Heidegger provides a framework to discuss "what being is," even if we must, unfortunately, omit the complicated ethics and racialization from that discussion.

102. Saldanha, "Reontologising Race," 1.

103. Saldanha, "Reontologising Race," 1.

that is based not so much on what race is, but on race as a hermeneutics of bodily identity. What this means, then, is, as Saldanha suggests, "race cannot be transcended, only understood and arranged."[104] It is more than just "race cannot be transcended," but race must not be transcended—the ontological structure of race is a system that "cannot be transcended," but only "understood and arranged" in terms of race being an embodied and material event. This approach to the ontology of race takes Anderson's *Beyond Ontological Blackness* (1995) further than Anderson is willing to go—rather than arguing for a deontology of race, as Anderson does, Saldanha argues for a reontology of race in much the same vein as M. Shawn Copeland's *Enfleshing Freedom*, which is contingent on the bodily demands of race.

M. Shawn Copeland's *Enfleshing Freedom*

M. Shawn Copeland's *Enfleshing Freedom: Body, Race, and Being* (2010), from its foreword section, proposes that theological anthropology should address the historical perception and treatment of Black women's bodies "by framing theological inquiry around [them, in order to] point out both the pitfalls of human conduct and interactions and the potential for transformation found in the Christian faith."[105] In terms of Copeland's argument about the subjectivity and objectification of Black female bodies, African American theological discourse must revolve around the body by "highlighting the manner in which the materiality of the black woman's concrete, perceptive flesh impacts and informs both theological language and conduct."[106] In light of this, not only does Copeland suggest that Black female bodies, "because they are female and black, black and female," are discarded, used, and defiled,[107] but there exists, from that fact, the Christian question of what being human means on the body.[108] This notion, then, is utilized by Copeland in explaining how the relationship between being human and the body are explicated through being a woman in Black skin and the Black female body. What makes the Black woman's body the central concern for Copeland's *Enfleshing Freedom* as the starting point for theological anthropology is through "allow[ing] us to interrogate the impact of [the Black woman's bodily] demonization in history, religion, culture, and society."[109]

From there, Copeland proceeds to consider the theological anthropological relation between the social body and the physical body as a means of "opt[ing] for the concrete and aims to do so without absolutizing or essentializing particularly

---

104. Saldanha, "Reontologising Race," 1.
105. Copeland, *Enfleshing Freedom*, ix.
106. Copeland, *Enfleshing Freedom*, xi.
107. Copeland, *Enfleshing Freedom*, 1.
108. Copeland, *Enfleshing Freedom*, 1.
109. Copeland, *Enfleshing Freedom*, 2.

or jeopardizing a notion of personhood as immanent self-transcendence in act."[110] The focal point of this is undoubtedly encapsulated in race, by way of what Copeland denotes as the use of skin as horizon—this horizon is summated in "what and who is outside the range of that field [as being] eliminated from [one's] knowledge and interest, care and concern [to the extent that this] limited and limiting standpoint of skin as horizon reassures and is reassured in bias."[111] From this supposition, Copeland connects the body and the exemplification of race to being Black, where, in a negro-phobic society, Blackness "mutates as negation, non-being, nothingness [and] insinuates an 'other' so radically different that [those exhibiting a Blackness ontologically has their] very humanity discredited."[112] What this affords, then, is the quest for authenticity, where "the black struggle for [that] authenticity is coincident with the human struggle to be human and reveals black-human-being as a particular incarnation of universal finite human being."[113]

To address this Black struggle, Copeland argues for a Black body theology that enfleshes freedom through a form of theological anthropology that "interrogates the enfleshing of created spirit through the struggle to achieve and exercise freedom in history and society."[114] Speaking specifically in terms of the Black woman's struggle, Black bodily theology arises in response to "the reduction and objectification of black women [which] began with the seizure and binding of the body; the violent severing of the captive from community and personhood; imprisonment in dark and dank places below ground; packing and confinement in the slave ship; the psychic disorientation and trauma of the Middle Passage."[115] When considering this history of the Black female body, the fact that Copeland proposes these instances as "suspended out of time and in 'no place' further suggests what Martin Heidegger noted as the relationship between time, the realms of entities existing temporally and ontologically in a specific reality, and the underlying concept of space as a means of understanding the manner in which an existing entity exists.[116] Like Heidegger, and even Kierkegaard's belief in the subject and object respectively arriving at a truth while assuming a history,[117] Copeland is concerned with subjectivity and objectification.

So, to apply the interconnections Copeland makes between the body, race, and being in light of how Blackness is represented subjectively and objectified socially, it becomes evident that these interconnections embody a specific theological understanding of what it means to be human. This kind of theologizing is, as Copeland

110. Copeland, *Enfleshing Freedom*, 8.
111. Copeland, *Enfleshing Freedom*, 13.
112. Copeland, *Enfleshing Freedom*, 19.
113. Copeland, *Enfleshing Freedom*, 21.
114. Copeland, *Enfleshing Freedom*, 24.
115. Copeland, *Enfleshing Freedom*, 29.
116. Heidegger, *Being and Time*, 39.
117. Brown, *Subject and Object*, 34–82.

describes a Black body theology. Though this is explained in reference to Black woman's body, there remains the possibility of universally theologizing the apparent ways and means the body incorporates a social and physical identity by its relative being-in-the-world. This "being-in-the-world" is Heideggerian, where existence pertains "both to an understanding of something like a 'world,' and to the understanding of the Being of those entities which become accessible within the world."[118] With that, what Copeland puts forth theologically is not just a formulation of Blackness as comprising a combination of body, race, and being but presents a Kierkegaardian truth in its history that is distinctly human.

Political Approach

What Is Political Theology?

The term "political theology" can be defined more broadly as "an attempt to relate religion to the political character of the society in which it exists."[119] This is very true, indeed, particularly if the way religious character is shaped is by how political character is shaped, and vice versa. For Michael Kirwan, political theology "is meant to bridge [the] gap between gospel inspiration and specific political commitment."[120] More specifically, when considering that political theology reconciles the "theological" with the "political," this relation is relevant and necessary due to the worldwide nature of the church and of its theological enterprise.[121]

Such a theological enterprise, as Ched Myers contends, means to "argue that theology should be fundamentally politically grounded in context, content, and method."[122] To that end, it becomes important that, if theology is "politically grounded," the context, content, and method that it assumes, certainly, is skewed toward the public realm. In this case, theology speaks to that public realm in a voice that is distinctly its own.[123] In my view, theology uses a theological voice that articulates itself with contemporary political language. What this means is that, for theology to be political, it must engage "debates about theology, about the way a tradition has reasoned about God and God's relationship with the world."[124] However, it is more than just about being theologically literate. Instead, it is about developing and employing a certain skill set "to enter into a conversation that has been taking place

---

118. Heidegger, *Being and Time*, 33.
119. Ferguson and Wright, *New Dictionary of Theology*, 520.
120. Kirwan, *Political Theology*, 4.
121. Ferguson and Wright, *New Dictionary of Theology*, 522.
122. Myers, introduction to *Eerdmans Reader in Contemporary Theology*, 337.
123. Cavanaugh et al., *Eerdmans Reader in Contemporary Theology*, xviii.
124. Cavanaugh et al., *Eerdmans Reader in Contemporary Theology*, xviii.

across a diversity of contexts for generations."[125] I find this to mean that, as Kirwan asserts, faith has political implications and that to do theology calls for the person doing the theologizing "to imagine and work for a transformed world."[126] This transformed world, as the introduction to *An Eerdmans Reader in Contemporary Political Theology* suggests, has taken shape in the twentieth century in the wake of European wars.[127] Obviously, political theology, when operating in such a transformed world, is meant to serve the contingent needs of those that have been impacted by their transformed world. As Myers rightly ascertains, "political theology must be about where, how, and with whom we do our reflection."[128] But, the "where," the "how," and "with whom" occur in a variety of contexts.

Regardless of the contexts involved, political theology requires a special kind of vision[129] capable of analyzing and critiquing "political arrangements (including cultural-psychological, social and economic aspects) from the perspective of differing interpretations of God's ways with the world."[130] Perhaps this can be understood on two fronts when considering political theology. First, "theology" makes it possible to understand God's ways with the world and examine how human persons relate to God. But, "the political" makes it possible to understand "God's ways with the world" and how human persons relate to God in relation to the "use of structural power to organize a society or community of people."[131] Therefore, the relationship between "theology" and "the political" is, in my view, dialectic, where "theology" informs what it means to be "political" just as much as "the political" informs what it means to do "theology."

Not only is this a Hegelian dialectic with respect to how "theology" and "the political" inform one another, but, by simply invoking the term "political theology," the encounter between "theology" and "the political" denotes, as Hegel suggests in *Phenomenology of Spirit*, a "relation of the self-conscious individuals [where it] is such that they prove themselves and each other through a life-and-death struggle."[132] Though, admittedly, I am aware that Hegel is describing what has come to be labeled as the Lordship-Bondsman dialectic, and that "theology" and "the political" cannot be exactly correlated to what Hegel was articulating. That is, "theology" and "the political" cannot be bestowed with personhood in the same regard as the lordship and the bondsman. I am the first to concede that fact, and confess that there are limitations in such an application. Still, there is something very helpful in the Hegelian dialectic,

---

125. Cavanaugh et al., *Eerdmans Reader in Contemporary Theology*, xviii.
126. Kirwan, *Political Theology*, 3–4.
127. Cavanaugh et al., *Eerdmans Reader in Contemporary Theology*, xxiv.
128. Myers, introduction to *Eerdmans Reader in Contemporary Theology*, 341.
129. Cavanaugh et al., *Eerdmans Reader in Contemporary Theology*, xxiv.
130. Scott and Cavanaugh, introduction to *Blackwell Companion to Political Theology*, 1.
131. Scott and Cavanaugh, introduction to *Blackwell Companion to Political Theology*, 1.
132. Hegel, *Phenomenology of Spirit*, 113–14.

especially with the idea of two self-consciousnesses. In effect, if appropriating what Scott and Cavanaugh believe, "politics and theology are therefore two essentially distinct activities, one to do with public authority, and the other to do . . . with religious experience and the semiprivate associations of religious believers."[133] To that end, I would argue that "theology" and "the political," in fact, have inherent self-consciousnesses in the way that they function in our lives and the means by which we engage with them as separate entities. To use Hegel, "theology" and "the political," within political theology, do "prove themselves and each other" through a "life-and-death struggle," which is a struggle, in my view, where each balances out the other without completely obliterating one another in the process.

But, to move a little further beyond the Hegelian dialectic, I find that that "life-and-death struggle" synthesizes into one struggle, or one juxtaposed meaning. This is the Kantian dialectic that I have mentioned at the beginning of this paper. Instead of belaboring this point, I will argue that the two representations of "theology" and "the political" unite "to form a certain content"[134] that is purposely slanted toward a specific goal, or task.

Scott and Cavanaugh describe political theology in terms of having different goals and serving varied tasks.[135] One very important way that Scott and Cavanaugh define political theology is that its task "might be to relate religious belief to larger societal issues while not confusing the proper autonomy of each."[136] They go on to suppose that political theology shows particular reverence to the fact that "theology reflects and reinforces just or unjust political arrangements,"[137] which I would argue is critical to understanding the task of political theology.

The task, then, of political theology, as Scott and Cavanaugh assert, "might be then to expose the ways in which theological discourse reproduces inequalities of class, gender or race, and to reconstruct theology so that it serves the cause of justice."[138] Using terms such as "justice," "gender," "race," "class," and "inequality," I find that the task of political theology is advanced in reference to issues of power. That is to say, the powerless versus the powerful. What this means, as Myers rightly concludes, is that "for theology to be political . . . it must engage the Powers, [and] for politics to be theological, it must aspire to nonviolence"[139] when engaging "the Powers."

---

133. Scott and Cavanaugh, introduction to *Blackwell Companion to Political Theology*, 2.
134. Kant, *Critique of Pure Reason*, 111.
135. Scott and Cavanaugh, introduction to *Blackwell Companion to Political Theology*, 2.
136. Scott and Cavanaugh, introduction to *Blackwell Companion to Political Theology*, 2.
137. Scott and Cavanaugh, introduction to *Blackwell Companion to Political Theology*, 2.
138. Scott and Cavanaugh, introduction to *Blackwell Companion to Political Theology*, 2.
139. Myers, introduction to *Eerdmans Reader in Contemporary Theology*, 341.

Carl Schmitt's Political Theology

The fundamentals of "political theology," through a postmodern understanding of the term itself as the relationship between "the theological" and "the political," begins with the political thought of Carl Schmitt (1888–1985)—the manner in which we do "political theology" today, as it is currently articulated within the bounds of postmodernity, can undoubtedly be traced to its conceptualization in Schmitt's *Political Theology* (1922) and, later, his *The Concept of the Political* (1932). Indeed, though Schmitt's "political theology" is influenced by Mikhail Bakunin (1814–1876) and his use of the term in "The Political Theology of Mazzini and the International" (1871) and, to a certain extent, also influenced by Thomas Hobbes (1588–1679) and his *Leviathan* (1651), what is found more precisely in Schmitt speaks more directly to the relationship between modern theologizing and modern politics, which Schmitt contextualizes in a theologizing and politicizing about the Weimar Republic (or the "German Reich") and then Nazi Germany (or the "Third Reich").

Not only is Schmitt considered as the "leading jurist during the Weimar Republic"[140] during the pre-Nazi years of Germany, he is also considered, upon the rise of Nazism in 1933, as "the crown jurist of the Third Reich."[141] It is this latter consideration that overshadows the first, and rightfully so, such that Schmitt's support of Nazism becomes integral to how we come to understand his view of political theology. Yet, Schmitt's Nazism, as such, is complicated—just as it is rather complicated for Schmitt's contemporary Heidegger. Though Schmitt's brand of political theology is chiefly illustrated in *Political Theology* and *The Concept pf the Political*, both of which were published before Schmitt's allegiance to Nazism, these texts are reassessed in relation to another noteworthy text that was, in fact, written in a presumed advocacy of and influenced by Schmitt's Nazism: *Leviathan in the State Theory of Thomas Hobbes: Meaning and Failure of a Political Symbol* (1938)—here it is with his *Leviathan in the State Theory of Thomas Hobbes* that we have a more mature form of Schmitt's political theology calibrating the relationship between "the theological" and "the political" in terms of the development of the Nazi State. The maturity of this latter text is grounded on the complicated nature of Schmitt's Nazism—this latter text comes at the time when Schmitt, as it has been noted in George Schwab's introduction to the 1996 translation of the text, has "'left' the Nazi legal organizations that he had joined in 1933 and confined his activities to those primarily associated with a university career: teaching and writing."[142] Schwab contextualizes this with respect to "vitriolic attacks on [Schmitt]" made by the SS publication, *Das Schwarzes Korps* in December 1936, which strongly questioned Schmitt's allegiance to Nazism and used Schmitt's earlier criticisms of

---

140. Schmitt, *Political Theology*, vii.
141. Frye, "Carl Schmitt's Concept of the Political," 818–30.
142. Schmitt, *Leviathan in the State Theory of Thomas Hobbes*, ix.

Nazism against him as inculpatory evidence.[143] These attacks deeply embarrassed Schmitt, in one sense, and made his status in the Nazi Party tenuous, especially, as Schwab points out, "in the context of the rapidly emerging totalitarian one-party SS state."[144] In light of this, when contextualizing Schmitt's *Leviathan in the State Theory of Thomas Hobbes*, Schwab comes the following conclusion:

> What is argued is that Schmitt used his writings on Hobbes to provide an assessment of and a response to emerging political realities. Stated succinctly, because of the Nazi failure to heed his advice on the necessity of forging the new Germany into a qualitative total polity, Schmitt insinuated the demise of the Third Reich.[145]

Schmitt's envision of a "new Germany" is what drew Schmitt to Nazism, based on the idea that National Socialism could develop the Germany state "into a qualitative total polity"—the fact that, as Schmitt viewed it, Nazism did not actualize what Schmitt had hoped it would become underscores his complicated relationship with National Socialism. For that matter, stands to reason that Schmitt would be critical of "emerging political realities" set forth by Nazism and the extent to which "a new Germany" was less likely to reach its full fruition as Schmitt had hoped when he first aligned himself with Nazism in 1933. The promises of Nazism, the "emerging political realities," and Schmitt's desires for a "new Germany" were increasingly misaligned.

For Schmitt, this misalignment arises from his sentiment at the opening of *The Concept of the Political*, in which Schmitt proposes that "the concept of the state presupposes the concept of the political."[146] In particular, Schmitt finds, when defining "the political" as such, "in its literal sense and in its historical appearance the state us a specific entity of a people."[147] Said this way, Schmitt recognizes that, even before joining the Nazi Party in 1933, Nazism itself would give rise to "the political" insomuch as the Nazi Party becomes a representation of "the state."

It is from the relationship between "the state" and "the political" that the concept of sovereignty develops, as Schmitt argues at the opening of *Political Theology*. What allows "the sovereign" to venture from merely "the political" into "the theological" is predicated on the fact that "the sovereign is he who decides on the exception."[148] This is certainly so, when remembering that Nazism as "the political" and the Nazi Party "the state" positions Hitler as "the sovereign," or "the one who decides on the exception."

---

143. Schmitt, *Leviathan in the State Theory of Thomas Hobbes*, ix.
144. Schmitt, *Leviathan in the State Theory of Thomas Hobbes*, ix.
145. Schmitt, *Leviathan in the State Theory of Thomas Hobbes*, x.
146. Schmitt, *Concept of the Political*, 19.
147. Schmitt, *Concept of the Political*, 19.
148. Schmitt, *Political Theology*, 5.

We need not say, here, what Hitler as "sovereign" decided on as "the exception"—we need not look any further than Nazi concentration camps and the Holocaust for a practical example of Schmitt's understanding of sovereignty.

In this way, the rationalization of situating "the sovereign [as] he who decided on the exception," even we remain true to the genocide of some six million Jews, becomes a realization of "the theological." This orientation, as Schmitt argues in *Political Theology*, comes by way of the following proposition:

> All significant concepts of the modern theory of the state are secularized theological concepts not only because of their historical development—in which they were transferred from theology to the theory of the state, whereby, for example, the omnipotent God became omnipotent lawgiver—but also because of their systematic structure, the recognition of which is necessary for a sociological consideration of these concepts.[149]

Here, by recognizing that "all significant concepts of the modern theory of the state are secularized theological concepts," Schmitt's kind of theologizing about God becomes a theologizing about sovereignty, such that the sovereign's power itself is theological. It is the theological power of sovereign that allows for the existential meaning of "the state of exception" to orient itself theologically, in order to existentialize those that are included in the state from those that are excluded from it. At the intersection of "the theological" and "the political," the meaning of doing political theology, for Schmitt, is based on a theologizing of the sovereign, to the point that this kind of theologizing theologically transfigures the meaning of the state and the concept of the political—in turn, the meaning of the sovereign's act of engaging in the state of exception existentializes the theologizing of the sovereign.

John Howard Yoder's *The Politics of Jesus*

The question that John Howard Yoder situates as his basic thesis of *The Politics of Jesus* (1994), which he explicitly states as hinging on the following supposition: whether Jesus was in principle a political person.[150] Though, as Yoder asserts, such a supposition fuels debate in New Testament Studies, I do not see any room for debate on the issue. In my view, Jesus was, in fact, a political person and, as a political person, Jesus' ministry and teachings were, by principle, construed through political language meant to be subversive to the status quo and empower the powerless.

I say this, particularly, because language[151] is always a political act. The semantic choices of words, the linguistic string of those words, and the overall structure in a given

---

149. Schmitt, *Political Theology*, 36.
150. Yoder, *Politics of Jesus*, 13.
151. Language is, of course, written and oral. When considering the "language" of Jesus, whatever was written came out of an oral tradition. For the purposes of how I wish to use the term "language,"

sentence are all always meant to express a purposeful content. Any given sentence is a power relation between the addresser and the addressee across a plane of "meaning," where the dialectic that occurs is a political negotiation between the signifier-signified elements of every word. As Ferdinand de Saussure suggests, words are "signs" and, in them, there is a "signifier" in the way a word is represented as a visual collection of letters and a "signified" in the image that is conjured when the "signifier" of a word is presented as an object of understanding. Depending on the context of a given word, a "sign" can provide different notions of what is "signified." What becomes "signified," then, is always relative to the lived experiences, or personal histories, we bring to our encounter with words and, to that end, the creative act[152] that must be involved in our extrapolation of meaning. Meaning itself is political, since it must be extrapolated through language and the relativity of quantitative elasticity therein.

As a political person, Jesus is very much aware of the power of language and the power of meaning as inextricably linked political activities. Words have meanings, and those meanings are meant to "represent" an understanding of the existential limitations placed on our existence in the world—our "being," our "being-in-the-world," and the physical trappings of our "being" are all exemplified through our awareness of the power relations between the powerless and the powerful. For Jesus, language serves as a means to give voice to the powerless and, in turn, becomes a source for empowerment against the oppressive actions of the powerful. The politics of Jesus, as such—Yoder's own choice of title for his book is a political act in itself—is about the metaphysics of language and the ontology of empowerment through linguistic metaphysicality.

* * *

In reading the second half of John Howard Yoder's *The Politics of Jesus*, I was immediately interested in focusing this journal entry on his discussion of subordination. According to Yoder, the early church took a stance of subordination, where they put forth a set of rules to the Christian faithful about the roles they should play in society. This kind of concept, in my view, is about the dialectic relationship between the Christian and the world. In other words, in order to exist in the world as a Christian—to have what I might refer to as a Christian "being"—that existence is always predicated on what I will describe as certain transcendental ideas. The three "ideas" that Yoder points out are the following: the state, faith, and history. What I find particularly interesting about these three ideas is that they are, as I have stated, transcendental ideas that are predicated on a Husserlian notion that they must be bracketed as a means of finding and interpreting epistemological value in them. This means, then, that the concepts of

---

I will refer only to oral.

152. I use this term rather purposefully as a tip of the hat to Mikhail Bakhtin and, to a lesser extent, Gilles Deleuze.

"the state," "faith," and "history" are objects of transcendence that require a different degree of objectification than traditional objects such as materials objects. I find that Yoder is aware of this, at least on some very important level.

In my view, by drawing a dialectic relationship between Christian existence and the transcendental ideas of the state, faith, and history, there is credence in why the early church would define Christian existence in subordination with them, since our consciousness and our awareness of our existential limitations are construed through how well or how effective we embrace those three transcendental ideas. This is particularly the case, of course, if understanding that the way those three ideas are bracketed through Husserl's phenomenological reduction, they come to embody an inherent value that is relative to our lived experiences. To that end, then, Yoder is creating the following dialectics: Christian-state, Christian-faith, and Christian-history—all three shape what it means to exist as a Christian, but also do a great deal to structure human existence. I would only extend Yoder a bit further by suggesting that these dialectics are not only, as I have asserted, aspects of the existential limitations to the Christian existence, but also, to a more important degree, gesturing to the Heideggerian "being-in-the-world." It is this, I would argue, is at the heart of the "social ethic" that Yoder describes—a social ethic that not only addresses the individuality of "being" and the notion that that "being" is construed through the lived experience, but that "being" as Christian is one that is connected to the world: the state, faith, and history, all of which are transcendental ideas that inform Christian consciousness in a decidedly Hegelian way.

Reinhold Niebuhr's *The Children of Light and the Children of Darkness*

In chapters 1–3 of Reinhold Niebuhr's *The Children of Light and the Children of Darkness: A Vindication of Democracy and a Critique of Its Traditional Defenders* (1944), I was immediately struck by Niebuhr's discussion of his notions of "the children of light" and the "children of darkness" as, I would argue, respectively liberal and radical forms of democratic theory. What particularly interested me about Niebuhr's articulation of these notions is his relation to how such notions can be theoretically construed through German romanticism. To put it a little more accurately, however, I would extend that Niebuhr is really focusing on German Idealism, since Fichte and Hegel chiefly function as German Idealists.

The reason why I make this small distinction is to place Niebuhr's discussion of Fichte's and Hegel's theory of "democracy" as theories specifically created in response to Kant. It is, of course, very important to understand that both Fichte and Hegel arise in a post-Kantian period, reacting to what I would call Kant's universalist approach to perception: the idea that all of us perceive an object of understanding the same way. I only say this to argue that this "universalist" approach to perception is essentially what Fichte and Hegel disagree with as they begin to wrestle with the idea that experience plays a vital role in how any individual perceives any object of understanding. That is, experience becomes the means by which individuals shape meaning from what they perceive. For Fichte and Hegel, experience is woven into their sense of "democracy" and how a "democracy" is an experiential extrapolation of the individual perceived of within their community as much as it is of the community perceived of as a collection of individuals.

From this, I would contend that any notion Kant may have had about "democracy" was rather general and broad. I would even go so far to say that "democracy" was not in Kant's vocabulary, which is, perhaps, much of the reason why Niebuhr avoids any theoretical connection of Kant to Fichte and Hegel all together. Instead, since Niebuhr focuses exclusively on Fichte and Hegel, I would suggest that Niebuhr is very much aware that Kant was much more concerned with "ethics" as an object of understanding that is simply a "thing-in-itself" to all that perceive it as such. In other words, beliefs in "justice," "equality," and "rights" are "things-in-themselves" rather than objects of understanding construed to subjectivity and meaning. Obviously, the Kantian concept of ethics does not work very well with the concept of democracy that Fichte and Hegel theorized. But, Kant's concept of ethics becomes the ideological framework upon which Fichte and Hegel develop their own ethics—Fichte and Hegel push back against Kant's simplicity in order to conceive of "ethics" not only as a complicated dialectic between the community and the individual, but as an object of understanding that is relative to subjectivity and individualized meaning.

Niebuhr attests to this with his notions of the "children of light" and the "children of darkness," which seem to draw upon two experiential distinctions of the same object of understanding: democracy. Niebuhr's "children of light" and "children of darkness" embody opposing views of what "community" is and what an "individual" is. In effect, by Niebuhr invoking both Fichtean and Hegelian notions of "democracy" as two perspectives in understanding the development of the relationship between community and the individual, I find that Niebuhr understands, then, that there is a community-individual dialectic that is always at work in a democracy. This dialectic is what Fichte and Hegel focus on in terms of what they both call "The Right"—while Fichte discusses "The Right" in his *Foundations of Natural Right*, Hegel examines "The Right" in his *Philosophy of Right*. As Niebuhr would likely agree, Fichte and Hegel consider "The Right" as an object of understanding that has epistemological and aesthetic value in it: an idea that is relative to conception, subjectivity, and meaning. It is with this encounter with "The Right" that makes community, the individual, and democracy possible as three social constructions relative to theory and practice.

* * *

In chapter 4 of *The Children of Light and the Children of Darkness*, I wanted to focus this journal entry particularly on Niebuhr's discussion of a democratic civilization, and what "democratic" means. For Niebuhr, the task of a civilization that is decidedly "democratic" should be as follows: "to integrate the life of its various subordinate, ethnic, religious and economic groups in the community in such a way that the richness and harmony of the whole community will be enhanced and not destroyed by them."[153] This notion of "harmony," as Niebuhr puts it, is, obviously, touching on the idea of pluralism, where a pluralistic community functions with integration and inclusion.

But, the problem that I find in the idea of "harmony" is that it is an ideality, rather than a reality. In other words, "harmony," as a concept, is a kind of Platonic form: it is an idea that we can never truly or completely understand beyond its secondhand representation, even if it is an object of our understanding born from our will and presentation.[154] The most that can be done about "harmony" is have to it bracketed, or to place it in quotations as I have done as a way of qualifying it as a possibility. In my view, then, "harmony" is not congruent with the realities of a democratic community—communities that define themselves as "democratic" are conceived by conceptions of power and, in turn, filter that power through the power relations between the powerful and the powerless to such an extent that it is impossible to ascertain any true, qualitative "harmony." Niebuhr seems to be aware of the problem of power relations, particularly with regards to developing "genuine universalism."[155] However, in my view, I see "genuine universalism" as an ideal. It is an unattainable and ungraspable idea as long as religious, ethnic, and economic groups are defined in the first place. To say that groups can be stratified through grouping means that there is no "genuine universalism" between them—there is only a genuine and universal sentiment about the way groups function sociologically. For instance, when ethnic groups are presented as African American, White, Native American, Hispanic, Asian, and so forth, there is a specific, systematic meaning applied to each "ethnic" group that is purely a sociological construction. As such, these sociological distinctions are applied to the community in which each group is represented as a means of finding differences between them, which, as a result, draw upon the availability to or unavailability of power. Whether groups, when defined along ethnic lines, are in positions of superiority or inferiority with respect to the possibility of power, such distinctions become socioeconomic. In a given community with difference possibilities of power, the economic groups can be labeled broadly as the wealthy, the middle-class, and the poor.

---

153. Niebuhr, *Children of Light*, 124.

154. Here, I am referring to Arthur Schopenhauer's concept of the world being relative to will and presentation. In effect, that what we see in the world is based on our ability to will it into "being" and, then, our own individual possibility to "present" as an object of our understanding.

155. Niebuhr, *Children of Light*, 124.

Kathryn Tanner's *Economy of Grace*

Kathryn Tanner raises the concept of "theological economy" in *Economy of Grace* (2005). As such, Tanner describes "theological economy" as something that "enters into the present configuration of global capitalism to transform [global capitalism] at those points where the two fields cross each other in conflict." What is particularly profound about this assertion, and worthy of a bit of nuance, is the idea that "theological economy," as an object of understanding, can only be truly understood and embraced within a dialectic with global capitalism. This means, then, that both—"theological economy" and "global capitalism"—do, indeed, engage in a "conflict," which Tanner suggests, is predicated through "a clash" over "economic life." To that end, I would add that this "clash" over "economic life" is a clash over authenticity, where the two fields of "theological economy" and "global capitalism" each vie for representation not just in the world of ideas, but also in our lived experiences.

As Tanner rightly proposes, "theological economy and global capitalism are not parallel planes but fields that come together in struggle because of their different vectors, their movements in opposite directions." An important way that Tanner illustrates the "struggle" that ensues between "theological economy" and "global capitalism" is by equating the former to "moving up" particularly "in the direction of life," and the latter "moving down, in the direction of death." Obviously, "theological economy," as a means of "moving" up in the direction of life is about living an economic life in alignment with God.

Essentially, such an economic life is about longitudinal reference between the human and God, so that the human experience seeks a theological existence between the humanity's "being" and God's "Being." In other words, when embarking on a decidedly "theological" economic life, humanity's "being" not only has a much better chance to fully actualize and self-actualize their "being-ness," but can situate "being" within the situatedness of existential authenticity. In this regard, "theological economy" becomes a means through which authentic economic life can strive and survive the marginalizing, oppressive, and subversive aspects of a global capitalist system. Of course, when I say "strive and survive," Tanner offers the notion that a theological economy puts forth "viable theological proposal for changing the present system." This is true, particularly when taking into account, as Tanner continues to propose, that such a change arises out of "partial overlaps and clashes, as the theological principles of economy meet the workings of the capital system so as to infiltrate and subvert its usual operation." However, I am compelled to take Tanner just a bit further. In my view, perhaps, then, it becomes indispensably important to consider that "theological economy" confronts the capital system in order to open up the possibility for a different "usual operation." That is, the existence of "theological economy" subjugated under the premise that it should be the "usual operation" and the capital system is an "unusual operation."

EXISTENTIAL THEOLOGY
ANDREA SMITH'S *CONQUEST*

When considering Andrea Smith's *Conquest: Sexual Violence and American Indian Genocide* (2005), I wanted to particularly focus on Smith's notion of "sexual violence as a primary tool of genocide."[156] What seems pivotal to this notion, as Smith argues it, is the role of the body as a hegemonic object—the body as a tool for coercion, domination, and oppression. As such, the body, then, becomes the means by which power structures are established within the infrastructure of systems, and power paradigms are grounded between the powerful and the powerless. Essentially, the body is a Marxist commodity that has a value and exchange rate. As I am sure Smith would agree, the body, as a commodity, embodies something that can be valued and exchanged. What is valued and exchanged, I would argue, is power. In this case, when the body is relinquished by one person and repossessed by another, the power paradigm between those individuals drastically shifts—the body is bartered for power.

I find that understanding the role of the body as a means of exchanging power between the powerless and the powerful critical to interpreting Smith's concept of sexual violence. One way to understand Smith is to propose that having control of the body is essential to the relationship between the victimizer and the victimized. When the victimizer takes control of the body from the victimized, the victimizer assumes control of not just the body as a physical object, but assumes control of the victimized's selfhood. This, I believe, is another way to understand what Smith means by "sexual violence"—the sense that selfhood is exchanged with the same physical resonance as the body. To dominate, oppress, and coerce is to exert power over the self so that, as a result, selfhood becomes bartered, monetized, and commoditized.

If thinking about "sexual violence" as seizing control of the physical body and the metaphysical self, then Smith is offering an existential argument. In my view, in Smith, "sexual violence" becomes a method of meaning-making. I look at this not just in terms of the meaningfulness of the physical act of "sexual violence" for the victimizer and the victimized, but the phenomenological meaningfulness in the ramifications of one soul being subjected to the soul of another. It is in the latter sense that "sexual violence" has existential value—the shaping of "being-for-self" into "being-for-others." In effect, when a victimizer is subjected to a position of powerlessness by a victimizer, the victimized's selfhood is transformed into a "being-for-others." I tend to believe that Smith is operating under the same premise. But, also, and perhaps more importantly, the "being-for-others" of the victimized can be best illustrated through Hegel's lordship-bondsman dialectic, where the bondsman's self-consciousness is so inextricably linked in the personhood of the lordship that the bondman does not have a "being-for-self" but, instead, has a "being-for-others." So, "sexual violence," as Smith describes it, is Hegelian dialectic of power, powerlessness, and empowerment—within

---

156. See introduction to Smith's *Conquest*.

this dialectic, the body becomes objectified and, then, through that objectification, relegates two persons to hierarchal positionalities.

* * *

Here, I would like to focus on Smith's chapter 6, entitled "Spiritual Appropriation as Sexual Violence." In this chapter, Smith makes the following assertion: "Sexual violence . . . suggests that the violation of [physical and psychic] boundaries operates not on the physical but on the spiritual and psychic levels as well."[157] Here, this becomes very important to what Smith is offering about "spiritual appropriation," particularly arising as a result of sexual violence. In my view, what Smith seems to touch on is the sense that sexual violence, as a physical act, enacts more than just a superficial or explicit effect on the victim but, more importantly, ravages a victim's spiritual sense of self. When a victim recognizes their victimization through sexual violence, there arises an understanding that the victim's spiritual awareness has been changed. For me, I see this as an understanding of the victim's "being-in-the-world"—the Heideggerian notion that "being" is not construed simply or exclusively as a Kantian thing-in-itself, but, instead, that it is constituted "in-the-world."

Smith's concept of spiritual appropriation through sexual violence is rooted, first, in the knowledge of overarching power structures, changes in power paradigms between the victim and the victimizer, and the positionality of powerlessness. Of course, what makes Smith's concept particularly resonate with me is the degree to which sexual violence experienced by Native peoples is not just bodily or physical, but is also tied to violence against the land, nature, and the environment. For Native peoples, the human body and the land share a critical dialectic with one another, one that is linked across an existential plane of understanding. In other words, Native peoples define their identities—the facticities of their "being" and their "being-in-the-world"—in relation to land in which they live. Smith agrees with this, arguing that "native spiritualities are land based—they are tied to the landbase from which they originate."[158]

So, as Smith continues to rightly argue, "when the dominant society disconnects Native spiritual practices from their landbases, it undermines Native peoples' claim that the protection of the landbase is integral to the survival of Native peoples."[159] In this, I find that Smith is making a very fundamental connection, a connection that is immensely valuable to re-understanding what sexual violence is. In other words, what Smith outlines is that sexual violence is not just a performative act against the human body, but one that can be related to nature. I find this to be pivotal to conceptualizing, as Smith offers in the title of her book, what "conquest" of American Indian people looks like.

157. See ch. 6 in Smith's *Conquest*.
158. Smith, *Conquest*, ch. 6.
159. Smith, *Conquest*, ch. 6.

Essentially, for the victimizer to truly victimize the victim, especially a victim that is a Native people, the victimizer must disconnect and undermine the Native peoples' relationship with their land. What this means, of course, is not just physically ravaging the human body as a means of appropriating dominance, but ravaging the land. As I am sure Smith would agree, when the land of Native people is raped, pillaged, and plundered by a victimizer, a more intrinsic, more existential sense of self is also violated. As a result, the facticities of "being" and "being-in-the-world" become reconstituted into some of the following facticities of existence: "being-victimized," "being-landless," and "being-powerless."

Giorgio Agamben's *Homo Sacer*

In his introduction to *Homo Sacer* (1995), Giorgio Agamben proposes that the "the protagonist of [*Homo Sacer*] is bare life, that is, the life of *homo sacer* (sacred man), who *may be killed and yet not sacrificed*, and whose essential function in modern politics we intend to assert."[160] Agamben's interpretation of "the life of homo sacer" is derived from "an obscure figure of archaic Roman law,"[161] but is particularly appropriated with respect to how human life, in the general sense, is included in or excluded from the overarching political structure, in the narrow sense. When I say human life "in the general sense," I am referring to what Agamben calls "the bare life"—it is a simple form of human existence that, as Agamben suggests, "is originally situated at the margins of the political order."[162] Conversely, human life "in the narrow sense" is denoted by a political order, or a structural politicization that functions, in part, "along with the disciplinary process by which State power makes man as a living being into its own specific subject."[163] The analytical possibility of human life existing in "the general sense" as bare life and "the narrow sense" as political life is respectively represented with *zoē* and *bios*.

But, more importantly, the relationship between *zoē* and *bios* seems tied to the dialectic between essence and existence. If so, does Agamben view *zoē* as "essence" or "existence"? In other words, if we understand that *zoē* precedes *bios*—or that *zoē* opens up the possibility for *bios*—does Agamben ascribe to the traditional notion of *essence preceding existence*, or the Sartrean reversal of *existence preceding essence*? I think this is a very important distinction to make, even if charting Agamben's posthumanistic project along the lines of Karen Barad's "mattering" of essence and existence "becoming" together.[164] If essence is *zoē*, then *bios* as existence concretizes "being" by building upon

---

160. Agamben, *Homo Sacer*, 12.
161. Agamben, *Homo Sacer*, 12.
162. Agamben, *Homo Sacer*, 12.
163. Agamben, *Homo Sacer*, 13.
164. See Karen Barad's "Posthumanist Performativity."

it. On the other hand, if existence is *zoē*, that is existence is "bare" because the essence of bios concretizes "being" in a Sartrean way into something meaningful.

Clearly, Agamben's notions of essence and existence are situated in "scientific" and "political" representations—bare life as *zoē* is "bare" because it is only scientifically represented by something that exists outside a "system," while *bios* is politically represented by something that can exist both inside and outside of a "system." This latter sense—that is, political representation—is the means by which *zoē* performs in the world, particularly a world construed by Baradian onto-epistemological performativity. If following Agamben's conceptualization a bit further, the existentialities (or the possibilities of meaning-making by performative means) of *zoē* and *bios* "in large measure corresponds to the birth of modern democracy, in which man as a living being presents himself no longer as an *object* but as the *subject* of political power."[165]

When considering "the birth of modern democracy," Agamben defines modern democracy—as opposed to classical democracy—"as a vindication and liberation of *zoē*, and that it is constantly trying to transform its own bare life into a way of life and to find, so to speak, the *bios* of *zoē*."[166] To be clear, Agamben envisions modern democracy as a power-based structure capable of ultimately providing a Derridan "freeplay" or Baradian "agential realism" for the *bios* of *zoē*. That is to say, Agamben's notion of the *bios* of *zoē*, or what I would term as the political existence for bare life, is grounded not on the objectification of *zoē* by the *bios*, but instead, on the subjectivization of *zoē* through the *bios*. Note the difference between *by the bios* and *through the bios*. For Agamben, the goal of modern democracy should be to vindicate and liberate *zoē*, but also function at a "historico-philosophical level, since it alone will allow us to orient ourselves in relation to the new realities and unforeseen convergences of the end of the millennium."[167]

With these "new realities and unforeseen convergences," the means by which any vindication and liberation of *zoē* becomes possible is through biopolitics—in order to "make it possible to clear the way for [biopolitics]," Western politics must construct an existential link between *zoē* and *bios*. Yet, just as Agamben argues, Western politics "has not succeeded," since Western politics—which operates in opposition to biopolitics—is "founded on the *exceptio* of bare life."[168] Agamben's new politics—one of "both modern totalitarianism and the society of mass hedonism and consumerism"—is based on Carl Schmitt's definition of sovereignty, the possibility of a "sovereign" capable of deciding on "the state of exception," and the extent to which sovereignty exists paradoxically.

Agamben is correct to suggest that there is a "paradox" to sovereignty, since the role of the sovereign is both outside and inside the juridical order. Yet, this paradox

165. Agamben, *Homo Sacer*, 13.
166. Agamben, *Homo Sacer*, 13.
167. Agamben, *Homo Sacer*, 13.
168. Agamben, *Homo Sacer*, 13.

is essential—albeit, the ethical lynchpin—to Agamben's post-humanism ethically interpreted through a politicalized lens. This is because, when viewed through a politicalized lens, the sovereign must stand outside the juridical order and still belong to it, since the political structure to which the sovereign operates within and beyond grants the sovereign *freeplay*.

Not only does the sovereign exist in a politicalized construct to, first and foremost, stabilize it and make determinations about who should be included in or excluded from the *bios*, but that same sovereignty ek-sists due to an exception that is *existentially exceptional*. This sort of exception, in itself, allows the sovereign to bestow a *state of exception* that separates the sovereign's *state* from that *exception*—without the sovereign's ability to exist in a *freeplay*, or have an *agential realism*, the ability to include and exclude from the *bios* would be impossible.

The logic of exception (that is, to say who is included or excluded from the "good life" of political existence), then, is the logic of sovereignty—for the sovereign to grant a "state of exception," the sovereign must exist within his/hers own implied *state of exception* that is *existentially apolitical*. In effect, the only manner in which a sovereign can include or exclude anyone from the *bios* is from this apolitical position—this *existentially apolitical* position (a position that is both within and beyond the sovereign's political structure) is post-humanistic. Though Agamben's post-humanism must be apolitical in one sense, to a greater degree, the apolitics of the sovereign is undoubtedly based on the necessity of having *no exteriorized other* in much the same sentiments as Baradian ethics theorizes, even for the positionality (or, perhaps "historicality," as in the historical situations of all contributing roles to the *bios*) of the sovereign with respect to all over which it holds sovereignty.

Miroslaw Volf's *Exclusion and Embrace*

There are two concepts from Miroslaw Volf's *Exclusion and Embrace* (1996) that I found particularly interesting, inextricably linked, and worthy of nuance: (1) the cross, the self, and the other, and (2) distancing and belonging.

What runs beneath the two concepts is existence, or "being"—what it means to exist is about what it means to "know" existence for what it is, what it means to perceive that existence in terms of time and historicity, and what it means to translate that existence into the limitations of one's existential situation. All these things are important when encountering the cross, the self, and the other, since the sum totality of all the facticities of our existence open the possibility, as Martin Heidegger would certainly agree, of recognizing the cross, the self, and the other as three very distinct objects of understanding that all yield very different epistemological and phenomenological value and meaning. Perhaps, I would go so far as to say that "being" sets the parameters to and the rules for how we encounter the cross, the self, and the other—we situate our situatedness in our self, or within our selfhood, and reflect that situatedness on the situatedness of the cross and the other. This is accomplished, as Volf rightly asserts, through distancing and belonging: to distance and to belong is about the situatedness of identity.

In my view, what Volf is suggesting through his explication of identity is that we are selves, while "the cross" and "the other" validate our selfhood self-referentially as much as they affirm themselves as pseudo-selves and points of objectification. To that end, the self, when we perceive it as such, allows us to, first, refer to "the other" as a projection of otherness which exists outside of our own existence. In other words, by ontologically construing "the other" as an object of our understanding that exists through exteriority, we place an identity in "the other" and, in turn, perceive that "the other" places the same sense of identity in us. This is what Volf is arguing as "otherness"—or, as I would argue a bit further, the other's "otherness" is shaped through our field of perception, the givenness of the other's identity and situatedness, and the ability of the other's situatedness to add nuance to our own situatedness and identity.

In same regard, the cross offers a kind of otherness similar to that of "the other," but, as Volf would concur, the cross represents an idea that must be apperceived. Of course, "the cross" also has its own situatedness, but is situated outside our field of perception. What I mean is that "the other" and "the self" can, indeed, be perceived through measures of reason and empirical study. However, experience is the only way to perceive "the cross," which not so much about "perceiving," but, more aptly, "apperceiving"—that is, bracketing an idea as ideality in order to become aware that the identity of the cross is experiential for us, where it ultimately transcends our perceivable reality.

There lies a "problematik" to the meaning of otherness, whereby otherness cannot always be quantified, or even objectified. In some cases, otherness can only be qualified as an idea and that "idea," as such, then, has to be bracketed as object of understanding. I am thinking particularly of Husserl's phenomenological reduction, whereby the only way that we can understand something transcendent is by "bracketing" it, or reducing its transcendence to something more epistemologically accessible. Not to say that something transcendent does not have a certain epistemological quality to it—it is just that objects of transcendence can only be "apperceived" through a phenomenological awareness of them. The "problematik" is that certain forms of otherness can only be apperceived, where that apperception of them engages our awareness of them differently depending on the experiences and history we bring into our encounter of them.

This seems to be what Volf is most concerned with when confronting the "otherness" of oppression, justice, and truth. There is, in fact, something problematic in them. We each encounter oppression, justice, and truth differently, either viewing them through our own experiences of them, the nature in which we are aware that other people have experienced them, and the degree to which we idealize what we think they are in society—these three things, as "ideas," can only be conceptualized as "others," but share a problematic stature in the human consciousness that is relative to how they are defined, appropriated, and interpreted contextually.

To say that anything is "oppression," "justice," and "truth" means that they must be individualized, qualified within some concrete situational context in order to proceed toward human quantification. In other words, as objects of understanding, oppression, justice, and truth are idea existing only in ideality. There is no true reality in which oppression, justice, and truth "are," as such—what I mean is that they do not have a concretized existence in themselves outside of the means and ways in which they are used and applied. When we affirm that something is oppressive, or something is a form of justice, or that something is truth, we affirm, first to ourselves, that they have relevance in the world of ideas and that, in turn, within the world of ideas they are possible quantities. What we make of oppression, justice, and truth is based on the meaning we make out of them as "ideas"—the fact that they are not factual by their nature, but only "factical," particularly in the sense that they have ontical groundings. I find that this is directly in line with what Kierkegaard describes as "truth is subjectivity," where any idea can only be objectified through our own will as a subjective figure in the world and the extent to which we formulate a meaning from that idea.

* * *

In light of continuing to discuss Miroslav Volf's *Exclusion and Embrace: A Theological Exploration of Identity, Otherness, and Reconciliation*, I wanted to focus particularly on chapter 6's discussion on "deception" and "truth."

Previously, I made an important connection between chapters 4 and 6 and the meaning of otherness as a "problematik." To that end, the "problematik" I chose to focus on was "oppression" and "justice"—"otherness can only be qualified as an idea and that 'idea,' as such, then, has to be bracketed as object of understanding." I find that the same can be said of truth. Though, to some extent, I did mention in that previous journal that "truth" must be "qualified within some concrete situational context in order to proceed toward human quantification," it is possible, however, for truth to be misconstrued through either deception or self-deception. Here, the "problematik" of truth's "otherness" is not just the nature in which any of us arrive at truth—either by forming it into "a truth" or assuming that it is "The Truth"—but through the possibility of what Jean-Paul Sartre asserted as "bad faith."

For Sartre, "bad faith" is about self-deception, where we develop a truth about something that we know is not entirely "true" and, in turn, through an "untruth," find a kind of meaning in it for ourselves. In other words, it is about appropriating a faith in an untruth with the intent of deceiving oneself. Whether that deception occurs within the self or comes from outside the self, the self still must somehow conceptualize what the truth is and what the truth is not. Nevertheless, to appropriate a "bad faith" is, as Volf seems to argue, about "insert[ing] something of one's own" into what Volf refers to as "the act of witnessing"—perhaps, more importantly, when we witness something, attempt to draw a meaning from that experience, and discover gaps or gray areas within that experience as we proceed toward ascertaining the truth, we "insert" whatever is necessary to make "truth" as full-fleshed as possible, even if that means deceiving ourselves about our situatedness with respect to the nature of the experience experienced.

Volf addresses the notion by making a particularly interesting and important connection to Michel Foucault and the idea that knowledge is power. What I would offer as a bit of nuance to Volf's argument is that, when knowledge is power, knowledge always has an epistemological value to it, from which we empower ourselves in "knowing." But, the question I would pose is the following: What about "ideas" that do not necessarily have a fixed epistemological value, such as "truth"? In this case, to consider "truth," as such, as something that has an experiential epistemological value to it, I find that problem inherent in "truth" and stating "truths" is that it must always be predicated as a "truth claim," where our subjectivity and meaning shapes what we "know" about "truth."

JACQUES DERRIDA'S *THE POLITICS OF FRIENDSHIP*

At the conclusion of *The Politics of Friendship* (1994), Jacques Derrida offers the following question about the relationship between the concept of friendship and the political context in which friendship must conceptually exists: "When will we be ready for an experience of equality that would be a respectful test of [the concept of] friendship, and that would at last be just, just beyond justice as law, that is, measure up to its immeasure?"[169] In this question, Derrida is, in one sense, certainly presenting a dialectic between *what friendship is* and *how politics must represent itself conceptually through friendship*. Yet, in another sense, more narrowly, friendship itself, if appropriating Arthur Schopenhauer, is merely a representation shaped by the "will." So, in this narrow sense, there is a dialectic between friendship and the world. Together, though this apparent dialectic hinges on the experience of equality—a Hegelian "play of forces" between friends—there arises a need to "respectful[ly] test" the extent to which friendship grounds itself between selves. What is grounded, as Derrida rightly notes, is "just beyond justice as law," but what exactly does Derrida mean? How can friendship, even as a conceptualization of the experience of equality, be measured "just beyond justice as law"? In other words, Derrida comes to an ideological and theoretical impasse here—it brings him to a rather difficult question of how friendship is grounded fundamentally in the experience of whether quality can "measure up to its immeasure." The answer for Derrida, as he seems to suggest, lies in democracy, which undoubtedly underscores Derrida's "politics of friendship." I wish

---

169. Derrida, *Politics of Friendship*, 306.

to depart from Derrida here, because arriving at the answer of "democracy" veers away *from the question of the meaning of friendship itself*. To be sure, any politics of friendship only goes so far—its limitations are seated in a contextual framework, or an Alhusserian ideological state apparatus. Not only is this reductive to the meaning of friendship, but it never answers the question of the meaning of friendship itself. Is it even possible for democracy itself to become "measure[d] up to its immeasure," if we concede that it is, at first, an idea that must exist "just beyond justice as law"? That is, democracy does not shape "justice as law," but rather, it is shaped by "justice as law." Democracy is not an essence from which "justice as law" locates its existence in the world. Instead, "justice as law" has an essence that "measure[s] up to its immeasure," by giving an account of itself through democracy's existence in the world. But, what is democracy? The facticity of democracy itself points to the facticity of "justice as law" and, ultimately, is oriented toward the facticity of friendship, as an ideology that governs the superstructure of "justice as law" and the infrastructure of democracy. What this means, then, is that friendship, as a concept that is "just beyond justice as law" must be interpreted beyond the ideological state apparatus to *a rhetoric of friendship between related Kierkegaardian selves*.

Louis Althusser: Ideology, the Ideological, and State Apparatuses

In the section of the *Critical Theory* collection devoted to Marxist theory, we are provided with a sample of Louis Althusser's "Ideology and Ideological State Apparatuses," which argues, straightforwardly, that "ideology represents the imaginary relationship of individual to their real conditions of existence."[170] By beginning here, we arrive at Althusser's "central thesis" grounded on "the structure and functioning of ideology"— it contains two theses delineated along what Althusser describes as the "negative" and the "positive": while the former is invested in how the object is "represented in the imaginary form of ideology," the latter is devoted to "the materiality of ideology."[171] What might this mean, then, in reference to how Althusser conceives of "the negative" and "the positive" aspects of his conceptualization of ideology?

I would argue that this question is central to Althusser's "central thesis," particularly when considering what kind of Marxist approach Althusser is employing (structural Marxism) and, by extension, what form of Marxism his approach is in opposition to (humanistic Marxism)—what Althusser advocates is a kind of empirical examination of structure objectively based on the capitalist production, aligning more with "later Marx" in *Das Kapital* of 1867–1894 and opposes alienation of individual freedom of "early Marx" in *Economic and Philosophic Manuscripts* of 1844. I have placed "later Marx" and "early Marx" in scare quotes, because it has been argued, most notably by Georg Lukács in *The Young Hegel* (1948), that there is a clear division between Karl Marx's

---

170. Althusser, "Ideology and Ideological State Apparatuses," 450.
171. Althusser, "Ideology and Ideological State Apparatuses," 450.

early philosophical influences and the later development of his political thought—on one hand, in his early period, what has been labeled as "young Marx" is overwhelmingly influenced by Hegel (and Hegelian dialectics) and expressed in Marx's theory of alienation, but on the other hand, what has been called "mature Marx" develops into a more political and economic thought oriented toward modes of production. To be clear, "young Marx" is represented by Humanistic Marxism, while "mature Marx" is expressed by Structural Marxism—not only is it fair to suggest that, for Althusser, "ideology" is based on a specific rearticulation of structuralism and more deeply concerned with Structural Marxism, but, by opposing Humanistic Marxism, Althusser's theoretical approach to the "ideological state apparatus" provides specific functional rearticulations of deconstruction and psychoanalysis.

Allow me to return to how Althusser advances the notion of ideology as having both negative and positive ramifications, respectively situated in *ideology as imaginary* and *ideology as material*. What makes the latter—*ideology as material*—a "positive" part of ideology is rooted in the manner in which "ideology" and the "ideological state apparatus" come together for the sake of (capitalist) production and reproduction, or what Althusser calls "the reproduction of the relations of production."

Though Althusser makes this assertion before the *Critical Reader* begins its sample, it is an immensely "critical question," according to Althusser, as an entry point of "Ideology and Ideological State Apparatuses" essay itself—the roles of "ideology" and "ideological state apparatuses" hinge on, in Althusser's argument in the essay included in the collection entitled *Lenin and Philosophy and Other Essays* (1968), "the ultimate condition of production [which] is therefore the reproduction of the conditions of production."[172]

What is produced and reproduced is "labour power"—as such, with respect to *ideology as material*, Althusser contends that "it is not enough to ensure for labour power the material conditions of its reproduction if it is to be reproduced as labour power."[173] In effect, this "labour power" is material insofar as it is produced as a "condition of production," but it is more than just material, because it is reproduced, particularly as a means of production that sustains "ideology" through reproduction.

So, again, "labour power" is both produced and reproduced as a materiality that becomes, in the end, ideological in nature. More specifically, Althusser describes the reproduction (and production) of "labour power" in the following way:

> The reproduction of labour power thus reveals as its *sine qua non* not only the reproduction of its "skills" but also the reproduction of its subjection to the ruling ideology or of the "practice" of that ideology ... for it is clear that *it is in the forms and under the forms of ideological subjection that provision is made for the reproduction of the skills of labour power.*[174]

172. Althusser, *Lenin and Philosophy*, 127.
173. Althusser, *Lenin and Philosophy*, 131.
174. Althusser, *Lenin and Philosophy*, 133.

This suggests, then, that not only does *labour power*, as Althusser considers it, produce and reproduce itself, but, through that production and reproduction, it produces and reproduces *ideology*. Moreover, ideology produces and reproduces itself by, in turn, producing and reproducing "forms of ideological subjection." If we refer back to *ideology as material*, we find that *labour power* has a materiality that produces/reproduces itself through what I would call "tangible work" (or what Marx calls "*Grundisse*") and, simultaneously, produces/reproduces ideology by creating/sustaining the "subjection to the ruling ideology or of the practice of that ideology." Notions of "subjection," "ruling ideology," and "the practice of that ideology" all point to Althusser's conceptualization of an "ideological state apparatus"—to this end, the production/reproduction of labour power and the production/reproduction of ideology both produce/reproduce an "ideological state apparatus" through the proliferation of "infrastructure" and "superstructure."

According to Althusser, *infrastructure* and *superstructure* form a framework upon which the "State Apparatus" is precisely built with and maintained by *labour power, subjection, ruling ideology*, and *the practice of that ideology*. Althusser defines "infrastructure" as the "economic base," or "the unity of the productive forces and relations of production"[175]—this is realized by *labour power*. Superstructure, on the other hand, is described by Althusser as "contain[ing] two 'levels' or 'instances': the politico-legal (law and the State) and ideology (different ideologies, religious, ethical, legal, political, etc.)"[176]—which are manifested in *subjection, ruling ideology* and *the practice of that ideology*. These elements are essential to what a "superstructure" is and does, and Althusser makes this case by asserting, "I believe that it is possible and necessary to think what characterizes the essential of the existence and nature of the superstructure on the basis of reproduction."[177] This, then, leads Althusser to make the "basic thesis" that it is not possible to pose questions about how *infrastructure* supports *superstructure*, and the extent to which *superstructure* supports a *State Apparatus* "except from the point of view of reproduction."[178]

Is "reproduction," then, more important to Althusser's prescriptive notion of *ideology as material*? And, if so, does this inform Althusser's understanding of *ideology as imaginary*, with respect to taking a descriptive approach, when such an approach has as its "greatest disadvantage"[179] that it is always metaphorical?

I would like to push back against Althusser here, by focusing, now, on his notion of *ideology as imaginary*, and addressing what Althusser means by the "negative" thesis of "representation" in the imaginary form of ideology. This brings me back to reconsidering Althusser's thesis at the beginning of the sample in the *Critical Reader*:

175. Althusser, *Lenin and Philosophy*, 134.
176. Althusser, *Lenin and Philosophy*, 134.
177. Althusser, *Lenin and Philosophy*, 136.
178. Althusser, *Lenin and Philosophy*, 136.
179. Althusser, *Lenin and Philosophy*, 136.

"Ideology represents the imaginary relationship of individuals to their real conditions of existence."[180] So, first, the question is this: how does Althusser's thesis respond to structuralism, deconstruction, and psychoanalysis? Althusser's response to structuralism is clear, particularly if we assess an *ideological state apparatus* as a structural representation of an *ideology*—that *ideology*, then, is represented in *labour power, subjection, ruling ideology*, and *the practice of that ideology*. Though *labour power* is not imaginary, since it can be tangible, are not *subjection, ruling ideology*, and *the practice of that ideology* all imaginary, at least fundamentally? Is it possible to see these elements as validating Althusser's thesis? I would say so. But, more importantly, is it possible to view these elements, even if fundamentally imaginary, as critical points of departure for Althusser from deconstruction and psychoanalysis?

If holding firm to Althusser's definition of the *ideological state apparatus*, I would argue that it is also, through its *ideology*, something that oppresses, suppresses, and represses—the function of the *ideological state apparatus* "oppresses" the structure of a given society with the rationality of *labour power*, "suppresses" any spirit of meaning through *ruling ideology* and *subjection* so that "reality" is outside the state, and "represses" the appetitive needs of the lower rungs of society by *practicing ideology*.

To pursue this a bit further, I will need to take the very descriptive approach that Althusser believes is "the greatest disadvantage"—allow me to consider what *an ideological state apparatus* is and does through Socrates's correlation of the balanced soul to a balanced society in Plato's *The Republic*. In brief, Socrates argues that a soul contains rational, spirited, and appetitive parts, and, in order to be "balanced," the rational part must rule the other two. Socrates correlates this framework to a republic that contains a philosopher king, auxiliary, and workers, which can only be "balanced" if the philosopher king rules the other two classes. Socrates's "Republic" is a "representation"—it embodies what Althusser's thesis calls "the imaginary relationship of individuals to their real conditions of existence." But, more importantly, along with Socrates's conceptualization of the soul, we arrive at Althusser's Marxist notions of structuralism with respect to oppression, deconstruction with respect to suppression, and psychoanalysis with respect to repression.

Slavoj Žižek: "Trauma" and "Symptom"

The relationship between Slavoj Žižek and theology has been well-researched, particularly and at its most explicit in Adam Kotsko's *Žižek and Theology* (2008). Through Kotsko's study, Žižek's "theology" is assessed in reference to and in relation with the thought of Hegel, Lacan, and Marx. Not only is this an excellent means of contextualizing Žižek's general influences, but it also becomes a means to further contextualize what kind of theologizing Žižek is concerned with explicating. What

---

180. Althusser, "Ideology and Ideological State Apparatuses," 450.

Hegel, Lacan, and Marx contribute to Žižek's theologizing can be outlined and explained in a wide variety of ways, when attending to the various means of focusing on Hegelianism, Lacanianism, and Marxism—in each, there is a history of ideas, in which Žižek situates his own thought and attunes that thought to a specific kind of thinking through the respective thought of Hegel, Lacan, and Marx. Indeed, Kotsko recognizes that Hegel, Lacan, and Marx, in themselves, contribute to Žižek's thought in ways that sometimes intersect and sometimes provide stark contractions. This is especially so when laying a foundation for what can be meant by Žižek's "theologizing," if we take into account that "theologizing" itself can be taken differently by Hegelianism, Lacanianism, and Marxism—the meaningfulness of theologizing to Hegel, to Lacan, and to Marx are all up for debate, to which Žižek's "theologizing," if you will, can litigate at the margins of each.

An important way to litigate Hegel, Lacan, and Marx from the standpoint of Žižek's theologizing is by way of ascertaining how "the theological" and "the political" come to bear in that kind of theologizing. Kotsko assesses what can be construed as Žižek's "political theology," though he does not explicitly refer to it as such, in sections devoted to "ideology critique," "subjectivity and ethics," "the Christian experience," "dialectical materialism," and "theological responses"—all are punctuated, in part, on an existential dialogue between "the theological" and "the political," though "the political," for Kotsko, is part of a larger matrix of concerns for "the theological." What becomes all the more apparent with Kotsko is that, even when acknowledging the contributions of Hegel, Lacan, and Marx to Žižek's theologizing, there is certainly more than can be said about the nature of "the political" in Žižek, and how Hegel, Lacan, and Marx speak to and are, in themselves, spoken to with Žižek's theologizing.

In a certain sense, the way that "the political" works through Hegel, Lacan, and Marx on the way to Žižek is with the notion of the dialectic: the Hegelian dialectic, as it is stands in relation to the Kantian version, the Marxist dialectic, as it stands in relation to the Hegelian version, and the Lacanian "dialectic," as the "mirror stage," as it stands in relation to both Hegel and Sigmund Freud. In my article "Dialectics and Hegelian Negation in Slavoj Žižek's *Enjoy Your Symptom*: Fighting the Fantasies of Trauma, Identity, Authority, and Phallophany" (2019), I discuss dialectics more broadly through the use of Hegel, Lacan, and Marx, as well as Kierkegaard, though I ground these understandings in terms of a dialectic between "trauma" and the "symptom." In this regard, when reading *Enjoy your Symptom* (2007), I argue that "Slavoj Žižek presents the notion of 'trauma' as critical to understanding the scope and meaning of the 'symptom.'"[181] It seems to me that the relationship between "trauma" and "symptom" requires a kind of theologizing about God that must be "political" in nature—to define Žižek's political theology, as such, means tempering the direct influences of Hegel, Lacan, and Marx, as well as the indirect influence of Kierkegaard, on the manner with which we can say that Žižek theologizes about God.

181. Woodson, "Dialectics and Hegelian Negation," 2.

Yet, recently, in Bojan Koltaj's *Žižek Reading Bonhoeffer: Towards a Radical Critical Theology* (2019), Koltaj explicitly discusses Žižek's "political theology," doing so with Hegel, Lacan, and even Kierkegaard in mind, but without any mention of Marx. As thoroughgoing as Koltaj's assessment of Žižek's "political theology" is, what makes Žižek's theologizing "political" has as much—if not mostly—to do with Marxism as it does with the contributions of Hegel and Lacan. Koltja's lack of a Marxist voice in his understanding of Žižek's "political theology" begs the question if, as it is presented, there can even be a "political theology" for Žižek without Marx. In my view, while Hegelianism and Lacanianism are not overtly political and, arguably, do not directly contribute to what can be meant by "the political," Marxism not only allows us to politicize the meaning of Hegelian dialectics, but it makes it possible to view Lacanianism through a political lens predicated on a means of handling a dialectical structure.

Because of this, when we speak about "trauma" and "symptom" as a case in dialectics, we do so with the understanding that both are theologically-comported and, as such, require a kind of theologizing to fully understand them—through Hegelianism, Lacanianism, Marxism, and even Kierkegaardianism, Žižek's "political theology" is one that theologizes about God from the standpoint of the relationship between "trauma" and "symptom." What it means to be human, then, is grounded in "trauma" and "symptom," so that human existence itself is situated by "trauma" and situates itself in "symptom"—both politicize what it means to be human in terms of how we handle "trauma" and manage "symptom." The extent to which we handle "trauma" and manage "symptom" occurs through how we theologize about God, and how, in doing so, overcome a "negation" attempting to "negate" the meaning of our humanity by distancing us from God's existence. To theologize about God by way of Žižek's "political theology" means theologizing the meaning of "symptom" as it physically manifests itself in the meaning of human existence and, then, theologizing the meaning of "trauma" as it psychologically manifests itself in the connectedness with God's existence.

Ethical Approach

Understanding the Ethical as Fichte's "Right"

"Right" exists beyond human existence as a point of transcendence that human existence uses as a means of measurement, self-actualization, and teleological significance. In this way, *Right* is what existence uses as a point of cosmic destination, which is transcendent to "being-Human." Since *Right* is a transcendental idea, as Immanuel Kant argues in *Critique of Pure Reason*, it is a pure concept of reason.[182] The "pure" aspect to any concept, or object—that is, when it is a "transcendental idea"—is one predicated on *a priori* understanding of its "is-ness" and "there-ness" as that which is *Right*. Because of this, *being-Human* conceives of *Right* as an object of understanding.

182. Kant, *Critique of Pure Reason*, 315.

As such, this kind of object of understanding is something that is represented, or objectified, prior to all experience—we apprehend *Right* before actually experiencing it.[183] This *a priori* concept, through the process of a more rigorous experiential objectification, according to Kant, "indicates the synthetic unity which alone makes possible an empirical knowledge of objects."[184] What this means, then, is that, when human existence encounters *Right* as an object of understanding, in its transcendence, there is an initial knowledge of it as a "mere logical form" before there is a deeper, deliberative knowledge of it as an "empirical form." Knowledge of an *a priori* object of understanding, as Kant argues, "[is] not to be obtained by mere reflection but only by inference."[185] So, what arises here is the relationship between sense and reference,[186] where what can be logically inferred about an a priori object of understanding becomes an empirical point of reference. Not only do sense and reference come to bear upon what *Right* is, but there are the deontological dimensions of human existence that perceives, understands, and grasps *Right*, and there are ethics involved in the encounter between *Right* and *being-Human*. If it is possible to argue that *Right* is a transcendent object of understanding that we must conceive, understand, and grasp, what kind of ethics do we use, if *Right* must fall into truth-related parameters. I would argue that this is a kind of natural law—it is something that is set up through the ascetic, deontological value of *being-Human*, and a recognition of its link to the "highest good." What makes the "highest good" possible is, as Johann Fichte asserts in *The Foundation of Natural Right*, when "each free being makes it a law for himself to limit his freedom through the concept of the freedom of all others."[187] Fichte's idea of "each free being" is grounded on the universality of freedom. The nature and purpose of human existence are as *being-Human* through the intersection between *Right* and the "natural law" of "being-Human-in-the-world"—Fichte's *Right* and *being-Human* are existentially actualized in the "highest good" and *natural law* grounded on the purpose of the world, worldhood, and worldliness.

Alasdair MacIntyre's *After Virtue*

In his *After Virtue* (1981), I find that the central argument Alasdair MacIntyre makes is with the integral thesis: "language and the appearance of morality persist even though the integral substance of morality has to a large degree been fragmented and then in part destroyed."[188] What MacIntyre suggests, then, is that there is a

---

183. Here, "apprehends" is similar to "apperceives."

184. Kant, *Critique of Pure Reason*, 315.

185. Kant, *Critique of Pure Reason*, 308.

186. I am thinking particularly of Gottlob Frege's notions of "sense" and "reference," which, of course, owe their theory and praxis to Kant. Frege, "On Sense and Reference," 61.

187. Fichte, *Foundation of Natural Right*, 85.

188. MacIntyre, *After Virtue*, 5.

lack of consistency between what he denotes as contemporary moral attitudes and arguments,[189] where these important elements of moral claims, morality, and value judgments are, at their most fundamental, only appearances. As "appearances," MacIntyre believes that the morality statements that are made explicitly in terms of the language used to appropriate them, express them, and articulate them are only semantic gestures that inadequately get to the "integral substance of mortality," which he believes never becomes as fully realized as it should be.

For MacIntyre, this problem arises out of the expression of disagreements, which become "the most striking feature of contemporary moral utterance."[190] And, within this notion, he further denotes that "the most striking feature of the debates in which these disagreements are expressed is their interminable character."[191] There is no doubt, here, that what MacIntyre is proposing is that certain "debates" of extreme moral value have no end to them, meaning, in other words, that they are issues that are debated from perpetual perspectives. If there are, I would argue, two sides to any one issue, where either side has taken a firm moral stance to their logical point of view, it is impossible for either side to claim that their logical point of view is the most logical, or, as I am sure MacIntyre would agree, the most moral. Perhaps, as MacIntyre rightly theorizes, "there seems to be no rational way of securing moral agreement in our culture."[192] To say this, ultimately, is to say that certain debates[193] of moral value exist, chiefly, as disagreements. This is particularly the case with respect to war. The idea that a war can be labeled as a "just war" is always relative to the side doing the labeling, which is, essentially, the side that believes that the war they are engaging in has an extreme moral value and that the judgment made about the necessity of the war will prove, in the end, to bring about an essential good. A "just war," as MacIntyre explains, "is one in which the good to be achieved out-weighs the evils involved in waging the war."[194] This, of course, is a true extrapolation of anything perceived as being "just." However, when I think about the "other side" of any given "just" action, event, or situation, I must consider the possibility that there will be a voice that will never perceive anything good coming out of something labeled as "just" in general and, as result, would find all "just" causes, in whatever form, to be unjust. Therefore, as MacIntyre would resoundingly agree, this is a moral argument that gives way to a moral disagreement. More importantly, I think it is an issue that involves so much more than just a moral disagreement but, instead, manifests from fundamental

189. MacIntyre, *After Virtue*, 5.
190. MacIntyre, *After Virtue*, 6.
191. MacIntyre, *After Virtue*, 6.
192. MacIntyre, *After Virtue*, 6.

193. I say "certain debates" because I wonder if it can be accurately stated that "all debates" have moral value to them and, thusly, present lasting disagreements that are expressed without end. Maybe I am thinking idealistically here, but, perhaps, there are some debates, even of some relative ethical or moral value, that some consensus is possible.

194. MacIntyre, *After Virtue*, 6.

differences in the application of the term "just" and the meaning that the term itself is meant to convey when it is appropriated in any given context by any given person in the position of labeling meaning. What I mean is this: to say that anything is "just" denotes that the side labeling it as "just" has certain moral parameters ascribed to it, for it, and through it that make a "just" thing different from something that is "unjust," which, in turn, informs its own moral parameters.

What happens, then, when something that is described as "just" informs the definition of what can be called "unjust," and vice versa by proxy, there exists a plane of immanence, where the seemingly distinct meanings evident in both are inseparable.[195] For something to be labeled as "just," there must be an antithesis, and to say that something is "unjust" suggests that it, also, has an antithesis. As MacIntyre would agree, what links the definition of "just" to that of "unjust" becomes the very thing that unravels moral arguments made on behalf of explaining something as being "just" or something being "unjust." It is, if I may appropriate Kierkegaard's pseudonym Anti-Climacus, "a relation which relates itself to its own self, or it is that in the relation (which accounts for it) that the relation relates itself to its own self."[196] I say this to propose that this relation that relates, inseparability, or connectedness between moral terms such as "just" and "unjust" is at the heart of the problem with any moral argument—it is apparent in the inability to justify one over the other, since both are, inevitably, factually doomed by the semantics of their arguments. Just as MacIntyre rightly points out, "in an argument in which any attempt is made to derive a moral or evaluative conclusion from factual premises something which is not in the premises, namely the moral or evaluative element, will appear in the conclusion. Hence, any such argument must fail."[197] If extending MacIntyre's point a bit further, he finds, then, that it is not just that moral arguments fail since the moral conclusions that bind them cannot be justified, but that "the loss of the possibility of such justification signals a correlative change in the meaning of moral idioms."[198] Though MacIntyre would indicate, as moral idioms, "just" and "unjust" do not have the same meanings as they did in the classical tradition,[199] I would argue that, in fact, their meanings have not changed. They are, I believe, constant moral variables. If anything has changed, it is the social, psychological, cultural, racial,

---

195. Here, I am adapting the concept of the plane of immanence by Gilles Deleuze. Deleuze theorized that a plane of immanence exists between a subject and an object, because that plane is "itself actualized in an object and a subject which it attributes itself." The most important thing about this concept is that it expresses the connectedness of a subject and an object through their inherent inseparability, through the notion that the subject interacts with an object as much as the object interacts with the subject. I find this critical to understanding the semantics of "just" and "unjust," where, for the sake of argument, the former informs the latter as much as the latter informs the former. Deleuze, *Pure Immanence*, 31.

196. Anti-Climacus, *Sickness unto Death*, 1.

197. MacIntyre, *After Virtue*, 54.

198. MacIntyre, *After Virtue*, 56.

199. MacIntyre, *After Virtue*, 56.

and historical contexts in which the concepts of "just" and "unjust" are utilized. It is not, as MacIntyre proposes, that "the moral concepts and arguments at this point in history [have] radically chang[ed] their character so that they become recogni[z]ably the immediate ancestors of the unsettlable, interminable arguments of our own culture,"[200] but, alternately, it is a case of what "is" no longer being what "is" anymore, and what was "ought" not being what was once "ought."

If taking MacIntyre at face value, the moral concepts of "just" and "unjust" had to develop—or, as he proposes, had to "change their character"—into what our culture recognizes them to be through "a posteriori,"[201] rather than the knowledge of them existing as such by "a priori."[202] I believe the latter to be more plausible: that what our culture defines as "just" and "unjust" has always been a moral element available in the classical culture's moral vocabulary, even if the terms themselves were not explicitly used. They have, unquestionably, been implicit within the oldest articulations and utterances of moral and ethical language. What has occurred, as MacIntyre accurately points out, which I find validates my aforementioned premise, is that "moral judgments [have] change[d] their import and meaning." Not only is this true, but it addresses the notion that a change in contexts have warranted a modification in moral and ethical language, in order to make certain that the best possible meaning of a moral concept can be injected as accurately as possible into a moral judgment, not to mention in any given moral argument. In turn, what I would suggest this means is that, whatever previous semantic equivalents of "just" and "unjust" that may have been present in the oldest morality language, each semantic generation had to negate itself periodically in order to better affirm itself by, first, differing from itself, then deferring itself, and, finally, constituting itself through what Jacques Derrida theorized as "différance."[203] What I am, essentially, arguing is that foundational meaning has always been there for concepts such as "just" and "unjust," but, through the passage of time, that foundational meaning had to be deconstructed in the wake of the availability of more articulate morality language and humanity's increasingly-stratified moral and ethical experience.

Perhaps, when discussing the meanings applied to the words "just" and "unjust," it become relevant to consider what Jacques Derrida theorized about word meaning, suggesting that "from the moment that there is meaning[,] there are nothing but signs [since] we think only in signs."[204] These "signs"—a more linguistic name for "words," pertaining to how they function semantically as standalone

---

200. MacIntyre, *After Virtue*, 56.

201. Knowledge derived from experience. Kant, *Critique of Pure Reason*, 27.

202. I am applying Kant's articulation of "a priori" as "a necessary condition of every cognition that is to be established upon 'a priori' grounds [so] that it shall be held to be absolutely necessary." In using Kantian language, I find moral concepts, or ideas, "necessary conditions" that are "absolutely necessary" to how we interact with the world. Kant, *Critique of Pure Reason*, 7.

203. Derrida, *Writing and Difference*, 95.

204. Derrida, *Of Grammatology*, 50.

entities and within the structure of a sentence capable to conjuring images when evoked[205]—contain what Ferdinand de Saussure ascertained as the signified and the signifier: a concept and a sound image, respectively.[206] In short, "signs" are the basic elements toward which meaning is, ultimately, as Derrida suggests, reduced. What this means is that once meaning is ascribed to any one thing in particular, that particular thing that has been ascribed that meaning, in effect, loses its meaning. This is due to what Derrida describes as "ruining the notion of the sign [when] its exigency is recognized in the absoluteness of its right."[207] To say this, Derrida is putting forth the supposition that there is no "absoluteness" that can be affixed to a word, and no "right" meaning by which anything can be labeled. I offer this as a way to explain not only the fact that "just" and "unjust" have been implicit in our culture's moral and ethical language, but that they become dichotomous concepts that, in seeking to own the truth and be altogether factual in their own rights, cancel one another out when conversing in argument.

MacIntyre would agree with this, I believe, since both sides of the "just-unjust" moral argument propose to be more factual than the other. It is here, as MacIntyre explicitly states, where moral arguments fail, since they are presented as moral judgments, until it "begins to appear implausible to treat moral judgments as factual statements."[208] This is, specifically, the case when considering the "just war" example again, where anyone that believes a war to be "just" interprets the inherent problems that arise from war—such as the killing of innocent people as collateral damage, for instance—as being essential to the founding of peace once a "just" war has ended. With that said, obviously, for the side of the argument that would refuse to call any war "just," the mere engagement in conflict is considered unethical, irrational, and immoral when that conflict inflicts death and human suffering.

To step back and put this on a more generalized footing, anything that is considered as "just" is, I find, ideologically based on a moral issue that inherently envelopes concepts of "right," "justice," and "fairness," which, by no means, is an all-inclusive list of synonymous terminology. Nevertheless, the connectedness is inextricable, because the uses of such concepts are based on the contexts in which they are used, the processes by which they are appropriated through language, and the value judgments that are made by those that chose to label them as such. This means, as far as I am concerned, and as far as MacIntyre would acknowledge, that moral, or ethical, concepts are contingent on subjectivity, where it is possible, then,

---

205. What I am suggesting, here, is that every word that we hear affords us with a specific meaning when we see or hear it, whether we see or hear words in or out of the contexts of a sentence. This is what Derrida is articulating when he states that "we think only in signs." Signs are the fundamental parts of language. This can be looked at through the Aristotelian model of essence preceding existence: in this case, when thinking about meaning and the sign, the sign precedes meaning.

206. Saussure, *Course in General Linguistics*, 66.

207. Derrida, *Of Grammatology*, 50.

208. MacIntyre, *After Virtue*, 57.

to conceive of any one point of view as a truth-claim. To use the term "truth-claim" is not the same as invoking the word "truth." I would, moreover, insert Kierkegaard, in writing under the pseudonym Johannes Climacus, here by injecting the notion that subjectivity is truth, where "subjective reflection turns in towards subjectivity, wanting in this inner absorption to be truth's reflection."[209] The fact that, as Kierkegaard's Johannes describes, there exists a "truth's reflection," undoubtedly, proposes that the way anyone approaches the concepts of "right," "justice," or "fairness" is in relation to not only how they find those concepts enacted in the world, but how they chose to reflect those concepts back into the world.

This is the crux of the truth-claim, because it is, essentially, not only a "claim" about the truth, but something that can never be proposed as The Truth.[210] As I am sure MacIntyre would concur, the truth is plural, not singular—it cannot be objectified, but is always relative to experience. To attain any version of the truth means possessing "a truth," where, in terms of expressing it through a truth-claim, it arises from what Gilles Deleuze calls an "immanent" event, which "is actualized in a state of things and of the lived that make it happen."[211] Specifically, just to approach any construction of a truth-claim means that it has been created through the creative act of the spirit, which, accordingly to Nikolai Berdyaev, becomes relegated by the creative act of knowing.[212] MacIntyre would agree with this, I believe, particularly, if considering that, as he asserts, "there is in our society no established way of deciding between these claims [since] moral argument appears to be necessarily interminable."[213] It is from these truth-claims and the interminable nature of the moral arguments in them that MacIntyre rightly contends that "from our rival conclusions we can argue back to our rival premises."[214] When these truth-claims materialize into "rival premises," MacIntyre further proposes that the assertions and counter-assertions, when in conflict, when either side wants to force the moral value of their truth-claim on their opponent's, produce a "slightly shrill tone"[215] between parties engulfed in a moral debate. I would agree with this, since the "shrill tone," as MacIntyre calls it, arises between opposing factions on either side of a debate that are both unwilling to validate the other's truth-claim made from a moral judgment as it is personified in a moral argument.

The fact that there even exists this "shrill tone" between moral arguments demonstrates that "moral judgments lose any clear status and the sentences which express

---

209. Climacus, *Concluding Unscientific Postscript*, 165.

210. I use this term, in capital letters, to denote a kind of truth that is true to all individuals, so that it is a constant truism. This is not a possible, nor a plausible conception.

211. Deleuze, *Pure Immanence*, 31.

212. What Berdyaev express is that knowing, no matter what degree that knowing occurs, is a creative act in itself. Berdyaev, *Meaning of the Creative Act*, 155.

213. MacIntyre, *After Virtue*, 8.

214. MacIntyre, *After Virtue*, 8.

215. MacIntyre, *After Virtue*, 8.

them in a parallel way lose any undebatable meaning."[216] This is, undoubtedly, true. This is, particularly, evident when considering, as MacIntyre further postulates, to which I concede in agreement, that "such sentences become available as forms of expression for an emotivist self."[217] If I were to consider Derrida again, it becomes possible, then, to further ascertain that moral judgments made by an emotivist self attempt to place so high of a qualitative value on their truth-claim that their underlying moral argument loses its meaning. It becomes, as MacIntyre states, "undebatable," since what exists at the ideological hub of the moral argument that the emotivist self advocates is not strictly factual, but, frankly, emotional.

Against MacIntyre

For this section, I would like to address the history of rights language as it is conceived and argued by Alasdair MacIntyre in *After Virtue* and assert that the main problem in MacIntyre's argument is his notion of "rights." What I would like to offer, then, is that MacIntyre's argument is not just incorrect, but it is infused with contradictions and misrepresentations of the history of the concept of "rights." As a result, when MacIntyre seeks to suggest what "rights" are—or, perhaps, what "rights" are not—he does so through an unfortunate belief system that I will coin as illogical negativism.

When considering *After Virtue*, the best place to begin arguing against MacIntyre is with his belief that "rights" are "alleged to belong to human beings . . . which are cited as a reason for holding that people ought not to be interfered with in their pursuit of life, liberty and happiness."[218] It is at this point in MacIntyre's argument where he makes his intentions overt and explicit: rights are "alleged." In saying that rights are "alleged," MacIntyre is entirely missing what "rights" are. They are not "alleged," where they are philosophically laced with conjecture and estimation that must be proven beyond a shadow of doubt in the court of public opinion and in the world of ideas. No, there is no need for conjecture about "rights" no more than there is a need for "rights" to be proven. When we invoke the name of "rights," we are instantly aware of them not just subjectively, but objectively. We understand what "rights" are when we consider them in relation to ourselves and how we engage the world. But, also, we grasp the ideality of "rights" as the glue that holds society together when we conceptualize how the world should treat us individually.

The proof, as it were, is in humanity as "humanity" and society as "society." It is the sense that humanity and society are always pluralistic notions: to be human is to be so in relation to another human and the enumeration of "being human" in society. In this, there is a constant relation between "rights" and human beings. So, what is the point that MacIntyre is pushing forward about "rights" and the relationship between "rights"

216. MacIntyre, *After Virtue*, 57.
217. MacIntyre, *After Virtue*, 57.
218. MacIntyre, *After Virtue*, 68–69.

and human beings? I think a good place to begin to answer this question is by using the aforementioned court example. If we take MacIntyre's argument a bit further, we might even go so far as to say, if using the court example, that evidence must be presented and judged upon for validity in accordance with a parameter, in order for us to determine beyond a reasonable doubt that "rights" are there or not there. MacIntyre seems poised to rule that "rights" are never there. But, the problem with MacIntyre's ruling that "rights" are "alleged" and that they do not belong to human beings is that the evidence of "rights" existing as such is self-evident in human existence.

For MacIntyre, "there are no self-evident truths." I would not completely disagree with MacIntyre here. However, I will say that MacIntyre seems to concentrate more on the "truth" in "self-evident truths" than the "self-evident" part. To say that "rights" are "self-evident" is to say that they can be universally objectified regardless of one's subjectivity. In effect, we always know what "rights" look like, even if we refuse to recognize them. "Rights" are, for instance, objectified through concepts of justice and equality, just to name a couple. The objectification of "rights" can be best explained through Immanuel Kant's notion of pure reason and the "thing-in-itself." As Kant describes in his *Critique of Pure Reason*, a "thing-in-itself" is something that is "completely determined."[219] What Kant means as "completely determined" is that what we see in a "thing-in-itself" is literally what we see, and that "what is seen" is nothing more than a universal set of elements that can "be seen" by everyone. These "things-in-themselves" are what they are and what we know about them is not based on our experiential understanding. So, if we say that "rights" are "things-in-themselves," we can explain why we are so appalled by human rights violations by third-world countries or, on a smaller scale, why we cringe at the thought of an infant being abused by an adult. These "things" have a certain effect on us. We sense in them something immoral, unethical, and particularly uncivilized. We label immoral, unethical, and uncivilized things as "immoral," "unethical," and "uncivilized," because we are aware that a universal standard has not been adhered to. However, I will concede that such labels are relative to the one that is applying that label.

As MacIntyre would likely agree, "rights" are not "truths." In extending MacIntyre a bit further, a very important point worth making is this: "rights" are not "truths" any more than a "Right" is a "Truth." That is to say, no matter how "immoral," "unethical," or "uncivilized" something may be, we each have a choice to validate or refute what we see. Each of us utilizes our subjectivity as an agent to objectify objects as we so desire. Our agency is experiential.

In saying that, it is possible to find problems in Kantian reason, which, of course, directly led to German Idealism in tandem with Romanticism and the injection of experience into what we can say we "know." Rather than simply saying that all knowledge is "a priori"[220] in a Kantian way, we must concede that what we "know" is "posteriori"

---

219. Kant, *Critique of Pure Reason*, 490.

220. Just for sake of clarity, I am thinking of the term along the lines of the notion that knowledge

and predicated on experience.[221] To this end, one important post-Kantian, Georg Wilhelm Friedrich Hegel, in his *Phenomenology of Spirit*, argues that what we know is based on our "sense-certainty."[222] In a similar ideological vein similar to Hegel, another important post-Kantian, Arthur Schopenhauer, describes in *The World Is Will and Representation* that what we know is regulated by "will" to the extent that "the world is my representation."[223] Both Hegel and Schopenhauer ascribe to the notion that human agency dictates how we objectify any object of understanding. "Rights," as an object of understanding, is relative to what we choose to accept or reject. Whether arguing this from Hegel's "sense-certainty" or Schopenhauer's "will," we arrive at the same ideological summation: we are just as entitled to be rational as we are to being irrational.

MacIntyre's subjectivity as a thinking human being gives him the "right" to conclude that rights are "alleged" and that they do not belong to human beings. Here, we might call this MacIntyre's "sense-certainty" about "rights" or, in another sense, MacIntyre's "will" to represent "rights" in any way he chooses. This is the contradiction in MacIntyre's argument. Because MacIntyre uses, as I would call it, "illogical negativism" to argue against the inherent existence of "rights," he fails to realize that his subjectivity has come to bear on his logic. This subjectivity is a "right" in itself. It is his inherent "right" to believe as he wishes. And, does that not say, then, that his agency to argue against rights belonging to human beings is something that belongs to him as a "right"? I would say it does. I would say that his "right to subjectivity," if reappropriating his own verbiage, is something that "ought not to be interfered with in [his] pursuit of life, liberty and happiness."[224] This is just as much an issue in his contention that "the concept [of rights] lacks any means of expression . . . before about 1400,"[225] where he fails to understand that he is so steeped in his own "right to subjectivity" that he has made his subjective belief into the same self-evident truth he refutes.

The question that begs to be answered is this: Why has MacIntyre presented a self-evident truth about the nonexistence of the concept of "rights" before 1400, when he asserts that "there are no self-evident truths"? From that question, we might ask the following: Is he not contradicting his own words? In my view, he is definitely contradicting himself. But, setting aside any sense that this is done intentionally or unintentionally, I would like to simply focus on the ramifications of his contradiction.

I would argue that he has a specific historicized view of what the concept of "rights" is and, therefore, projects that historicized view to all of history as a self-evident truth.

---

is not dependent on any authority given to the evidence of experience. Honderich, *Oxford Guide to Philosophy*, 45.

221. I am using this term to signify a kind of knowledge or justification that depends decidedly on evidence, or some form of warrant, from sensory experience. Moser, *Concise Routledge Encyclopedia of Philosophy*, 1.

222. Hegel, *Phenomenology of Spirit*, 58–66.

223. Schopenhauer, *World Is Will and Representation*, 3.

224. MacIntyre, *After Virtue*, 69.

225. MacIntyre, *After Virtue*, 69.

Perhaps, it is possible to argue that MacIntyre is simply wrong. Quite frankly, it might even be easy to dismiss his mark of 1400 as some arbitrary point in history based mainly on his personal affinity for Thomas Aquinas and the High Medieval Philosophical period as a point in time when they approached the "rights" thing correctly. I would readily subscribe to either of these assessments. But, where would that leave us when we grapple with MacIntyre's seemingly blatant oversight? It affords us the opportunity to say that either explanation does not truly explain what MacIntyre's suggesting.

Either way, it would not be too far-fetched to say that there are some obvious gaps in MacIntyre's reasoning. We have to concede that, of course. The obvious gap, as it were, is between what he defines as "rights" at the time he was writing *After Virtue* and how he believes the concept was represented before 1400. He bases this argument on "there [being] no expression in any ancient or medieval language correctly translated by our expression 'a right.'"[226] I would not venture to say that MacIntyre is totally inaccurate here. If giving him the benefit of the doubt, maybe it is plausible that there is no word in any ancient or medieval languages that can be directly translated into "a right" in English. But, that does not mean that I am willing to take MacIntyre's assertion in its totality. Instead, I think it is important to focus on his careful use of the word "right" and how that word is an ideality. This is the key to understanding what he means and, in turn, confronting his own ideality of the concept of "a right."

Generally, much of MacIntyre's problem with the concept of "a right" is accredited to his subjective conceptualization of the historicity of the word. In this regard, he completely ignores language as a necessary semantic vehicle in which "a right" can become expressed. For MacIntrye, the word is the same throughout history. He seems to be ideologically fixated on the notion that the way he uses "right" is the same as it has always been used through the course of human history. This is a very wrong assumption. "A right," as I have mentioned earlier, is an ideality. As such, it is something that cannot be objectified in the same manner as we would objectify a chair, or a table, or each another. Unlike physical objects that we, as humans, can encounter firsthand with the use of our senses, we cannot encounter the physicality of "a right." In effect, "a right" is a transcendent object that exists beyond the concretized-physical as an "idea" of the imagination—it must be encountered secondhand in a Platonic sense. We do not interact with "a right" as we would with a chair, or a table, or each another. Rather, we encounter "a right" across a plane of understanding, where the only way we can objectify what "a right" is and make it "known" to us is by bracketing it. As an ideality with universality, we must use what Edmund Husserl denotes as "phenomenological reduction" to understand what "a right" is. In Husserl's *Ideas*, part 1, he asserts that any "phenomenological reduction" has the intent of limiting the universality of something, so that that "something" can be better understood or comprehended.[227] In light of this, even though MacIntyre has the ability to phenomenologically-reduce "a right"

---

226. MacIntyre, *After Virtue*, 69.
227. Husserl, *Ideas Pertaining to a Pure Phenomenology*, 60–62.

to the word "right," it does not mean that the concept of "a right" has not been "reduced" to different verbiage before MacIntyre's mark of 1400.

Essentially, MacIntyre has ignored the extent to which any concept of "a right" has a history to it and that historicity is predicated by specific moments in time and the "rights language" appropriated therein. What I mean is that it would be irresponsible to say that the way we use "right" now—or, during MacIntyre's time, for that matter—is analogous to what might have been used before 1400. Such correlations are just as dangerous and small-minded as trying to consider the New Testament out of its historical context, in order to rationalize why women should not be pastors and why slavery is acceptable.

What looms very largely in MacIntyre's concept of "a right" and the history of the human condition is he exhibits a major disconnect between the present and the past. On one hand, I would argue that he is erroneously linking the two across an ideological bridge build on the concept of "a right," where it becomes possible for him dismiss the existence of "a right" before 1400. But, on the other hand, MacIntyre is, in fact, concretizing "a right" through his own language and use of the term, rather than yielding to the possibility that his own "rights language" is not a universal language spoken throughout the course of human history. I do not know if I am prepared to say that MacIntyre's disconnect is from his own hubris or just a simple oversight. It can be argued quite effectively either way. But, what remains at issue here is this: "rights," as a concept, cannot exist outside of rights language, since rights language is the only thing that can concretize or "phenomenologically reduce" the concept of "a right" from its transcendent ideality.

"Rights," as MacIntyre rightly reports, are "conferred by positive law or custom on specific classes of person."[228] I would agree with this. It becomes a bit surprising that these are MacIntyre's words, when trying to reconcile these words with what comes directly after where he proposes that rights are "alleged" and do not belong to human beings and so forth. If we take MacIntyre's assertion about "positive law," there is no doubt that he does understand what "rights" are, how "rights" come into existence, and the role that "rights" plays in society.

So, why would he contradict himself by alternatively contending that "there are no such rights, and belief in them is one with belief in witches and in unicorns?"[229] Furthermore, he suggests that this "truth is plain"[230]—this can be taken to mean that it is a plain truth that witches and unicorns should not be believed in any more than rights. Does this not contradict what he has mentioned about "self-evident truths?" I find that it does. But, what extends from such a troubling contradiction is the refusal to recognize that he is doing precisely what he says should not be done—he

---

228. MacIntyre, *After Virtue*, 68.
229. MacIntyre, *After Virtue*, 69.
230. MacIntyre, *After Virtue*, 69.

is subjectivizing his notion of witches, unicorns, and "rights" and projecting it as a self-evident truth.

Aside from the fact that witches and unicorns are ideas, MacIntyre's use of the two ideas in his argument does not refute their existence, but simply positions those ideas as a point of negation to concretize his argument. For instance, for an atheist to say that God does not exist, it is first essential for that atheist to use the idea of God as a point of negation, which, in turn, becomes the crux of their argument. What such an atheist misses is that, by suggesting that God does not exist, such a proposition contains logical positivism within it—God remains an object of understanding in that proposition, even if it is an object that is being negated. This is what MacIntyre is doing: he proposes that "rights" are no more real than witches and unicorns, all the while, what still remains latent in such an opinion, is that he has subconsciously bracketed ideas of "rights," witches, and unicorns to make his point. In fact, by simply invoking the words, MacIntyre has given them authentic existence in the world of ideas and human imagination, no matter how transcendent of an ideality they may be.

When we use the word "rights," we are bestowing upon that word a sense of its historicity within the broader world of ideas and human imagination. MacIntyre does not understand this. The concept of "a right" cannot be reduced to "rights" any more than it could be reduced to verbiage before 1400. This is because the concept of "a right" needs rights language to express it—it needs language that can concretize it and bracket it into something that can be readily understood. As a concept, in order to express what "a right" is means it must be couched in the human experience, a linguistic experience. I am reminded of Martin Heidegger's notion that "language is the house of being"—language concretizes the "being-ness" of everything the moment we are able to apply a word to a concept. This is particularly relevant to the concept of "a right," which has its "being" housed in the history of "rights language."

In terms of its historicity, rights are, indeed, "conferred," because they are endowed to humanity through the facticity of human existence. In other words, when we exist in the world, when we come to terms with the facticity of our existence as a "being" in a world of other "beings," when we realize that our being has parameters shaped to our individual experiences as "being human," we are first confronted with our "rights." I find this to be what MacIntyre means by "positive law." His sense, which I would wholeheartedly agree with, is that "being human" invokes a logical positivism: the sense that "being human" and recognizing one's humanity contains a positivity to it. That positivism is logically "conferred" upon humanity and the belief that a human not only has the right to be human, but that a human has certain "rights" inherent in their humanity. I would argue that one of these rights—perhaps, the most important of all—is the right to exist. When I say the "right to exist," I mean the "right to live," once that life has been brought into existence. Essentially, it is the "right to be." The only way to express such idealities is with and through language—such expressions, as "rights language," have a history that is just as long as the human condition.

The Theology of the Philosophy of "Rights" Language

Here, when considering "philosophy of rights language," I find that it is prudent to first discuss "the philosophy of rights" before embarking on an explanation of the rights language that sustains the concept of "rights."

To begin with that concept of "rights" is to begin with a fundamental conceit: rights are real. "Rights" must be believed in and, as Alan Dershowitz rightly asserts in his *Rights from Wrongs*, "our rights are purported to be factual."[231] What such a proposition means is that we must concede that "rights" are structures of ideality that are "what they are" due to our extension of their existence into the world. But, when we say what "rights" are, we are really outlining "rights" in the following inquisitive fashion: who has "rights," how do "rights" function in the world, where is the existence of "rights" both inside and outside of the human imagination, and why have "rights" come into existence within the societal sphere? In my view, these are the four foundational dimensions to any definition of "rights"

So, when we give dimensionality to "rights," we are, as I mentioned in my previous essay, objectifying "rights" and making them known to ourselves as an object of understanding by "bracketing" them as "something." I use this is in reference to Edmund Husserl's *Ideas*, part 1, which extends the notion of "phenomenological reduction"—an intentional act of limiting the universality of something, so that that something can be better comprehended.[232] This makes it possible to use the word "rights" in a concretized sense. But, more importantly, if we follow the dimensionality of "rights," we arrive at another question, one that permeates after we have phenomenologically-reduced "rights" from its ideality to something concretized: where do rights come from? Dershowitz poses this question and suggests that "the answer to this question is important because the source of our rights determine their status as well as their content."[233] With this, Dershowitz has made an excellent point. He has, in effect, encapsulated the duality of "rights"—the fact that to say we have "rights" is something liberating and, at the same time, something strangely confining. In other words, when we speak of "rights," we must reckon with both the qualitative and quantitative aspects of the concept.

In terms of the qualitative, as Dershowitz contends, there exists a "status" in "rights"—or, what I might call a contextualization of "rights." This kind of contextualization is based on the aesthetic value of "rights," where we use tangible ways to say that "rights" are happening in the world through ideas such as equality and justice. For example, if one person kills another person, when the first person is tried, convicted, and sentenced for the murder, we can conclude, then, that justice has taken place. More aptly, perhaps, we can say that the murdered person's "rights" to live were

---

231. Dershowitz, *Rights from Wrongs*, 1.
232. Husserl, *Ideas Pertaining to a Pure Phenomenology*, 60–62.
233. Dershowitz, *Rights from Wrongs*, 1.

infringed upon by the murderer and the murderer was held accountable for that encroachment. If I follow this example a bit further, while we quantify the "rights" of the murdered, we also quantify the "rights" of the murderer by affording the murderer "rights" in the judicial system: the right to a fair trial, the right to an attorney, the right to due process, etc. This addresses the quantitative aspect of "rights." I find this to be what Dershowitz denotes as the "content" of rights, or the extent to which "rights" are enumerated and quantified. In either regard, what Dershowitz has very poignantly pointed to is that any philosophy of "rights" does not strictly revolve around their content or context in society. Instead, the inevitable question is, as Dershowitz posits, "What are the sources of our rights?"[234]

There are two ways to answer such a question: one that is decidedly theological, the other that is secular and philosophical. Setting aside the theological for now and for the purposes of this paper, I will concentrate only on the philosophical. So, philosophically speaking, the "sources" of "rights" could be argued as being inherent in or endowed into the "human spirit." I prefer to think of this "human spirit" in the manner that Soren Kierkegaard, under the Anti-Climacus pseudonym, describes at the outset of *The Sickness unto Death*:

> A human being is spirit. But what is spirit? Spirit is the self. But what is the self? The self is a relation that relates itself to itself or is the relation's relating itself to itself in the relation. . . . A human being is synthesis of the infinite and the finite, of the temporal and the eternal, of freedom and necessity.[235]

The human spirit, as Kierkegaard explains, is a self and that "self" is a "relation." This selfhood, as such, contains a dialectic within itself along a variety of internalized, self-reflective and self-actualizing levels—the self is steeped in relating to itself, relates itself to itself, and is within a relation. What arises from the human spirit and its overarching selfhood, as Kierkegaard contends, is a human being predicated by a synthesis "of freedom and necessity." Within this, I find that Kierkegaard is articulating an understanding of the philosophy of "rights"—the sense that, I would argue, for the human being to be a spirit and, then, for a spirit to be a self, human selfhood's ability to relate to itself as such is by way of the freedom and necessity of "rights." This "freedom" and "necessity" work in conjunction across a kind of bilateral-actualization, so that human selfhood can recognize that the "freedom" to relate to itself is a "necessity" just as much as the "necessity" to relate to itself is a "freedom."

My intent in using Kierkegaard's notions of "freedom" and "necessity" is to set up the sense that, when we speak of philosophizing about "rights," we are promoting a philosophical justification of "rights." For Kierkegaard, I would argue that his notion of "rights" were justified in and through human selfhood's freedom and necessity—not only the freedom to relate to itself, but the necessity to relate to itself. The ability to do

---

234. Dershowitz, *Rights from Wrongs*, 5.
235. Kierkegaard, *Sickness unto Death*, 13.

both, at the same time, is the definition of human selfhood. Nevertheless, as Andrew Fagan asks, "Do human rights require philosophical justification?" It would seem, then, in my view, that Fagan is pushing beyond the Kierkegaardian philosophy of "rights" and settling on the "validity of rights." In other words, just to say that our freedom and necessity arise out of our rights is not enough when addressing how "rights" are valid, why "rights" are valid, what makes "rights" valid, and where do "rights" become valid. We, as Fagan asserts, "cannot settle the question of the philosophical validity of human rights by appealing to purely empirical observations upon the world."[236] I would agree with this, since any validity in human rights must be discovered intrinsically, not only in an extrinsic fashion. But, from there, Fagan extends the following: "As a moral doctrine, human rights have to be demonstrated to be valid as norms and not facts."[237] So, for Fagan, there are two approaches to the question of the validity of human rights: "the interests theory approach" and "the will theory approach."

While "the interests theory approach" argues that the principal function of human rights is to protect and promote certain essential human interests, "the will theory approach" centers on a single human attribute: the capacity for freedom.[238] It is safe to say, then, that both approaches are more normative than factual, if we follow Fagan's argument about how the validity of human rights should be demonstrated. If we further Fagan's assertion, then it is possible to ascertain that human interests and the human capacity for freedom both have normative societal qualities. In effect, human interests and the human capacity for freedom come to bear in normative society where their existences have tangible exchange values as commodities. Human interests are shared just as the human capacity for freedom is shared. It is here where I will dissent from Fagan's argument. In my view, to say that human interests or the human capacity for freedom feed into a normative society means conceding that both have been concretized in society. The moment issues of "interest" or "freedom" are concretized, they become factual in the world—in this sense, they become known quantities. Their validities, as such, are demonstrated as facts that human beings can be understood, comprehended, and applied in individualized "subjectivized" ways. That means, too, that, though "interests" and "freedom" are internal manifestations articulated from one's subjectivity, they can only be shared in a normative marketplace once they have been deemed as factual. A norm is not a "norm" unless it has been claimed as a facticity and an object of understanding. In some sense, as I have already argued, it is about bracketing as Husserl illustrates through phenomenological reduction: "interests" and "freedom" are bracketed or "reduced" and, in doing so, their idealities become factual as cognitively graspable.

In this regard, I would contend that human interests are developed from the human capacity for freedom and the human capacity for freedom promotes human

---

236. See Andrew Fagan's *Human Rights* (2009).

237. Fagan, *Human Rights*.

238. Fagan, *Human Rights*.

interests. I find the two to be inextricably linked, rather than personified separately through individual theories. Fagan makes this point as well, suggesting that there are "potential philosophical benefits attainable through combining various themes and elements found within these . . . philosophical approaches to justifying human rights."[239] So, in fact, if the "interests theory" and "will theory" approaches are combined, perhaps that combination can be illustrated in the following manner: when the human capacity for freedom comes into existence as such, it lends itself to the capacity to recognize self-interest and, then, acknowledge the self-interests of others, where the recognition of others having their own self-interests denotes that they, too, have a capacity for freedom. Even though Fagan argues that such a combination has its strengths and weaknesses, I would argue in favor of its overwhelming strength that subjugates any possible for weakness. These strengths to what I will call the "interests-will theory" are precisely evident in Johann G. Fichte's and Georg W. F. Hegel's concepts of "right" in their respective works *Foundations of Natural Right* and *Elements of Philosophy of Right*.

First, allow me to discuss Fichte. For Fichte, he sets up his approach to the concept of "right" as a deduction and an inference—what can be deduced from "right" and what can be inferred from "right." In terms of deduction, Fichte asserts that "if a rational being is to posit itself as such, then it must ascribe to itself an activity whose ultimate ground lies purely and simply within itself."[240] This "activity," Fichte describes, "reverts into itself in general [as] the mark of a rational being." What can be derived from this, through inference, is that a "rational being" has, as Fichte ascertains, "[the] capacity to exercise free efficacy, the rational being posits and determines a sensible world outside of itself."[241] Now, similarly, Hegel is undoubtedly influenced by Fichte when Hegel proceeds to argue for an "abstract right," one that is linked to "an abstract will [that] is the individual will of a subject [to the extent that it] has definite ends, and, as exclusive and individual, has these ends before itself as an externally and directly presented world."[242]

What arises out of this Fichtean-Hegelian notion of right is "Right." This is particularly important in promoting what I coin as an "interests-will theory" approach to the philosophical justification of human rights—it is the sense that a dialectic forms between humans and "Right" and, consequently, humans, as "rational beings," validate "rights" when "Right" validates human existence. From the point of view of human existence, "Right" is justified the moment that human existence self-justifies itself. It is a dialectical justification: when one is validated, the other is, and when one is justified, the other is. Essentially, when I suggest that there is a natural "human-Right" dialectic—and, specifically, a connectedness between human existence and the existence of "Right"—I

239. Fagan, *Human Rights*.
240. Fichte, *Foundations of Natural Right*, 18.
241. Fichte, *Foundations of Natural Right*, 24.
242. Hegel, *Philosophy of Right*, 43.

am ascribing to the existence of Natural Law as "Right," from which all human rights emanate naturally. In effect, human existence and the existence of Right-Natural Law mutually affect one another as beings, just as Plato explains in *The Sophist*.[243] Such a proposition falls in line with one of the three forms of human utterance that Margaret MacDonald's outlines in "Natural Rights": assertions or expressions of value.[244] MacDonald fleshes out the uniqueness of such propositions by stressing:

> Propositions about natural law and natural rights are not generalizations from experience, nor deductions from observed facts subsequently confirmed by experience. Yet they are not totally disconnected from natural fact. For they are known as entailed by the intrinsic or essential nature of [humanity].[245]

Evidently, when propositions are based on assertions or expressions of value, those propositions become the "intrinsic or essential nature" of humanity. They are, in a sense, value statements, or statements that have aesthetic value inherent in them. Consider, for example, how Fichte and Hegel describe "Right"—both employ the use of assertions or expressions of value in their propositions, where they are both articulating the intrinsic or essential nature of humanity through their own intrinsic or essential nature for understanding it.

As intrinsic or essential as "rights" are to human nature, they must be articulated. That means, of course, that "rights" are only understood when they are explained and only when those explanations are linguistically situated. Such explanations, as Fichte and Hegel do in their respective understandings of "Right," require the use of language. If we are to follow Martin Heidegger's assertion in *On the Way to Language* about language being the house of being,[246] then we can say that "rights" are given their "being-ness" in language. Language "houses" what "rights" are, how "rights" function, and where "rights" come into existence. "Rights" are, as such, qualitative and, when restricted to that existential dimension, they contain an ideality that transcends human understanding. It is only when "rights" are quantified with words that "rights" materialize in the world as "something" with an authentic existence. That is to say, the true authenticity of "rights" is not so much situated in the human consciousness but, instead, extrapolated in the situatedness of meaningful and purposeful discourse.

Any philosophizing about "rights" requires language. Whether we are speaking of words, statements, or propositions, "rights" language concretizes what "rights" are. For instance, when we use terms such as "justice" and "equality," we understand that those words, in their simplicity, have implicit meanings to them. In the same sense,

---

243. In the *Sophist* dialogue, Plato explains "being" as anything which possesses any sort of power to affect another, or to be affected by another, if only for a single moment, however trifling the cause and however slight the effect. To that end, it has real existence. The definition of being, then, is simply power. Hamilton and Cairns, *Collected Dialogues of Plato*, 957–1017.

244. MacDonald, "Natural Rights," 23.

245. MacDonald, "Natural Rights," 25.

246. Heidegger, *On the Way to Language*, 63.

when we bring forth "rights" or say that something is "Right," we do so with certain connotations in mind. But, the problem is, of course, that one person's definitions of "justice," "equality," "rights," and "Right" may not be another's. That is because the words themselves are subjective, and the way in which they can be defined depend greatly upon how they are objectified. So, this reverts to what I have mentioned earlier in this essay about content and context—for two people with their own subjective experiences and their individualized abilities to objectify the world to agree on what a "right" is, context is critical. Context is given not in individual words, but in statements and propositions. As a case in point, in using the term "justice," for the term to have meaning, it must be situated in a complete proposition such as: one man was served justice for killing another man. Now, even in this proposition, "justice" is rather ambiguous, where it yields at least three of the following meanings: (1) the man was arrested for the crime, (2) the man was charged with a crime, and (3) the man was convicted of the crime. None of these meanings change what "justice" is, in terms of its fundamental content—however, they only add dimensions to the way in which "justice" can be contextualized. In any of the cases, how "justice" is defined depends on how a subjective experience comes to bear upon the objectification of the word. This is essentially what the philosophy of rights language is all about—it is the fact that no matter how particular and focused "rights" language attempts to be, because it is contingent so much on subjectivity and language, it contains a great deal of problematic linguistic elasticity.

In "Rights Theory and Rights Practice," Primus makes this point when he describes "rights" language as being, on one hand, a social practice, but, on another, a limited linguistic practice. In the former, Primus rightly contends that a theory of rights is "a theory that [is] located [in] the consistency among rights not in a set of analytic properties but in the way that the concept is used in social practice."[247] What this means is that we do not know what "rights" are exclusively from what Primus calls "analytic properties" or even through theoretical conjectures, but from how they function in the world. We know what "rights" are by seeing "rights" in action. We understand that "rights" are as they are when they adhere to a certain set of constitutive rules that, in turn, underlie their performative acts in the real world. However, as Primus notes, when "rights" language is examined through social practice, it has its limitations, since "analyzing rights discourse as a linguistic practice requires having some way of knowing what uses of language counts as part of the practice and what uses of language do not."[248] Therein lies the problem—as Primus accurately argues, rather than examining every "right" that occurs in the English language, "we want to explore not just the word, but a concept."[249] But, of course, the problem here is that, when we use the word "right," it summons forth a plethora of

247. Primus, "Rights Theory," 28.
248. Primus, "Rights Theory," 32.
249. Primus, "Rights Theory," 32.

"right" words that are both in- and out-of-context. To this end, I would argue that every social practice is construed through social discourse and, as a result, all social discourse is limited by human expression. In this regard, "rights" language is liberating but, at the same time, it is confining.

Toward a Theology of "Right": Moving beyond Christian Smith

For this section, I would like to extend Christian Smith's "Does Naturalism Warrant a Moral Belief in Universal Benevolence and Human Rights?" (2011) by first answering the question raised in the title. I will begin there with: yes—essentially, even if we assume the presence of a naturalistic universe, our most paramount concern in that universe is that it is ideologically governed by some form of moral belief in "universal benevolence and human rights."

Even if we believe that a naturalistic universe, as Smith asserts, is "one that has come to exist by chance,"[250] its existence after the fact comes under some degree of regulation, some historicized order, some hierarchy of understanding that affords us the opportunity to conceive of that naturalistic universe as an object of our understanding. To do so, we must recognize both the inner machinery of that universe and ramifications of it on human existence and, in turn, reconcile the relationship that human existence has with it. This requires, as Smith points out, a "moral belief"—a belief that, though there is "no ultimate, inherent meaning or purpose" in a naturalistic universe coming into being, "any meaning or purpose that exists for humans . . . is constructed by and for humans themselves."[251] In order to further encapsulate what Smith means by "moral belief," I intend to offer what I would like to coin a "Theology of Right": the sense that humanity and "Right" have a dialectic with one another through "being-Right," where "being" becomes predicated on what Smith calls "universal benevolence and human rights."

For Smith, the central question is this: "If we in fact live in the naturalistic cosmos that much of science tells us we occupy, do we have good reasons for believing in universal benevolence and human rights as moral facts and imperatives?" What I find Smith to be pointing out is relationship between human existence and a "naturalistic cosmos." Particularly, his question is wrestling with not only the sense that a naturalistic universe comes into being of its own volition, but that, perhaps, human existence is a by-product of that volition. In effect, it is the assumption that, because of purposeless and meaningless inherent in the existence of a naturalistic universe, there is an underlying purposelessness and meaninglessness in human existence. This, of course, is problematic and all the more reason why it is essential for human existence to be affirmed by some moral fact or imperative. Such an affirmation, as Smith rightly

---

250. Smith, "Does Naturalism Warrant a Moral Belief," 292.
251. Smith, "Does Naturalism Warrant a Moral Belief," 292.

contends, comes to bear in "many believers in naturalism [being] passionate and devoted believers in human dignity, universal benevolence, and human rights."[252] Why is this so? Well, my contention, in following up Smith, is that human existence cannot be as naturalistic as the universe—though the facticity of a naturalistic universe may not be moral, the facticity of human existence must be in a Heideggerian sense, particularly since a naturalistic universe situates humanity within a moral situatedness that harbors existential meaning.[253]

To say that human existence should "have good reason" to believe in universal benevolence and human rights, as Smith posits in a question more intrinsic to the first, means that there should be something "rationally warranted in asserting and championing such moral claims and imperatives."[254] Given in this is the following supposition: since human existence cannot completely "rationalize" its existence from a naturalistic universe, it must "rationalize" itself from some other source in a more meaningful manner. Human existence must tease out something explicit in the implicitness of its existence, something that validates "being-in-the-world" and self-validates "being-for-self." This is where moral claims and imperatives come into play. As Smith would likely agree, I would argue that moral claims and imperatives concretize human existence into an authentic existence and "being"—they make it possible for "being" to ascertain value and meaning as decidedly existential value and existential meaning.

The problem with discovering existential value and existential meaning in human existence as "being-in-the-world" and "being-for-self," not to mention "being-for-others," is that the same kind of value and meaning is projected upon "the universe." Perhaps, this would not be so if human existence and the existence of the universe were separate, autonomous existential entities. We know that this is not the case, since they are inextricably linked. Human existence is "human existence" when it is situated temporally and spatially in "the universe." But, more importantly, human existence and the existence of "the universe" share a historicized sense of being: the sense that they both come into existence by and through a shared history and then, that underlining joint-historicity grants existential value and existential meaning to both. Such an argument aligns with Smith's notion that "a belief in universal benevolence and human rights as moral fact and obligation does not make particular sense, fit well with, or naturally flow from the relatives of a naturalistic universe."[255] Smith makes

---

252. Smith, "Does Naturalism Warrant a Moral Belief," 294.

253. Just as a word of note, rather than arguing Sartre's view of human existence as one based on meaning-making on behalf of humanity in spite of the lack of meaning in a world of nothingness, I am specifically arguing Heidegger's sense of "being" as one that contains meaning in the facticity of existence itself. This is one of the chief differences between Sartre's existentialism and Heidegger's, even though Heidegger both rejected Sartre's existentialism and having his philosophy as categorized as "existentialism."

254. Smith, "Does Naturalism Warrant a Moral Belief," 294.

255. Smith, "Does Naturalism Warrant a Moral Belief," 294.

a great point here. Not only would I agree with it, but I would contend that when we speak of "moral belief" and a "naturalistic universe," we are having two very different conversations—in the former, we are interested in meaning-making, while, in the latter, we are conceding to the impossibility of meaning-making. In that particular vein, Smith surmises the following:

> One who believes in a naturalistic cosmos is, it seems to me, perfectly entitled to believe in and act to promote universal benevolence and human rights, but only as an arbitrary, subjective, personal preference—not as a rational, compelling, universally binding fact and obligation. The person who lives in a naturalistic universe may certainly choose to affirm universal benevolence and human rights. But they might equally reasonably choose some other, quite or radically different moral position.[256]

What Smith is suggesting here, then, is that, even through a naturalistic perspective, one may be able to affirm or reject the idea of universal benevolence and human rights, but, they still must affirm some moral position, whatever it might be.

This "moral position," in whatever form it takes, becomes, if I may use Smith's words, "a rational, compelling, universally binding fact and obligation." In other words, one who believes in a naturalistic cosmos may use their "arbitrary, subjective, personal preference" to subjectivize some other objective reality predicated on some other sense of morality. However, what remains at the core of their subjectivity and objectification is the choice of "something" moral, "something" obligatory, "something" rational: there must be some moral milieu to it all capped off by a transcendent facticity. That is to say, anyone holding a naturalistic perspective must accept the facticity of some moral mechanism running through the veins and arteries of a Husserlian "life-world." Smith makes this case by highlighting that some moral mechanism, as I have called it, serves to sustain the status quo of someone with a naturalistic perspective. It is the sense that, as Smith notes, if "intellectual honesty does not grant residents of a naturalistic universe warranted moral belief in universal benevolence and human rights,"[257] then there certainly is a necessity to believe in "something" of moral quality that possesses existential value and existential meaning.

A "moral position" is always made, whether formal or informal, covertly or overtly. The "moral" stance that is always taken is constantly steeped in some greater multidimensional sense of meaning-making, which reaches beyond a naturalistic universe. Essentially, a naturalistic universe, as such, is the lowest common denominator of human existence—it is only the foundation upon which greater meaning and value is constructed for human selfhood, "being," and existential personae. When assuming a "moral position," one that may or may not be nominally conceding "universal benevolence and human rights," everything must converge there, nonetheless. That point of

---

256. Smith, "Does Naturalism Warrant a Moral Belief," 294.
257. Smith, "Does Naturalism Warrant a Moral Belief," 294.

convergence, one shared by a naturalistic perspective and others, is the connectedness between "being" and a "moral position." My contention is that this connectedness is dialectical in nature: it is respectively between the physical positionality of "being" and the transcendent positionality of the "Right."

Through the "being-Right" dialectic, I intend to use the term "Right" in an all-encompassing manner, combining Smith's notion of "universal benevolence and human rights" into one word of ideality. My concern is with what "Right" is and how, in turn, "Right" underscores both the horizontal and vertical aspects of human societal existence—I view this as a twofold sense of "being human": the horizontal reference toward "Right" as a point of qualification that self-authenticates "being," and the vertical reference with others' "being-Right" as points of quantification that enumerates a Heideggerian "being-in-the-world."

If I were to take up the mantel from Smith and become employed in his interest, as Smith asserts, "in sustaining and strengthening the modern moral commitments to universal benevolence and human rights,"[258] then such an undertaking requires circumspection. Be that as it may, it requires incorporating a perspective about human rights that can be shared by the totality of the human experience, a totality linked by the same "existentiality"—it requires focusing on an existential cause that can get a consensus. Such a cause, as Smith finds in his conclusion, would be extrapolated through "an articulation of some truly rational and compelling account for high moral standards of benevolence and rights."[259] In my view, what Smith is groping for is certainly graspable in the "being-Right" dialectic—the sense that "being" and "Right" are two inextricably linked existences engaged in an ethical dialogue grounded on theological foundations.

There is a relatedness between "being" and "Right" that arises within a dialectic of ethical obligation. But, I would argue, as I am sure Smith would agree, that "being" also has certain ethical obligations to itself and to others. This is particularly so when considering that all existing things construed through a Husserlian "life-world" revolve around the notion of living together and how that "living together" is an apparent commonality between all "beings."[260] When "being" is oriented toward "self" and toward "others," what we are considering, then, is what Jean-Paul Sartre describes as being-for-self and being-for-others.[261] What lies at the core of this consideration is the sense is the possibility of becoming "dialogic." I consider "dialogic" as Mikhail Bakhtin does, where it is embodied in "forces that serve to unify and centralize the verbal-ideological world."[262] These "forces" that Bakhtin describes are particularly extrapolated through the relatedness between intersubjective beings in a Husserlian "life-world."

258. Smith, "Does Naturalism Warrant a Moral Belief," 317.
259. Smith, "Does Naturalism Warrant a Moral Belief," 317.
260. Husserl, *Crisis of European Sciences*, 108–10.
261. Sartre, *Being and Nothingness*, 548.
262. Bakhtin, *Dialogic Imagination*, 270.

What these "forces" do is position intersubjective beings as entities of intentionality in very much the same manner that Edmund Husserl describes in *The Crisis of European Sciences and Transcendental Phenomenology: An Introduction to Phenomenological Philosophy*.[263] Hence, in a decidedly Husserlian way, I think that, through intentionality, intersubjective beings recognize their "intented-ness" to the point that one "being" becomes the epistemological ultimacy of the other "being," and vice versa. In light of this epistemological ultimacy, beings become "dialogic" with one another, functioning not just on their own individual subjectivity and personal abilities to objectify reality, but applying that subjectivity transitively toward the relatedness shared with other subjective beings in the "life-world" community.

In this kind of "life-world" community, the ethical obligation one "being" has toward another "being" is linked dialectically by what Aristotle calls, in his *Nicomachean Ethics*, the "highest good."[264] As Aristotle suggests, this "highest good" is evident in

> every art and every inquiry, and similarly, every action and every intention [that] is thought to aim at some good [so that everyone has] expressed themselves well in declaring the good to be that at which all things aim.[265]

What I take this to mean, therefore, is that all of us have an ethical obligation toward the "highest good" and that, as Aristotle seems to propose, we collectively and individually have a dialectic with the "highest good." Not only is the "highest good" something that we each strive for as a personal aim, but it is also a communal aim. The "highest good," as such, is "good" for the self and for others. To some extent, if extending Aristotle a bit further, the "highest good" can be viewed as the "one thing" that validates relatedness, becomes the nucleus of the "forces" that Bakhtin offers about "dialogism," and holds together the Husserlian "life-world" as a community of selves and others. The "highest good," then, is, in fact, a moral commitment, as Smith suggests—it is also something that, as Smith contends, "let[s] us say that we want on moral grounds to eliminate slavery, child abuse, political imprisonment and torture, the sex trade, and the like."[266] Smith is conceiving of Aristotle's "highest good." When Smith offers the following conception—"Let us suppose that it is not only perhaps beneficial but also truly good for people to be interpersonally kind, thoughtful, and fair to other people"[267]—I find that Smith is conceiving of the Aristotlean "highest good" as a kind of Tillich-like "ultimate concern."

Let me be clear: for the "highest good" to be an "ultimate concern," I am proposing that the "highest good" is "Right." The universality of "Right" is in the possibility of it being anything to anyone. When I speak of "Right," I could just as easily be referring to

263. Husserl, *Crisis of European Sciences*, 85.
264. In terms of Bekker numbers, this occurs in 1094a. Aristotle, *Nicomachean Ethics*, 1–2.
265. This is in the same Bekker-numbered section of 1094a. Aristotle, *Nicomachean Ethics*, 1.
266. Smith, "Does Naturalism Warrant a Moral Belief," 317.
267. Smith, "Does Naturalism Warrant a Moral Belief," 317.

equality as I could be to justice. As I mentioned to some extent in my previous essay, "Right" could be exemplified in a murderer being arrested, tried, and convicted of a crime—this, of course, would be the view of the family of the murdered one, but also, alternatively, about the right to due process and a fair trial. In some other non-crime-based sense of "Right," it might be possible to say there is something "Right" about a child given up for adoption being adopted by a loving, caring family. In yet another sense, when I say "Right," I could apply the concept to civil liberties, such as freedom of speech, freedom of assembly, freedom of religion, freedom of free press, and other freedoms—what makes all of these "Right" is that they enumerate the ways in which a citizen, as a "being" of the state, should be treated in a civilized, democratized society. In all these instances, as Smith would likely agree, there is a "modern moral commitment" being made. It is the belief that there is a "highest good" and that all "beings" should be afforded an opportunity at realizing that "highest good."

What makes the "highest good" possible is, as Johann Fichte asserts in *The Foundation of Natural Right*, when "each free being makes it a law for himself to limit his freedom through the concept of the freedom of all others."[268] This sense of "each free being" is based on the universality of freedom that is afforded to every "being" by the Aristotlean "highest good." There is no doubt that what Fichte is arguing for is that the "highest good" can be equated as a law, albeit a natural law, that provides the parameters for freedom. Freedom is the key to how I wish to describe what Fichte is doing: it is the notion that every "being" enters the world with an inherent ability to be free, but must, to some extent, be aware of what that freedom is when it functions and operates in the Husserlian "life-world." It becomes important for freedom, if appropriating Fichte, to be grounded in a law that regulates "the concept of the freedom for all others." When I think about freedom as a "modern moral commitment," I think it is prudent to say that law and "Right" are interchangeable. That stands to suggest, I would contend, that, though we all have a "being-Right" dialectic, the way that we each encounter the concept of freedom as "Right" is subjective, whereby it is contextualized differently depending on the lived experience of the one that encounters freedom. Undoubtedly, Smith would agree with this. To this end, when Fichte considers the notion of "law," I find he is doing so not just to provide a regulatory manner in which we each conceptualize what freedom is for ourselves, but how freedom should be realized and objectified for and upon others. One important way that Fichte illustrates what he means by "law" is with the following:

> I think of myself as both subject to the law and not subject to it: *I think of myself* as subject to the law *in general* but as not subject to it in this particular case. In consequence of the former, I act in *accordance with right*, under the command of the law, and thus I possess a *right*.[269]

268. Fichte, *Foundation of Natural Right*, 85.
269. Fichte, *Foundation of Natural Right*, 88.

In this illustration, when Fichte suggests that he is both subject and not subject to the law, he is arguing that the concept of law is a transcendent concept. When we encounter "law," we are really encountering it as "Law," as something that is subjective to the context in which it is applied. There is both a generality and particularity to what "Law" is, as Fichte rightly argues. But, nevertheless, "being" encounters "Law" across a plane of understanding based on "Freedom"—this is the dialectical relationship between "being" and "Law" as "Right."

More importantly concepts of "Law/Right" and "Freedom" are predicated on, according to Fichte, how we act "in accordance with right." In other words, when we engage in any action of moral credence, in terms of Smith's sense of "modern moral commitment," we do so having recognized the existence of "Right" as, according to Smith, a "truly rational and compelling account for high moral standards of benevolence and rights."

I would argue that "being" shares a dialectic with "rights" as "Right." When Fichte concedes that he is both subject to the law and also not subject to it and, therefore, acts "in accordance with right," I believe he is visualizing what is "in accordance with right" as something that encompasses and calibrates the calculus of "Right" and freedom. To be "in accordance with right" means gesturing toward a highest reality, or toward an ideality that transcends laws and freedom, and becomes extrapolated in notions of equality, justice, love, and power. In some sense, when we act "in accordance with right," we are acting in accordance with Aristotelean "highest good." This "highest good" looms within what is "in accordance with right." To this extent, as I am sure Smith would agree, when "being" has a dialectic with "Right," it is translated through an ethical obligation, the necessity for subjective truth, the elasticity of objective reality, and a relatedness across historicity.

When considering a "being-Right" dialectic, ethical obligation, subjective truth, the elasticity of objective reality, and historicity becomes the key components to how Georg Wilhelm Friedrich Hegel outlines "Right" in his *Philosophy of Right* published in 1821, almost thirty years after Fichte's *The Foundation of Natural Right*, with the following:

> When we speak of right, we mean not only civil right, which is the usual significance of the word, but also morality, ethical observance and world-history. These belong to this realm, because the conception taking them in their truth, brings them all together.[270]

Not only do I find it apparent in Hegel's definition of "Right" that he is concerned with the "being-Right" dialectic, but I would argue that Hegel is ascribing certain features and traits to "Right" that have decidedly theological and ethical leanings. What we have in Fichte, Hegel, and myself, as we all describe "Right," is what rights language looks like. It is about concretizing the ideality of "Right" quantitatively into language.

270. Hegel, *Philosophy of Right*, 40.

When we make, as Smith states, "modern moral commitments to universal benevolence and human rights," we must make "moral commitments" to rights language as well. We do so every time we attempt utterances of rights language, since "Right" does not come into existence until "being" has been seated "Right" in the semantic and linguistic structures of the language of "being."

This is why Heidegger's assertion in *On the Way to Language* about language being the house of being[271] is so significant and critical to my argument about "being-Right," as I extend Smith's. In this regard, "rights language" is precisely what Smith believes is needed: rights language is "an articulation of some truly rational and compelling account for high moral standards of benevolence and rights." In order for us to truly conceptualize "Right," we must do so through a "being-Right" dialectic predicated on meaningful, contextualized rights language.

---

271. Heidegger, *On the Way to Language*, 63.

CONCLUSION

Theologizing Beyond the Question of the Meaning of Existential Theology

Toward Posthumanism

The question of the meaning of existential theology, when it reaches its fullest extent and its farthest implications to what it means to be human, becomes a kind of theologizing that reaches the concerns of posthumanism. If *the question of the meaning of existential theology* is, to a certain degree, about negotiating the relationship between human existence and God's existence, such a negotiation is grounded on how human existence is defined in relation to what can be ascertained, from the human standpoint, about God's existence. In doing so, when addressing the limitations and contexts of human existence, these limitations and contexts are often extended to how we understand God's existence as that which is beyond our own. Yet, what remains at the core of any theologizing about God is the parameters of human existence—to theologize from a human perspective is just as much about the meaning of God's existence as it is about the meaning of human existence. These parameters, whether we are considering existential theology in terms of its themes, its European traditions, its countertraditions, or its postmodern traditions, *the question of the meaning of existential theology* can be existentialized further than postmodernity. To go further than postmodernity means questioning what it means to be human and questioning "humanity" itself as pivotal to *the question of the meaning of existential theology*. These further questions about what it means to be human and what it means to theologize about God place existential theology against what it takes to think the thought of posthumanism—the dialogue between existential theology and posthumanism must reckon with three posthumanist thinkers: Bruno Latour, Rosi Braidotti, the posthumanizing of Sylvia Wynter, Catherine Malabou, and Cary Wolfe, and the extent to which each of them expand what it means to theologize about God from a posthumanist standpoint.

CONCLUSION: THEOLOGIZING BEYOND THE MEANING OF EXISTENTIAL THEOLOGY

"What It Means to Be Human" and Bruno Latour's Posthumanism

In *We Have Never Been Modern* (1991), Bruno Latour proposes that "our intellectual life is out of kilter,"[1] to the extent that what becomes "out of kilter" poses a crisis between the scientific and political representations of "the nature of things." This sort of "crisis," as Latour describes it, comes to bear on "epistemology, the social sciences, the sciences of texts [since] all have their privileged vantage point, provided that they remain separate."[2] What this means, then, is that each discipline, as such, attempts to interpret "the nature of things," but does so from epistemologically independent "vantage points." Though these "vantage points" are concerned with interpreting/understanding *the nature of things* in a general sense, Latour contends that, when interpreted/understood through a specific "vantage point," what we can ever know about *the nature of things* is ultimately limited by "vantage points."

As Latour suggests, there is, in fact, a problem here—that is, a "crisis"—since, I would argue, *the nature of things* must be interpreted/understood through "vantage points" just as much as these "vantage points" construct their respective epistemologies on *the nature of things*. To be clear, when Latour is speaking of *the nature of things*, he is speaking precisely of objects that must be interpreted/understood through "rhetoric, textual strategies, writing, staging, [and] semiotics—all these are really at stake."[3] What is exactly "at stake" here, for Latour? Each "vantage point" has interpreting/understanding "at stake." That is to say, Latour recognizes that what is "at stake" is the possibility for *the nature of things* to be misinterpreted/misunderstood, rather than strictly interpreted/understood—according to Latour, this leads to a series of misunderstandings hinging on *the nature of things* being "segmented into three components corresponding to our critics' habitual categories [where] they turn [*the nature of things*] into nature, politics, or discourse."[4]

More specifically, though "nature, politics, [and] discourse" individually allow *the nature of things* to be interpretable/understandable, this individuation ignores that *the nature of things* are, as Latour proposes, "more supple than the notion of system, more historical than the notion of structure, [and] more empirical than the notion of complexity."[5] This informs Latour's conceptualization of *the nature of things*—it is the extent to which the meaning of *the nature of things*, as either interpretable/understandable or a misunderstanding, is not individually-dependent on "nature, politics, or discourse," but is grounded in a "thread of these interwoven stories."[6] Because of

---

1. Latour, *We Have Never Been Modern*, 5.
2. Latour, *We Have Never Been Modern*, 6.
3. Latour, *We Have Never Been Modern*, 5.
4. Latour, *We Have Never Been Modern*, 3.
5. Latour, *We Have Never Been Modern*, 3.
6. Latour, *We Have Never Been Modern*, 3.

this "thread," interpretation and misunderstanding are "at stake," but what also remains "at stake" is what Latour notes as

> a new form that has a simultaneous impact on the nature of things and on the social context, while it is not reducible to the one or the other.[7]

This "simultaneous impact" is through interpretation/misunderstanding, which, in a general sense, gives *the nature of things* a meaning that ventures beyond "rhetoric, textual strategies, writing, staging, [or] semiotics."[8] Nevertheless, in a narrow sense, Latour is clear that this "simultaneous impact" is not reducible to *the nature of things* or "on the social context"—any reduction to "one or the other" does not account for the "simultaneous impact" of "nature, politics, [and] discourse" on *the nature of things* itself.

Not only does Latour locate a problem in the relationship between *the nature of things* and "the simultaneous impact" of epistemology, the social sciences, and the science of texts on the meaning of *the nature of things*, but he highlights the fact that "the creatures we are pursuing cross all three spaces"[9]—in other words, as individualized as any one "vantage point" can be toward making-meaning out of *the nature of things*, the meaning of *the nature of things* "cross[es] all three spaces," presenting a "crisis." Latour views this "crisis" by suggesting that, because "the creatures we are pursuing cross [the] three spaces [of epistemology, the social sciences and the science of texts]," he believes "we are no longer understood."[10] This poses another problem for how the meaning of *the nature of things* "cross[es] all three spaces," not just in the extent to which "they remain separate,"[11] but in terms how any meaning made from *the nature of things* situates meaningfulness in us.

It is through critiquing why "we are no longer understood" that Latour further critiques "humanism" with respect to "modernity," through what he calls "The Modern Constitution." These two terms—*humanism* and *modernity*—are constituted together, since, as Latour argues, "modernity is often defined in terms of humanism, either as a way of saluting the birth of 'man' or as a way of announcing his death."[12] In other words, under "The Modern Constitution," *modernity* and *humanism* are inextricably linked, but, more importantly, *humanism* becomes a constituent of *modernity*—this constituency, by "saluting the birth of [the human]" and "announcing [the human's] death," salutes/announces the Anthropocene as both the literal and figurative center of the structure of *modernity*. To be sure, *humanism* is a referent to *modernity*, as much as *modernity* provides the structure in which *humanism* flourishes. Latour seems to make

---

7. Latour, *We Have Never Been Modern*, 5.
8. Latour, *We Have Never Been Modern*, 5.
9. Latour, *We Have Never Been Modern*, 6.
10. Latour, *We Have Never Been Modern*, 5.
11. Latour, *We Have Never Been Modern*, 5.
12. Latour, *We Have Never Been Modern*, 13.

note of this, suggesting that, due to the manner in which modernity salutes/announces the birth/death of the human, "we were never modern."

"What It Means to Be human" and Rosi Braidotti's Posthumanism

In the introduction to *The Posthuman* (2013), Rosi Braidotti poses a series of "main questions" that serve as guiding lanes of philosophical/theoretical inquiry for the book—these four questions all hinge, more specifically, on the meaning of the following question: "What is the posthuman?"[13] As Braidotti suggests, in asking this question, or even proposing the possibility of such a concept, this means that there are "intellectual and historical itineraries that may lead us to the posthuman."[14] What this means, then, is that the "posthuman"—as an idea related directly to what Braidotti calls the "posthuman condition"—has been a spectre looming behind "a crucial aspect of our historicity."[15] This historicity can be viewed as a semiotic chain of meaning-making events—these "intellectual and historical itineraries," as Braidotti calls them—lead humanity to an event of Deleuzean immanence, whereby becoming "posthuman" develops out of the existential need to define *what it means to be human* as "being." In effect, *what it means to be human* means, for Braidotti, recognizing that "being" is not teleological, but transformational. There is no final Aristotlean cause to *what it means to be human*, since "being" transforms itself through progressive phases, by which "being" is always becoming.

Becoming posthuman means rethinking about *what it means to be human* and actuating "being" as ever-changing, ever-progressing ontology. Braidotti's notion of the posthuman is an ontology of becoming, attempting to reconceptualize human metaphysics—like Heidegger's *Being and Time*, Braidotti's project deconstructs and decentralizes *what it means to be human* by delimiting "being" and focusing on the actuality of "being" in a Husserlian life-world. In a Whiteheadian way, the posthuman is more of an actual entity in a life-world than human being, since the former better articulates *what it means to be human* than the latter. Braidotti provides a solution for *what it means it human* in the posthuman approach, which views the life-world as "boundaries between the categories of the natural and the cultural [which] have been displaced and to a large extent blurred by the effects of scientific and technological advances." *What it means to be human* is not structured around any specific Kantian categorical imperatives, but is, more accurately, epistemologically construed through the progressive proliferation of ontologies about the concept of the human. In other words, as Braidotti suggests, "the effects of scientific and technological advances" have allowed *what it means to be human* to venture from the narrow to the inclusive—this sort of decategorization from "the effects of scientific and technological advances," Braidotti writes, "starts from the

13. Braidotti, *Posthuman*, 3.
14. Braidotti, *Posthuman*, 3.
15. Braidotti, *Posthuman*, 3.

assumption that social theory needs to take stock of the transformational concepts, methods and political practices brought about by this change in paradigm."[16] This brings about what Braidotti terms the "posthuman condition"—it is *what it means to be human* after "the effects of scientific and technological advances."

Braidotti's posthuman stance is situationally grounded on the posthuman condition as "a crucial aspect of our historicity," not just as a means of developing a posthuman hermeneutics of "being," but, as Braidotti argues, "to provide adequate representations of our historical situation."[17] The historical situation of *what it means to be human* is encased in history, a tension between the past and the future—"being" is encased in the present as a totality of historical facts and historicized by a Wittgensteinian case in the directions of both antecedence and posterity.

Because *what it means to be human* is linked to a question of historicity, Braidotti's approach, as she admits, "rests on the binary opposition between the given and the constructed." This kind of binary opposition is evidenced in Braidotti's reference to Simone de Beauvior's statement about how woman becomes woman. But, also, to be clear, this issue of binaries can be traced through the Western philosophy and rests on the doorstep of subject-object distinctions. Binaries are not just in Plato's "Form" or even the Allegory of the Cave, but in some of Aristotle's more convoluted discussions of rhetoric as the counterpart to dialectic, and even in Cartesian dualism, Kantian epistemology, Hegelian/Fichtean dialectics, Schopenhauer's notion of the world as will and representation, and Saussure's sign as a signifier-signified relationship. Each of these examples—and many others, of course—set up an existential opposition between "the given" and "the constructed"—it is an opposition that Braidotti's posthuman wishes to replace with "a non-dualistic understanding of nature-culture interaction."[18]

What is "given" and what is "constructed" are problematic in their own right, and especially problematic when speaking across a dialectic—Heidegger points this out in his deconstruction of metaphysics, the meaning of the forgotten question of Being post-Plato's *Sophist*, and the necessity for addressing the analytical possibilities of *Dasein*. In this vein, Braidotti's posthuman is more concerned with what "being" looks like in a Husserlian phenomenologically bracketed life-world—or, what Heidegger coins as "being-in-the-world"—as "a non-dualistic understanding of nature-culture interaction" posited by Braidotti's brand of monistic philosophy.

When *what it means to be human* becomes posthuman in a Husserlian-Heideggerian life-world of deconstituted binaries, we arrive at two very important questions to Braidotti's project: "Where does the posthuman condition leave humanity?" and "What new forms of subjectivity are supported by the posthuman?"[19] A way into these

16. Braidotti, *Posthuman*, 3.
17. Braidotti, *Posthuman*, 3.
18. Braidotti, *Posthuman*, 3.
19. Braidotti, *Posthuman*, 3.

questions rests, in part, on a fundamental Spinoza-Leibniz monistic stance about "being" and *what it means to be human*. Yet, any answer to Braidotti's question must gesture toward the theoretical dehumnanization of *what it means to be human* in order to rehumanize "being," in praxis, into a posthuman condition that, just as Braidotti proposes, "stresses . . . the self-organizing (or auto-poietic force) of living matter."[20]

Even if stressing "the self-organizing" of living matter, particularly as posthuman "becoming," the degree to which posthuman "engenders its own forms of inhumanity" means an engendering of *what it means to be human* into what it means to be "inhuman." This poses an unavoidable problem and a theoretical flaw that problematizes posthuman praxis. Part of the problem is that, for posthuman to be truly "posthuman," and ultimately engender "its own forms of inhumanity,"[21] these "forms" are undeniably structural within the construction of what can be described as *what it means to be inhuman*—not only does this mean that, though the posthuman intends to promote a "non-dualistic understanding of nature-culture interaction" in a monistic scope, do we not arrive at Kierkegaardian dialectics of the relation of selves within a selfhood? Would this mean that, like the problem with *what it means to be human* under the heel of binary oppositions, for Braidotti's posthuman to function theoretically in posthuman times, concessions have to be made about the analytical possibilities of the posthuman?

Though I would not go as far as Foucault and other French theorists about the impossibility of escaping structure (and even binary oppositions), I do view Braidotti's posthuman project as running into the same pitfalls as Heidegger's *Being and Time*—the inability to avoid metaphysics.

"What It Means to Be Human" and Sylvia Wynter's Posthumanism

In reading the collection, as edited by Katherine McKittrick, entitled *Sylvia Wynter: On Being Human as Praxis* (2014), I am confronted with the following question: How does this collection contribute or critique posthumanism, particularly with respect to Agamben (or, even to a lesser extent, hold dialogue with Butler's *Giving an Account of Oneself*)? In other words, perhaps the question should be considered from the standpoint of suggesting that posthumanism is a way of thinking about being—with this in mind, how might *On Being Human as Praxis* be read in this mode of thinking tracing a particular errand?

Like Agamben's *Homo Sacer*, does *On Being Human as Praxis* consider that "being as praxis"—or what I could crudely call "being-in-the-world" in a Heideggerian sense—is devoted to interpreting "being" in reference to a systematized life-world? I am thinking of a *life-world*—to simply borrow from Husserl and Schutz, rather than

20. Braidotti, *Posthuman*, 3.
21. Braidotti, *Posthuman*, 3.

carrying in tow any of their respective philosophical baggage—that is categorized as "modes of being," or modes of *being as praxis*. That is, when we say *being as praxis*, we are not speaking of *being as theory*, but, instead, we are recognizing that the moment we speak of "being" we are speaking of it as it is in "praxis"—"being" is always "practical being," then, which is situated in political structures, social hierarchies, cultural contexts, and gender constructions. To say this, of course, we are conceding that "being" can only be translated as *being-in-the-world*—when we think of being in a posthumanistic way, we are thinking of "what being human" looks like in "praxis." Though I am using Heidegger's *being-in-the-world* to denote *what being human is in praxis*, a posthumanistic approach purposely abandons the continental philosophical approach, especially since any Heideggerian language is a bit problematic, even if grounding that terminology in *Being and Time* as a flawed text that does not explicitly address politics, society, culture, and gender. A clear line of critique for the posthumanistic approach against Heidegger is that *Being and Time* does not address practical being, as such—though Heidegger describes *being-in-the-world*, it avoids the deeply-ethical territory that can be found in Heidegger's "Black Notebooks." Practical being is *being human as praxis*. It is clear that, on the surface, if we are evoking the notion of *being human as praxis*, then we are conceding certain assumptions upfront, which revolve around the sentiment that any philosophy of being must be formulated as a conceptualization of practical being—this is a posthumanistic imperative. Not only does Wolfe and Agamben both understand this imperative respectively as notion of "law" and "sovereignty," *being human as praxis*—in the vein of Sylvia Wynter—incorporates this imperative.

One way to read Wynter's posthumanistic imperative and her underlying conceptualization of *being human as praxis* can be linked to her anticolonial vision, which "is not, then, teleological—moving from colonial oppression outward and upward toward emancipation—but rather consist of knots of ideas and histories and narratives that can be legible in relation to one another."[22] If understanding Wynter's "anti-colonial vision," we must not misunderstand it to be a way of moving away from "colonial oppression," but struggling through the messiness of colonialism. This messiness is grounded in the "knots of ideas and histories and narrative" and the extent to which all anticolonial figures, regardless of their individualized situations, share a common relation with colonialization and with one another. It is an "intellectual" struggle for the anti-colonial figure, which, through Wynter's experiences, "emerge[s] not as *inciting* the political vision put forth in her writings but rather as *implicit to* a creative-intellectual project of reimagining what it means to be human and thus rearticulating who/what we are."[23] For Wynter, the process of rearticulation is important not just to her anticolonial vision but to her post-humanistic imperative, particularly since it is focused on "relationality and interhuman narratives." Through Wynter's posthumanistic imperative,

22. McKittrick, *Sylvia Wynter*, 12.
23. McKittrick, *Sylvia Wynter*, 12.

CONCLUSION: THEOLOGIZING BEYOND THE MEANING OF EXISTENTIAL THEOLOGY

her anticolonial vision is read as "the question-problem-place of blackness"—it is not just about *what it means to be human* but more precisely about *being human as praxis*. Wynter's notion of Blackness is "positioned not outside and entering into modernity but rather the empirical-experiential-symbolic site through which modernity and all of its unmet promises are enabled and made plain."[24] In particular, Wynter's sense of Blackness—perhaps extending Victor Anderson's concept of ontological Blackness "beyond" Platonic-Aristotlean ontology[25]—is rooted in her unique experience as a Black woman, whereby *being human as praxis* is articulated against feminism and employs a Black feminist (or Womanist) perspective.

How might Wynter's interpretations of femininity and Blackness be read as a way of doing posthumanism, and a necessary extension of Agamben's *Homo Sacer*? In other words, is Wynter's post-humanistic approach to *being human as praxis* a way of articulating the specific "struggle" of a unique experience shaped by political structures, social hierarchies, cultural contexts, and gender constructions? Would Wynter view these "systems" themselves as post-humanistic, or do they become, as they are, constituents that presents *being human as praxis* into posthumanism? I think these questions must be answered, first, once understanding that Wynter's interpretations of femininity and Blackness through a post-humanistic lens is not meant to isolate such an experience outside or away from "being," or *what it means to be human*. On the contrary, her posthumanistic interpretations intend on "speak[ing] to the interrelatedness of our contemporary situation and our embattled histories of conflicting and intimate relationalities"[26]—it is the underlying assumption that *being human as praxis* is translated through the same unavoidable, inescapable superstructures against which Wynter's interpretations of femininity and Blackness are read. Yet, Wynter's experience is no different from other beings in our life-world, when considering the "interrelatedness" of beings that share *being-in-the-world* and the communal nature of our "contemporary situation."

"What It Means to Be Human" and Catherine Malabou's Posthumanism

In the introduction to *What Should We Do with Our Brain?* (2004), because "we can say that there exists a constitutive historicity of the brain," Malabou suggests that "the aim of this book is precisely to awaken a consciousness of this historicity."[27] Malabou situates her argument by resisting the continuing tradition of understanding the relationship

---

24. McKittrick, *Sylvia Wynter*, 12.

25. In *Beyond Ontological Blackness*, Victor Anderson's seems to define "ontological blackness" within and against a traditional, continental philosophical framework, though it can be argued that what Anderson is moving "beyond" is a kind of ontology that is post-human.

26. McKittrick, *Sylvia Wynter*, 13.

27. Malabou, *What Should We Do with Our Brain?*, 2.

between the brain and consciousness as "one and the same thing," and ultimately proposing that "we must constitute this strange critical entity, at once philosophical, scientific, and political, that would be a *consciousness of the brain*."[28] To constitute the brain in this manner means defining what identity is and giving a Butler-like account of identity—as something at the intersectionality of the philosophical, the scientific, and the political—with respect to the brain's history. However, as Malabou contends, "it's not just that the brain has a history . . . but that it is a history."[29]

What this means, in particular, is that the brain is a historical being grounded on the historicity of the consciousness, which is consistent with Hegel's concept of *Geistes* in *Phenomenology of Spirit*—Marabou seems to agree with one of the possible interpretations of *Geistes*, which is as an entity that is both historical and ahistorical. If there is a "structural bond" within what defines identity as such, this "bond" is, on one hand, historical (tied to the temporal), but on the other, ahistorical (capable of temporal flexibility). The degree to which the brain "is" history points to a sense that it is *in history*, and also *beyond history*—in other words, because we can say, as Malabou writes, "that there exists a constitutive historicity of the brain," are we not saying that there is something unique about how the brain operates alongside history? Is the consciousness of the brain, then, based on a phenomenological history—something capable of operating "within" the structure of history and, simultaneously, "outside" historical structures. I use the terms "within" and "outside" loosely. It is, of course, impossible to get "outside" of history without stepping "within" another situational sense of history. But, if we consider "history" with respect to Hegel's *Geistes*—making special note of *Geistes* lending the literal, plural translation of "spirit," or "mind"—Malabou's structural understanding of the consciousness of the brain theoretically aligns with Deleuze and Guattari's "rhizome" and the extent to which there is no single structurally-bound consciousness of the brain, but a plurality of "plateaus" at which the brain operates historically and ahistorically, temporally and atemporally.

Malabou seems to make this point, proposing that "the work proper to the brain that engages with history and individual experience"[30] is *plasticity*—especially for Malabou, the term holds special significance when discussing the consciousness of the brain. Malabou appropriates the term in the following manner:

> To talk about the plasticity of the brain means to see in it not only the creator and receiver of form but also an agency of disobedience to every constituted form, a refusal to submit to a model.[31]

The point that Malabou makes here about the brain's plasticity is an important point that underlies her notion of "flexibility" (which is evident in her title). Plasticity and

---

28. Malabou, *What Should We Do with Our Brain?*, 2.
29. Malabou, *What Should We Do with Our Brain?*, 1.
30. Malabou, *What Should We Do with Our Brain?*, 4.
31. Malabou, *What Should We Do with Our Brain?*, 6.

flexibility are complicatedly synonymous, particularly as a way of describing how the brain both works within a structure while not being confined to that structure—Malabou is careful to denote a difference between plasticity and flexibility, offering the following distinction: "What flexibility lacks is the resource of giving form, the power to create, to invent or even to erase an impression, the power of style."[32]

To be clear, the brain is tied to a limiting structure—a material one, in fact—that is not necessarily based on "flexibility." For Malabou, "flexibility is a vague notion, without tradition, without history,"[33] and this "vague notion" becomes ultimately inadequate. It is not about considering "what we could stand [but] about what we could create"[34]—this kind of plasticity, then, has unlimited neurological capabilities that change our understanding of the brain's materiality. For the brain to be "creator and receiver of form," it must, on one hand, be historical and temporal as "receiver of form," abiding to the structural status quo of modeling "neuronal connections, made possible by our individual experience, skills, and life habits, by the power of impression of existence in general."[35] Yet, in another sense, when the brain acts as "creator," through its plasticity, exhibits "an agency of disobedience to every constituted form," it takes an ahistorical-atemporal turn—as Malabou rightly asserts, plasticity opens "the possibility of fashioning by memory, to the capacity to shape a history."[36]

Is this plasticity, then, similar to Hegel's *Geistes*? Can we read *Geistes* through Malabou's plasticity, as the means by which the consciousness of the brain interacts with history existentially, specifically if we read into her sense of plasticity "ha[ving] a long philosophical past"?[37] Like Malabou's notion that "true plasticity of the brain means insisting on knowing what it can do and not simply what it can tolerate,"[38] Hegel's *Geistes* employs a kind of plasticity invested in "making its history, becoming the subject of its history."[39] However, in moving beyond Hegelian phenomenology (and even eclipsing Husserlian phenomenological εποχη), Malabou's plasticity of the brain accounts for

> the connection between the role of genetic nondeterminism at work in the constitution of the brain and the possibility of a social and political nondeterminism, in a word, a new freedom, which is to say: a new meaning of history.[40]

---

32. Malabou, *What Should We Do with Our Brain?*, 12.
33. Malabou, *What Should We Do with Our Brain?*, 13.
34. Malabou, *What Should We Do with Our Brain?*, 13.
35. Malabou, *What Should We Do with Our Brain?*, 6.
36. Malabou, *What Should We Do with Our Brain?*, 6.
37. Malabou, *What Should We Do with Our Brain?*, 13.
38. Malabou, *What Should We Do with Our Brain?*, 13.
39. Malabou, *What Should We Do with Our Brain?*, 13.
40. Malabou, *What Should We Do with Our Brain?*, 13.

This "new freedom" and "new meaning of history" is decidedly post-Hegelian and post-Husserlian, since the brain refuses "to submit to a model," and its plasticity grants "freeplay" within the constraints of history and time—both of which are problematic in Hegel and Husserl.

"What It Means to Be Human" and Cary Wolfe's Posthumanism

In anticipation of *Before the Law: Humans and Other Animals in a Biopolitical Frame* (2012), Wolfe's 2010 article entitled "Before the Law: Animals in a Biopolitical Context" uses the example of factory farming and the Spanish Parliament decision to grant fundamental rights to great apes, in order to make a larger point about the question of justice and "the problem of ethical standing for non-human animals."[41] This question, as Wolfe outlines it, is situated in appeals to the rights model for nonhuman animals, particularly with respect to legal pragmatism and animal rights philosophy—more specifically though, Wolfe's chief concern is to evaluate recent work in biopolitical theory as a way "to rearticulate not just ethical but also the political status of our treatment of non-human animals."[42]

For Wolfe, biopolitical theory is comprised of what I would describe as the intersectionality (or existentiality) of biopolitics and biophilosophy, which, when considering recent work in the field,

> throws into striking relief the limitations of legal and political liberalism and its grounding philosophical assumptions for coming to terms not only with the ethical and legal status of non-human animals, but also with the *political* status of how we treat them in and through material practices and *dispositifs* that are of a piece with biopolitics in its specifically modern form.[43]

Yet, though Wolfe recognizes that there are "limitations" inherent in the "prevailing legal doctrine," he suggests, more frankly, that these "limitations," as such, are related to a "considerable disagreement about the satisfactoriness of the 'rights' framework for protecting the ethical standing of non-humans."[44] What ultimately arises out of this disagreement is "a growing disjunction between existing legal doctrine and the question of justice for (at least some) non-human animals."[45] To be clear, this poses a significant problem, not just for how we conceive of existing legal doctrine, but how that doctrine measures the question of justice for nonhuman animals. This problem, Wolfe points out, is grounded in the notion that existing legal doctrine does not serve the question of justice for nonhuman animals—the existing legal doctrine

41. Wolfe, *Before the Law*, 8.
42. Wolfe, *Before the Law*, 8.
43. Wolfe, *Before the Law*, 9.
44. Wolfe, *Before the Law*, 9.
45. Wolfe, *Before the Law*, 11.

does more to serve the existential needs of humanity than it does for nonhuman animals, and, in turn, becomes an inadequate superstructure by which the question of justice for nonhuman animals is measured. Because of this, nonhuman animals experience a rather unsatisfactory sense of "rights"—it is only an arbitrary degree of "rights," so to speak, that is not aligned with a Hegelian-Fichtean "Right" perhaps—if we measure that access to "rights" in terms of providing protection and ensuring an ethical standing for nonhuman animals.

What do we mean by "ethical standing"? Are we, first and foremost, suggesting that the ethical standing of nonhuman animals is not generally analogous to humanity? In other words, do nonhuman animals and humanity share an "ethical standing," in a general sense, as Agamben's notion of bare life or "zoē"? Or, is there something altogether different about how we measure the ethical standing of nonhuman animals and that of humanity—not just in terms of what can be considered "zoē," but also as "bios"? In the narrow sense, if what we think of as humanity's ethical standing is incomparable to nonhuman animals—simply because we are applying an ethics to nonhuman animals that are not congruent to existential value/concerns of humanity—are we conceding that means of measuring both have a kind of sliding scale, or, if appropriating Derrida, are contingent on free-play within the structure we call ethical standing?

Essentially, the possibility of ethical standing and the overarching ethical structure within which standing is measured is not comparable between nonhuman animals and humanity—this is due, at least in part, on how we define "existing legal doctrine." That is to say, the existing model that delineates what is considered "legal" (and what is not), specifically in terms of predefined doctrinal statements of legality. As Wolfe rightly argues, nonhuman animals should not be held to the standards of existing legal doctrine, since that doctrine is decidedly anthropocentric and constructed especially around ensuring humanity's ethical standing. Yet, the degree to which existing (and anthropocentric) legal doctrine is used to measure the ethical standing of nonhuman animals presents a "disjunction" between what is used to evaluate their "rights" and how those "rights" are evaluated. Wolfe cites this "disjunction" as critical not just to how biopolitics should work generally with respect to the concept of rights, but pivotal to any narrow formulation of a "'rights' framework for protecting the ethical standing of non-human animals." This becomes especially important, then, when "our knowledge about [nonhuman animals'] ethically relevant characteristics and capacities (to suffer, to communicate, to engage in complex forms of social behavior and bonding) increases dramatically every year."[46]

What this ultimately points to is the necessity of "our ethical responsibility to animals,"[47] and through an acknowledgment of Jacques Derrida and Cora Diamond in particular, Wolfe suggests that

46. Wolfe, *Before the Law*, 11.
47. Wolfe, *Before the Law*, 12.

> it is our shared vulnerability and finitude as embodied beings that forms the foundation of our compassion and impulse toward justice for animals—a vulnerability that gets "deflected," as Diamond puts it, by the rights model, the kinds of argument it deploys (pro or con), and its emphasis on agency, reciprocity, and the like.[48]

It is clear, then, that the rights model is a structure that does not appeal to the vulnerability and finitude of nonhuman animals as "embodied being" as it does to humanity. But, more importantly, if following Wolfe a bit further, is it not possible to suggest that the current rights model only makes nonhuman animals all the more vulnerable? Is our "compassion and impulse towards justice for animals" based on our conceptualization of nonhuman animals are "embodied beings" capable of being grounded in Agambenian "bare life" and becoming "zoē"? Or, do we base our understanding of what justice looks like for nonhuman animals on a belief that their "finitude" is more finite than our own?

The only way to answer the above questions is to step outside the rights model. That means, of course, not just deconstructing what we know as the rights model but construct a new "rights model"—at least, something rebuilt, reorganized, and reconceptualized, which subscribes to the "vulnerability and finitude" of nonhuman animals. But, the problem remains, right? To step outside the rights model means being situated, ultimately, within another. Even if we deconstruct (in a Heideggerian or Derridian kind of way) our historical understanding of the rights model in order to construct a new model with its own historicality, are we not simply falling back into the same fundamental paradox?

Wolfe certainly thinks so, proposing that, particularly in light of what I have called a fundamental paradox to the rights model,

> our ethical obligations to animals by deploying the rights model misses the point, not just because the question is thicker and more profound than the thin if-P-then-Q propositions of a certain style of analytic philosophy, but also because "when genuine issues of justice and injustice are framed in terms of rights, they are thereby distorted and trivialized."[49]

Not only does Wolfe note Diamond's assertion about the link between rights and a system of entitlement, but he proposes that this link is not concerned, to quote Cora Diamond, "with the evil done to a person, but with how much he or she gets compared to other participants in the system."[50] Like Diamond, Wolfe believes there is more to it. Through Diamond, Wolfe agrees with the idea that "what is crucial to our sense of the injustice done to animals is the embodiment and vulnerability we share with them, which ground our horror at the brute subjection of the body that they

---

48. Wolfe, *Before the Law*, 12.
49. Wolfe, *Before the Law*, 13.
50. Wolfe, *Before the Law*, 13.

CONCLUSION: THEOLOGIZING BEYOND THE MEANING OF EXISTENTIAL THEOLOGY

so often endure."[51] Consequently, Wolfe envisions taking "the discussion of animals, ethics, and law into a different register, one that does not take for granted, much less endorse, our current legal structures for confronting [questions of injustice]: namely, the context of biopolitics."[52] An important part of this "discussion" centers, for Wolfe, on "the question of the body and entitlement, and the political and juridical power over life itself."[53] Wolfe is right to see this as "fundamental," which he affirms both with Agamben's *The Open: Man and Animal*, *Homo Sacer*, and *State of Exception*, as well as Judith Butler's *Precarious Life: The Powers of Mourning and Violence*. In particular, Wolfe highlights Butler, who

> asserts that the fundamental question that needs to be reopened in the current political context is "Whose lives count as lives? And finally, What makes for a grievable life? Despite our differences in location and history," she continues, "my guess is that it is possible to appeal to a 'we,' a community of those who deserve ethical consideration by virtue of their embodied vulnerability and exposure."[54]

Though Wolfe is careful to say he admires and shares Butler's "impulses," he finds that her "effort . . . runs aground precisely on the question of non-human beings."[55] What "runs aground" in Butler, according to Wolfe, is the supposition that the dangers and vulnerabilities that accrue from the fact of embodiment are "limited to a 'common human vulnerability.'"[56] In other words, Wolfe is critiquing Butler's disconnection between nonhuman lives and grievable lives in terms of the former "counting as" the latter—which is especially apparent in Wolfe's example of "many millions of people griev[ing], and griev[ing] deeply, for their lost animal companions."[57] What undergirds Wolfe's reading of Butler is not, as he points out, the problem "that animals have an ontologically and existentially different relationship to their finitude than we do"—noted very poignantly in Wolfe's invoking of Heidegger's "being-towards-death."[58] Rather, Wolfe argues that Butler "is at pains to separate herself from such an ontology in many of her key theoretical and methodological commitments"—even though it appears that Wolfe seems unwilling to make that venture as well. Instead, Wolfe considers Butler's "key problems" to be situated, on one hand, on Butler's notion of ethics and of community tied to a "reciprocity" model that can be traced, in its extreme form, to the contractualism of John Rawls (as voiced in his *Theory of*

---

51. Wolfe, *Before the Law*, 13.
52. Wolfe, *Before the Law*, 13.
53. Wolfe, *Before the Law*, 13.
54. Wolfe, *Before the Law*, 14.
55. Wolfe, *Before the Law*, 14.
56. Wolfe, *Before the Law*, 14.
57. Wolfe, *Before the Law*, 14.
58. Wolfe, *Before the Law*, 14.

Justice), and on the other, on Butler's notion of subjectivity which "remains too committed to the primacy of 'agency' for ethical standing."[59] These notions of ethics and subjectivity come to bear at the intersectionality (or existentiality) of dehumanization, Western civilization, and the production of the human. Wolfe makes this point by quoting Butler in the following:

> Dehumanization becomes the condition for production of the human to the extent that a "Western" civilization defines itself over and against a population understood as, by definition, illegitimate, if not dubiously human.[60]

However, Wolfe's critique of Butler, with respect to the above quote, rests on the notion that

> as long as the automatic exclusion of animals from ethical standing remains intact simply because of their species, such a dehumanization via animalization will be readily available for deployment against *whatever* body that happens to fall outside the ethnocentric "we."[61]

The fact that "dehumanization via animalization" even occurs means that the ethical standing of animals (nonhuman animals, to be sure) is always at jeopardy, since the "ethnocentric 'we'" remains the means of measure. This calls Agamben to mind, if assigning ethical standing to notions of "zoē" and "bios"—in particular, how we understand either as ontological representations of biopolitics via biophilosophy. With this in mind, even though Wolfe acknowledges that Butler calls for "a politics that seeks to recognize the sanctity of life, of all lives"—a sort of politics subscribing to biopolitics via biophilosophy—Wolfe argues that Butler

> needs to expand her call across species lines, to declare the human/animal distinction irrelevant, strictly speaking, to such a call; but to do so, she would need to move away from the centrality of reciprocity and agency to ethical and political standing that we find in *Precarious Life*.[62]

Because he is intent on moving away "from the centrality of reciprocity and agency to ethical and political standing," through finding irrelevance in human/animal distinctions, Wolfe seems poised to decidedly enter into ontological territory—the same territory he criticized Butler for not entering, and yet, unwilling to enter himself. Still, Wolfe is clearly aware that any hope for truly conceptualizing ethical and political standing is through the use of ontology. It is for this reason, perhaps, that Wolfe discards the term "context" in favor of "frame" in the 2012 *Before the Law: Humans and Other Animals in a Biopolitical Frame*—unlike "context," the term "frame" affords

---

59. Wolfe, *Before the Law*, 14.
60. Wolfe, *Before the Law*, 16.
61. Wolfe, *Before the Law*, 16.
62. Wolfe, *Before the Law*, 16.

CONCLUSION: THEOLOGIZING BEYOND THE MEANING OF EXISTENTIAL THEOLOGY

Wolfe the ability to genealogically situate his approach to ontology in Agamben and carry it forward through Foucault and Heidegger.

By way of Heidegger in particular, Wolfe employs "enframing"—a modified version of "frame" found more explicitly in later Heidegger than early Heidegger—as having a twofold effect, which he describes in the following way: "Not only is human being cut off from a more authentic relation to the natural world, it is also cut off from an authentic relationship to itself." Enframing, then, for Wolfe's notion of a "biopolitical frame," is contingent on a "decisive ontological distinction between those who are fully human and those who are less than human, those others who have been so fundamentally distanced from Being."[63] To this end, Wolfe's enframing assumes an ontological agency of meaning-making proportions not just for Agamben's "zoē," but for "bios"—enframing allows "being," whether for humanity or nonhuman animals, to exist in "a more authentic relation to the natural world" so that "being" can have, ultimately, "an authentic relationship to itself," which is situated (or even grounded) by an existential elasticity similar to Derrida's freeplay and Barad's agential realism.

---

63. Wolfe, *Before the Law*, 2.

—————————— APPENDIX A ——————————

An Introduction to Robert Boyle's *The Excellency of Theology, Compared with Natural Philosophy* (1665)

IN THE PREFACE TO Robert Boyle's *The Excellency of Theology, Compared with Natural Philosophy*, the publisher presents an advertisement to the reader noting that "the following discourse was written in the year 1665, while the author, to avoid the great Plague that then raged London, was reduced with many others to go into the country, and frequently to pass from place to place, unaccompanied with most of his books."[1] What follows, then, is the publisher's further contextualization of the work as strictly correspondence the author, Robert Boyle, did not intend for publication as much for fear of compromising the welfare of the work's subject matter as for an apprehension of its contents being used against him by ideological opponents. But, aside from what might be nothing more than subtle propaganda on behalf of the publisher, which, of course, is often common in other literatures of the period, what remains important about the contextualization of Robert Boyle's *The Excellency of Theology* is that it was written in the aftermath of two very significant events in British history: one, as mentioned by the publisher in the preface, is the Great Plague of 1665, and the other is, undoubtedly, the Restoration of Charles II in 1660—both of these events have substantial contextual influence over the purpose of Robert Boyle composing *The Excellency of Theology*.

As mentioned by the publisher in the preface to the Robert Boyle's text, the Great Plague ravaged London in 1665. Originally, it began in the summer of that year with an outbreak of smallpox that had become "so rife in such a short time . . . that between the church and the pound, a distance not above [one hundred and twenty paces], about forty families were afflicted by it."[2] What also occurred during that summer was a proliferation of flies that swarmed in houses so frequently that the multitudes lined the walls of homes. This led to an eventual infestation of ants that covered the thoroughfares, and a further infestation of frogs in every conceivable,

---

1. Boyle, *Excellency of Theology*, 1.
2. Bell, *Great Plague in London in 1665*, 15.

APPENDIX A: *THE EXCELLENCY OF THEOLOGY, COMPARED WITH NATURAL PHILOSOPHY*

shadowy street ditch,[3] which was, in large part, due to the relative unclean conditions of city streets[4] and the unsatisfactory advances in sanitary science[5] as much as it can be evidenced in a noticeable drought that had been so severe that "the level of saturation in the ground fell unprecedentedly low."[6] As a result, what began as isolated cases of small pox before manifesting as a full-blown infection in the air, many families began to shut themselves in their homes with the intent of shutting out the disease—these are best represented in the numbers who, with the alarm of the infection entering their shut-away families, stopped up the keyholes of their doors, and avoided communication with anyone, whether exhibiting plague symptoms or not.[7] This did little, however, to prevent the swelling of the initial infection—something that would have been, perhaps, isolated in widely scattered areas during irregular times and seasons—into a vast epidemic that, though it "began in out-parishes, or suburbs, and only after slow progress became lodged in the city,"[8] allowed London to "become a Plague [center] from which only peril radiated."[9]

The plague, then, passed quickly through London from household to household, since, by 1665, "[the city] was home to at least 450,000 persons, with visitors and transients raising the total population to around 500,000."[10] Therefore, since London was such a densely populated city—having "exceeded in population all the capitals and major cities of Europe except Paris and had drawn almost even with that great metropolis"[11]—and the infection was so communally contagious, and, subsequently, there was such a lack of sufficient, systematic medical care to remedy the potential fatal symptoms that arose from the infection, the number of plague burials and the number of infected parishes increased exponentially during August 1 to September 5, 1665, where all 130 parishes were infected and recorded triple-digit deaths in relation to the same numbers recorded in the previous period from May 2 to June 13, 1665, where only twelve parishes were infected and only single-digit deaths had been recorded.[12]

The infected and the dead became largely populated by the poor,[13] since they were committed by their poverty to stay in London and, quite frankly, be beholden to

---

3. Bell, *Great Plague in London in 1665*, 15.
4. Bell, *Great Plague in London in 1665*, 11.
5. Consider the following: "And London had learned nothing [from the plague that occurred 40 years before the Great Plague of 1665]. Sanitary science had not been borne." Bell, *Great Plague in London in 1665*, 9.
6. Bell, *Great Plague in London in 1665*, 15.
7. Bell, *Great Plague in London in 1665*, 154–55.
8. Bell, *Great Plague in London in 1665*, 154–55.
9. Bell, *Great Plague in London in 1665*, 136.
10. Moote and Moote, *Great Plague*, 26.
11. Moote and Moote, *Great Plague*, 26.
12. Moote and Moote, *Great Plague*, 61.
13. When looking for the plague's first signs, "one must look among the poor, whose squalid

whatever fate lay for them with the plague. However, for the well-to-do and the rich, there was a contrasting "means of prevention not afforded to the poor, something that experience had taught to be more effective than medicine: they could fly from the infected city before the Plague, taking that precaution with no unnecessary delay."[14] These individuals escaped London and the plague to take harbor in the country, accumulating in, namely, the outlying districts and suburbia that they believed held security and safety against the spread of infection and, more importantly, in response to the drastic increase in plague burials and a lack of medical competency with plague symptoms, avoided certain death.

Having fled the plague and the accompaniment of certain death in London, Boyle took refuge in Oxford,[15] where, like other plague refugees, he, undoubtedly, viewed the incident of the plague in terms of its wider theological implications. That is, more intuitively, as more than just an event that occurred by happenstance in nature but, instead, as a God-related occurrence. As with many confronted with the plague, specifically those, like Boyle, that survived it, it was easy to find the hand of God in the plague as much as it was convenient to overlay an opinion that God brought the plague as judgment on a sinning people. For Boyle, conversely, the plague represented much more than the case of humanity's sin and God's punishment, whereby there was the common assumption that "if a plague struck a community, these fervent believers called for repentance and hoped that God would remove the Destroying Angel's hand."[16] Boyle, consequently, perceived the plague not just in terms of theology but bilaterally through the lens of science, explicitly as something that had to be explained, first, with God being the first prime cause of the plague and, second, by God allowing the plague to manifest itself through the forces of nature, of which God himself had created.[17] Theologically speaking, to follow Boyle's line of argument a bit further, God was the spiritual embodiment of the plague, the calculus within the gestation of the infection, as well as the existential embodiment of the natural conditions under which the plague could be allowed to exist, the mechanics within the infrastructure of nature that made the plague a possible reality.

Perhaps, it wouldn't be too much to suggest that Boyle's understandings of the way that God works in the plague and jointly works in nature comes into focus more keenly in the wake of a Restoration England. Under Restoration England, many were still reeling from the regicide of Charles I's execution,[18] still making sense of the

---

conditions of life when herded together in undrained and dirty tenements and hovels, or underground cellars, offered to [the plague] a ready lodgment." See Bell, *Great Plague in London in 1665*, 8–9.

14. Bell, *Great Plague in London in 1665*, 53.

15. This is known by way of correspondence written between Boyle and Oldenburg, in June 14, 1665. See MacIntosh, *Excellencies of Robert Boyle*, 31.

16. Moote and Moote, *Great Plague*, 67–68.

17. Moote and Moote, *Great Plague*, 67–68.

18. What this means is that "the trauma of regicide left few royalists with faith in the providences of God; the much deeper sense of betrayal experienced by the radicals in 1660 largely explains their

experiment with the monarchial-abolished republic of Oliver Cromwell's ill-fated Protectorate,[19] and still readjusting under the restored kingship of Charles II. By 1660, then, just five years before the outbreak of the Great Plague, when Charles II was restored to his father's throne, there was a relatively wide acceptance of the world "as the domain of sin and of imperfectability."[20] By extension, Christianity became depoliticized and demystified to the point that the role God played wasn't stringently limited to the scientific annals of nature and life, but became more theological as "the creator who set things going, and the spirit who worked within the individual."[21] Not only did this theological shift in a Restoration-ripened, cultural-social climate lead to an array of religious disputes, a greater diversity of religious opinions, and an explosion of different religious sects,[22] but, for Boyle, it presented the opportunity to distinguish God from nature—more specifically, in that case, perhaps in reverence to the human suffering caused by the plague and the changes in the political climate that reached into the religious atmosphere after the Restoration, Boyle sought to draw a clear and distinct ideological boundary line between theology and natural philosophy in his *The Excellency of Theology*.

Having already well established himself as a prominent scientist in the field of natural philosophy, Boyle is best considered as a lay theologian, which was "a status [that] was recognized in the seventeenth century and has been acknowledged ever since."[23] Not only was Boyle unabashedly aware of his relative laity as a theologian, but he embraced it, believing that "because he was a layman, his theological writings would be taken more seriously than they would be if he were a clergyman."[24] What this meant for Boyle was that he could speak about theological concerns from a lay theologian's point of view while maintaining his scientist's footing in natural philosophy.[25] This

---

political quiescence thereafter. [As a result of this], psychologically, the pain of betrayal after such visible testimonies of divine favour was too great." See Morgan, *Oxford History of Britain*, 3:138.

19. Following Charles I's execution on January 30, 1649, for high treason against the Ancient Constitution of England, Parliament abolished the monarchy along with the House of Lords, and on May 19, 1649, declared that the people of England "are and shall be, and are hereby constituted to be a Commonwealth and Free State, and shall from henceforth to be governed as a Commonwealth and Free by the supreme authority of this nation, the representatives of the people in Parliament." England's experiment in republican rule had begun. See Herman, *Short History of Early Modern England*, 230.

20. See Morgan, *Oxford History of Britain*, 3:138.

21. Morgan, *Oxford History of Britain*, 139.

22. See Seaward, *Restoration, 1660–1668*, 40–42.

23. See Wojcik, *Robert Boyle*, 1.

24. Specifically, Wojcik cites a quote from Boyle's *Reason and Religion*, where Boyle writes, in part, "Perhaps my being a secular person may the better qualify me to work on those I am to deal with, and may make my arguments, though not more solid in themselves, yet more prevalent with men, that usually . . . have a particular pique at the clergy, and look with prejudice upon whatever it taught by men, whose interest is advantaged by having what they teach believed." Wojcik, *Robert Boyle*, 3.

25. Robert Boyle is considered to be "one of the most prolific scholars among those who combined a deep interest in science and religion in late seventeenth-century England. He wrote much on natural philosophy, religion, and theology. In certain important ways, Boyle resembles a medieval

stands to reason why, in terms of his voluminous writings, Boyle's "theological concerns are so interwoven with his thoughts on natural philosophy that it is impossible to classify some work as either primarily theological or as concerned primarily with natural philosophy."[26] Boyle's interweaving of theological concerns and his thoughts on natural philosophy are evidenced most noticeably in *The Excellency of Theology*, where the text, at its best, attempts to compare and contrast theology, as the study of divinity, with natural philosophy, as the study of nature. Both are, consequently, examined in the context of understanding God: theology as understanding God in the systematic research of scripture and tradition, and natural philosophy as understanding God through what is yielded from the scientific research of nature.

In the comparison of theology and natural philosophy—that is, the explicit contrasting of the two as subjectively engaging in two different objectifying intellectual endeavors[27]—Boyle's *The Excellency of Theology*, generally, wholly separates theology from natural philosophy. How Boyle proceeds to do this in the work is, first, by "[upholding] the study of theology as not only worthwhile in itself, but as preferable even to the study of natural philosophy,"[28] and, second, seemingly more poignantly, by considering that both theology and natural philosophy, as Boyle chooses to define them, lack something substantive in their own rights. Therefore, theology and natural philosophy, for Boyle, become inadequate structures through which he contends to understand the relationship between God and nature. In effect, it is not only evident that "Boyle's natural philosophy is not about God,"[29] but it is further apparent, perhaps, more notably, that Boyle's concept of theology is fully about nature as the essential platform through which humankind explicates, interprets, and perceives a knowledge about God. This is at the ideological heart of Boyle's argument in *The Excellency of Theology*. Rather than strictly utilizing either theology or natural philosophy individually, Boyle operates within a theological-philosophical discipline, where he asserts, "that to the knowledge [about] God there needs no other [than] Natural Theology."[30]

Natural Theology, then, becomes the theological-philosophical meeting point for Boyle's concepts of theology and natural philosophy. Here, when working from that meeting point, Boyle explores something that not only transcends the subjects of God, but does so, too, with nature. In effect, by working from what should be two diametrically opposed theological perspectives toward something more theologically

---

theologian-natural philosopher." Grant, *History of Natural Philosophy*, 299.

26. Wojcik, *Robert Boyle*, 2.

27. Consider this: "Classifying theology as a science . . . made theology a separate discipline that used rational arguments to arrive at its conclusions. As theology became an independent scientific discipline, philosophy, and natural philosophy, also became autonomous disciplines that used rigorous reasoning from fundamental scientific principles. Thus did natural philosophy and theology become separate principles." See Grant, *History of Natural Philosophy*, 248.

28. MacIntosh, *Excellencies of Robert Boyle*, 38.

29. Grant, *History of Natural Philosophy*, 299.

30. Boyle, *Excellency of Theology*, 4.

intermediary, Boyle examines in *The Excellency of Theology* how humankind should develop a knowledge about God from God's tangible works in nature.[31] But, moreover, and more importantly, what Boyle postulates, within the natural theology argument, is how humankind can extrapolate from their knowledge about God something contemplatively existential about human selfhood.

Human selfhood, when translated in Boyle's natural theology, is crafted in relation to the problem of evil. The problem of evil, as a reoccurrence in humankind, becomes the epitome of selfhood. Specifically, for natural theology, the "[aim is] to demonstrate the existence of God, to establish the principal [that the] divine attributes, to vindicate God's relation to the world as that of the Creator to the creature and, finally, to throw what light it can on the action of divine providence in regard of man and on the problem of evil."[32] The problem of evil, in itself, presents the notion of morality and links morality to the "divine providence" of God as the existential determiner of what is moral for "a selfhood." This aim was, undoubtedly, Boyle's aim in *The Excellency of Theology*, whereby, as Boyle suggests that the existence of God affords us with the discovery of our own souls.[33] What Boyle's natural theology ascertains is that, through the inherent existence of God and what can be inherently gleaned from the representation of God objectively in nature, selfhood is developed by way of certain "informations [God] is pleased to vouchsafe us, touching [God's] own nature and Attributes, [which] are exceedingly preferable to any account, [so] that we can give our selves of [God], without [God]."[34] To this end, the "information" Boyle refers to is inherent in nature, inherent in God, inherent in humankind, inherent in the problem of evil in humankind, and inherent in the degree to which selfhood is derived from the relationship humankind forges with God. These inherencies, as a result, become distinctly existential, describing the dimensions and limitations of selfhood within the context of being and nothingness—when applying Boyle's terms, being is "our selves of God" and nothingness is "without God," where the evidence of the existence of God in nature represents a divine selfhood, which is "furnished [to humankind] by the intrinsic light or evidence of the beings of [humankind] experience[s]"[35] as indicative of humankind's selfhood.

---

31. When considering the discipline of natural theology, "[the natural theologian studies] God according to what existing things can tell [humankind] about him." Holloway, *Introduction to Natural Theology*, 17.

32. See Joyce, *Principles of Natural Theology*, 1.

33. Boyle, *Excellency of Theology*, 13.

34. Boyle, *Excellency of Theology*, 3.

35. Holloway, *Introduction to Natural Theology*, 17.

APPENDIX B

Pluralism and Ecumenism

The Development of Pluralistic Theology and Ecumenical Ecclesiology in the Nineteenth-Century European Religious Culture

IN ORDER TO PROPERLY explore the dynamics of religious/confessional/interdenominational coexistence over the course of the nineteenth century, specifically through the rise of pluralism and ecumenism, the development of religious culture in Europe, as a whole, is greatly influenced by the decline of Enlightenment ideals, marked notably by the French Revolution of 1789. In beginning here with what has been coined as a "Radical Enlightenment," the advancement of the concept of separating the affairs of church from the state and the advocacy of general religious tolerance ushered in both a pluralistic theology (what can be called "religious pluralism") and what I wish to call "ecumenical ecclesiology." While the former refers to an interdenominational understanding of theology that fundamentally decenters any exclusivist denominational soteriology by offering an inclusivist eschatology, the latter focuses on the roles that different churches play intra-denominationally within their different religious traditions. These notions of "pluralistic theology" and "ecumenical ecclesiology," as I have defined them, chiefly arise from the denominational influence of Christianity in Europe, evidenced precisely in the emergence of liberal theology, or "liberal Christianity," which, by the end of the eighteenth century, saw the intra-denominational proliferation of philosophically diverse religious movements informed by varying biblical hermeneutical approaches. This approach became known as biblical criticism, predicated on not just replacing dogma and bias with an interpretative judgment based on reason, but reconstructing history by placing its meaning within a contemporary perspective—the former is denoted as higher criticism, while the latter is referred to as lower criticism. In light of this, biblical criticism's avoidance of intradominatiomal dogma and an investment in the making of contemporary meaning allows the denominational influence of Christianity in Europe to lead interdenominational engagement with non-Christian religions, such as Judaism and Islam—it is out of liberal theology's biblical criticism that pluralistic theology and ecumenical ecclesiology became possible, especially as a means of officially bringing an end to the notion of Christendom, by which the Catholic Church had been viewed as the established religion at the center of religious culture in Europe. Not only did this cause a shift in the Church's previous geopolitical power—particularly if we understand that the Holy See wielded ecclesiastical concordats with sovereign states—but it allowed for the emergence of the theologies of Protestantism and Eastern Orthodoxy (or Orthodox Christianity), as well as the theologies and ecclesiologies of Judaism and Islam. What resulted, then, by the nineteenth century, was a pluralism and ecumenism that created substantial diversity generally in European religious culture but, more narrowly, allowed for the development of interreligious dialogue that both secured the coexistence of Catholicism, Protestantism, Orthodoxy Christianity (of Eastern Europe), Judaism (in Hungary), and Islam (in Turkey within Southeastern Europe) within the rootedness of respective religious communities and unique traditions and brought about, by 1893, the inauguration of the Parliament of World Religions, convened at the World Columbian Exposition, as a means of pursuing an interfaith and interbelief dialogues. From these dialogues, there arises the branch of theology of religions, which evaluates religion as a phenomena, but does so by adjudicating between pluralism, inclusivism, and exclusivism about the nature of God (or "theology proper") and the meaning of salvation (in relation to harmatiology, soteriology, and eschatology).

APPENDIX C

"The March of God in the World"

American Ideological Monumentality, Hegel's State, and the Second Great Awakening

AMERICAN IDEOLOGICAL MONUMENTALITY OF the nineteenth-century can be viewed contemporaneously through the religious movement, the Second Great Awakening (ca. 1790–1840), when considering that the overall American canonization of nineteenth-century social, political, and legal ideas represents a counter-monumentalism against the European ideological monumentality of the Enlightenment of the previous eighteenth century. Not only did the Enlightenment, as a chiefly European intellectual and philosophical movement, initiate monumentally big ideas in the monuments of rationalism and deism, both are responsible for the embodiment in three "public" monuments that serve at the intersectionality of culture: the social, the political, and the legal. What makes the social, the political, and the legal each a "public monument" is that they are created, allowed to exist, and sustained in the religious and philosophical public sphere—this informs eighteenth-century European ideological monumentality as much as it does the counter-monumentalism of nineteenth-century American ideological monumentality. On one hand, while Rene Descartes (1596–1650) begins the monumentality of European enlightenment thinking and Immanuel Kant (1724–1804) canonizes that monumentality by attempting to fundamentally synthesize rationalist with deist thinking in Critique of Pure Reason (1781), on the other hand, the emergence of Georg W. F. Hegel (1770–1831) begins a counter-monumentalism in *Phenomenology of Spirit* (1807) against Kantianism, which becomes canonized in Hegelianism and, in turn, develops into the monumentality of German Idealism (or post-Kantianism), by way of the "public" monument of Hegel's last published work, *Elements of the Philosophy of Right* (1820). Though German, this text is a "public" monument for American ideological monumentality of the nineteenth-century, since, in light of the Second Great Awakening, it provides an understanding of the State as "the march of God in the world," as a monumentality, based on the public monuments of patriarchy, the Second Party System and slavery as they become respectively personified in the American monumentalities of "the social," "the political," and "the legal."

─── APPENDIX D ───

The Hermeneutical Significance of the Doctrine of Creation to Theological Thought

From Karl Barth and Emil Brunner to Paul Tillich and Karl Rahner

THE DOCTRINE OF CREATION—OR viewed as religious cosmology, with relation to theological anthropology, Mariology, angelology, notions of heaven and hell, and theodicy—has a centralized significance to theological thought. On one hand, while the doctrine of creation broadly informs an understanding of the connectedness between theology proper, Christology, the Trinity, and Pneumatology, the doctrine of creation, on the other hand, is also essential to specifically working out the interrelated issues of hamartiology, soteriology, and eschatology. Yet, when interpreting the manner in which the doctrine of creation functions within theological thought, there arises a need to consider the doctrinal demands of "creation" in terms of a "high hermeneutic" and a "low hermeneutic." To be clear, though the significance of the doctrine of creation generally comes to bear on the whole of theological thought, whether it is interpreted through a "high hermeneutic" or a "low hermeneutic" calls forth a specific emphasis on adequately working out the respective meanings of divinity and humanity, if considering that the difference between a high hermeneutic and a low hermeneutic is similar to the difference between a high Christology and a low Christology. When viewed this way, applying a high hermeneutic to the doctrine of creation seeks to interpret, in a "high" mode, theology proper, Christology, the Trinity, and Pneumatology (i.e., the role of God in theology), while applying a low hermeneutic to the doctrine of creation focuses on hamartiology, soteriology, and eschatology (i.e., the role of the human in theology) from a relatively "low" mode. Because of this, the hermeneutical significance of the doctrine of creation shifts theological thought, by necessity, within the framework of a systematic theology, which is primarily evident in the "high hermeneutic" handling of creation in the dialectical theologies of Karl Barth and Emil Brunner, in relation to the "low hermeneutic" approach to creation in the philosophical theologies of Paul Tillich and Karl Rahner. Under what has been labeled as "dialectical theology," creation figures hermeneutically in Barth's fourteen-volume *Church Dogmatics* (1932–1967) as functionally situated between God and "Reconciliation," while, in his three-volume *Dogmatics* (1949, 1952, 1962), Brunner places creation alongside "redemption" and functionally situated between God and a relationship between church, faith, and "consummation." However, by way of a philosophical theology (or an existential theology), creation figures hermeneutically in Tillich's three-volume *Systematic Theology* (1951, 1957, 1963) within the "actuality of God" through a broader question of the meaning of being, while, in *Foundations of Christian Faith* (1976), Rahner places creation between God's "self-communication" predicated on the meaning of "man as event."

––––––––– APPENDIX E –––––––––

Paul as Tragic Hero and the Use of the Soliloquy

––––––––– An Exegesis of Acts 20:17–38 –––––––––

As Paul's third speech, Acts 20:17–38 is specifically addressed to Christians and does so in the form of a literary soliloquy, where Paul presents both a theology and an apologia: a philosophy and defense. Paul's theology as an apologia not only expresses that Paul is "serving the Lord with all humility and with tears, enduring the trials that came to me" (20:19a–b) but, moreover, that, regardless of "the plots of the Jews" (20:19c), Paul "did not shrink from doing anything helpful, proclaiming the message to you and teaching you publicly and from house to house" (20:20). For Paul, by his being "a captive to the Spirit" (20:22a), reiterating the theological importance of Jews and Greeks "repent[ing] towards God and [assuming] faith toward our Lord Jesus" (20:21) becomes just as important as defending to the Ephesian elders why "I lived among you the entire time from the first day that I set foot in Asia" (20:18b–c).

What becomes significant, then, about Paul's massage to the Ephesian elders is that, while it interrupts the "we" structure employed in Acts 20:7–16, which is subsequently picked up again in Acts 21, it is chiefly concerned with Paul providing an orderly account of himself and a defense of his ministry.

Particularly in soliloquy, as a format of accounting for and defending himself, Paul makes an impassioned plea to the Ephesian elders to "keep watch over yourselves and over all the flock" (20:28). This plea, in the capable hands of Luke, employs the uses of rhetoric to persuade toward what is justly concerned, arouse a passion for doing just acts as a Christian, and soliciting empathy in the justness of Paul's authority. Not just through the apparent utilization of Aristotle-influenced literary concepts of rhetoric but also those of poetics—this is in relation to Paul representing a tragic hero that assumes distinctive, tragedy-infused language—the Paul that Luke advances is a tragic figure to arouse hope, passion, and preservation among the Ephesian faithful.

Similarly to Luke's dedication to Theophilus in Luke 1:4, Luke's Paul depicted in Acts 20:17–38 wants to extrapolate "the truth concerning things about [himself and what it means to be a Christian operating in the Christian faith] which [Christians] have been [already] instructed." This truth is more than just about the truth of the kingdom (20:26b) but about Paul embracing the tragic reality that "I am on my way to Jerusalem, not knowing what will happen to me there, except that the Holy Spirit testifies to me in every city that imprisonment and persecutions are waiting for me" (20:22b–23). As uncertain as he is with regards to what will happen to him when he leaves Ephesus for Jerusalem, Paul, for Luke, is a tragic hero. To say "tragic hero" does not strictly mean "tragic" in the sense of some tragic virtue or tragic flaw that predicts or foreshadows a tragic hero's undoing, fall, or death—this, of course, is the Shakespearean tragic hero in terms of some unavoidable, human failing in a Shakespearean hero's personality. Paul, throughout the second half of Acts and, specifically, within the passage at study in this exegesis, is not a Shakespearean hero, but is, for all practical purposes, much closer to the Aristotle version of a tragic hero. In that respect, then, what Luke does with Paul as a tragic hero is present a man ruled by such unshakable, superhuman convictions about faith and truth. Paul is a man that is fully aware of his awaiting tragedy but, nevertheless, sees that tragedy simply as validation of his heroism and his heroic deeds in teaching the Christian faith to the Ephesians so that he might become an example to others of a heroic life well lived.

Just as Jesus Christ is rendered as a tragic hero in the Gospel of Luke,[1] Luke's Paul in Acts 20: 17–38 displays a significant amount of humanity while exuding something transcendent of that humanity. Since Paul does not know what awaits him in Jerusalem, he is aware of the worst possible scenarios: imprisonment and persecution. But, more importantly, by the fact that Paul suggests that none of the Ephesian elders "will ever see [his] face again" (20:25c), Paul seemingly points to an awareness of death possibly awaiting him, as well. This, undoubtedly, leads Paul to reflect on the manner with which he has lived his life as it comes to bear on the means with which the Holy Spirit testifies to him of how his life will come to an end. This is precisely behind Paul "not [needing to] count my life of any value to myself" (20:24a) if it means that he will not "finish [his] course and the ministry that [he] received from the Lord Jesus, to testify to the good news of God's grace" (20:24b–c). Knowing that the Ephesian elders "will [never] see [his] face again" (20:25c), Paul is worried that there will be a power vacuum in the Ephesian church. In the case of such an event, Luke's Paul knows that the truth concerning himself and his teaching will be threatened in his absence, which is a kind of death of his teachings that is more important to him than death itself—this is fundamentally analogous to Luke's Jesus, as previously noted, in Luke 23:28, with Jesus saying, "Daughters of Jerusalem, do not weep for me, but weep for yourselves and for your children."

---

1. This is in reference to the depictions of Jesus in the Gethsemane scene of Luke 22:42–44, the crucifixion scene of Luke 23:28, and the death of Jesus in 23:46. All three of these scenes make Jesus a tragic hero that wrestles with his heroism but, also, is fully aware of the necessities of that heroism even in the face of tragedy.

It becomes apparent, therefore, that Paul is not concerned with the Ephesian elders weeping for him or for what might happen to him in Jerusalem but, instead, wants them to "weep for [themselves] and for [their] children" by keeping watch over themselves and over their flock (20:27). To do this, Paul believes that "the Holy Spirit has made [the Ephesian elders] overseers, to shepherd the church of God that he obtained with the blood of his own Son" (20:28). For Luke's Paul, there is an uneasy wariness of, once Paul has gone, "savage wolves [coming] in among [the elders], not sparing the flock" (20:29). These savage wolves, for Paul, will threaten the integrity of the truth because they "will come distorting the truth in order to entice the disciples to follow them" (20:30) and they will need to be alert (20:31a). To distort the truth means to compromise the truth to disastrous proportions and, for Paul as a tragic hero that "worked with [his] hands to support [himself] and [his] companions" (20:34) in an effort to instill the truth in Ephesus, this is of a greater concern than his possible imprisonment, persecution, or death. Here, Luke's Paul as a tragic hero is aware of his heroic legacy as it has been manifested in his heroic deeds for the Ephesians. Paul's work, therefore, is what he wants to leave behind. Paul addresses this directly with: "In all this I have given you an example that by such work we must support the weak, remembering the words of the Lord Jesus, for he himself said, 'It is more blessed to give than to receive'" (20:35).

Even though the Gospels do not include Jesus having said, "It is more blessed to give than to receive," the essence of this Pauline saying within Acts 20:17–38, frankly, epitomizes Luke's necessity of Paul being a tragic heroic figure whose heroic deed is meant to impart what it means to live an exemplary Christian life. As an articulation of the Christian life, Paul's tragic soliloquy is meant to induce "much weeping among [the Ephesian elders]" (20:37) not just because of what Paul says to them (20:38a) or that Paul would not see the Ephesian elders again (20:38b) but because of Luke's Paul's status as a tragic hero.

APPENDIX F

Vision, Seeing, and Sight

— An Exegesis of Acts 9:1–22 —

IN ACTS 9:1–22, THE conversion of Saul is presented as a divinely inspired transformational event of revelation. What makes this event particularly significant is that it depicts the conversion of a persecutor of the followers of Christ into a follower and advocate of the teachings of Jesus Christ. This conversion, then, lays the thematic groundwork for not only the eventual, nomenclatural shift from Saul to Paul but, more importantly, the theological shift of a Jewish man's traditional Judaic principles and beliefs—a way of life that would have deemed the teachings of the Christ's disciples as a theological affront to Judaism—to a Christ-inspired man that adopts the principles and beliefs that forerun Christianity. Saul's theological shift, as it is depicted in Acts 9:1–22, is outlined by a systematic, christological framework: the relationship between the act of sinning, the grace of God, and the opportunity of a sinner, through the power in the grace of God, being afforded salvation through the acceptance of Christ. The missing interrelational component, however, in the way this passage outlines a systematic, christological framework is Saul's request for forgiveness, which is considered the christological impetus for God's grace. In the place of a request for forgiveness, Saul's metaphysical vision on the road to Damascus functions as this impetus. Whether spiritual or physical, concepts of vision, seeing, and sight all become important thematic recurrences throughout this passage, where these concepts often invoke transformational agency.

At the beginning of the passage, at Acts 9:2, where Saul, who has already been described in a visually-interpretive manner as "breathing threats and murder against the disciples of the Lord,"[1] goes to the high priest and "asked him for letters to the synagogues at Damascus." These letters provide visual proof for Saul's authority to apprehend "any who belonged to the Way, men or women [so that] he might bring them bound to Jerusalem." To bring "any who belonged to the Way" bound to

---

1. Acts 9:1.

Jerusalem represents the physical manifestation of their identification as fugitives. If brought to Jerusalem in such an ocular way at the hand of Saul, not only would Saul be viewed as a champion of the Jewish faithful, but those that "belonged to the Way" would be perceived as pariahs and outcasts. Perception, for Saul, becomes important: what is seen, what is perceived, and what is interpreted embody a kind of succinct validation for him.

By Acts 9:3, when Saul is "going along and approaching Damascus" to carry out further visual persecution against Christians, "a light from heaven flashed around him" causing Saul to fall to the ground, where he hears a voice saying to him, "Saul, Saul, why do you persecute me?"[2] When Saul asks, "Who are you, Lord," he is requesting visual proof. What Saul receives accordingly is the reply of, "I am Jesus, whom you are persecuting. But get up and enter the city, and you will be told what you are to do."[3] It is here, perhaps, that it can be ascertained that Saul sees something that serves as visual validation for the voice belonging to Jesus. For Saul to request visual proof, it would be likely that this proof would be manifested in some interpretative, tangible way. To that end, more specifically, if "the men who were traveling with [Saul] stood speechless because they heard the voice but saw no one,"[4] Saul, upon hearing that voice, "saw" something, even if what he "saw" can be better categorized as spiritual rather than physical. In following that line of logic, it stands to reason that what Saul perceives and interprets from what he "saw" in his spiritually induced mind's eye was enough validation to, eventually, physically blind Saul. Though this infirmity, perhaps, handicaps Saul so that he has to be "led by the hand and brought"[5] to Damascus, it presents an opportunity for Saul to meditate and fast over the "three days he was without sight [where he] never ate nor drank."[6] This christological, three-day period of meditation and fasting further affords Paul/Saul's a spiritual vision of "a man named Ananias [who will] come in and lay his hands on [Saul] so that [Saul] might regain his sight."[7]

The man named Ananias, who has been instructed by the Lord to "get up and go to the street called Straight, and at the house of Judas look for a man of Tarsus named Saul,"[8] receives a joint vision. In response to this vision, Ananias is hesitant to do as the Lord instructs based on secondhand knowledge from those that have seen "how much evil [Paul/Saul] has done to [the Lord's saints in Jerusalem."[9] To assist Ananias in "seeing" the importance of what the Lord wants him to do, the Lord says, "Go, for

2. Acts 9:4.
3. Acts 9:5.
4. Acts 9:7.
5. Acts 9:8.
6. Acts 9:9.
7. Acts 9:12.
8. Acts 9:10–11b.
9. Acts 9:13.

[Saul] is an instrument whom I have chosen to bring my name before the Gentiles and kings and before the people of Israel; I myself will show [Saul] how much be must suffer for the sake of my name."[10] The things that the Lord "will show" Saul serve as validations for Saul's divine purpose.

In Acts 9:17, Ananias locates Saul and lays hands on him, saying, "Brother Saul, the Lord Jesus, who has appeared to you on your way here, has sent me so that you may regain your sight and be filled with the Holy Spirit." Since Saul is physically blind, he has no visual proof that Ananias is who he claims to be beyond the "letters to the synagogues at Damascus" that would still be assumedly in Saul's possession. So, Saul's validation of Ananias occurs by way of his aforementioned vision: what Saul has spiritually "seen." Once Ananias carries out his divine purpose upon Saul, "something like scales fell from [Saul's] eyes, and his sight was restored. Then, [Saul] got up and was baptized."[11] The regaining of Saul's physical sight, then, becomes significant, because it is personified as a new way of "seeing," a regenerated means of vision structured by a spiritual-theological awakening. In turn, to highlight Saul's spiritual-theological awakening, his being baptized illustrates a visual necessity for Saul to see and be seen by physically engaging in the practice of the purification of his sins. Following this baptism, Saul embarks on a fellowship with the disciples in Damascus and "immediately he began to proclaim Jesus in the synagogues saying 'He is the Son of God.'"[12] Here, Saul's fellowship with the same persons that he had previously "breath[ed] threats and murder against" as well as his physical presence in the synagogues exalting what he had once condemned invokes a specific visual of change, transcendence, and transformation.

This visual would have been shocking to those that witnessed it. Therefore, it stands to reason that "all who heard [Saul] were amazed and said, 'Is not this the man who made havoc in Jerusalem among those who invoked [the name of Jesus as the Son of God]? And has he not come here for the purpose of bringing them before the chief priests?'"[13] The conflict here, quite frankly, is between what Saul was seen as being in the past and what he is being seen as in the present—in this, it becomes problematic for "all who heard him" to see Saul as a champion of Jesus. Nevertheless, as Acts 9:22 states, since "Saul became increasingly more powerful and confounded the Jews who lived in Damascus by proving that Jesus was the Messiah," it illustrates how Saul was seen in the Jewish and Christian communities through the ways and means by which he saw and choice to show others that "Jesus was the Messiah."

The evidence of Acts 9:1–22 being preoccupied with the concepts of vision, seeing, and sight assumes a similar stylistic, literary trope in reference to where this passage fits into literary contexts of what comes before it and what occurs afterward.

10. Acts 9:15–16.
11. Acts 9:18.
12. Acts 9:20.
13. Acts 9:21.

First, in Acts 8:36–38, like Saul's conversion on the road to Damascus, Philip and the eunuch are going along the road when they, too, experience an event of transformation. Vision, seeing, and sight play an important role in 8:36–38 when Philip and the eunuch see a body of water along the road and Philip envisions that body of water as a means of converting the eunuch—the visual act of baptizing the eunuch ensues, where, once Philip is said to be "snatched away"[14] by the Spirit of the Lord, the eunuch goes on his way rejoicing in seeing something revelatory and attaining a newfound sight in that revelation. Second, when considering Acts 9:23–31, concepts of vision, seeing, and sight all come to bear in Saul's ability to escape the Jews in Damascus plotting to kill him when "their plot became known to Saul,"[15] perhaps, arguably, in the form of a vision. Seeing and sight, more specifically, are employed physically when "[those that were with Saul] were watching the gates day and night so that they might kill him."[16] Again, in 9:26, seeing and sight are exemplified in Saul attempting to join the disciples in Jerusalem in light of those that "were all afraid of him, for they did not believe that he was a disciple." Not only does this passage express the inability of the disciples to see Saul as being anything more than a persecutor but a greater inability to understand Saul's vision and resulting conversion on the road to Damascus. This misperception of Saul, or an underlying ineffectiveness with physical seeing and sight, is perceived differently on behalf of the apostles who seem able to spiritually see Saul's intentions enough to bring Saul down to Caesarea and send him to Tarsus once the Hellenists Saul argued with were attempting to kill him.[17]

Visions, seeing, and sight are essential concepts toward understanding how Acts 9:1–22 functions not just in its literary context but in it theological-ideological context. What can be ascertained, then, from the employing of these concepts is the addressing of certain conflicts existing in the human hermeneutical process in relation to the negotiation of the spiritual and the physical. What is seen physically is not always exemplified in what is seen spiritually, and vice versa. In this respect, visions, seeing, and sight further explore the connotations of what kind of evidence can be derived from what may not be seen[18] as well as the ability of walking by faith and not by sight.[19]

14. Acts 8:39.
15. Acts 9:24.
16. Acts 9:24.
17. Acts 9:29–30.
18. Heb 11:1.
19. 2 Cor 5:8.

APPENDIX G

Christophanic Moments, Ontological Proof, and Existential Truth in the Conversion of Saul

An Exegesis of Acts 9:1–18

ACTS 9:1–18 DEPICTS THE conversion of Saul as a divinely inspired event of transformational proportions and theological significance. Strictly in terms of being a transformational event, what happens to Saul, first, is a change in identity: from a Jewish man traditional Judaic principles and beliefs to a Christ-inspired man that adopts the principles and beliefs that constitute Christianity. More specifically, having "breath[ed] threats and murder against the disciples of the Lord" (9:1), Saul becomes a standard-bearer for the same "disciples of the Lord" whom he had persecuted by wanting to "[bring] them bound to Jerusalem" (9:2). This, of course, leads to the theological significance of Saul's transformation. In it, it becomes possible for a known persecutor of those "who belonged to the Way" to become a follower of "the Way" on the heels of divinely inspired event. The event that occurs on the road to Damascus lays the thematic groundwork not only for the eventual, nomenclatural shift from Saul to Paul, but the theological shift in Saul's thinking.[1] Essentially, the event can be viewed as a christophanic[2] moment of ontological proof[3] for Saul of the existence of

---

1. By this, I mean to say that Saul becomes something more than just a Jew, as well as something more than a man "breathing threats and murder against the disciples of the Lord" but becomes a Jewish Christian focused on carrying out the very charge the resurrected Jesus placed in his disciples to "go therefore and make disciples of all nations, baptizing them in the name of the Father and of the Son and of the Holy Spirit, and teaching them to obey everything that I have commanded you" (Matt 28:19–20a).

2. This is a derivative of the term "christophany." The term, itself, is an NT adaptation of "theophany," specifically involving the appearance of Christ to man, rather than the appearance of God to man. Ferguson and Wright, *New Dictionary of Theology*, 681.

3. I use this term as an adaptation of the theological concept of "ontological argument," which is an argument for God which moves from the definition of God's nature as a perfect being to the conclusion that God exists. To say "ontological argument" is to conceive of proofs for the existence of God and is to distinguish this by claiming to be a genuinely a priori argument. So, to appropriate "ontological argument" into "ontological proof" means to examine, specifically, the means by which proof,

317

Jesus Christ from a divinely-inspired vision, from which he, ultimately, develops an existential truth[4] about his being-in-itself[5] and his being-in-the world.[6]

Paul's Vision and the Christophanic Moment

After 9:1–2, Saul is described as "going along and approaching Damascus" (9:3a) when "suddenly a light from heaven flashed around him" (9:3b). In this, it is possible to ascertain that, if taking "a light" at face value, what "[Saul] saw, within the light, [was] Jesus himself, in Jesus's risen and glorified body."[7] Though this is not explicitly expressed in 9:3, the fact that "a light from heaven [suddenly] flashed around [Saul]" would arguably make it plausible that Saul, being surprised by the sudden appearance of the light, would have sent his eyes searching for the origin of that light. What would Saul have seen within that light? Even if Saul looked into that light for a moment, it was within that moment—a moment of actually seeing "Jesus's risen and glorified body" suspended within that light—that Saul would have been overcome by the vision itself. This is particularly the case if taking into account that a "light from heaven" signifies a divine revelation. More specifically, "the light" could be interpreted as a "lightning-swift light brighter than Syria's noonday sun [which] could only be the shekinah glory [that is] indicative of the divine presence."[8] To say all of this, then, is to suggest that Saul is aware of the magnitude of such a divine presence to the extent that "he fell to the ground" (9:4). Undoubtedly, what can be gleaned from Saul's action is his awareness of the theophanic implications within this encounter, since the light is not only "brighter than the sun, [but] has

---

whatever form it may manifest itself, presents the most basic possibility of ascertaining "being" within that proof. Reese, *Dictionary of Philosophy and Religion*, 400.

4. Though this means that the truth is subjective, it also derives from the notion that the individual and universal exist in its individuality. That is to say that the "truth" is not a kind of reality any more than it corresponds to a given reality. Instead, to say "existential truth" is to suggest that there is a meaning of reality for the individual based on how the individual chooses to perceive, interpret, or define it. Berdyaev, *Truth and Revelation*, 27.

5. Martin Heidegger uses this term when explaining how a being uses existence to establish selfhood. For Heidegger, this occurs only when the basic structures of human existence, or what he calls "dasein," has been adequately worked out with explicit orientation toward the problem of "being" itself. Being-in-itself, then, is an existential justification that is gained from the interpretation of human existence. To use this term in reference to Saul, I am working under the assumption that, by Saul eventually changing his name to Paul, he is aware of an essential change in his being-in-itself, whereby it becomes inadequate to continue to call himself Saul after his conversion. Heidegger, *Being and Time*, 37.

6. "Being-in-the-world" is a term coined by German existentialist Martin Heidegger in *Being and Time*, where he analyzes this original, unitary phenomenon into the following three constituent elements: (1) in the world, (2) the being that is in the way of being-in-the-world, and (3) being-in as such. For Heidegger, "dasein," which is the German word for existence, is the being that is in-the-world. Gordon, *Dictionary of Existentialism*, 37; 100.

7. Dummelow, *Commentary on the Holy Bible*, 830.

8. Howley et al., *New Layman's Bible Commentary*, 1354.

surround[ed] [Saul's] companions as well as himself."[9] If assuming that Saul does not know what or who he sees within that light,[10] the fact that Saul "heard a voice saying to him, 'Saul, Saul, why do you persecute me'" (9:4b–c) would only add credence to the possibility that Saul is experiencing a Moses-like moment, where "the voice from the light . . . recalls the voice from the bush in Exodus 3:3 and from [Mount] Sinai in Exodus 19:16–20."[11] To interject this is to explain why, in 9:5a, Saul asked, "Who are you, Lord?" By merely addressing whatever he sees within that light as "Lord," it is conceivable to suggest that "Saul does not yet know it is Jesus who is Lord, [even if] he recognizes that he is involved in a theophany."[12]

It is not until receiving the reply of "I am Jesus, whom you are persecuting" (9:5b) that Saul realizes—to whatever extent or capacity therein—that he is involved in a christophanic moment. This, in effect, can be lifted theologically from the reply Saul receives that provides "a revelation which meant that, in one tremendous moment of time, Saul had to identify the Lord Jehovah of the OT whom he zealously sought to serve, with Jesus of Nazareth whom he ferociously persecuted in the person of His saints."[13]

Christophanic Moment as Ontological Proof

In Saul's christophanic moment, he is given ontological proof of the post-death, resurrected existence of Jesus so that "the actual sight of the Lord's person [implies] that [Saul] became a witness of the Lord's resurrection."[14] Being a witness as he is, Saul becomes privy to "the burden of the revelation [that] is not information about Jesus, but a commission for Saul."[15] To say this is to suggest that it is not enough for Saul to have his christophanic moment any more than it is merely sufficient to connect that moment to the ontological proof of the existence of the resurrected Jesus. In this, Saul is meant to discover the ontological proof of the Way's validity, as well as proof of the wrongheadedness of his persecution. It means that the proof presented to Saul is meant to arouse within him the same zeal he used to persecute those that belonged to the Way. Because Saul is told further by the voice he hears to "get up and enter the city, and you will be told what you are to do" (9:6), the ontological proof of what Saul sees and hears changes Saul's sense of being. This occurs in two ways: his being-in-itself and his being-in-the world. On one hand, Saul is changed by way of his being-in-itself, where, in a single christophanic moment of ontological proof, Saul is able to

9. Johnson, *Acts of the Apostles*, 163.
10. That is, working from the notion that Saul seeing Jesus's "risen and glorified body" within the light.
11. Johnson, *Acts of the Apostles*, 163.
12. Johnson, *Acts of the Apostles*, 163.
13. Howley et al., *New Layman's Bible Commentary*, 1354.
14. Irwin, *Irwin's Bible Commentary*, 451.
15. Johnson, *Acts of the Apostles*, 163.

separate his former existence as a persecutor of the Way from a new existence as a member of the Way. Specifically, Saul's realization—or, more aptly, his revelation—of his christophanic experience as ontological proof presents him with a past that must be compartmentalized into the past so that his present and future may position him to be "told what [he is] to do." To that extent, Saul's being-in-the-world is changed, particularly if considering that being-in-the-world involves "[an] immersed character of human existence insofar as it relates to being, [by] opening up the clearing in which beings can be encountered in meaningful relations."[16] For Saul, while these relations[17] are interpersonal,[18] his "being-in-the-world" is affected by an existential meaning derived from those interpersonal relations, which, in turn, become relative to how Saul is meant to affect other beings.[19] In other words, Saul's christophanic experience is not meant to stand alone. Instead, it explains the connection[20] between Saul's christophanic experience on the road to Damascus and the Ananias's vision, where Ananias is told to "get up and go to the street called Straight, and at the house of Judas look for a man of Tarsus named Saul" (9:11).

Ontological Proof as Existential Truth

The christophanic experience of Ananias overrides Ananias's previously held ontological proof of what Ananias knows of Saul already. From this, Ananias has developed an existential truth about Saul that he understandably expresses to the voice he hears by saying "Lord, I have heard from many about this man, how much evil he has done to your saints in Jerusalem and here he has authority from the chief priests to bind all who invoke your name" (9:13–14). What Ananias is articulating, quite frankly, is fear

---

16. Gordon, *Dictionary of Existentialism*, 37; 100.

17. The term "relations" or, in the singular form, "relation," is a concept of human existence or the nature of a being that stresses specific relations for self-realization. These relations are necessary conditions or constitutive elements for realizing a dimension of humanity such as true selfhood, the authentic self, freedom, engagement, and true personality. Gordon, *Dictionary of Existentialism*, 397.

18. To this end, "interpersonal" can also mean "impression," as in an exchange of impressions that occurs between two beings engaged in interpersonal contact. What this further points to, then, when considering what happens to Saul, is the idea of existence and external existence as it is outlined by David Hume in *Treatise on Human Nature*. Hume suggests, in this work, that a being never remembers any idea or impression without attributing existence to it because the idea of existence must either be derived from a distinct impression, conjoined with every perception or object of our thought, or must be the very same with the idea of the perception or object. What this can be applied to is the impression Saul has of the resurrected Jesus and the perception of what it is that that impression comes to mean in terms of its idea. Hume, *Treatise on Human Nature*, 41.

19. In the *Sophist* dialogue, Plato explains "being" as anything which possesses any sort of power to affect another, or to be affected by another, if only for a single moment, however trifling the cause and however slight the effect. To that end, it has real existence. The definition of being, then, is simply power. Hamilton and Cairns, *Collected Dialogues of Plato*, 957–1017.

20. Just as the Lord has appeared to Saul on the road, so he speaks to Ananias in a vision. Laymon, *Interpreter's One-Volume Commentary on the Bible*, 740.

of Saul. This fear is an existential fear[21] that has developed from what he had learned by word of mouth about Saul's exploits. In this fear, there is resistance and hesitation.[22] Also, there is a reluctance to do as the Lord has instructed, where "Ananias' reluctance, which appears to be an affront to the risen Christ [personified in the voice Ananias hears], serves to emphasize the greatness of [Saul's] conversion."[23] Of course, Ananias is not aware of Saul's conversion any more than he is of the "greatness" of it. What Ananias needs is further christophanic intervention and ontological proof in order to ascertain an existential truth in why he should "look for" Saul in the first place. This is why the Lord tells Ananias, "Go, for he is an instrument whom I have chosen to bring my name before Gentiles and kings and before the people of Israel" (9:15). Particularly, in being informed that Saul is "an instrument whom [the Lord] has chosen," Ananias is given ontological proof of Saul's election "in spite of [Saul's] past."[24] So, with this proof in hand that becomes nurtured in the existential truth of what Saul has become and the purpose that Ananias must serve, Ananias "went and entered the house [of Judas and] laid his hands on Saul" (9:17).

By the time this occurs, Saul has already lost his sight on the heels of his christophanic experience (9:8), where "for three days he was without sight, and neither ate nor drank" (9:9). Though the time between Saul's experience on the road to Damascus and the moment when Ananias meets him in the house of Judas suggests that the "the three days' rest was necessary so that Saul might recover from the shock and meditate on the meaning of the celestial encounter before receiving further messages,"[25] it can also be construed as the necessity for further ontological proof to reach a different level of existential truth. For Saul, the christophanic experience is only the first step to his overall transformation. Losing his sight is an existential truth,[26] where, as he "recover[s] from the shock and meditate[s] on the meaning of the celestial encounter before receiving further messages," Saul must be afforded further ontological proof of his commission, or election, to being "an instrument whom [the Lord] has chosen." Ananias's role, here, is to provide just that, since he is "probably the head of the Christian body of Damascus."[27] Undoubtedly, this stands to reason why Ananias and Saul

---

21. Heidegger refers to this kind of fear as a "state-of-mind" that arises from seeing, or perceiving, the fearsomeness in the potentiality of the object of fear "drawing close" or "coming close" within the existential spatiality of being-in-the-world. Heidegger, *Being and Time*, 180.

22. According to Luke Johnson, human hesitancy is legitimate, but can be overturned by the command of the Lord. Johnson, *Acts of the Apostles*, 164.

23. Laymon, *Interpreter's One-Volume Commentary*, 740.

24. Laymon, *Interpreter's One-Volume Commentary*, 740.

25. Howley et al., *New Layman's Bible Commentary*, 1354.

26. By this, I mean to suggest that Saul's loss of vision represents the existential truth of his life of sin by being a persecutor of those that belonged to the Way. Losing his vision, specifically, suggests that eyes must be renewed in order to carry out his mission as "an instrument of the Lord."

27. Dummelow, *Commentary on the Holy Bible*, 830.

would have corresponding visions[28] but, more poignantly, places them at a theological junction. In other words, Ananias's authority in the Damascus church is meant to legitimize Saul's authority. Here, with Ananias having "laid his hands on Saul and [saying], 'Brother Saul, the Lord Jesus who appeared to you on your way here, has sent me so that you may regain your sight and be filled with the Holy Spirit'" (9:17), Saul is given further ontological proof. Not only is this in reference to the christophanic experience he had on the road to Damascus but, moreover, that his blindness was for a purpose. From this, Saul is presented with another degree[29] of existential truth—it is the truth that what happened to him happened for a reason and that he is to be empowered by being "filled with the Holy Spirit."

Existential Truth and Paul's Apostleship

Once Ananias has "laid hands on Saul" and "scales fell from his eyes and his sight was restored" (9:18), what Saul sees when "his sight was restored" is an existential truth about his existence. Though it might be regarded as "simply a symbolic way to describe the miracle,"[30] it is also possible to interpret this phenomenon as metaphorical rather than literal, where "the light that blinded [Saul] paradoxically relieved him of his spiritual blindness."[31] No matter how it is interpreted, as previusly mentioned, it is based on Saul's christophanic experience, which involved a change in his sense of being through his being-in-itself and his being-in-the-world. This is, of course, personified in Saul's baptism which, as Paul states in Acts 22:16, permits him to "have [his] sins washed away." Not only does it allow Saul to "be fully incorporated into the life of the community [but] the baptism completes [Saul's] ritual passage out of the sacral state he was in since his vision, a return to profane existence signaled by his taking of food."[32] From there, having reestablished his existence, Saul establishes his apostleship.

---

28. Laymon, *Interpreter's One-Volume Commentary on the Bible*, 740.

29. In interjecting "another degree," I mean to propose that existential truth is not all-encompassing, or all-actualizing. Instead, there is a continual actualization process that occurs between ontological proof and existential truth. To say this I mean to assert that only a certain amount of ontological proof provides a certain amount of existential truth. It is proportional. When considering this in terms of what happens to Saul, for example, he is given only a degree of ontological proof to be afforded the appropriation of an equivalent degree of existential truth, respectively. This logic is an extrapolation and reinterpretation of Nikolai Berdyaev's concept of knowledge as a function of the growth of being, and that being is developed from the creative act of the spirit. Berdyaev, *Meaning of the Creative Act*, 42.

30. Laymon, *Interpreter's One-Volume Commentary*, 740.

31. Johnson, *Acts of the Apostles*, 165.

32. Johnson, *Acts of the Apostles*, 165.

Bibliography

Ackerman, Denise M. "From Mere Existence to Tenacious Endurance." In *African Women, Religion, and Health*, edited by Isabel A. Phiri and Sarojini Nadar, 221–42. Maryknoll: Orbis, 2006.

Agamben, Giorgio. *Homo Sacer: Sovereign Power and Bare Life*. Stanford: Stanford University Press, 1995.

Akoto, Dorothy. "Women and Health in Ghana and the Trokosi Practice." In *African Women, Religion, and Health*, edited by Isabel A. Phiri and Sarojini Nadar, 96–110. Maryknoll: Orbis, 2006.

Althusser, Louis. "Ideology and Ideological State Apparatuses." In Parker, *Critical Theory*, 449–61.

———. *Lenin and Philosophy and Other Essays*. Translated by Ben Brewster. New York: Monthly Review, 2001.

Anderson, James F., ed. *An Introduction to the Metaphysics of St. Thomas Aquinas*. Washington, DC: Regnery Gateway, 1953.

Anderson, Victor. *Beyond Ontological Blackness: An Essay on African American Religious and Cultural Criticism*. New York: Bloomsbury, 2016.

Anselm, Saint. *Monologion and Proslogion: With the Replies of Gaunilo and Anselm*. Translated by Thomas Williams. Indianapolis: Hackett: 1995.

Anti-Climacus. *The Sickness unto Death: A Christian Psychological Exposition for Upbuilding and Awakening*. Princeton: Princeton University Press, 1941.

Apostle, Hippocrates G., ed. *Aristotle's Metaphysics*. Des Moines: Peripatetic, 1979.

Aquinas, Thomas. *The Summa Theologiae of Saint Thomas Aquinas*. Vol. 1. Scotts Valley, CA: NovAntiqua, 2008.

Ariew, Roger, and Daniel Garber, eds. *G. W. Leibniz: Philosophical Essays*. Indianapolis: Hackett, 1989.

Aristotle. *Nicomachean Ethics*. Translated by Hippocrates G. Apostle. Grinnell: Peripathetic, 1975.

———. *Nicomachean Ethics*. Translated by Terence Irwin. Indianapolis: Hackett, 1985.

Augustine, Saint. *Confessions and Enchiridion*. Translated by Albert C. Outler. Louisville: Westminster, 1955.

Aumann, Antony. "Kierkegaard on Indirect Communication, the Crowd, and a Monstrous Illusion." In *International Kierkegaard Commentary*, vol. 22, *The Point of View*, edited by Robert L. Perkins, 295–324. Macon: Mercer University Press, 2010.

Bakhtin, Mikhail M. *The Dialogic Imagination: Four Essays*. Austin: University of Texas Press, 1981.

———. *Problems of Dostoyevsky's Poetics*. Translated by Caryl Emerson. Minneapolis: University of Minnesota, 1984.

Barrett, William. *Irrational Man: A Study of Existential Philosophy*. New York: Anchor, 1958.

Barth, Karl. *Evangelical Theology: An Introduction*. Grand Rapids: Eerdmans, 1963.

———. *The Humanity of God*. Louisville: Westminster John Knox, 1960.

Barthes, Roland. "The Death of the Author." In *The Norton Anthology of Theory and Criticism*, edited by Vincent B. Leitch, 1322–26. New York: Norton, 2010.

Beauvoir, Simone de. *The Second Sex*. Translated by Constance Borde and Sheila Malovany-Chevallier. New York: Knopf, 2010.

Bell, Walter G. *The Great Plague in London in 1665*. London: Bodleyhead, 1924.

Berdyaev, Nikolai. *The Destiny of Man*. Translated by Natalie Duddington. London: MacLehose, 1937.

———. *The Divine and the Human*. Translated by R. M. French. London: Bles, 1949.

———. *The Meaning of the Creative Act*. Translated by Donald A. Lowrie. New York: Harper, 1955.

———. *The Russian Idea*. Translated by R. M. French. London: Bles, 1947.

———. *Truth and Revelation*. Translated by R. M. French. New York: Collier, 1962.

———. "Truth of Orthodoxy." *Wheel* 8 (2017) 47–53.

Bethune, George W. *Expository Lectures on the Heidelberg Catechism*. New York: Sheldon, 1864.

Blount, Brian K. *Then the Whisper Put on Flesh: New Testament Ethics in an African American Context*. Nashville: Abingdon, 2001.

Bonhoeffer, Dietrich. *Act and Being: Transcendental Philosophy and Ontology in Systematic Theology*. Translated by Hans-Richard Reuter. Minneapolis: Fortress, 2009.

Boyle, Robert. *The Excellency of Theology, Compar'd with Natural Philosophy*. London: Anchor in the Lower Walk of the New Exchange, 1674.

Bradley, Anthony B. *Liberating Black Theology: The Bible and the Black Experience in America*. Wheaton: Crossway, 2010.

Braidotti, Rosi. *The Posthuman*. Malden, MA: Polity, 2013.

Bretall, Robert, ed. *A Kierkegaard Anthology*. Princeton: Princeton University Press, 1973.

Brown, James. *Subject and Object in Modern Theology*. New York: Macmillan, 1953.

Buber, Martin. *Good and Evil: Two Interpretations*. New York: Scribner, 1953.

Cain, Seymour. *Gabriel Marcel*. South Bend, IN: Gateway, 1963.

Calvin, John. *The Institutes of the Christian Religion*. Translated by Henry Beveridge. Grand Rapids: Christian Classics Ethereal Library, 2002.

Cannon, Katie G. *Black Womanist Ethics*. Atlanta: Scholars, 1988.

Cavanaugh, William T., et al., eds. *An Eerdmans Reader in Contemporary Theology*. Grand Rapids: Eerdmans, 2012.

Climacus, Johannes. *Concluding Unscientific Postscript to Philosophical Crumbs*. Edited by Soren Kierkegaard. Translated by Alastair Hannay. New York: Cambridge University Press, 2009.

Cobb, John B. *The Structure of Christian Existence*. Louisville: Westminster, 1967.

Coffey, Peter. *Ontology; or, The Theory of Being*. London: Longmans, Green, 1914.

Coleman, Monica. *Making a Way out of No Way: A Womanist Theology*. Minneapolis: Fortress, 2008.

Collins, Patricia H. *Black Feminist Thought: Knowledge, Consciousness, and the Politics of Empowerment.* New York: Routledge, 1990.

Cone, James H. *The Black Church and Marxism.* New York: Institute for Democratic Institutions, 1982.

———. *Black Theology and Black Power.* New York: HarperCollins, 1969.

———. *A Black Theology of Liberation.* Maryknoll: Orbis, 1986.

———. *God of the Oppressed.* New York: HarperCollins, 1975.

Copeland, M. Shawn. "Black Political Theologies." In *The Blackwell Companion to Political Theology*, edited by Peter Scott and William T. Cavanaugh, 271–87. Malden, MA: Blackwell, 2004.

———. *Enfleshing Freedom: Body, Race, and Being.* Minneapolis: Fortress, 2010.

Copleston, Frederick. *A History of Philosophy.* Vol. 6, *Wolff to Kant.* Westminster, MD: Newman, 1960.

Cunningham, William. *The Reformers and the Theology of the Reformation.* Carlisle: Banner of Truth, 1967.

Deleuze, Gilles. *Pure Immanence: Essays on a Life.* Translated by Anne Boyman. New York: Zone, 2001.

Derrida, Jacques. *Of Grammatology.* Translated by Gayatri Chakravorty Spivak. Baltimore: John Hopkins University Press, 1998.

———. *The Politics of Friendship.* London: Verso, 2006.

———. *Writing and Difference.* Translated by Alan Bass. New York: Routledge, 2001.

Dershowitz, Alan. *Rights from Wrongs: A Secular Theory of the Origins of Rights.* New York: Basic, 2009.

Dostoyevsky, Fyodor. *The Brothers Karamazov.* Translated by Richard Pevear and Larissa Volokonky. New York: Farrar, Straus and Giroux, 1990.

———. *Notes from the Underground.* Translated by Constance Garrett. Norwalk, CT: Heritage Club, 1997.

———. *The Possessed.* Translated by Constance Garrett. New York: Macmillan, 1916.

Douglas, Kelly B. *Sexuality and the Black Church: A Womanist Perspective.* Maryknoll: Orbis, 1999.

Du Bois, W. E. B. *Darkwater: Voices from within the Veil.* New York: Harcourt, Brace and Howe, 1920.

———. *The Souls of Black Folk: Essays and Sketches.* Chicago: McClurg, 1903.

Dummelow, J. R., ed. *A Commentary on the Holy Bible.* New York: Macmillan, 1949.

Duns Scotus, John. *Philosophical Writings.* Translated by Allan Wolter. Indianapolis: Hackett, 1987.

———. *A Treatise on God as First Principle.* Translated by Allan Wolter. Chicago: Franciscan Herald, 1966.

Ennis, Paul P. *The Moody Handbook of Theology.* Chicago: Moody, 1989.

Ericksen, Robert P. *Theologians under Hitler: Gerhard Kittel, Paul Althaus and Emanuel Hirsch.* New Haven: Yale University Press, 1985.

Evans, James H. *We Have Been Believers: An African-American Systematic Theology.* Minneapolis: Fortress, 1992.

Fagan, Andrew. *Human Rights: Confronting Myths and Misunderstandings.* Northampton, MA: Elgar, 2009.

Ferguson, Sinclair B., and David F. Wright, eds. *New Dictionary of Theology.* Downers Grove: InterVarsity, 1988.

BIBLIOGRAPHY

Fichte, Johann G. *An Attempt at a Critique of All Revelation*. Translated by Garrett Green. New York: Cambridge University Press, 2009.

———. *Foundations of Natural Right*. Translated by Michael Baur. New York: Cambridge University Press, 2000.

———. *Foundations of Transcendental Philosophy*. Translated by Daniel Breazeale. Ithaca, NY: Cornell University Press, 1992.

———. *The Science of Knowledge*. Translated by Peter Heath and John Lachs. New York: Cambridge University Press, 1982.

Foucault, Michel. "What Is an Author?" In *The Norton Anthology of Theory and Criticism*, edited by Vincent B. Leitch, 1475–90. New York: Norton, 2010.

Frege, Gottlob. "On Sense and Reference." In *Translations from the Philosophical Writings of Gottlob Frege*, edited by Peter Geach and Max Black, 56–78. Oxford: Blackwell, 1960.

Friedan, Betty. *The Feminine Mystique*. New York: Norton, 1963.

Frye, Charles E. "Carl Schmitt's Concept of the Political." *Journal of Politics* 28 (1966) 818–30.

Fulton, Ann. *Apostles of Sartre: Existentialism in America 1945–1963*. Evanston, IL: Northwestern University Press, 1999.

Furst, Lilian R., and Peter N. Skrine. *Naturalism*. London: Methuen, 1971.

Gebara, Ivone. "Women Doing Theology in Latin America." In *With Passion and Compassion: Third World Women Doing Theology*, edited by Virginia Fabella and Mercy A. Oduyoye, 125–34. Maryknoll: Orbis, 1988.

Gilson, Étienne. *God and Philosophy*. New Haven: Yale University Press, 1941.

Gonzalez, Justo L. *Manana: Christian Theology from a Hispanic Perspective*. Nashville: Abingdon, 1990.

———. *The Story of Christianity*. Vol. 1, *The Early Church to the Dawn of the Reformation*: New York: Harper Collins, 1984.

———. *The Story of Christianity*. Vol. 2, *The Reformation to the Present Day* New York: Harper Collins, 2010.

Gordon, Haim, ed. *Dictionary of Existentialism*. Westport, CT: Greenwood, 1999.

Gordon, Lewis, ed. *Existence in Black: An Anthology of Black Existential Philosophy*. New York: Routledge, 1997.

Grant, Edward. *A History of Natural Philosophy: From the Ancient World to the Nineteenth Century*. New York: Cambridge University Press, 2007.

Grene, Marjorie. "The German Existentialists" *Chicago Review* 13 (1959) 49–58.

Hamilton, Edith, and Huntington Cairns, eds. *The Collected Dialogues of Plato*. Princeton: Princeton University Press, 1982.

Harrelson, Walter J., et al., eds. *The New Interpreter's Study Bible: New Revised Standard Version with the Apocrypha*. Nashville: Abingdon, 2003.

Harvey, Van A. *A Handbook of Theological Terms*. New York: Collier, 1964.

Hegel, Georg W. F. *Lectures on the Philosophy of Religion: The Lectures of 1827*. One-volume ed. Translated by R. F. Brown et al. Berkeley: University of California Press, 1988.

———. *Phenomenology of Spirit*. Translated by A. V. Miller. New York: Oxford University Press, 1977.

———. *Philosophy of Right*. Translated by S. W. Dyde. Amherst, MA: Prometheus, 1996.

Heidegger, Martin. *Being and Time*. Translated by John Macquarrie and Edward Robinson. New York: Harper and Row, 1962.

———. *German Existentialism*. Translated by Dagobert D. Runes. New York: Philosophical Library, 1965.

———. *Identity and Difference.* Translated by Joan Stambaugh. Chicago: University of Chicago Press, 1969.

———. *On the Way to Language.* Translated by Peter D. Hertz. New York: Harper and Row, 1971.

The Heidelberg Catechism: Text of Tercentenary Edition. Cleveland: German Publishing House of the Reformed Church, 1877.

Hemming, Laurence. "Reading Heidegger: Is God Without Being? Jean-Luc Marion's Reading of Martin Heidegger in God Without Being." *New Blackfriars* 76 (July/August 1995) 343–50.

Herberg, Will, ed. *Four Existentialist Theologians: A Reader from the Works of Jacques Maritain, Nicolas Berdyaev, Martin Buber, and Paul Tillich.* Garden City: Double Day, 1958.

Herman, Peter C. *A Short History of Early Modern England: British Literature in Context.* Malden, MA: Wiley-Blackwell, 2011.

Holloway, Maurice R. *An Introduction to Natural Theology.* New York: Appleton-Century-Crofts, 1957.

Honderich, Ted, ed. *The Oxford Guide to Philosophy.* New York: Oxford University Press, 2005.

Hopkins, Dwight N. *Being Human: Race, Culture, and Religion.* Minneapolis: Fortress, 2005.

Horner, Robyn. *Jean-Luc Marion: A Theo-logical Introduction.* New York: Ashgate, 2005.

Horton, Walter M. *Christian Theology: An Ecumenical Approach.* New York: Harper and Row, 1958.

Howley, G. C. D., et al., eds. *The New Layman's Bible Commentary: In One Volume.* Grand Rapids: Zondervan, 1979.

Hume, David. *Treatise on Human Nature.* London: At the White Hart near Mercer's Chapel in Cheapside, 1739.

Husserl, Edmund. *The Crisis of European Sciences and Transcendental Phenomenology: An Introduction to Phenomenological Philosophy.* Translated by David Carr. Evanston, IL: Northwestern University Press, 1997.

———. *Ideas Pertaining to a Pure Phenomenology and to a Phenomenological Philosophy.* Translated by F. Kersten. Boston: Nijhoff, 1983.

Iannone, A. Pablo. *Dictionary of World Philosophy.* New York: Routledge, 2001.

Irigaray, Luce. "This Sex Which Is Not One." In Parker, *Critical Theory*, 257–63.

Irwin, C. H. *Irwin's Bible Commentary.* Philadelphia: Winston, 1927.

James, William. *The Meaning of Truth.* Amherst: Prometheus, 1997.

———. *Pragmatism.* New York: Prometheus, 1991.

Johnson, Luke T. *The Acts of the Apostles.* Sacra Pagina 5. Collegeville: Liturgical, 1992.

Joyce, George H. *Principles of Natural Theology.* New York: Longmans, Green, 1923.

Kant, Immanuel. *Critique of Judgment.* Translated by Werner S. Pluhar. Indianapolis: Hackett, 1987.

———. *Critique of Practical Reason.* Translated by Werner S. Pluhar. Indianapolis: Hackett, 2002.

———. *The Critique of Pure Reason.* Translated by J. M. D. Meiklejohn. Hazleton, PA: Penn State University, 2010.

———. *Critique of Pure Reason.* Translated by Norman Kemp Smith. New York: St. Martin's, 1929.

———. *Grounding for the Metaphysics of Morals: With On a Supposed Right to Lie Because of Philanthropic Concerns*. Translated by James W. Ellington. Indianapolis: Hackett, 1993.

———. *Lectures on Philosophical Theology*. Translated by Allen W. Wood and Gertrude M. Clark. Ithaca: Cornell University Press, 1978.

———. *The One Possible Basis for a Demonstration of the Existence of God*. Translated by Gordon Treash. Lincoln: University of Nebraska Press, 1979.

———. *Opus postumum*. Translated by Eckart Förster and Michal Rosen. New York: Cambridge University Press, 1993.

Kaufmann, Walter, ed. *The Basic Writings of Nietzsche*. New York: Modern Library, 1968.

———. *Existentialism from Dostoyevsky to Sartre*. New York: World, 1956.

———. *The Will to Power*. New York: Random House, 1967.

Kierkegaard, Soren. *Concluding Unscientific Postscript to Philosophical Crumbs*. Translated by Alastair Hannay. New York: Cambridge University Press, 2009

———. *The Point of View*. Translated by Howard V. Hong and Edna H. Hong. Princeton: Princeton University Press, 1998.

———. *The Point of View for My Work as an Author: A Report to History and Related Writings*. Translated by Walter Lowrie. New York: Harper and Row, 1962.

———. *Sickness unto Death: A Christian Psychological Exposition for Upbuilding and Awakening*. Translated by Howard V. Hong and Edna H. Hong. Princeton: Princeton University Press, 1983.

Kirwan, Michael. *Political Theology: An Introduction*. Minneapolis: Fortress, 2009.

Kuitert, Harry M. *The Reality of Faith: A Way between Protestant Orthodoxy and Existential Theology*. Grand Rapids: Eerdmans, 1968.

Lacan, Jacques. "The Signification of the Phallus." In *Ecrits: A Selection*, translated by Bruce Fink, 271–80. New York: Norton, 2002.

Latour, Bruno. *We Have Never Been Modern*. Cambridge: Harvard University Press, 1991.

Law, David R. "A Cacophony of Voices: The Multiple Authors and Readers of Kierkegaard's *The Point of View for My Work as an Author*." In *International Kierkegaard Commentary*, vol. 22, *The Point of View*, edited by Robert L. Perkins, 12–47. Macon: Mercer University Press, 2010.

Laymon, Charles M., ed. *The Interpreter's One-Volume Commentary on the Bible*. Nashville: Abingdon, 1982.

Lehan, Richard. *Realism and Naturalism: The Novel in an Age of Transition*. Madison: University of Wisconsin Press, 2005.

Leibniz, G. W. *Philosophical Essays*. Translated by Roger Ariew and Daniel Garber. Indianapolis: Hackett, 1989.

Leitch, Vincent B., and William E. Cain, eds. *The Norton Anthology of Theory and Criticism*. New York: Norton, 2010.

Levinas, Emmanuel. *Otherwise than Being: Or Beyond Essence*. Translated by Alphonso Lingis. Pittsburgh: Duquesne University Press, 1981.

Liefeld, Walter L. "The Hellenistic 'Divine Man' and the Figure of Jesus in the Gospels." *Journal of the Evangelical Theological Society* 16 (1973) 195–205.

Luther, Martin. *Christian Liberty*. Philadelphia: Lutheran Publication Society, 1903.

———. *On the Bondage of the Will*. Translated by Henry Cole. London: Bensley, 1823.

MacDonald, Margaret. "Natural Rights." *Proceedings of the Aristotelian Society* 47 (1946) 225–50.

MacGregor, Geddes, ed. *Dictionary of Religion and Philosophy*. New York: Paragon, 1989.

BIBLIOGRAPHY

MacIntosh, John J., ed. *The Excellencies of Robert Boyle: The Excellency of Theology and the Excellency and Grounds of the Mechanical Hypothesis*. Buffalo, NY: Broadview, 2008.

MacIntyre, Alasdair. *After Virtue: A Study in Moral Theory*. Norte Dame: University of Norte Dame Press, 1981.

Macquarrie, John. *An Existentialist Theology: A Comparison of Heidegger and Bultmann*. London: Clowes, 1955.

———. *Principles of Christian Theology*. New York: Scribner, 1977.

Malabou, Catherine. *What Should We Do with Our Brain?* New York: Fordham University Press, 2008.

Malone, Mary T. *Women and Christianity*. Vol. 1, *The First Thousand Years*. Maryknoll: Orbis, 2000.

———. *Women and Christianity*. Vol. 3, *From the Reformation to the 21st Century*. Maryknoll: Orbis, 2003.

Marcel, Gabriel. *Approaches to God*. Translated by Peter O'Reilly. New York: Macmillan, 1954.

———. *Being and Having: An Existentialist Diary*. Translated by James Collins. New York: Harper and Row, 1965.

———. *The Mystery of Being*. Vol. 2. Translated by G. S. Fraser. London: Harvill, 1951.

———. *The Philosophy of Existentialism*. Translated by Manya. New York: Citadel, 2002.

Marion, Jean-Luc. *God without Being*. Translated by Thomas A. Carlson. Chicago: University of Chicago Press, 1991.

———. *In Excess: Studies of Saturated Phenomena*. Translated by Robyn Horner and Vincent Berraud. New York: Fordham University Press, 2002.

Maritain, Jacques. *Existence and the Existent*. New York: Paulist, 2015.

———. *Man and the State*. Washington, DC: Catholic University of America Press, 1951.

———. *The Person and the Common Good*. Translated by John J. Fitzgerald. Notre Dame: University of Norte Dame, 2016.

Martin, Ross, and Supriya M. Ray. *The Bedford Glossary of Critical and Literary Terms*. New York: Bedford / St. Martin's, 2009.

Marx, Karl. *On Religion*. Translated by Saul K. Padover. New York: McGraw-Hill, 1974.

Marx, Karl, and Friedrich Engels. *Karl Marx and Friedrich Engels: Selected Works*. Vol. 1. Translated by W. Lough. Moscow: Progress, 1969.

Massey, Lesly F. *Women and the New Testament: An Analysis of Scripture in Light of New Testament Era Culture*. Jefferson, NC: McFarland, 1989.

McKeon, Richard, ed. *The Basic Works of Aristotle*. New York: Modern Library, 2001.

McKim, Robert. *On Religious Diversity*. New York: Oxford University Press, 2012.

McKittrick, Katherine, ed. *Sylvia Wynter: On Being Human as Praxis*. Durham: Duke University Press, 2014.

Migliore, Daniel. *Faith Seeking Understanding: An Introduction to Christian Theology*. Grand Rapids: Eerdmans, 1991.

Mignolo, Walter. "Epistemic Disobedience, Independent Thought, and De-Colonial Freedom." *Theory, Culture, and Society* 26 (2009) 159–81.

Miller, Jacques-Alain, ed. *On Feminine Sexuality: The Limits of Love and Knowledge*. Translated by Bruce Fink. Seminar of Jacques Lacan 20. New York: Norton, 1998.

Mirsky, Prince D. S. *Contemporary Russian Literature, 1881–1925*. New York: Knopf, 1972.

Mooney, Edward F. "The Perils of Polarity: Kierkegaard and MacIntyre in Search of Moral Truth." In *Kierkegaard after MacIntyre: Essays on Freedom, Narrative, and Virtue*, edited by John J. Davenport and Anthony Rudd, 233–63. Chicago: Open Court, 2001.

Moote, A. Lloyd, and Dorothy C. Moote. *The Great Plague: The Story of London's Most Deadly Year*. Baltimore: Johns Hopkins University Press, 2004.

Morgan, Kenneth O. *The Oxford History of Britain*. Vol. 3. New York: Oxford University Press, 1992.

Moser, Paul K., ed. *Concise Routledge Encyclopedia of Philosophy*. New York: Routledge, 2000.

Musser, Donald W., and Joseph L. Price, eds. *A New Handbook of Christian Theology*. Nashville: Abingdon, 1992.

Myers, Ched. Introduction to *An Eerdmans Reader in Contemporary Theology*, edited by William T. Cavanaugh et al., 337–41. Grand Rapids: Eerdmans, 2012.

Nabokov, Vladimir. *Lectures on Russian Literature*. New York: Harcourt Brace Jovanovich, 1981.

Niebuhr, Reinhold. *The Children of Light and the Children of Darkness: A Vindication of Democracy and a Critique of Its Traditional Defense*. Chicago: University of Chicago Press, 2011.

———. *The Nature and Destiny of Man*. Vol. 1, *Human Nature*. New York: Scribner, 1941.

Ockham, William of. *Philosophical Writings*. Translated by Philotheus Boehner. Indianapolis: Hackett, 1990.

Oden, Amy, ed. *In Her Words: Women's Writings in the History of Christian Thought*. Nashville: Abingdon, 1994.

Parker, Robert D., ed. *Critical Theory: A Reader for Literary and Cultural Studies*. New York: Oxford University Press, 2012.

Pax, Clyde. *An Existential Approach to God: A Study of Gabriel Marcel*. The Hague: Nijhoff, 1972.

Pictet, Benedict. *Christian Theology*. London: Seeley and Burnside, 1836.

Primus, Richard A. *The American Language of Rights*. New York: Cambridge University Press, 2004.

Pui-lan, Kwok. *Introducing Asian Feminist Theology*. Sheffield, UK: Sheffield, 2000.

Reese, William L. *Dictionary of Philosophy and Religion: Eastern and Western Thought*. Atlantic Highlands, NJ: Humanities, 1980.

Richardson, David B. *Berdyaev's Philosophy of History: An Existentialist Theory of Social Creativity and Eschatology*. The Hague: Martinus, 1968.

Ricoeur, Paul. *Oneself as Another*. Chicago: University of Chicago Press, 1992.

Roberts, J. Deotis. *A Black Political Theology*. Philadelphia: Westminster, 1974.

Sartre, Jean-Paul. *Being and Nothingness: A Phenomenological Essay on Ontology*. Translated by Hazel Barnes. New York: Citadel, 2001.

Saussure, Ferdinand de. *Course in General Linguistics*. Translated by Wade Baskin. Edited by Charles Bally and Albert Sechehaye. New York: Philosophical Library, 1959.

Scarry, Elaine. *On Beauty and Being Just*. Princeton: Princeton University Press, 1999.

Schelling, Friedrich W. J. *Philosophical Inquires into the Nature of Human Freedom*. Translated by James Gutmann. La Salle: Open Court, 1936.

———. *Philosophy and Religion*. 1804. Translated by Klaus Ottmann. Putnam, CT: Spring, 2010.

———. *System of Transcendental Idealism*. 1800. Translated by Peter Heath. Charlottesville: University Press of Virginia, 2001.

Schillebeeckx, Edward. *Jesus: An Experiment in Christology*. New York: Crossroad, 1986.

Schiller, F. C. S. *Humanism: Philosophical Essays*. New York: Macmillan, 1903.

BIBLIOGRAPHY

Schmitt, Carl. *The Concept of the Political*. Translated by George Schwab. Chicago: University of Chicago Press, 1995.

———. *The Leviathan in the State Theory of Thomas Hobbes*. Translated by George Schwab. Westport, CT: Greenwood, 1996.

———. *Political Theology: Four Chapters on the Concept of Sovereignty*. Translated by George Schwab. Chicago: University of Chicago Press, 1985.

Schopenhauer, Arthur. *The World as Will and Presentation*. Translated by David Carus and Richard E. Aquila. New York: Routledge, 2016.

———. *The World as Will and Representation*. Translated by E. F. J. Payne. Indian Hills, CO: Falcon's Wing, 1958.

Scott, Peter, and William T. Cavanaugh. Introduction to *The Blackwell Companion to Political Theology*, edited by Peter Scott and William T. Cavanaugh, 1–3. Malden, MA: Blackwell, 2004.

Seaward, Paul. *The Restoration, 1660–1688*. New York: St. Martin's, 1991.

Shaw, Joseph M. *Readings in Christian Humanism*. Minneapolis: Fortress, 2009.

Shook, John R., ed. *Pragmatic Naturalism and Realism*. New York: Prometheus, 2003.

Smith, Andrea. *Conquest: Sexual Violence and American Indian Genocide*. Durham, NC: Duke University Press, 2015.

Smith, Christian. "Does Naturalism Warrant a Moral Belief in Universal Benevolence and Human Rights?" In *The Believing Primate: Scientific, Philosophical, and Theological Reflections on the Origin of Religion*, edited by Michael J. Murray and Jeffrey Schloss, 292–31. New York: Oxford University Press, 2009.

Sohm, Rudolph. *A History of Christianity*. New York: Hunt and Eaton, 1891.

Spanos, William V. *A Casebook on Existentialism*. New York: Harper and Row, 1968.

Spivak, Gayatri. "Can the Subaltern Speak? Speculations on Widow Sacrifice." In Parker, *Critical Theory*, 675–93.

Sweetman, Brendan. *The Vision of Gabriel Marcel: Epistemology, Human Person, the Transcendent*. New York: Rodopi, 2008.

Thomas, J. Heywood. Review of *Christian Existentialism: A Berdyaev Anthology*, selected and translated by Donald A. Lowrie. *Scottish Journal of Theology* 19 (March 1966) 91.

Tillich, Paul. *The Courage to Be*. New Haven: Yale University Press, 1952.

———. *A History of Christian Thought: From Judaic and Hellenistic Origins to Existentialism*. New York: Simon and Schuster, 1968.

———. *Systematic Theology*. Vol. 1, *Reason and Revelation, Being and God*. Chicago: University of Chicago Press, 1951.

———. *Systematic Theology*. Vol. 2, *Existence and the Christ*. Chicago: University of Chicago Press, 1957.

———. *Systematic Theology*. Vol. 3, *Life and Spirit: History and the Kingdom of God*. Chicago: University of Chicago Press, 1963.

Tiryakian, Edward A. "Existential Phenomenology and the Sociological Tradition." *American Sociological Review* 17 (1965) 674–88.

Tolstoy, Leo. *The Death of Ivan Ilyich*. New York: Crowell, 1886.

———. *My Confession and the Spirit of Christ's Teachings*. New York: Crowell, 1887.

———. *What Is Art?* New York: Crowell, 1899.

Townes, Emile M. *Womanist Ethics and the Cultural Production of Evil*. New York: Palgrave, 2006.

Tucker, Robert, ed. *The Marx-Engels Reader*. New York: Norton, 1978.

Underhill, Evelyn. *The Life of the Spirit and the Life of Today*. New York: Dutton, 1922.

Urban, Linwood. *A Short History of Christian Thought*. New York: Oxford University Press, 1995.

Urquhart, William S. *Humanism and Christianity: Being the Croall Lectures of 1938–1939*. Edinburgh: T. & T. Clark, 1945.

Valliere, Paul. *Modern Russian Theology: Bukharev, Soloviev, Bulgakov; Orthodox Theology in a New Key*. London: Bloomsbury, 2014.

Volf, Miroslav. *Exclusion and Embrace: A Theological Exploration of Identity, Otherness, and Reconciliation*. Nashville: Abingdon, 1996.

Walker, Theodore. *Mothership Connections: A Black Atlantic Synthesis of Neoclassical Metaphysics and Black Theology*. Albany: State University of New York Press, 2014.

West, Cornel. "Black Theology and Marxist Thought." In *Black Theology: A Documentary History, 1966–1979*, edited by Gayraud S. Wilmore and James H. Cone, 543–51. Maryknoll: Orbis, 1979.

———. "Dispensing with Metaphysics in Religious Thought." In *Prophetic Fragments: Illuminations of the Crisis in American Religion and Culture*, 267–70. Trenton: Eerdmans, 1988.

———. *Prophesy Deliverance: An Afro-American Revolutionary Christianity*. Louisville: Westminster, 2002.

———. "Prophetic Theology." In *Beyond Eurocentrism and Multiculturalism*, vol. 2, *Prophetic Reflections: Notes on Race and Power in America*, 223–38. Monroe, ME: Common Courage 1993.

Wiener, Philip P., ed. *Leibniz Selections*. New York: Scribner, 1951.

Wiles, Maurice, and Mark Santer, eds. *Documents in Early Christian Thought*. New York: Cambridge University Press, 1975.

Williams, Delores. *Sisters in the Wilderness: The Challenge of Womanist God-Talk*. Maryknoll: Orbis, 2013.

Williard, George W., ed. *The Commentary of Dr. Zacharias Ursinus on the Heidelberg Catechism*. Cincinnati: Elm Street, 1888.

Witherington, Ben. *Women and the Genesis of Christianity*. New York: Cambridge University Press, 1990.

Wittgenstein, Ludwig. *Tractatus Logico-Philosophicus*. Translated by C. K. Ogden. Mineola, NY: Dover, 1999.

Wojcik, Jan W. *Robert Boyle and the Limits of Reason*. New York: Cambridge University Press, 1997.

Wolfe, Cary. "Before the Law: Animals in a Biopolitical Context." *Law, Culture and the Humanities* 6 (2010) 8–23.

Woodson, Hue. "Between Activism, Religiosity, and the Public Sphere: The Intellectual Insurgency of bell hooks." *Journal of African American Studies* 23 (2019) 187–202.

———. "Dialectics and Hegelian Negation in Slavoj Žižek's Enjoy Your Symptom: Fighting the Fantasies of Trauma, Identity, Authority, and Phallophany." *International Journal of Žižek Studies* 13 (2019).

———. *Heideggerian Theologies: The Pathmarks of John Macquarrie, Rudolf Bultmann, Paul Tillich, and Karl Rahner*. Eugene, OR: Wipf & Stock, 2018.

———. *A Theologian's Guide to Heidegger*. Eugene, OR: Wipf & Stock, 2019.

Yoder, John H. *The Politics of Jesus: Vicit Agnus Noster*. Grand Rapids: Eerdmanns, 1972.

Names Index

Ackerman, Denise, 196–97
Agamben, Giorgio, 244–46, 287–89, 293, 295–97
Akoto, Dorothy, 195–96
Althaus, Paul, 70
Althusser, Louis, 250–53
Anderson, Victor, 34, 205, 217–20, 228–29, 289
Anselm, 13, 28–31, 73–74
Aquinas, Thomas, 5, 9–11, 13–15, 31–32, 34, 51, 58, 61, 64, 66, 265
Aquino, Maria, 202–3
Aristotle, 12, 29, 31–32, 34, 44, 51, 174–75, 278, 286, 310, 311
Athanasius of Alexandria, 21, 24
Augustine, 9–11, 13, 15–22, 25–26, 28, 31–32, 35, 205

Baeumler, Alfred, 88
Bakhtin, Mikhail, 96, 173, 175, 196–97, 237, 277–78
Bakunin, Mikhail, 234
Baldwin, James, 184
Balthasar (Urs von), Hans, 63
Barad, Karen, 244, 297
Barrett, William, 2, 94
Barth, Karl, 4–5, 8, 37–38, 89, 113–14, 118–119, 308–9
Barthes, Roland, 48
Bauer, Bruno, 86
Beauvoir, Simone (de), 137, 152–54, 157, 160, 164, 165, 166, 167
Berdyaev, Nikolai, 6–12, 16–18, 45, 56, 92–93, 104–8, 261, 318, 322
Blount, Brian, 125–28
Bonhoeffer, Dietrich, 8–11, 13, 67, 89–91, 255
Boyle, Robert, 299, 301–4
Bradley, Anthony, 130–33, 184
Braidotti, Rosi, 282, 285, 286, 287
Brown, James, 4–6, 116, 188, 230

Brunner, Emil, 308–9
Buber, Martin, 4, 6–11, 16, 19, 56
Bukharev, Aleksandr, 92–93
Bulgakov, Sergei, 92–93
Bultmann, Rudolf, viii–ix, 3–11, 63–64, 69–70, 200
Burns, J. Patout, 204–5
Butler, Judith, 137, 171–73, 178, 287, 290, 295–96

Calvin, John, 13, 38–39, 42–43
Camus, Albert, 94
Cannon, Katie, 181–84
Chantal, Jane F. (de), 146
Cobb, John B., 11–12
Cochrane, Arthur, 5
Coleman, Monica, 192–94
Collins, Patricia H., 2, 170–71, 178–84
Colonna, Vittoria, 146
Cone, James H., 110–20, 131–34, 181, 184, 222
Copeland, M. Shawn, 110, 177, 205, 229–31

de la Cruz, Juana I., 146
Deleuze, Gilles, 47, 63, 122, 155–56, 216, 237, 258, 261, 290
Derrida, Jacques, 47–48, 63, 122, 154, 159, 166, 198–99, 214, 225, 249, 250, 259–60, 262, 293, 297
Dershowitz, Alan, 268–69
Descartes, Rene, 51, 61, 307
Dostoyevsky, Fyodor, 92–97, 104
Douglas, Kelly B., 188–89
Du Bois, W. E. B., 113, 122, 129, 205–210, 219
Duns Scotus, 28–31

Evans, James, 109–110, 121–25

Feuerbach, Ludwig, 86

333

NAMES INDEX

Fichte, Johann, 70, 72, 78–82, 84, 91, 238–39, 255–56, 271–72, 279–80
Foucault, Michel, 48, 171, 249, 287, 297
Frazier, E. Franklin, 117
Frege, Gottlöb, 225
Freud, Sigmund, 6, 164–67, 254
Friedan, Betty, 137, 152–54, 156–57, 159, 166–67, 170

Gebara, Ivone, 201–2
Gilroy, Paul, 129
Gilson, Etienne, 5, 11, 66
Gonzalez, Justo, 21–28, 40–43, 62, 123–25
Gordon, Lewis, 35–36, 46, 153, 205, 210, 219–20, 318, 320
Gregory of Nyssa, 21, 23, 28, 51, 205
Grene, Majorie, 1–3, 53, 67–69
Grimké, Sarah, 149
Guyon, Madame Jeanne, 146

Hegel, Georg W. F., 9–11, 32–33, 51, 62, 70, 72, 80, 82–84, 86–87, 91, 93, 104, 159, 175, 197–99, 227, 232–33, 238–39, 242, 250–51, 253–55, 264, 271–72, 280, 290–92, 307
Heidegger, Martin, vii–ix, 1–6, 9–10, 13, 35–36, 46, 51, 53, 56, 63–65, 67–71, 88–89, 123, 153–55, 161, 176, 202–3, 210, 225, 228, 230–31, 234, 246, 267, 272, 275, 281, 285–86, 287, 288, 295, 297, 318, 321
Henderson, Ian, 3–4
Herberg, Will, 6–8, 56–59, 61, 108
Herder (von), Johann G., 71–72
Heschel, Abraham, 10
Hirsch, Emmanuel, 70
Hitler, Adolf, 68–70, 87, 90–91, 235–36
Hobbes, Thomas, 234–35
hooks, bell, 184–86, 218
Hopkins, Dwight N., 205, 221–23
Husserl, Edmund, 51, 62–63, 68, 173–74, 238, 247, 265, 268, 270, 277–78, 287, 292

Ignatius of Loyola, 51
Irenaeus of Lyons, 21, 24
Irigaray, Luce, 137, 162, 164–71

James, William, 2, 4, 11, 45, 48, 56, 109–111, 116–17, 121, 123, 131–32, 184, 212
Jaspers, Karl, 1–2, 5, 67–68, 88
Jenkins, David, 8
Jesus (Christ), 10, 13, 19–24, 35, 36, 39, 102, 112, 114, 116, 121, 126–28, 140, 142, 146, 222, 236–37, 310–20, 322

Kant, Immanuel, 9–11, 44–45, 48, 51, 70–82, 84–85, 91, 93, 104, 154, 157–58, 216, 233, 238–39, 255–56, 259, 263, 307
Kaufmann, Walter, 17, 19, 94, 175
Kierkegaard, Soren, 1–6, 8–9, 11, 14–15, 17, 38, 43–49, 52, 58, 67–68, 82, 94, 95, 122, 185, 230, 248, 254–55, 258, 261, 269
King (Jr.), Martin L., 110–11, 113
Kittel, Gerhard, 70
Koltaj, Bojan, 255
Kotsko, Adam, 253–54
Kuitert, Harry, 8
Kwok, Pui-lan, 200

Lacan, Jacques, 164, 166–67, 253–55
Larsen, Nella, 205, 212
Latour, Bruno, 282–84
Leibniz, Gottfried, 15, 33, 38, 71–72, 110, 287
Levinas, Emmanuel, 123, 225, 227
Locke, Alain, 220
Long, Eugene, 8
Löwith, Karl, 88
Lowrie, Donald, 11, 48, 105
Lukács, Georg, 250
Luther, Martin, 13–15, 25, 32–33, 39, 40–43, 142

MacIntyre, Alasdair, 256–67
Macquarrie, John, viii–ix, 3–11, 18, 37, 63–64, 118–19, 200
Magdalene, Mary (of Magdala), 102, 140–41
Major, Clarence, 213
Malabou, Catherine, 282, 289–91
Malcolm X, 110–11, 113
Marcel, Gabriel, 1, 2, 50–56, 67, 105
Marion, Jean-Luc, 50, 51, 62–66
Maritain, Jacques, 6–11, 50–51, 56, 57, 58, 59, 60, 61
Martin, Bernard, 5–6, 8, 15–16, 25, 32–33, 36, 39–41, 46, 51, 53, 63, 68, 99, 110–11, 113, 123, 142, 153, 202, 210, 230, 246, 267, 272, 318
Marx, Karl, 51, 70, 82, 85–87, 160, 242, 250–55
Merleau-Ponty, Maurice, 62
More, Thomas, 1, 12, 14, 25, 72, 79, 107, 111, 112, 117–18, 140, 152, 159, 176, 178, 181, 197–98, 206, 223, 231, 251, 257, 268, 280, 283, 317–18
Morrison, Toni, 189–90, 205, 214
Mott, Lucretia, 150

Nabokov, Vladimir, 98–101, 103
Niebuhr, Reinhold, 13, 37, 38, 238–40
Niethammer, Friedrich, 12

NAMES INDEX

Nietzsche, Friedrich, 1–3, 11, 17, 19, 51, 67, 70, 71, 82, 87–89, 93–94, 104, 175

Oduyoye, Mercy, 197–99
Origen, 21–23, 25, 28, 51
Ortega y Gasset, Jose, 10

Palmer, Phoebe, 150
Pascal, Blaise, 13, 50–51
Petre, Maude, 150
Plato, 12, 21, 153–54, 226, 253, 272, 286, 320
Pseudo-Dionysius, 51

Rahner, Karl, viii–ix, 5–11, 63–64, 308–9
Rawls, John, 295
Ricoeur, Paul, 62, 210
Roberts, J. Deotis, 111, 117–21, 132, 134
Rosenzweig, Franz, 10

Saldanha, Arun, 205, 224–29
Sartre, Jean-Paul, 1–3, 5, 52–58, 60–61, 67, 87, 94, 134, 154, 165, 173, 248, 275, 277
Saussure, Ferdinand (de), 237, 260, 286
Scarry, Elaine, 216–17
Schelling, Friedrich, 51, 70, 72, 80–84, 91
Schleiermacher, Friedrich, 13, 51, 70, 72, 202
Schmemann, Alexander, 92–93
Schmitt, Carl, 234–36, 245
Schopenhauer, Arthur, 38, 70, 82, 84–85, 93, 224, 240, 249, 264, 286
Shestov, Lev, 10
Slaatte, Howard, 8
Smith, Andrea, 242
Smith, Christian, 274
Socrates, 226, 253
Soloviev, Vladimir, 92–93
Spivak, Gayatri, 116, 137, 161–64, 190
Stanton, Elizabeth Cady, 149
Strauss, David, 86

Tanner, Kathryn, 241
Teilhard de Chardin, Pierre, 50–51, 62
Teresa of Ávila, 146
Tertullian, 25–28, 142
Thurman, Wallace, 205, 209
Tillich, Paul, viii–ix, 5–11, 16–19, 24–25, 27–28, 35, 41–42, 56, 63–64, 67–70, 88–89, 113–14, 118–19, 124, 175, 200, 203, 278, 308–9
Tolstoy, Leo, 92–93, 97–104, 106
Townes, Emile, 189–93
Tracy, David, 66, 222

Underhill, Evelyn, 137, 150–52
Urquhart, William, 12
Ursinus, Zacharias, 34

Vahanian, Gabriel, 89
Valliere, Paul, 92–93
Volf, Miroslav, 246–49
Voltaire, 33

Walker (Jr.), Theodore, 129–30
Wallace, Michelle, 176–77, 205, 209
Washington (Jr.), Joseph R., 117, 133
West, Cornel, 132–36
William of Ockham, 28–31
Williams, Delores S., 186–88
Wilmore, Gayraud, 117
Wittgenstein, Ludwig, 110, 155–56
Wolfe, Cary, 282, 288, 292–97
Wolff, Christian, 71–72
Wynter, Sylvia, 282, 287–89

Yoder, John H., 236–38
Young, Norman, 6, 8, 86, 250

Žižek, Slavoj, 253–55
Zwingli, Ulrich, 39, 41–42

335

Subject Index

a priori, 29, 74, 208, 255–56, 259, 263, 317
absoluteness, 81, 260
absurdism, 94
Act and Being (Bonhoeffer), 89–91
Acts of Paul and Thecla, 140–41
aesthetic, 45, 216–18, 222–23, 239, 268, 272
Age of Enlightenment, 71
androcentric, 149
anthropological, 93, 125, 177, 216–17, 221–22, 229
anthropo-logocentrism, 115
anti-Christianity, 88
anti-Thomistic, 53
apperceiving, 247
Approaches to God (Maritain), 61
Aristotlean, 228, 278–79, 285, 289
Attempt at a Critique of All Revelation (Fichte), 78–80
authenticity, 11, 36, 115, 120, 176, 188, 218, 222, 230, 241, 272

bad faith, 248
bare life, 244–45, 293–94
Barmen Declaration of Faith, 89
Being and Time (Heidegger), 10, 288,
being for others, 153, 157
being for self, 153, 155, 157
being of God, 5, 91
being-for-others, 173, 242, 277
being-in-the-world, 35, 110, 123, 153, 161, 173, 175–77, 197, 199–200, 202–3, 207, 210–11, 213, 215, 225, 231, 238, 243–44, 275, 277, 286–89, 318, 320–22
being-Right, 174–75, 274, 277, 279–81
being-Womanist, 173–75
Beyond Ontological Blackness (Anderson), 217–19
binary, 169, 218–19, 286–87

biophilosophy, 292, 296
biopolitics, 245, 292–93, 295–96
Black Atlantic, 129–30
Black Church, 111, 117, 133, 175, 188–89, 211
Black Consciousness movement, 111
Black elitism, 208
Black existence, 113–14, 207, 209
Black existential sociology, 208–9
Black femininity, 176–77
Black feminism, 165, 170, 177, 181, 184–85
Black feminist thought, 170–71, 178–81, 183
black identity, 132, 220
Black intellectualism, 185–86
Black Political Theology, A (Roberts), 117–21
Black Power, 111–12, 116–18
Black sexuality, 188–89
black suffering, 121, 219–20
Black theologian, 112, 114, 117, 119–20
Black theology, 110–21, 130–34, 136, 181, 184, 187, 189–90, 193, 211, 219–20, 222–23
Black Theology of Liberation (Cone), 112–15
Black Feminist Thought (Collins), 178–81
black womanhood, 193
Black Womanist Ethics (Cannon), 181–84
Blackness, 109–122, 129–35, 171, 173, 175, 176–77, 181–82, 189, 205–7, 209–215, 217–20, 223, 228–31, 289
blaxploitation, 116–17, 189
body theology, 177, 230–31
bondsman, 159, 161, 197–98, 232, 242
bracketing, 247, 265, 268, 270

Calvinist, 39, 42–43
Candide (Voltaire), 33
Cartesian, 51, 60, 286
Cartesianism, 60
catechization, 34
categorical imperative, 77, 224

337

SUBJECT INDEX

Catholic thought, 50, 56, 105
Catholicism, 10, 12, 50, 51, 53–54, 58, 70, 104, 306
causation, 31
Christian existentialism, 11, 13
Christian humanism, 11–13
Christian philosophy, 11, 13
Christian theologians, 25, 85, 148
Christian thought, 10, 11, 26, 92, 135, 145, 147, 150
Christology, 27, 114, 177, 222, 308
Church Dogmatics (Barth), 5, 309
Civil Rights movement, 111
coexistence, 32, 33, 305–6
colonial, 161–64, 288
coloniality, 163–64
color line, 206–7, 210, 213
communion, 24, 26, 151
Confessing Church, 89–91
consciousness, 55, 62, 80, 87, 99, 103, 106, 110, 113, 122, 132, 151–52, 159, 163, 176, 179, 181–82, 198, 206–7, 210–11, 218, 228, 238, 242, 248, 272, 289–91
contractualism, 295
Corinthians (First Epistle of), 138
cosmotheology, 74
Counter-Enlightenment, 72
Courage to Be (Tillich), 5, 68, 89, 175
creative act, 106–7, 261, 322
creative activity, 107
Critique of Pure Reason (Kant), 72, 74–76

Darkwater (Du Bois), 207–9
death of God, the, 11, 82
dehumanization, 115, 177, 207, 296
dehumanized, 115
de-linking, 164
democracy, 59, 238–39, 245, 249–50
demythology, 6, 7
deontological, 256
Devils (Dostoyevsky), 95–97
dialectical feminism, 137
dialectical materialism, 160, 254
dialectics, 33, 153–54, 156, 218, 238, 251, 254–55, 286, 287
dialogic, 173–75, 196, 277–78
dialogism, 175, 278
différance, 122–23, 154, 159, 198–99, 259
direct communication, 43–47
discrimination, 183, 197, 209
divinity, 65, 73, 116
doctrine, 17, 19, 21, 23–24, 26–29, 31, 34– 35, 37, 39–43, 54, 60, 83, 99, 105–6, 124, 128, 138, 140, 142, 144–45, 200, 270, 292–93, 308–9
double-self, 206

early church, 13, 15, 21, 24, 26–28, 51, 141–42, 237–38
economics, 86, 131
egalitarian, 143
empowerment, 111, 117, 134, 155, 175, 181–82, 184, 189, 200–201, 221, 237, 242
Enfleshing Freedom (Copeland), 229–31
enframing, 297
epistemology, 12, 59–60, 90, 105, 162, 163, 181, 182, 206, 213, 221, 224, 227, 283, 284, 286
eschatology, 108, 114, 305–6, 308
estrangement, 35, 124
ethical responsibility, 293
ethical standing, 292–93, 296
Ethics (Aristotle), 8, 12, 44, 52, 89, 125, 173–74, 181–83, 189–92, 278
evil, problem of, 14, 16–17, 20, 193, 304
exegesis, 127, 311
existence, 1–3, 8, 11–18, 20, 22–23, 26, 29–38, 46–47, 50–51, 53, 55, 58–59, 61–62, 65, 69–70, 72–75, 78, 80–81, 85, 87, 90, 92, 96, 97, 103, 106, 108–110, 112–17, 119, 122, 124–25, 130–31, 135–36, 144, 149–56, 159, 171, 173–74, 176–78, 181, 187–88, 190–201, 204–211, 214–15, 217–21, 223, 228, 231, 237–38, 241, 244–48, 250, 252–53, 255–56, 263–64, 266–68, 271–72, 274–77, 280–82, 291, 304, 317, 318–20, 322
Existence and the Existent (Maritain), 60–61
Existence in Black (Gordon), 219–20
existential epistemological perspective, 151
existential phenomenological stance, 151
existential situation, 109–112, 154, 158, 175, 182, 203, 210, 215, 246
existential theology, vii–ix, 1–14, 15–49, 50–108, 110–203, 205–281, 282–97, 309
existentialism, 1–4, 6–9, 11, 13, 51–54, 57–61, 67–69, 73, 82, 93–95, 105–6, 134, 137, 153, 165, 223, 275
existentialist, 2–8, 52–54, 56–58, 67–69, 92, 94, 105, 210, 318
existentialist theologian, 6–8
existentializing, 13, 29, 114, 118, 192, 211, 219
Existenzphilosophie, 67
experience, 8, 13, 36, 53, 57, 85, 110–15, 119, 121–23, 125–26, 132, 140–41, 143–44, 147, 149, 152, 155–56, 165, 170–71, 177–79, 181–82, 186–87, 190–93, 195, 197,

338

201, 206, 209–210, 214, 216–17, 219, 228, 233, 238–39, 241, 247, 249, 254, 256, 259, 261, 264, 267, 272–73, 277, 279, 289–91, 293, 301, 304, 316, 320–22

facticities, 173, 203, 243–44, 246
facticity, 110–11, 155–56, 158–60, 175, 197, 199, 201, 250, 267, 270, 275–76
faith, 11–12, 14–15, 20, 21, 25–28, 32–35, 38–43, 79, 92–93, 98, 104, 111, 134, 140–42, 144–48, 174–75, 181–83, 186–88, 201–2, 219, 229, 232, 237–38, 248, 301, 309–311, 316
female sexuality, 167–68, 170
femaleness, 136–37, 153–56, 158, 164, 186
femininity, 136–37, 150, 152, 164, 166, 170, 173, 176–77, 186, 289
feminist theology, 14, 136, 137, 187, 193, 197, 202
first sin, 37
forgiveness, 13, 20–22, 24–26, 35, 40–41, 313
freeplay (Derrida), 225, 245–46, 292, 297
Freudian, 164–70
friendship, 249–50
Führer, 69
Führerprinzip, 70

Geistes (Hegel), 290–91
German Existentialism (Heidegger), 68
German Evangelical Church, 89–91
German Idealism, 78, 80, 82–85, 91, 238, 263, 307
German romanticism, 238
gnostic, 147
Gnosticism, 24, 26, 142
God, 1–3, 5, 8–18, 20–45, 47, 50, 51, 53, 56, 59, 61, 63–66, 71–85, 87–92, 95–97, 99, 100–101, 105–8, 110–25, 128–39, 142–43, 146–47, 149, 172–73, 175, 180–89, 191–94, 200–205, 208–9, 211, 216–21, 223, 231–32, 236, 241, 254–55, 267, 282, 301–4, 306–7, 308–313, 315, 317, 331
God is dead (Nietzsche), 82, 88–89
God-Talk, 9, 118, 186
God Without Being (Marion), 66
goodness, 15–20, 23, 29, 32–34, 45, 66
groundedness, 13, 204–5

Harlem Renaissance, 209
Hegelian, 33, 153, 158–59, 161, 197–98, 227–28, 232–33, 238–39, 242, 249, 251, 254, 255, 271, 286, 291–93
Hegelianism, 254–55, 307
hermeneutical, 110, 112, 202, 207, 308–9, 316

hermeneutics, 28, 112, 113, 115, 171, 202, 225, 227, 229, 286
highest good, 34, 75, 174–75, 256, 278–80
historicality, 175, 201, 246, 294
historicity, 175, 201, 246, 265, 266, 267, 275, 280, 285, 286, 289, 290
hominization, 62
Homo Sacer (Agamben), 244–46
homoousian, 24
House of Romanov, 104
human nature, 18, 32, 37, 77, 209, 221, 272
human rights, 195–96, 263, 270–72, 274–77, 281
humanism, 11–13, 41, 52, 115, 208, 215, 246, 284
humanists, 41
Husserlian, 125, 173–75, 216, 237, 276–79, 285–86, 291–92

ideality, 240, 247–48, 262, 265–68, 272, 277, 280
ideological state apparatus, 161, 164, 250–253
ideology, 18, 26, 68–69, 88, 101–3, 125, 138–39, 153, 156–57, 161, 163, 167–68, 177, 224, 226, 228, 250–54
illogical negativism, 262, 264
imaginary, 168–69, 250–53
imago Dei, 14, 116, 204, 211
immanence, 47, 156, 258, 285
immanent event, 47, 122, 155, 216
immanent process, 228
imperialist theater, 161–64
incarnation, 24
infrastructure, 97, 99, 198–99, 242, 250, 252, 301
intellectualism, 184–86
interpretation, 17, 35, 42, 46, 91, 102, 117, 125–26, 128, 140, 165, 166, 223, 244, 284, 318
intersubjective, 173–74, 208, 277–78

jouissance, 166
justice, 15, 37, 61, 200, 216, 233, 239, 247–50, 260–61, 263, 268, 272–73, 279–80, 292–94
justification, 14–15, 39–43, 46, 219, 258, 264, 269–71, 318

Kantian, 61

Lacanian, 164–65, 167–70, 254
Lacanianism, 254–55
Law/Right, 280
Lectures on Philosophical Theology (Kant), 72, 74
Letter to the Colossians, 139
Letter to the Ephesians, 139
liberal theology, 137, 305, 306
liberalism, 148, 292

339

liberation, 14, 111–12, 115–17, 120–21, 126–27, 130–32, 133, 165, 175, 177, 188, 215, 220, 222, 245
life world, 175
life-world, 174–75, 276–79, 285–87, 289

Making a Way out of No Way (Coleman), 192–94
Marcionism, 141
marginalization, 112, 117, 122, 125, 177, 184, 187, 199, 207, 215
Marxism, 82, 132–34, 135, 250–51, 254–55
Marxist thought, 133–36
material event, 227, 229
materiality, 221, 224–29, 250–52, 291
materiality of race, 224–27
matriarchy, 184
Meaning of the Creative Act (Berdyaev), 106–7
medieval, 13, 25–28, 31, 51, 137, 141–45, 265, 302
mere existence, 196–97
metaphysics, 12, 51, 59–60, 63–65, 71, 74, 105, 115, 123, 130, 136, 237, 286–87
modernism, 102–4
modernity, 50, 66, 129, 284–85, 289
monastic life, 28, 142–43
Monasticism, 25, 142
Montanism, 26, 142
moral philosophy, 44, 47–48
moral theism, 74
Mothership Connections (Walker), 129–30
mystery, 32–33, 55–56, 66, 108, 142

National Socialism, 68–71, 88, 90–91, 235
National Socialist, 68–69, 90
natural theology, 8, 20, 30, 41, 304
naturalism, 99, 101–4, 275
Nazi ideology, 88
Nazi Party, 69, 70, 88, 235
Nazism, 68–70, 87, 234–35
negation, 17, 230, 255, 267
Neo-Socratic, 52
neo-Thomist, 60, 64
New Testament, 6, 70, 125–28, 138–39, 141, 236, 266, 329
New Testament ethics, 126–27
New Testament theology, 126
nominalists, 41
non-being, 16–17, 57, 230
nonhuman, 292–97
non-Thomistic, 53
nothingness, 176, 230, 275, 304

objectification, 122, 137, 151, 177, 202, 213, 215, 217, 229–30, 238, 243, 245, 247, 256, 263, 273
On Religion (Marx), 85–86
ontological, 16, 17, 28–29, 31, 35, 57–59, 73, 74, 91, 102, 136, 172, 173, 175, 176, 195, 196, 200, 215, 217–20, 226, 228–29, 289, 296, 297, 317, 319–22
ontological argument, 28–29
ontological blackness, 217–20, 289
ontological proof, 74, 317, 319–22
ontological structure, 228–29
ontologist, 57
ontology, 7, 9, 29, 51, 57–60, 176, 200, 213, 221, 224, 229, 237, 285, 289, 295–97
ontotheology, 74, 123
oppressed, 112, 114–15, 120, 126–27, 134, 165, 171, 211, 212
Opus postumum (Kant), 77–79
Other, 91, 133, 153–54, 224, 227, 251, 292, 296
Otherness, 123, 153, 154, 224, 225, 227, 248

pan-Africanism, 208
papal power, 28
paradox, 11, 16, 245, 294
passing, 123, 211–12
patriarchal hegemony, 189
patriarchy, 137, 157, 165, 184, 199, 307
Pauline tradition, 138
performativity, 245
personalism, 7, 57–60, 105–6
phallic function, 166–70
phallocentric, 137, 164
phallocentrism, 164, 168
phallogocentrism, 165, 168
phenomenological, 9, 63–64, 125, 152, 214, 215, 238, 242, 247, 265, 268, 270, 290–91
phenomenology, 51, 52, 62–64, 153, 207, 291
Phenomenology of Spirit (Hegel), 33, 82, 159, 197–99, 227, 232, 264, 290, 307, 326
philosophizing, 1, 2, 6, 9–10, 63, 70–72, 76, 82, 84, 88, 92, 129–30, 218, 269, 272
philosophy of language, 9, 210
Pietism, 148
plasticity, 225, 290–92
Platonic, 23, 175, 240, 265, 289
political philosophy, 60
political theology, 14, 109–110, 121, 231–34, 236, 254–55
Politics (Aristotle), 12, 59, 178
positive Christianity, 70, 87, 89
posthuman, 285–87
posthumanism, 282, 287, 289
posthumanistic, 244, 288–89

SUBJECT INDEX

posthumanizing, 282
post-Kantian, 84, 238, 264
Post-Kantianism, 84
postmodern blackness, 217–18
powerlessness, 21, 109–111, 128, 134, 161, 175, 242–243
pre-Constantinian, 13, 25
primitive Christianity, 10
privileged signifier, 166
Prophesy Deliverance (West), 135
prophetic, 90, 121, 135–36, 141
prophetic Christianity, 135–36
Prophetic Theology, 136
Proslogion (Anselm), 29
Protestantism, 10, 12, 70, 142, 149, 306
providence, 33, 74, 304
psychoanalysis, 164–65, 251, 253
purgatory, 26

race-centric, 123
racial discourse, 217, 224–26
racial identity, 124–25, 211, 219
racism, 114, 122, 124–25, 132–33, 193, 205, 209–211
rational cosmology, 71
rational psychology, 71
rational theology, 71, 83
rationalism, 11
rationalists, 74
realism, 94, 97–99, 101–4, 245–46, 297
Reformation, 13, 15, 25, 38, 90, 137, 142, 145–48
Reformed, 34, 38, 147–48
religiosity, 53, 116, 184–85
Renaissance, 12
reontology, 228–29
Republic (Plato), 12, 253
revelation, 13, 66, 77–78, 90, 114, 118, 149, 206, 313, 316, 318–20
rhizome, 290
righteousness, 37, 39, 42
Romantic nationalism, 72
Russian Nationalism, 104–5
Russian Orthodox Christian tradition, 92
Russian Orthodox Christianity, 92–93, 95, 98, 104
Russian Orthodox Church, 92–93, 104
Russian Orthodoxy, 10, 93, 104–5
Russian theology, 92

sacraments, 27
salvation, 12, 20–26, 35, 40–41, 135, 141, 142, 147, 149, 177, 193, 204, 205, 219, 306, 313
sanctification, 43

scholasticism, 28
second-wave feminism, 152–54
self-abnegation, 25
self-communication, 309
selfhood, 11, 14–15, 46, 109, 111, 137, 155, 157, 173, 175–78, 184, 195–96, 201, 208–9, 214, 221–23, 228, 242, 246–47, 269–70, 276, 287, 304, 320
Sexuality and the Black Church (Douglas), 188–89
Sisters in the Wilderness (Williams), 186–88
social oppression, 191
sociology, 131, 208–9
sovereign, 15, 235–36, 245–46, 306
sovereignty, 142, 235–36, 245–46, 288
spiritual, 12, 17, 22–23, 28, 36, 40, 100–104, 140, 143, 146, 150–52, 177, 186, 208, 214, 222–23, 243, 301, 313–16, 322
structural sin, 133
subaltern, 116, 161–64, 190
subalternity, 116–17, 137, 161–64, 190
subjection, 137–39, 149, 251–53, 294
subjectivity, 36, 106, 122, 174, 177, 202, 213, 215, 224, 229–30, 239, 248–49, 254, 260, 261, 263, 264, 270, 273, 276, 278, 286, 296
Summa Theologica (Aquinas), 14, 31
superstructure, 250, 252, 293
symptom, 254–55
System of Transcendental Idealism (Schelling), 80–81
Systematic Theology (Tillich), 5, 6, 18, 35, 68, 70, 89, 121, 124, 309

teleological (and teleology), 31, 73, 164, 196, 220, 255, 285, 288
tenacious endurance, 196–97
The Bluest Eye (Morrison), 214–15
The Brothers Karamazov (Dostoyevsky), 95–97
The Children of Light and the Children of Darkness (Niebuhr), 238–40
The Death of Ivan Ilyich (Tolstoy), 97–104
The Excellency of Theology (Boyle), 299–304
the exception, 51, 219, 235–36
The Gospel of Mary, 140–41
The Heidelberg Catechism, 14, 34, 36–38
The Other, 153, 169
The Point of View (Kierkegaard), 43–49
The Politics of Friendship (Derrida), 249–50
The Politics of Jesus (Yoder), 236–38
The Sickness unto Death (Kierkegaard), viii, 17, 95, 269
The Sophist (Plato), 153, 272
The Souls of Black Soul (Du Bois), 205–7

SUBJECT INDEX

The World as Will and Representation (Schopenhauer), 84, 224, 286
theios aner, 137, 140, 141
theodicy, 15, 32–34, 191, 193, 308
theologia archetypa, 76
theological, 1–7, 9–10, 14, 23, 27–28, 30, 32, 35, 41, 42, 50, 51, 53, 55–58, 62–67, 69–72, 84–93, 95, 97, 101, 108, 109–119, 123–26, 129–30, 132, 134, 136–37, 142, 147–48, 150, 152, 172–73, 175, 177, 181–82, 184, 186–88, 192, 193, 200–202, 204–5, 208–9, 213, 215, 219–23, 229–31, 233–36, 241, 254, 269, 277, 280, 301–3, 308, 310, 313, 315–17, 322
theological anthropology, 14, 114, 124, 125, 132, 204–5, 221, 223, 229, 230, 308
theological corrective, 187
theological economy, 241
theological language, 186, 187, 229
theological voice, 2, 9, 53, 65, 187, 231
theologize, 1, 3, 10–11, 13–14, 28, 59, 69, 83, 87, 89, 92, 111–16, 118–20, 129–30, 132, 134–37, 173, 180–82, 184–85, 187–88, 193, 217, 255, 282
theoretical philosophy, 71
theosophy, 33, 34
Thomism, 54, 57–60, 66
transatlantic slavery, 129
transcendence, 12, 55, 123, 129, 215–16, 218–19, 221, 230, 238, 247, 255–56, 315
transcendental, 34, 63, 74–78, 80, 84–85, 90, 91, 216, 237, 238, 255
transcendental reduction, 63
Trinitarian, 26–27
triple consciousness, 210

ungiven God, 122–23
Unitarianism, 70
unjust, 233, 257–60
unmoved mover, 29, 31

victimization, 177, 212, 215, 221, 243
victimology, 131–32, 184

Weimar Classicism, 72
Weimar Republic, 234
womanhood, 136–37, 142, 152–55, 157, 181–82, 186–89, 191–94
Womanism, 165, 170, 184–86
womanist, 14, 129, 130, 187–94
Womanist Ethics and the Cultural Production of Evil (Townes), 189–91
womanist theology, 14, 187, 188–89, 192–94
worldhood, 14, 59, 191, 194, 219–20, 224, 227, 256

Young Hegelians, 86

Lightning Source UK Ltd.
Milton Keynes UK
UKHW051254120223
416889UK00015B/453